THE *unofficial* GUIDE®

TO Walt Disney World® with Kids

5TH EDITION

BOB SEHLINGER *and* LILIANE J. OPSOMER
with LEN TESTA

WILEY

Please note that prices fluctuate in the course of time and that travel information changes under the impact of many factors that influence the travel industry. We therefore suggest that you write or call ahead for confirmation when making your travel plans. Every effort has been made to ensure the accuracy of information throughout this book, and the contents of this publication are believed to be correct at the time of printing. Nevertheless, the publishers cannot accept responsibility for errors or omissions, for changes in details given in this guide, or for the consequences of any reliance on the information provided by the same. Assessments of attractions and so forth are based upon the authors' own experiences; therefore, descriptions given in this guide necessarily contain an element of subjective opinion, which may not reflect the publisher's opinion or dictate a reader's own experience on another occasion. Readers are invited to write the publisher with ideas, comments, and suggestions for future editions.

Published by:
John Wiley & Sons, Inc.
111 River Street
Hoboken, NJ 07030-5774

Produced by Menasha Ridge Press

Cover design by Michael J. Freeland

Interior design by Vertigo Design

For information on our other products and services or to obtain technical support, please contact our Customer Care Department within the United States at 800-762-2974, outside the United States at 317-572-3993, or by fax at 317-572-4002.

John Wiley & Sons, Inc., also publishes its books in a variety of electronic formats. Some content that appears in print may not be available in electronic formats.

ISBN 978-0-470-09842-4

Manufactured in the United States of America

5 4 3 2 1

CONTENTS

LIST *of* MAPS

ACKNOWLEDGMENTS

THANKS TO OUR TEAM OF YOUNG PUNDITS, Idan Menin, Ian Geiger, Hannah Testa, and Katie Sutton for their unique wisdom and fun-loving attitude (gotta have attitude, right?). Lou Mongello created the theme-park trivia quizzes, and Disney historian Jim Hill provided insightful and funny glimpses of the World behind the scenes. Cartoons in the guide were created by artist Tami Knight, possibly the nuttiest person in Canada. Much appreciation to Eve Zibart for her characteristically droll comments concerning Walt Disney World attractions, hotels, and dining. For research and contributions concering family dynamics and child behavior, thanks to psychologists Karen Turnbow, Susan Corbin, Gayle Janzen, and Joan Burns. Kudos also to *Unofficial Guide* Research Director Len Testa and his team for the data collection and programming behind the touring plans in this guide.

Many thanks also to Ritchey Halphen, Holly Cross, Molly Merkle, and Susan Roberts for production and editorial work on this book. Annie Long earned our appreciation for her fine work and for keeping tight deadlines in providing the typography. Cartography was provided by Steve Jones, and the index was prepared by Ann Cassar.

THE
unofficial GUIDE®
ᵀᴼ Walt Disney World® with Kids

5TH EDITION

INTRODUCTION

▌ HOW COME "UNOFFICIAL"?

DECLARATION OF INDEPENDENCE

THE AUTHORS AND RESEARCHERS OF THIS GUIDE specifically and categorically declare that they are and always have been totally independent of the Walt Disney Company, Inc.; of Disneyland, Inc.; of Walt Disney World, Inc.; and of any and all other members of the Disney corporate family not listed.

The authors believe in the wondrous variety, joy, and excitement of the Walt Disney World attractions. At the same time, we recognize that Walt Disney World is a business, with the same profit motivations as businesses the world over. In this guide we represent and serve you, the consumer. If a restaurant serves bad food, or a gift item is overpriced, or a certain ride isn't worth the wait, we can say so, and in the process we hope to make your visit more fun, efficient, and economical.

WHY SO MANY BOOKS?

WE'VE BEEN WRITING ABOUT WALT DISNEY WORLD FOR 25 YEARS. When we started, Walt Disney World more or less consisted of the Magic Kingdom theme park and a few hotels. Since then, Walt Disney World has grown to the size of a city and is equally if not more complex. Our comprehensive *Unofficial Guide to Walt Disney World,* tipping the scales at more than 800 pages, still provides the most in-depth and objective coverage of any Walt Disney World guide and is our basic reference work on the subject.

As thorough as we try to make *The Unofficial Guide to Walt Disney World,* there is not sufficient space to share all of the tips and information that may be important and useful to some of our readers. Thus, we have developed five additional Walt Disney World guides, all designed to work in conjunction with what we call "the big book." Each of the five, including this guide for families with children, provides specialized information tailored to very specific Walt Disney World visitors. Although some tips from the big book (like arriving at the theme parks early) are echoed or elaborated herein, most of the information is unique and was developed especially for *The Unofficial Guide to Walt Disney World with Kids*. Just as there's not space in the big book for the family-oriented material presented here, we likewise can't cram all of the detailed information from *The Unofficial Guide to Walt Disney World* into this guide. Rather, the two guides are designed to work together and complement each other.

Besides *The Unofficial Guide to Walt Disney World* and *The Unofficial Guide to Walt Disney World with Kids,* the following titles are available:

Beyond Disney: The Unofficial Guide to Universal, SeaWorld, and the Best of Central Florida by Bob Sehlinger, Grant Rafter, and Katie Brandon

Inside Disney: The Incredible Story of Walt Disney World and the Man Behind the Mouse by Eve Zibart

Mini-Mickey: The Pocket-Sized Unofficial Guide to Walt Disney World by Bob Sehlinger

The Unofficial Guide to Walt Disney World for Grown-ups by Eve Zibart

Mini-Mickey is a nice, portable, *Cliffs Notes* version of *The Unofficial Guide to Walt Disney World*. Updated annually, it distills information from the more comprehensive guides to help short-stay or last-minute visitors quickly plan their limited hours at Walt Disney World. *Inside Disney* is a behind-the-scenes unauthorized history of Walt Disney World, and it is loaded with all the amazing facts and great stories that we can't squeeze into the big book. *The Unofficial Guide to Walt Disney World for Grown-ups* helps adults traveling without children make the most of their Disney vacation, and *Beyond Disney* is a complete consumer guide to the non-Disney attractions, restaurants, and nightlife in Orlando and central Florida. All of the guides are available on the Internet and at most bookstores.

THE MUSIC OF LIFE

ALTHOUGH IT IS COMMON in our culture to see life as a journey from cradle to grave, Alan Watts, a noted late–20th century philosopher, saw it somewhat differently. He viewed life not as a journey but as a dance. In a journey, he said, you are trying to get somewhere, and are consequently always looking ahead, anticipating the way stations, and thinking about the end. Though the journey metaphor is popular, particularly in the West, it is generally characterized by a driven, goal-oriented mentality: a way of living and being that often inhibits those who subscribe to the journey metaphor from savoring each moment of life.

When you dance, by contrast, you hear the music and move in harmony with the rhythm. Like life, a dance has a beginning and an end. But unlike a journey, your objective is not to get to the end, but to enjoy the dance while the music plays. You are totally in the moment and care nothing about where on the floor you stop when the dance is done.

As you begin to contemplate your Walt Disney World vacation, you may not have much patience for a philosophical discussion about journeys and dancing. But, you see, it is relevant. If you are like most travel guide readers, you are apt to plan and organize, to anticipate and control, and you like things to go smoothly. And, truth be told, this leads us to suspect that you are a person who looks ahead and is outcome-oriented. You may even feel a bit of pressure concerning your vacation. Vacations, after all, are special events and expensive ones as well. So you work hard to make the most of your vacation.

We also believe that work, planning, and organization are important, and at Walt Disney World they are essential. But if they become your focus, you won't be able to hear the music and enjoy the dance. Though a lot of dancing these days resembles highly individualized seizures, there was a time when each dance involved specific steps, which you committed to memory. At first you were tentative and awkward, but eventually the steps became second nature and you didn't think about them anymore.

Metaphorically, this is what we want for you and your children or grandchildren as you embark on your Walt Disney World vacation. We want you to learn the steps ahead of time, so that when you're on your vacation and the music plays, you will be able to hear it, and you and your children will dance with grace and ease.

YOUR PERSONAL TRAINERS

WE'RE YOUR WALT DISNEY WORLD PERSONAL TRAINERS. We will help you plan and enjoy your Walt Disney World vacation. Together we will make sure that it really is a vacation, as opposed to, say, an ordeal or an expensive way to experience heat stroke. Our objective, simply put, is to ensure that you and your children have fun.

Because this book is specifically for adults traveling with children, we'll concentrate on your special needs and challenges. We'll share our most useful tips as well as the travel secrets of more than 29,000 families interviewed over the years we've covered Walt Disney World.

So who are *we*? For starters, there's a bunch of us. Your primary trainers are Liliane and Bob. Helping out big time are Idan and Ian, also known as the I-Boys, and Hannah. Idan is 16 years old and comes from the Queens borough of New York. He plays rock guitar (loudly), has kind of a sweetly grunge style (secondhand clothes are the coolest, right?), and wears shoes large enough for eagles to nest in. Ian is a 12-year-old from Tampa. His surfer mop-head hair nearly covers his hazy blue peepers. He gets a kick out of playing soccer and hanging with his pet gecko, Iggie (not part of the I-Boys), and is addicted to saying "Sweet!" and "Awesome!"—punctuated with an occasional "Dude!" Hannah, age 8, lives near Winston Salem, North Carolina, really knows Disney, and will read you the riot act if you mess up. The rest of us work for her. The I-Boys and Hannah, needless to say, have a lot of

Idan   Ian   Hannah

opinions when it comes to Disney. So many, in fact, that they think Liliane and Bob are largely superfluous.

Liliane comes from Belgium and works in New York City. She's funny, very polite in the best European tradition, and puts more energy into being a mom than you'd think possible without performance-enhancing drugs. Optimistic and happy, she loves the sweet and sentimental side of Walt Disney World. You might find her whooping it up at the *Hoop-Dee-Doo Revue,* but you'll never see her on a roller coaster with Bob.

Speaking of whom, Bob is not exactly a curmudgeon, but he likes to unearth Disney's closely guarded secrets and show readers how to beat the system. His idea of a warm fuzzy might be the Rock 'n' Roller Coaster, but he'll help you save lots of money, find the best hotels and restaurants, and return home less than terminally exhausted. The caricatures below pretty much sum up the essence of Bob and Liliane.

BOB   **LILIANE**

If you're thinking the cartoons paint a somewhat conflicted picture of your personal trainers, you're right. Bob and Liliane—it must be admitted—have been known to disagree on a thing or two. Together, however, they make a good team. You can count on them to give you both sides of every story. As an analogy, Liliane will help you bask in the universal brotherhood theme of *It's a Small World*. Bob will show up later and help you get the infernal song out of your head. You get the idea.

 Oops, almost forgot: there's another team member you need to meet. Called a Wuffo, she's our very own character. She'll warn you when rides are too scary, too dark, or too wet. You'll bump into her throughout the book doing, well, what characters do. Why did we create our own character when Disney has dozens just sitting around? Simple—to avoid getting our butts sued! Incidentally, if you work for Disney, you're probably licking your chops at the thought of getting a Wuffo to star in one of your animated features. Yeah? I thought so. Have your agent call our agent, and we'll do lunch.

ABOUT *this* **GUIDE**

WALT DISNEY WORLD HAS BEEN OUR BEAT for more than two decades, and we know it inside out. During those years we have observed many thousands of parents and grandparents trying—some successfully, others less so—to have a good time at Walt Disney World. Some of these, owing to unfortunate dynamics within the family, were handicapped right from the start. Others were simply overwhelmed by the size and complexity of Walt Disney World; whereas still others fell victim to a lack of foresight, planning, and organization.

Walt Disney World is a better destination for some families than for others. Likewise, some families are more compatible on vacation than others. The likelihood of experiencing a truly wonderful Walt Disney World vacation transcends the theme parks and attractions offered. In fact, the theme parks and attractions are the only constants in the equation. The variables that will define the experience and determine its success are intrinsic to your family: things like attitude, sense of humor, cohesiveness, stamina, flexibility, and conflict resolution.

The simple truth is that Walt Disney World can test you as a family. It will overwhelm you with choices and force you to make decisions about how to spend your time and money. It will challenge you physically as you cover miles on foot and wait in lines touring the theme parks. You will have to respond to surprises (both good and bad) and deal with hyperstimulation.

This guide will forewarn and forearm you. It will help you decide whether a Walt Disney World vacation is a good idea for you and your family at this particular time. It will help you sort out and address the attitudes and family dynamics that can affect your experience. Most important, it will provide the confidence that comes with good planning and realistic expectations.

THE SUM OF ALL FEARS

EVERY WRITER WHO EXPRESSES an opinion is accustomed to readers who strongly agree or disagree: it comes with the territory. Extremely troubling, however, is the possibility that our efforts to be objective have frightened some readers away from Walt Disney World or made others apprehensive. For the record, if you enjoy theme parks, Disney World is as good as it gets, absolute nirvana. It's upbeat, safe, fun, eye-popping, happy, and exciting. If you arrive without knowing a thing about the place and make every possible

unofficial **TIP**
Be prepared to read experienced Disney World visitors' opinions of the parks in this book and to apply them to your own travel circumstances.

mistake, chances are about 90% that you'll have a wonderful vacation anyway. In the end, guidebooks don't make or break great destinations. Rather, they are simply tools to help you enhance your experience and get the most for your money.

As wonderful as Walt Disney World is, however, it's a complex destination. Even so, it isn't nearly as challenging or difficult as New York, San Francisco, Paris, Acapulco, or any other large city or destination. And, happily, there are numerous ways to save money, minimize hassle, and make the most of your time. That's what this guide is about: giving you a heads-up regarding potential problems or opportunities. Unfortunately, some *Unofficial Guide* readers add up the warnings and critical advice and conclude that Walt Disney World is too intimidating, too expensive, or too much work. They lose track of the wonder of Disney World and focus instead on what might go wrong.

Our philosophy is that knowledge is power (and time and money, too). You're free to follow our advice or not at your discretion. But you can't exercise that discretion if we fail to present the issues.

With or without a guidebook, you'll have a great time at Walt Disney World. If you let us, we'll help you smooth the potential bumps. We're certain we can help you turn a great vacation into an absolutely superb one. Either way, once there, you'll get the feel of the place and quickly reach a comfort level that will allay your apprehensions and allow you to have a great experience.

LETTERS AND COMMENTS FROM READERS

Many of those who use *The Unofficial Guide to Walt Disney World with Kids* write us to make comments or share their own strategies for visiting Walt Disney World. We appreciate all such input, both positive and critical, and encourage our readers to continue writing. Readers' comments and observations are frequently incorporated into revised editions of the *Unofficial Guide* and have contributed immeasurably to its improvement.

Privacy Policy

If you write us, you can rest assured that we won't release your name and address to any mailing-list companies, direct-mail advertisers, or other third party. Unless you instruct us otherwise, we will assume that you do not object to being quoted in a future edition.

How to Write the Authors

Bob and Liliane
The Unofficial Guide to Walt Disney World with Kids
P.O. Box 43673
Birmingham, AL 35243

When you write, be sure to put a return address on your letter as well as the envelope; sometimes envelopes and letters get separated. It's also a good idea to include your phone number.

You can also send us e-mail at **UnofficialGuides@MenashaRidge.com.** Remember, our work often requires that we be out of the office for long periods of time, and *Unofficial Guide* mail and e-mail are not forwarded to us when we're traveling. So forgive us if our response is a little slow; we will respond as soon as possible when we return.

A **QUICK TOUR** *of a* **BIG WORLD**

WALT DISNEY WORLD ENCOMPASSES 43 SQUARE MILES, an area twice as large as Manhattan and roughly the same size as Boston. Situated strategically in this vast expanse are the Magic Kingdom, Epcot, Disney-MGM Studios, and the Animal Kingdom theme parks; two water parks; two nighttime entertainment areas; a sports complex; several golf courses, hotels, and campgrounds; almost 100 restaurants; four large, interconnected lakes; a shopping complex; three convention venues; a nature preserve; and a complete transportation system consisting of four-lane highways, elevated monorails, and a system of canals.

THE MAJOR THEME PARKS

The Magic Kingdom

When people think of Walt Disney World, most think of the Magic Kingdom. It comprises Cinderella Castle and the collection of adventures, rides, and shows symbolizing the Disney cartoon characters. Although the Magic Kingdom is only one element of Disney World, it remains its heart. The Magic Kingdom is divided into seven areas or "lands," six of which are arranged around a central hub. First encountered is Main Street, U.S.A., which connects the Magic Kingdom entrance with the central hub. Clockwise around the hub are Adventureland, Frontierland, Liberty Square, Fantasyland, and Tomorrowland. Mickey's Toontown Fair, the first new land in the Magic Kingdom since the park opened, is situated along the Walt Disney

south orlando and walt disney world area

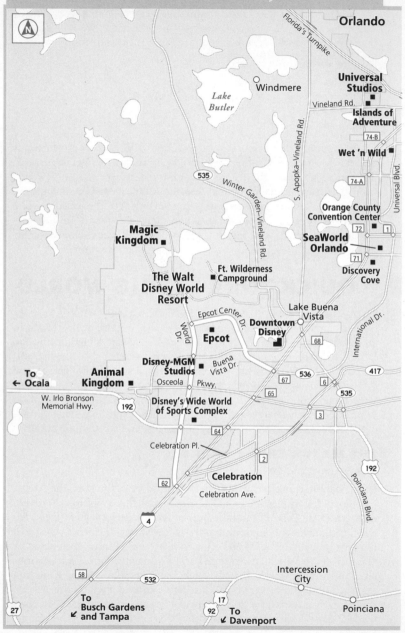

Orlando

Florida's Turnpike

Windmere

Lake
Butler

Universal
Studios

Vineland Rd.

Islands of
Adventure

74-B

Wet 'n Wild

S. Apopka–Vineland Rd.

74-A

535

Winter Garden–Vineland Rd.

Universal Blvd.

Orange County
Convention Center

72   1

Magic
Kingdom

SeaWorld
Orlando

71

The Walt
Disney World
Resort

Ft. Wilderness
Campground

Discovery
Cove

Epcot Center Dr.

Lake Buena
Vista

World
Dr.

Downtown
Disney

Epcot

68

International Dr.

Disney-MGM
Studios

Buena
Vista Dr.

To
← Ocala

Animal
Kingdom

Osceola   Pkwy.

536

67   6

417

W. Irlo Bronson
Memorial Hwy.

192

Disney's Wide World
of Sports Complex

65

535

3

64

Celebration Pl.

2

192

62

Celebration

Celebration Ave.

Poinciana Blvd.

4

58

532

Intercession
City

27

To
↙ Busch Gardens
   and Tampa

17

92   To
      ↙ Davenport

Poinciana

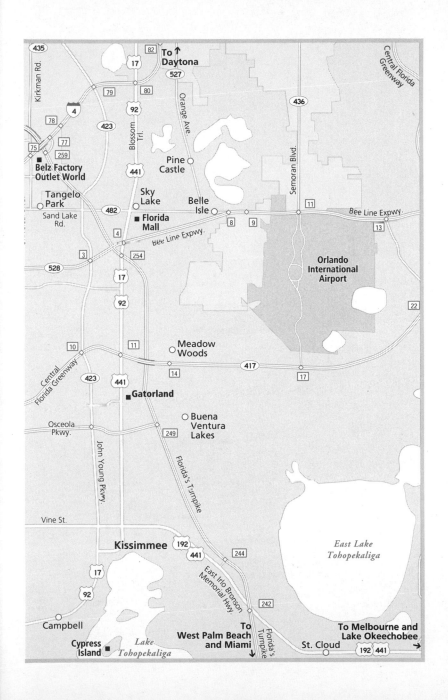

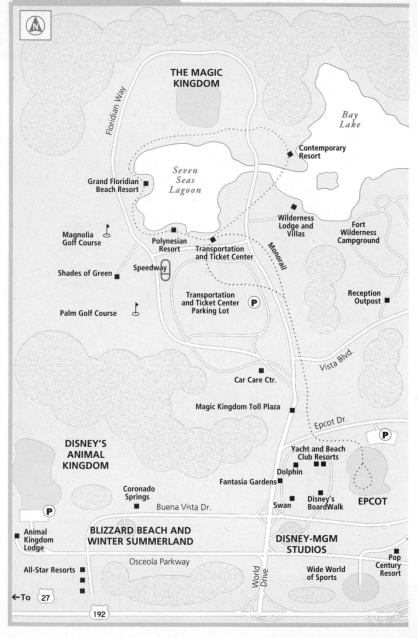

walt disney world

THE MAGIC
KINGDOM

*Bay
Lake*

Floridian Way

*Seven
Seas
Lagoon*

Contemporary
Resort

Grand Floridian
Beach Resort

Wilderness
Lodge and
Villas

Fort
Wilderness
Campground

Magnolia
Golf Course

Polynesian
Resort

Transportation
and Ticket Center

Monorail

Shades of Green

Speedway

Reception
Outpost

Transportation
and Ticket Center
Parking Lot

P

Palm Golf Course

Vista Blvd.

Car Care Ctr.

Magic Kingdom Toll Plaza

Epcot Dr.

P

DISNEY'S
ANIMAL
KINGDOM

Yacht and Beach
Club Resorts

Dolphin

Fantasia Gardens

Coronado
Springs

Swan

Disney's
BoardWalk

EPCOT

Buena Vista Dr.

P

Animal
Kingdom
Lodge

BLIZZARD BEACH AND
WINTER SUMMERLAND

DISNEY-MGM
STUDIOS

Pop
Century
Resort

All-Star Resorts

Osceola Parkway

*World
Drive*

Wide World
of Sports

←To 27

192

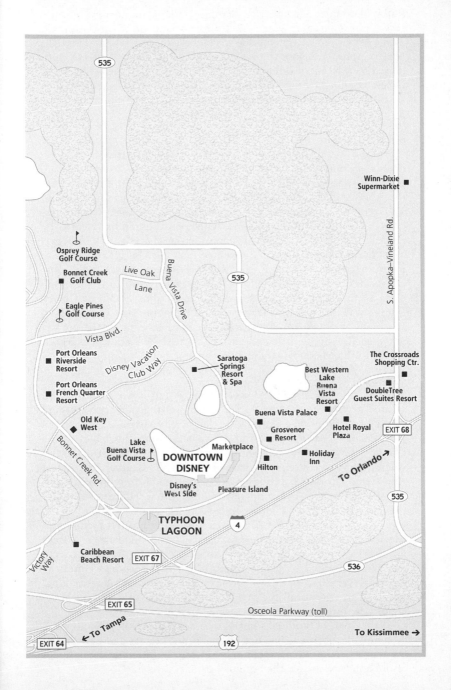

Railroad on three acres between Fantasyland and Tomorrowland. Access is through Fantasyland or Tomorrowland or via the railroad. Three hotels (the Contemporary, Polynesian, and Grand Floridian Beach resorts) are close to the Magic Kingdom and are directly connected to it by monorail and boat. Two additional hotels, Shades of Green (operated by the Department of Defense) and Disney's Wilderness Lodge Resort, are nearby but aren't served by the monorail.

Epcot

Epcot opened in October 1982. Divided into two major areas, Future World and World Showcase, the park is twice as big as the Magic Kingdom and comparable in scope. Future World consists of futuristic pavilions relating to different themes concerning humankind's creativity and technological advancement. World Showcase, arranged around a 41-acre lagoon, presents the architectural, social, and cultural heritages of almost a dozen nations, with each country represented by replicas of famous landmarks and local settings familiar to world travelers. Epcot is more education-oriented than the Magic Kingdom and has been repeatedly characterized as a sort of permanent World's Fair.

The five Epcot resort hotels—Disney's Beach Club and Villas, Disney's Yacht Club, Disney's BoardWalk and Villas, the Walt Disney World Swan and the Walt Disney World Dolphin—are within a 5- to 15-minute walk of Epcot's "back door," the International Gateway entrance. The hotels are also linked to the park by boat. Epcot is connected to the Magic Kingdom and its resort hotels by monorail.

Disney-MGM Studios

This 100-acre theme park opened in 1989 and is divided into two areas. The first is a theme park focusing on the past, present, and future of the motion picture and television industries. This section contains movie-theme rides and shows and covers about half of the Disney-MGM complex. Highlights include a re-creation of Hollywood and Sunset boulevards from Hollywood's Golden Age; movie stunt demonstrations; a children's play area; and four high-tech rides: *The Twilight Zone* Tower of Terror, Star Tours, the Rock 'n' Roller Coaster, and The Great Movie Ride.

The second Disney-MGM area is a working motion picture and television production facility encompassing three soundstages, a backlot of streets and sets, and creative support services. Public access to this area is limited to studio tours, which take visitors behind the scenes for crash courses on Disney animation and moviemaking, including (on occasion) the opportunity to witness the actual shooting of a feature film, television show, or commercial.

Disney-MGM Studios is linked to other Walt Disney World areas by highway and canal but not by monorail. Guests can park in the Studios' pay parking lot or commute by bus. Patrons staying in Epcot resort hotels can reach the Studios by boat.

Disney's Animal Kingdom

More than five times the size of the Magic Kingdom, the Animal Kingdom combines zoological exhibits with rides, shows, and live entertainment. The park is arranged somewhat like the Magic Kingdom, in a hub-and-spoke configuration. A lush tropical rain forest called The Oasis serves as Main Street, funneling visitors to Discovery Island at the center of the park. Dominated by the park's central icon, the 14-story-tall, hand-carved Tree of Life, Discovery Island is the park's center, with services, shopping, and dining. From Discovery Island, guests can access the theme areas: Africa, Asia, DinoLand U.S.A., and Camp Minnie-Mickey. Africa, the largest of the theme areas at 100 acres, features free-roaming herds in a re-creation of the Serengeti Plain. Guests tour in open-air safari vehicles.

Disney's Animal Kingdom has its own pay parking lot and is connected to other Disney World destinations by the Disney bus system. Although there are no hotels at the Animal Kingdom, the Animal Kingdom Lodge, All-Star, and Coronado Springs resorts are nearby.

THE WATER THEME PARKS

THERE ARE TWO MAJOR SWIMMING THEME PARKS in Walt Disney World: Typhoon Lagoon and Blizzard Beach. Typhoon Lagoon is distinguished by a wave pool capable of making six-foot waves. Blizzard Beach is the newest Disney water park and features more slides than Typhoon Lagoon. Both parks are beautifully landscaped, with great attention to aesthetics and atmosphere. Typhoon Lagoon and Blizzard Beach have their own adjacent parking lots and can be reached by Disney bus.

OTHER WALT DISNEY WORLD VENUES

Downtown Disney (Downtown Disney Marketplace, Pleasure Island, and Disney's West Side)

Downtown Disney is a large shopping, dining, and entertainment complex encompassing the Downtown Disney Marketplace on the east, the gated (that is, admission required) Pleasure Island nighttime entertainment venue in the middle, and Disney's West Side on the west. Downtown Disney Marketplace is home to the largest Disney character merchandise store in the world, upscale resort-wear and specialty shops, and several restaurants, including the tacky but popular Rainforest Cafe.

Part of the Downtown Disney complex, Pleasure Island is a six-acre nighttime entertainment center where one cover charge gets a visitor into any of eight nightclubs. The clubs have different themes and feature a variety of shows and activities. Music ranges from pop/rock to hip-hop to Celtic. For the hungry, there are several restaurants, including a much-hyped Planet Hollywood. There is a possibility that some or most of Pleasure Island will be closed permanently in 2007. Check **www.touringplans.com** for updates on the future of Disney's nightspots.

Disney's West Side combines nightlife, shopping, dining, and entertainment. Dan Aykroyd's House of Blues serves Cajun/Creole dishes in its restaurant and electric blues in its music hall. Bongos, a Cuban nightclub and cafe created by Gloria and Emilio Estefan, offers Caribbean flavors and rhythms. Wolfgang Puck Cafe, sandwiched among pricey boutiques (including a three-level Virgin Records megastore), is the West Side's prestige eatery. In the entertainment department, you'll find a 24-screen cinema; a permanent showplace for the extraordinary, 70-person cast of Cirque du Soleil; and DisneyQuest, a high-tech, interactive virtual reality and electronic games venue. Downtown Disney can be accessed via Disney buses from most Walt Disney World locations.

Disney's BoardWalk

Located near Epcot, Disney's BoardWalk is an idealized replication of an East Coast turn-of-the-20th-century waterfront resort. Open all day, the BoardWalk features upscale restaurants, shops and galleries, a brewpub, an ESPN sports bar, a nightclub with dueling pianos (New Orleans Pat O'Brien's–style), and a dance club. Although there is no admission fee for the BoardWalk per se, individual clubs levy a cover charge at night. Besides the public facilities, the BoardWalk fronts a 378-room deluxe hotel and a 532-unit timeshare development. The BoardWalk is within walking distance of the Epcot resorts and the International Gateway of the Epcot theme park. Boat transportation is available from Disney-MGM Studios, with buses serving other Disney World locations.

Disney's Wide World of Sports

Covering 200 acres, Disney's Wide World of Sports is a state-of-the-art competition and training facility consisting of a 7,500-seat ballpark, a field house, and venues for baseball, softball, tennis, track and field, beach volleyball, and 27 other sports. In addition to being the spring-training home of the Atlanta Braves, the complex hosts a mind-boggling calendar of professional and amateur competitions. Although Walt Disney World guests are welcome at the complex as paid spectators, none of the facilities are available for use by guests unless they are participants in a scheduled competition.

If you go for the cruise and Disney World package, visit the parks first, than sail away for Liliane more fun as well as some much deserved rest. *La dolce vita,* here I come.

The Mouse at Sea

The Disney Cruise Line operates three-, four-, and seven-day eastern and western Caribbean cruises from Port Canaveral, about an hour from Walt Disney World. These cruises can be packaged with a stay at Walt Disney World. The Disney cruises are perfect for families and for kids of all ages. Although the cruises are family-oriented, extensive children's programs and elaborate child-care facilities allow grown-ups plenty of opportunities to relax and do adult stuff.

DISNEYSPEAK POCKET TRANSLATOR

ALTHOUGH IT MAY COME AS A SURPRISE to many, Walt Disney World has its own somewhat peculiar language. Here are some terms you are likely to bump into:

DISNEYSPEAK	ENGLISH DEFINITION
Adventure	Ride
Attraction	Ride or theater show
Attraction Host	Ride operator
Audience	Crowd
Backstage	Behind the scenes, out of view of customers
Bull Pen	Queuing area
Cast Member	Employee
Character	Disney character impersonated by an employee
Costume	Work attire or uniform
Dark Ride	Indoor ride
Day Guest	Any customer not staying at a Disney resort
Face Character	A character that does not wear a head-covering costume (Snow White, Cinderella, Jasmine, and the like)
General Public	Same as day guest
Greeter	Employee positioned at an attraction entrance
Guest	Customer
Hidden Mickeys	Frontal silhouette of Mickey's head worked subtly into the design of buildings, railings, vehicles, golf greens, attractions, and just about anything else
In Rehearsal	Operating, though not officially open
Lead	Foreman or manager, the person in charge of an attraction
On Stage	In full view of customers
Preshow	Entertainment at an attraction prior to the feature presentation
Resort Guest	A customer staying at a Disney resort
Role	An employee's job
Security Host	Security guard
Soft Opening	Opening a park or attraction before its stated opening time
Transitional Experience	An element of the queuing area and/or preshow that provides a story line or information essential to understanding the attraction

PART ONE

BASIC CONSIDERATIONS

IS WALT DISNEY WORLD *for* YOU?

ALMOST ALL VISITORS ENJOY WALT DISNEY WORLD on some level and find things to see and do that they like. In fact, for many, the theme park attractions are just the tip of the iceberg. The more salient question, then (since this is a family vacation), is whether the members of your family basically like the same things. If you do, fine. If not, how will you handle the differing agendas?

A mother from Toronto wrote a couple of years ago describing her husband's aversion to Disney's (in his terms) "phony, plastic, and idealized version of life." Touring the theme parks, he was a real cynic and managed to diminish the experience for the rest of the family. As it happened, however, dad's pejorative point of view didn't extend to the Disney golf courses. So mom packed him up and sent him golfing while the family enjoyed the theme parks.

If you have someone in your family who doesn't like theme parks or, for whatever reason, doesn't care for Disney's brand of entertainment, it helps to get the attitude out in the open. Our recommendation is to deal with the person up front. Glossing over or ignoring the contrary opinion and hoping that "Tom will like it once he gets there" is naive and unrealistic. Either leave Tom at home, or help him discover and plan activities that he will enjoy, resigning yourself in the process to the fact that the family won't be together at all times.

DIFFERENT FOLKS, DIFFERENT STROKES

IT'S NO SECRET THAT WE AT THE *Unofficial Guides* believe thorough planning is an essential key to a successful Walt Disney World vacation. It's also no secret that our emphasis on planning rubs some folks the wrong way. One author's sister and her husband, for example, are spontaneous people and do not appreciate the concept of detailed planning or, more particularly, following one of our touring plans when they visit the theme parks. To them the most important thing is to relax, take things as they come, and enjoy the moment. Sometimes they arrive at Epcot at 10:30 in the morning (impossibly late for us *Unofficial Guide* types), walk around enjoying the landscaping and architecture, and then sit with a cup of espresso, watching other guests race around the park like maniacs. They would be the first to admit that they don't see many attractions, but experiencing attractions is not what lights their sparklers.

Not coincidentally, most of our readers are big on planning. When they go to the theme park they want to experience the attractions, and the shorter the lines, the better. In a word, they are willing to sacrifice some spontaneity for touring efficiency.

We want you to have the best possible time, whatever that means to you, so plan (or not) according to your preference. The point here is that most families (unlike my sister and her husband) are not entirely in agreement on this planning versus spontaneity issue. If you are a serious planner and your oldest daughter and husband are free spirits, you've got the makings of a problem. In practice, the way this and similar scenarios shake out is that the planner (usually the more assertive or type-A person) just takes over. Sometimes daughter and husband go along and everything works out, but just as often they feel resentful. There are as many ways of developing a win/win compromise as there are well-intentioned people on different sides of this situation. How you settle it is up to you. We're simply suggesting that you examine the problem and work out the solution *before* you go on vacation.

THE NATURE OF THE BEAST

THOUGH MANY PARENTS DON'T REALIZE IT, there is no law that says you must take your kids to Walt Disney World. Likewise, there's

Bob

Sehlinger's Law postulates that "the number of adults required to take care of an active toddler is equal to the number of adults present, plus one.".

no law that says you will enjoy Walt Disney World. And although we will help you make the most of any visit, we can't change the basic nature of the beast . . . er, mouse. A Walt Disney World vacation is an active and physically demanding undertaking. Regimentation, getting up early, lots of walking, waiting in lines, fighting crowds, and (often) enduring heat and humidity are as intrinsic to a Walt Disney World vacation as stripes are to a zebra. Especially if you're traveling with children, you'll need a sense of humor, more than a modicum of patience, and the ability to roll with the punches.

KNOW THYSELF AND NOTHING TO EXCESS

THIS GOOD ADVICE WAS MADE AVAILABLE to ancient Greeks courtesy of the oracle of Apollo at Delphi, who gave us permission to pass it along to you. First, concerning the "know thyself" part, we want you to do some serious thinking concerning what you want in a vacation. We also want you to entertain the notion that having fun

You can enjoy a perfectly wonderful time in the World if you are realistic, organized, and prepared.

Liliane

and deriving pleasure from your vacation may be very different indeed from doing and seeing as much as possible.

Because Walt Disney World is expensive, many families confuse "seeing everything" in order to "get our money's worth" with having a great time. Sometimes the two are compatible, but more often they are not. So, if sleeping in, relaxing with the paper over coffee, sunbathing by the pool, or taking a nap rank high on your vacation hit parade, you need to accord them due emphasis on your Disney visit (are you listening?), even if it means you see less of the theme parks.

Which brings us to the "nothing to excess" part. At Walt Disney World, especially if you are touring with children, less is definitely more. Trust us, you cannot go full tilt dawn to dark in the theme parks day after day. First you'll get tired, then you'll get cranky, and then you'll adopt a production mentality ("we've got three more rides and then we can go back to the hotel"). Finally, you'll hit the wall because you just can't maintain the pace.

Get a grip on your needs and preferences before you leave home, and develop an itinerary that incorporates all the things that make you happiest.

Bob

Plan on seeing Walt Disney World in bite-size chunks with plenty of sleeping, swimming, napping, and relaxing in between. Ask yourself over and over in both the planning stage and while you are at Walt Disney World: what will contribute the greatest contentedness, satisfaction, and harmony? Trust your instincts. If stopping for ice cream or returning to the hotel for a dip feels like more fun than seeing another attraction, do it—even if it means wasting the remaining hours of an expensive admissions pass.

The AGE THING

THERE IS A LOT OF SERIOUS COGITATION among parents and grandparents in regard to how old a child should be before embarking on a trip to Walt Disney World. The answer, not always obvious, stems from the personalities and maturity of the children, and the personalities and parenting style of the adults.

Walt Disney World for Infants and Toddlers

We believe that traveling with infants and toddlers is a great idea. Developmentally, travel is a stimulating learning experience for even the youngest of children. Infants, of course, will not know Mickey Mouse from a draft horse, but will respond to sun and shade, music, bright colors, and the extra attention they receive from you. From first steps to full mobility, toddlers respond to the excitement and spectacle of Walt Disney World, though of course in a much different way than you do. Your toddler will prefer splashing in fountains and clambering over curbs and benches to experiencing most attractions, but no matter: he or she will still have a great time.

Somewhere between 4 and 6 years of age, your child will experience the first vacation that he or she will remember as an adult. Though more likely to remember the comfortable coziness of the hotel room than the theme parks, the child will be able to experience and comprehend many attractions and will be a much fuller participant in your vacation. Even so, his or her favorite activity is likely to be swimming in the hotel pool.

As concerns infants and toddlers, there are good reasons and bad reasons for vacationing at Walt Disney World. A good reason for taking your little one to Walt Disney World is that you want to go and there's no one available to care for your child during your absence. Philosophically, we are very much against putting your life (including your vacation) on hold until your children are older.

Traveling with infants and toddlers sharpens parenting skills and makes the entire family more mobile and flexible, resulting in a richer, fuller life for all.

Liliane

Especially if you have children of varying ages (or plan to, for that matter), it's better to take the show on the road than to wait until the youngest reaches the perceived ideal age. If your family includes a toddler or infant, you will find everything from private facilities for breast-feeding to changing tables in both men's and women's restrooms to facilitate baby's care. Your whole family will be able to tour together with fewer hassles than on a day's picnic outing at home.

A bad reason, however, for taking an infant or toddler to Walt Disney World is that you think Walt Disney World is the perfect vacation destination for babies. It's not, so think again if you are contemplating Walt Disney World primarily for your child's enjoyment. For starters, attractions are geared more toward older children and adults. Even designer play areas like Tom Sawyer Island in the Magic Kingdom are developed with older children in mind.

By way of example, one author has a friend who bought a video camcorder when his first child was born. He delighted in documenting his son's reaction to various new experiences on video. One memorable night when the baby was about 18 months old, he taped the baby eating a variety of foods (from whipped cream to dill pickles) that he had never tried before. While some of the taste sensations elicited wild expressions and animated responses from the baby, the exercise was clearly intended for the amusement of Dad, not junior.

That said, let us stress that for the well prepared, taking a toddler to Walt Disney World can be a totally glorious experience. There's truly nothing like watching your child respond to the color, the sound, the festivity, and, most of all, the characters. You'll return home with scrapbooks of photos that you will treasure forever. Your little one won't remember much, but never mind. Your memories will be unforgettable.

Along similar lines, remember when you were little and you got that nifty electric train for Christmas, the one Dad wouldn't let you play with? Did you ever wonder who that train was really for? Ask yourself the same question about your vacation to Walt Disney World. Whose dream are you trying to make come true: yours or your child's?

My first memory of a trip to Walt Disney World is of sitting in the swimming pool of our hotel with a feather attached to my hair! I was 3 years old and so impressed by Frontierland that I truly believed I was an Indian. That feather was one of my most precious possessions for many months.

Idan

If you elect to take your infant or toddler to Walt Disney World, rest assured that their needs have been anticipated. The major theme parks have centralized facilities for infant and toddler care. Everything necessary for changing diapers, preparing formula, and warming bottles and food is available. At the Magic Kingdom, the Baby Center is next to the Crystal Palace at the end of Main Street. At Epcot, Baby Services is near the Odyssey Center, right of Test Track in Future World. At Disney-MGM Studios, Baby Care is in the Guest Relations Building left of the entrance. At the Animal Kingdom, Baby Changing/Nursing is in Discovery Island in the center of the park. Dads in charge of little ones are welcome at the centers and can use most services offered. In addition, men's rooms in the major theme parks have changing tables.

Baby supplies, including disposable diapers, formula, and baby food, are for sale, and there are rockers and special chairs for nursing mothers.

Liliane

Infants and toddlers are allowed to experience any attraction that doesn't have minimum height or age restrictions. But as a Minneapolis mother reports, some attractions are better for babies than others:

Theater and boat rides are easier for babies (ours was almost 1 year old, not yet walking). Rides where there's a bar that comes down are doable, but harder. Peter Pan was our first encounter with this type, and we had barely gotten situated when I realized he might fall out of my grasp. The standing auditorium films are too intense; the noise level is deafening, and the images inescapable. You don't have a rating system for babies, and I don't expect to see one, but I thought you might want to know what a baby thought (based on his reactions).

At the Magic Kingdom: Jungle Cruise—Didn't get into it. Pirates—Slept through it. Riverboat—While at Aunt Polly's, the horn made him cry. Aunt Polly's—Ate while watching the birds in relative quiet. Small World—Wide-eyed, took it all in. Peter Pan— Couldn't really sit on the seat. A bit dangerous. He didn't get into it.

Carousel of Progress—*Long talks; hard to keep him quiet; danced during song.* Walt Disney World Railroad—*Liked the motion and scenery.* Tiki Birds—*Loved it. Danced, clapped, sang along.*

At Epcot: Honey, I Shrunk the Audience—*We skipped due to recommendation of Disney worker that it got too loud and adults screamed throughout. Journey into Imagination—Loved it. Tried to catch things with his hands. Bounced up and down, chortled. The Land—Watchful, quiet during presentation. Gran Fiesta Tour—Loved it.*

The same mom also advises:

We used a baby sling on our trip and thought it was great when standing in the lines—much better than a stroller, which you have to park before getting in line (and navigate through crowds). My baby was still nursing when we went to Walt Disney World. The only really great place I found to nurse in the Magic Kingdom was a hidden bench in the shade in Adventureland in between the freezee stand (next to Tiki Birds) and the small shops. It is impractical to go to the baby station every time, so a nursing mom better be comfortable about nursing in very public situations.

Two points in our reader's comment warrant elaboration. First, the rental strollers at all of the major theme parks are designed for toddlers and children up to 3 and 4 years old, but are definitely not for infants. Still, if you bring pillows and padding, the rental strollers can be made to work. You can alternatively bring your own stroller, but unless it's collapsible, you will not be able to take it on Disney trams, buses, or boats.

In addition to providing an alternative to carrying your child, a stroller serves as a handy cart for diaper bags, water bottles, and other items you deem necessary.

Liliane

Even if you opt for a stroller (your own or a rental), we nevertheless recommend that you also bring a baby sling or baby/child backpack. Simply put, there will be many times in the theme parks when you will have to park the stroller and carry your child. As an aside, if you haven't checked out baby slings and packs lately, you'll be amazed by some of the technological advances made in these products.

The second point that needs addressing is our reader's perception that there are not many good places in the theme parks for breast-feeding unless you are accustomed to nursing in public. Many nursing moms recommend breast-feeding during a dark Disney theater presentation. This only works, however, if the presentation is long enough for the baby to finish nursing. *The Hall of Presidents* at the Magic Kingdom and *The American Adventure* at Epcot will afford you about 23 and 29 minutes, respectively. In addition, neither production includes noise or special effects that will frighten your infant, although you can expect fairly loud volume levels for narration and music. *Impressions de France* in the French pavilion at Epcot's World Showcase is only 18 minutes long but is very quiet and relaxing. For the time being, unfortunately, there are no theater presentations at the Animal Kingdom that offer sufficient quiet and adequate time to nurse. At the Disney-MGM Studios, *Voyage of the Little Mermaid* will work if your child can get filled up in 15 minutes.

Many Disney shows run back to back with only a minute or two in between to change the audience. If you want to breast-feed and require more time than the length of the show, tell the cast member on entering that you want to breast-feed and ask if you can remain in the theater and watch a second showing while your baby finishes.

If you can adjust to nursing in more public places with your breast and the baby's head covered with a shawl or some such, nursing will not be a problem at all. Even on the most crowded days, you can always find a back corner of a restaurant or a comparatively secluded park bench or garden spot to nurse. Finally, the baby centers, with their private nursing rooms, are centrally located in all of the parks except the Disney-MGM Studios.

Liliane

Infants are easy travelers. As long as they are fed and comfortable, there is really no limit to what you can do when on the road with little ones. Food plus adequate rest is the perfect formula for happy babies.

Walt Disney World for 4-, 5-, and 6-Year-Olds

Four-, five-, and six-year-olds vary immensely in their capacity to comprehend and enjoy Walt Disney World. With this age group, the go/no-go decision is a judgment call. If your child is sturdy, easygoing, fairly adventuresome, and demonstrates a high degree of independence, the trip will probably work. On the other hand, if your child tires easily, is temperamental, or is a bit timid or reticent in embracing new experiences, you're much better off waiting a few years. Whereas the travel and sensory-overload problems of infants and toddlers can be addressed and (usually) remedied on the go, discontented 4- to 6-year-olds have the ability to stop a family dead in its tracks, as this mother of three from Cape May, New Jersey, attests:

> *My 5-year-old was scared pretty bad on Snow White our first day at Disney World. From then on for the rest of the trip we had to coax and reassure her before each and every ride before she would go. It was like pulling teeth.*

If you have a retiring, clinging, and/or difficult 4- to 6-year-old who, for whatever circumstances, will be part of your group, you can sidestep or diminish potential problems with a bit of pretrip preparation. Even if your preschooler is plucky and game, the same prep measures (described later in this section) will enhance his or her experience and make life easier for the rest of the family.

Parents who understand that a visit with 3- to 6-year-old children is going to be more about the cumulative experience than about seeing it all will have a blast and wonderful memories of their children's amazement.

At age 5, Peter Pan and Captain Hook were my heroes, but I was way too scared to ride Peter Pan. It didn't make me feel bad, though. I kind of made my own attraction by running around doing my thing dressed like a pirate.

Idan

The Ideal Age

Although our readers report both successful trips as well as disasters with children of all ages, the consensus ideal children's ages for family compatibility and togetherness at Walt Disney World are 8 to 12 years. This age group is old enough, tall enough, and sufficiently stalwart to experience, understand, and appreciate practically all Disney attractions. Moreover, they are developed to the extent that they can get around the parks on their own steam without being carried or collapsing. Best of all, they are still young enough to enjoy being with mom and dad. From our experience, ages 10 to 12 are better than 8 and 9, though what you gain in maturity is at the cost of that irrepressible, wide-eyed wonder so prevalent in the 8- and 9-year-olds.

Walt Disney World for Teens

Teens love Walt Disney World, and for parents of teens the World is a nearly perfect, albeit expensive vacation choice. Although your teens might not be as wide-eyed and impressionable as their younger sibs, they are at an age where they can sample, understand, and enjoy practically everything Walt Disney World has to offer.

For parents, Walt Disney World is a vacation destination where you can permit your teens an extraordinary amount of freedom. The entertainment is wholesome, the venues are safe, and the entire complex of hotels, theme parks, restaurants, and shopping centers is accessible via the Walt Disney World transportation system. The transportation system allows you, for example, to enjoy a romantic dinner and an early bedtime while your teens take in the late-night fireworks at the theme parks. After the fireworks, a Disney bus, boat, or monorail will deposit them safely back at the hotel.

Because most adolescents relish freedom, you may have difficulty keeping your teens with the rest of the family. Thus, if one of your objectives is to spend time with your teenage children during your Disney World vacation, you will need to establish some clear-cut guidelines regarding togetherness and separateness before you leave home. Make your teens part of the discussion and try to meet them halfway in crafting a decision everyone can live with. For your teens, touring on their own at Walt Disney World is tantamount to being independent in a large city. It's intoxicating, to say the least, and can be an excellent learning experience, if not a rite of passage. In any event, we're not suggesting that you just turn them loose. Rather, we are just attempting to sensitize you to the fact that for your teens, there are some transcendent issues involved.

Most teens crave the company of other teens. If you have a solitary teen in your family, do not be surprised if he or she wants to invite a friend on your vacation. If you are invested in sharing intimate, quality time with your solitary teen, the presence of a friend will make this difficult, if not impossible. However, if you turn down the request to bring a friend, be prepared to go the extra mile to be a companion to your teen at Walt Disney World. Expressed differently, if you're a teen, it's not much fun to ride Space Mountain by yourself.

One specific issue that absolutely should be addressed before you leave home is what assistance (if any) you expect from your teen in regard to helping with younger children in the family. Once again, try to carve out a win/win compromise. Consider the case of the mother from Indiana who had a teenage daughter from an earlier marriage and two children under age 10 from a second marriage. After a couple of vacations where she thrust the unwilling teen into the position of being a surrogate parent to her stepsisters, the teen declined henceforth to participate in family vacations.

Many parents have written the *Unofficial Guide* asking if there are unsafe places at Walt Disney World or places where teens simply should not be allowed to go. Although the answer depends more on your family values and the relative maturity of your teens than on Walt Disney World, the basic answer is no. Though it's true that teens (or adults, for that matter) who are looking for trouble can find it anywhere, there is absolutely nothing at Walt Disney World that could be construed as a precipitant or a catalyst. Be advised, however, that adults consume alcohol at most Walt Disney World restaurants and that drinking is a very visible part of the Pleasure Island club scene. Also, be aware that some of the movies available at the cinemas at the West Side of Downtown Disney demand the same discretion you exercise when allowing your kids to see movies at home.

As a final aside, if you allow your teens some independence and they are getting around on the Walt Disney World transportation system, expect some schedule slippage. There are no posted transportation schedules other than when service begins in the morning and when service terminates at night. Thus, to catch a bus, for example, you just go to a bus station and wait for the next bus to your Disney World destination. If you happen to just miss the bus, you might have to wait 15 to 45 minutes (more often 15 to 20 minutes) for the next one. If punctuality is essential, advise your independent teens to arrive at a transportation station an hour before they are expected somewhere in order to allow sufficient time for the commute.

About **INVITING** *your* **CHILDREN'S FRIENDS**

IF YOUR CHILDREN WANT TO INVITE FRIENDS on your Walt Disney World vacation, give your decision careful thought. There's more involved here than might be apparent. First, consider the logistics of numbers. Is there room in the car? Will you have to leave something at home that you had planned on taking to make room in the trunk for the friend's luggage? Will additional hotel rooms or a larger condo be required? Will the increased number of people in your group make it hard to get a table at a restaurant?

If you determine that you can logistically accommodate one or more friends, the next step is to consider how the inclusion of the friend will affect your group's dynamics. Generally speaking, the presence of a friend will make it harder to really connect with your own children. So if one of your vacation goals is an intimate bonding experience with your children, the addition of friends will probably frustrate your attempts to realize that objective.

If family relationship building is not necessarily a primary objective of your vacation, it's quite possible that the inclusion of a friend will make life easier for you. This is especially true in the case of only children, who may otherwise depend exclusively on you to keep them happy and occupied. Having a friend along can take the pressure off and give you some much-needed breathing room.

If you decide to allow a friend to accompany you, limit the selection to children you know really well and whose parents you also know. Your Walt Disney World vacation is not the time to include "my friend Eddie from school" whom you've never met. Your children's friends who have spent time in your home will have a sense of your parenting style, and you will have a sense of their personality, behavior, and compatibility with your family. Assess the prospective child's potential to fit in well on a long trip. Is he or she polite, personable, fun to be with, and reasonably mature? Does he or she relate well to you and to the other members of your family?

Because a Walt Disney World vacation is not, for most of us, a spur-of-the-moment thing, you should have adequate time to evaluate potential candidate friends. A trip to the mall including a meal in a sit-down restaurant will tell you volumes about the friend. Likewise, inviting the friend to share dinner with the family and then spend the night will provide a lot of relevant information. Ideally this type of evaluation should take place early on in the normal course of family events, before you discuss the possibility of a friend joining you on your vacation. This will allow you to size things up without your child (or the friend) realizing that an evaluation is taking place.

By seizing the initiative, you can guide the outcome. Ann, a Springfield, Ohio, mom, for example, anticipated that her 12-year-old son would ask to take a friend on their vacation. As she pondered the various friends her son might propose, she came up with four names. One, an otherwise sweet child, had a medical condition that Ann felt unqualified to monitor or treat. A second friend was overly aggressive with younger children and was often socially inappropriate for his age. Two other friends, Chuck and Marty, with whom she had had a generally positive experience, were good candidates for the trip. After orchestrating some opportunities to spend time with each of the boys, she made her decision and asked her son, "Would you like to take Marty with us to Disney World?" Her son was delighted, and Ann had diplomatically preempted having to turn down friends her son might have proposed.

We recommend that you do the inviting, instead of your child, and that the invitation be extended parent to parent (to avoid disappointment, you might want to sound out the friend's parent before broaching the issue with your child). Observing this recommendation will allow you to query the friend's parents concerning food preferences, any medical conditions, how discipline is administered in the friend's family, how the friend's parents feel about the way you administer discipline, and the parents' expectation regarding religious observations while their child is in your care.

Before you extend the invitation, give some serious thought to who pays for what. Make a specific proposal for financing the trip a part of your invitation, for example: "There's room for Marty in the hotel room, and transportation's no problem because we're driving. So we'll just need you to pick up Marty's meals, theme park admissions, and spending money."

We suggest that you arrange for the friend's parents to reimburse you after the trip for things like restaurant meals and admissions. This is much easier than trying to balance the books after every expenditure.

A **FEW WORDS** *for* **SINGLE PARENTS**

BECAUSE SINGLE PARENTS GENERALLY are also working parents, planning a special getaway with your children can be the best way to spend some quality time together. But remember, the vacation is not just for your child—it's for you, too. You might invite a grandparent or a favorite aunt or uncle along; the other adult provides nice company for you, and your child will benefit from the time with family members. You might likewise consider inviting an adult friend.

Though bringing along an adult friend or family member is the best option, the reality is that many single parents don't have friends, grandparents, or favorite aunts or uncles who can make the trip. And while spending time with your child is wonderful, it is very difficult to match the energy level of your child if you are the sole focus of his or her world.

One alternative: try to meet other single parents at Walt Disney World. It may seem odd, but most of them are in the same boat as you; besides, all you have to do is ask. Another option, albeit expensive, is to take along a trustworthy babysitter (18 or up) to travel with you.

The easiest way to meet other single parents at the World is to hang out at the hotel pool. Make your way there on the day you arrive, after traveling by car or plane and without enough time to blow a full admission ticket at a theme park. In any event, a couple of hours spent poolside is a relaxing way to start your vacation.

If you visit Walt Disney World with another single parent, get adjoining rooms; take turns watching all the kids; and, on at least one night, get a sitter and enjoy an evening out.

Throughout this book we mention the importance of good planning and touring. For a single parent, this is an absolute must. In addition, make sure that every day you set aside some downtime back at the hotel.

Finally, don't try to spend every moment with your children on vacation. Instead, plan some activities for your children with other children. Disney educational programs for children, for example, are worth considering. Then take advantage of your free time to do what you want to do: read a book, have a massage, take a long walk, or enjoy a catnap.

"HE WHO HESITATES IS LAUNCHED!"
Tips and Warnings for Grandparents

SENIORS OFTEN GET INTO PREDICAMENTS caused by touring with grandchildren. Run ragged and pressured to endure a blistering pace, many seniors just concentrate on surviving Walt Disney World rather than enjoying it. The theme parks have as much to offer older visitors as they do children, and seniors must either set the pace or dispatch the young folks to tour on their own.

An older reader from Alabaster, Alabama, writes:

> *The main thing I want to say is that being a senior is not for wussies. At Disney World particularly, it requires courage and pluck. Things that used to be easy take a lot of effort, and sometimes your brain has to wait for your body to catch up. Half the time, your grandchildren treat you like a crumbling ruin and then turn around and trick you into getting on a roller coaster in the dark. What you need to tell seniors is that they have to be alert and not trust anyone. Not their children or even the Disney people, and especially not their*

grandchildren. When your grandchildren want you to go on a ride, don't follow along blindly like a lamb to the slaughter. Make sure you know what the ride is all about. Stand your ground and do not waffle. He who hesitates is launched!

If you don't get to see much of your grandchildren, you might think that Walt Disney World is the perfect place for a little bonding and togetherness. Wrong! Walt Disney World can potentially send children into system overload and precipitates behaviors that pose a challenge even to adoring parents, never mind grandparents. You don't take your grandchildren straight to Disney World for the same reason you don't buy your 16-year-old son a Ferrari: handling it safely and well requires some experience.

Begin by spending time with your grandchildren in an environment that you can control. Have them over one at a time for dinner and to spend the night. Check out how they respond to your oversight and discipline. Most of all, zero in on whether you are compatible, enjoy each other's company, and have fun together. Determine that you can set limits and that they will accept those limits. When you reach this stage, you can contemplate some outings to the zoo, the movies, the mall, or the state fair. Gauge how demanding your grandchildren are when you are out of the house. Eat a meal or two in a full-service restaurant to get a sense of their social skills and their ability to behave appropriately. Don't expect perfection, and be prepared to modify your behavior a little, too. As a senior friend of mine told her husband (none too decorously), "You can't see Walt Disney World sitting on a stick."

If you have a good relationship with your grandchildren and have had a positive one-on-one experience taking care of them, you might consider a trip to Walt Disney World. If you do, we have two recommendations. First, visit Walt Disney World without them to get an idea of what you're getting into. A scouting trip will also provide you an opportunity to enjoy some of the attractions that won't be on the itinerary when you return with the grandkids. Second, if you are considering a trip of a week's duration, you might think about buying a Disney package that combines four days at Walt Disney World with a three-day cruise on the *Disney Magic* or the *Disney Wonder*. In addition to being a memorable experience for your grandchildren, the cruise provides plenty of structure for children of almost every age, thus allowing you to be with them but also to have some time off. Call the Disney Cruise Line at ☎ 800-951-3532 or visit **www.disneycruise.com**.

A Dozen Tips for Grandparents

1. It's best to take one grandchild at a time, two at the most. Cousins can be better than siblings because they don't fight as much. To preclude sibling jealousy, try connecting the trip to a child's milestone, such as finishing the sixth grade.

2. Let your grandchildren help plan the vacation, and keep the first one short. Be flexible, and don't overplan.

3. Discuss mealtimes and bedtime. Fortunately, many grandparents are on an early dinner schedule, which works nicely with younger children. Also, if you want to plan a special evening out, be sure to make the reservation ahead of time.

4. Gear plans to your grandchildren's age levels, because if they're not happy, you won't be happy.

5. Create an itinerary that offers some supervised activities for children in case you need a rest.

6. If you're traveling by car, this is the one time we highly recommend headphones. Kids' musical tastes are vastly different from most grand-parents'. It's simply more enjoyable when everyone can listen to his or her own preferred style of music, at least for some portion of the trip.

7. Take along a night-light.

8. Carry a notarized statement from parents for permission for medical care in case of an emergency. Also be sure you have insurance information and copies of any prescriptions for medicines the kids may be on. Ditto for eyeglass prescriptions.

9. Tell your grandchildren about any medical problems you may have so they can be prepared if there's an emergency.

10. Many attractions and hotels offer discounts for seniors, so be sure you check ahead of time for bargains.

11. Plan your evening meal early to avoid long waits. And make advance reservations if you're dining in a popular spot, even if it's early. Take some crayons and paper to keep kids occupied.

12. If planning a family-friendly trip seems overwhelming, try Grandtravel, a tour operator/travel agent aimed at kids and their grandparents (call ☎ 800-247-7651 or visit **www.grandtrvl.com**).

ORDER *and* DISCIPLINE *on the* ROAD

OK, OK, WIPE THAT SMIRK OFF YOUR FACE. Order and discipline on the road may seem like an oxymoron to you, but you won't be hooting when your 5-year-old launches a screaming stem-winder in the middle of Fantasyland. Your willingness to give this subject serious consideration before you leave home may well be the most important element of your pretrip preparation.

Discipline and maintaining order are more difficult when traveling than at home because everyone is, as a Boston mom put it, "in and out" (in strange surroundings and out of the normal routine). For children, it's hard to contain excitement and anticipation that pop to the surface in the form of fidgety hyperactivity, nervous energy, and sometimes, acting out. Confinement in a car, plane, or hotel room only exacerbates the situation, and kids are often louder than normal, more aggressive with siblings, and much more inclined to push the envelope of parental patience and control. Once in the theme parks, it doesn't get much better. There's more elbow room, but there's also overstimulation, crowds, heat, miles of walking. All this coupled with marginal or inadequate rest can lead to meltdown in the most harmonious of families.

The following discussion was developed by leading child psychologist, Dr. Karen Turnbow, who has contributed to the *Unofficial Guides* for years and who has spent many days at Walt Disney World conducting research and observing families.

Sound parenting and standards of discipline practiced at home, applied consistently, will suffice to handle most situations on vacation. Still, it's instructive to study the hand you are dealt when traveling. For starters, aside from being jazzed and ablaze with adrenaline, your kids may believe that rules followed at home are somehow suspended when traveling. Parents reinforce this misguided intuition by being inordinately lenient in the interest of maintaining peace in the family. While some of your home protocols (cleaning your plate, going to bed at a set time, and such) might be relaxed to good effect on vacation, differing from your normal approach to discipline can precipitate major misunderstanding and possibly disaster.

Children, not unexpectedly, are likely to believe that a vacation (especially a vacation to Walt Disney World) is expressly for them. This reinforces their focus on their own needs and largely erases any consideration of yours. Such a mind-set dramatically increases their sense of hurt and disappointment when you correct them or deny them something they want. An incident that would hardly elicit a pouty lip at home could well escalate to tears or defiance when traveling.

Discuss your vacation needs with your children and explore their wants and expectations, as well, before you depart on your trip.

Liliane

The stakes are high for everyone on a vacation; for you because of the cost in time and dollars, but also because your vacation represents a rare opportunity for rejuvenation and renewal. The stakes are high for your children, too. Children tend to romanticize travel, building anticipation to an almost unbearable level. Discussing the trip in advance can ground expectations to a certain extent, but a child's imagination will, in the end, trump reality every time. The good news is that you can take advantage of your children's emotional state to establish pre-agreed rules and conditions for their conduct while on vacation. Because your children want what's being offered sooooo badly, they will be unusually accepting and conscientious regarding whatever rules are agreed upon.

According to child psychologist Dr. Karen Turnbow, successful response to (or avoidance of) behavioral problems on the road begins with a clear-cut disciplinary policy at home. Both at home and on vacation the approach should be the same, and should be based on the following key concepts:

1. LET EXPECTATIONS BE KNOWN. Discuss what you expect from your children but don't try to cover every imaginable situation. Cover expectations in regard to compliance with parental directives, treatment of siblings, resolution of disputes, schedule (including wake-up and bedtimes), courtesy and manners, staying together, and who pays for what.

2. EXPLAIN THE CONSEQUENCES OF NONCOMPLIANCE. Detail very clearly and firmly the consequence of not meeting expectations. This should be very straightforward and unambiguous. If you do X (or don't do X), this is what will happen.

3. WARN YOUR KIDS. You're dealing with excited, expectant children, not machines, so it's important to issue a warning before meting out discipline. It's critical to understand that we're talking about one unequivocal warning rather than multiple warnings or nagging. These undermine your credibility and make your expectations appear relative or less than serious. Multiple warnings or nagging also effectively passes control of the situation from you to your child (who may continue to act out as an attention-getting strategy).

4. FOLLOW THROUGH. If you say you're going to do something, do it. Period. Children must understand that you are absolutely serious and committed.

5. BE CONSISTENT. Inconsistency makes discipline a random event in the eyes of your children. Random discipline encourages random behavior, which translates to a nearly total loss of parental control. Long-term, both at home and on the road, your response to a given situation or transgression must be perfectly predictable. Structure and repetition, essential for a child to learn, cannot be achieved in the absence of consistency.

Although the above are the five biggies, there are several corollary concepts and techniques that are worthy of consideration.

First, understand that whining, tantrums, defiance, sibling friction, and even holding the group up are ways in which children communicate with parents. Frequently the object or precipitant of a situation has little or no relation to the unacceptable behavior. A fit may on the surface appear to be about the ice cream you refused to buy little Robby, but there's almost always something deeper, a subtext that is closer to the truth (this is the reason why ill behavior often persists after you give in to a child's demands). As often as not the real cause is a need for attention. This need is so powerful in some children that they will subject themselves to certain punishment and parental displeasure to garner the attention they crave.

To get at the root cause of the behavior in question requires both active listening and empowering your child with a "feeling vocabulary." Active listening is a concept that's been around a long time. It involves being alert not only to what a child says but also to the context in which it is said, to the language used and possible subtext, to the child's emotional state and body language, and even to what's not said. Sounds complicated, but it's basically being attentive to the larger picture, and more to the point, being aware that there is a larger picture.

Helping your child to develop a feeling vocabulary consists of teaching your child to use words to describe what's going on. The idea is to teach the child to articulate what's really troubling him, to be able to identify and express emotions and mood states in language. Of course learning to express feelings is a lifelong experience, but it's much less dependent on innate sensitivity than being provided the tools for expression and being encouraged to use them.

It all begins with convincing your child that you're willing to listen attentively and take what he's saying seriously. Listening to your child, you help him transcend the topical by reframing the conversation to address the underlying emotional state(s). That his brother hit him may have precipitated the mood, but the act is topical and of secondary importance. What you want is for your child to be able to communicate how that makes him feel, and to get in touch with those emotions. When you reduce an incident (hitting) to the emotions triggered (anger, hurt, rejection, and so on), you have the foundation for helping him to develop constructive coping strategies. Not only are being in touch with one's feelings and developing constructive coping strategies essential to emotional well-being, but they also beneficially affect behavior. A child who can tell his mother why he is distressed is a child who has discovered a coping strategy far more effective (not to mention easier for all concerned) than a tantrum.

Children are almost never too young to begin learning a feeling vocabulary. And helping your child to be in touch with, and try to communicate, his emotions will stimulate you to focus on your feelings and mood states in a similar way.

SIX MORE TIPS

UNTIL YOU GET THE ACTIVE LISTENING and feeling vocabulary going, be careful not to become part of the problem. There's a whole laundry list of adult responses to bad behavior that only make things worse. Hitting, swatting, yelling, name calling, insulting, belittling, using sarcasm, pleading, nagging, and inducing guilt (as in: "We've spent thousands of dollars to bring you to Disney World and now you're spoiling the trip for everyone") figure prominently on the list.

Responding to a child appropriately in a disciplinary situation requires thought and preparation. Following are key things to keep in mind and techniques to try when your world blows up while waiting in line for Dumbo.

I. BE THE ADULT. It's well understood that children can punch their parents' buttons faster and more lethally than just about anyone or anything else. They've got your number, know precisely how to elicit a response, and are not reluctant to go for the jugular. Fortunately (or unfortunately) you're the adult, and to deal with a situation effectively, you must act like one. If your kids get you ranting and caterwauling, you effectively abdicate your adult status. Worse, you suggest by way of example that being out of control is an acceptable expression of hurt or anger. No matter what happens, repeat the mantra, "I am the adult in this relationship."

2. FREEZE THE ACTION. Being the adult and maintaining control almost always translates to freezing the action, to borrow a sports term. Instead of a knee-jerk response (at a maturity level closer to your child's than yours), freeze the action by disengaging. Wherever you are or whatever the family is doing, stop in place and concentrate on one thing and one thing only: getting all involved calmed down. Practically speaking, this usually means initiating a time-out. It's essential that you take this action immediately. Grabbing your child by the arm or collar and dragging him toward the car or hotel room only escalates the turmoil by prolonging the confrontation and by adding a coercive physical dimension to an already volatile emotional event. If for the sake of people around you (as when a toddler throws a tantrum in church) it's essential to retreat to a more private place, chose the first place available. Firmly sit the child down and refrain from talking to him until you've both cooled off. This might take a little time, but the investment is worthwhile. Truncating the process is like trying to get on your feet too soon after surgery.

3. ISOLATE THE CHILD. You'll be able to deal with the situation more effectively and expeditiously if the child is isolated with one parent. Dispatch the uninvolved members of your party for a Coke break or have them go on with the activity or itinerary without you (if possible) and arrange to rendezvous later at an agreed time and place. In addition to letting the others get on with their day, isolating the offending child with one parent relieves him of the pressure of being the group's focus of attention and object of anger. Equally important, isolation frees you from the scrutiny and expectations of the others in regard to how to handle the situation.

4. REVIEW THE SITUATION WITH THE CHILD. If, as discussed above, you've made your expectations clear, stated the consequences of failing those expectations, and have administered a warning, review the situation with the child and follow through with the discipline warranted. If, as often occurs, things are not so black and white, encourage the child to communicate his feelings. Try to uncover what occasioned the acting out. Lecturing and accusatory language don't work well here, nor do threats. Dr. Turnbow suggests a better approach (after the child is calm) is to ask, "What can we do to make this a better day for you?"

5. FREQUENT TANTRUMS OR ACTING OUT. The preceding four points relate to dealing with an incident as opposed to a chronic condition. If a child frequently acts out or throws tantrums, you'll need to employ a somewhat different strategy.

Tantrums are cyclical events evolved from learned behavior. A child learns that he can get your undivided attention by acting out. When you respond, whether by scolding, admonishing, threatening, or negotiating, your response further draws you into the cycle and prolongs the behavior. When you accede to the child's demands, you reinforce the effectiveness of the tantrum and raise the cost of capitulation next time around. When a child thus succeeds in monopolizing your attention, he effectively becomes the person in charge.

To break this cycle, you must disengage from the child. The object is to demonstrate that the cause and effect relationship (that is, tantrum elicits parental attention) is no longer operative. This can be accomplished by refusing to interact with the child as long as the untoward behavior continues. Tell the child that you're unwilling to discuss his problem until he calms down. You can ignore the behavior, remove yourself from the child's presence (or visa versa), or isolate the child with a time-out. The important thing is to disengage quickly and decisively with no discussion or negotiation.

Most children don't pick the family vacation as the time to start throwing tantrums. The behavior will be evident before you leave home and home is the best place to deal with it. Be forewarned, however, that bad habits die hard, and that a child accustomed to getting attention by throwing tantrums will not simply give up after a single instance of disengagement. More likely, the child will at first escalate the intensity and length of his tantrums. By your consistent refusal over several weeks (or even months) to respond to his behavior, however, he will finally adjust to the new paradigm.

Tantrums are about getting attention. Giving your child attention when things are on an even keel often preempts acting out.

Liliane

Children are cunning as well as observant. Many understand that a tantrum in public is embarrassing to you and that you're more likely to cave in than you would at home. Once again, consistency is the key, along with a bit of anticipation. When traveling, it's not necessary to retreat to the privacy of a hotel room to isolate your child. You can carve out space for time-out almost anywhere: on a theme park bench, in a park, in your car, in a restroom, even on a sidewalk. You can often spot the warning signs of an impending tantrum and head it off by talking to the child before he reaches an explosive emotional pitch.

6. SALVAGE OPERATIONS. Children are full of surprises, and sometimes the surprises are not good. If your sweet child manages to make a mistake of mammoth proportions, what do you do? This happened to an Ohio couple, resulting in the offending kid pretty much being grounded for life. Fortunately there were no injuries or lives lost, but the parents had to determine what to do for the remainder of the vacation. For starters, they split the group. One parent escorted the offending child back to the hotel where he was effectively confined to his guest room for the duration. That evening, the parents arranged for in-room sitters for the rest of the stay. Expensive? You bet, but better than watching your whole vacation go down the tubes.

A family at Walt Disney World's Magic Kingdom theme park had a similar experience, although the offense was of a more modest order of magnitude. Because it was their last day of vacation, they elected to place the child in time-out, in the theme park, for the rest of the day. One parent monitored the culprit while the other parent and the siblings enjoyed the attractions. At agreed times the parents would switch places. Once again, not ideal, but preferable to stopping the vacation.

PART TWO

GETTING *your* ACT TOGETHER

Visiting Walt Disney World is a bit like childbirth—you never really believe what people tell you, but once you have been through it yourself, you know exactly what they were saying!

—Hilary Wolfe, a mother and *Unofficial Guide*
reader from Swansea, United Kingdom

GATHERING INFORMATION

IN ADDITION TO THIS GUIDE, we recommend that you obtain the following:

1. **THE WALT DISNEY TRAVEL COMPANY FLORIDA VACATIONS BROCHURE AND VIDEO/DVD** This video/DVD and brochure describe Walt Disney World in its entirety, list rates for all Disney resort hotels and campgrounds, and describe Disney World package vacations. They're available from most travel agents or by calling the Walt Disney Travel Company at ☎ 407-828-8101 or 407-934-7639. Be prepared to hold. When you get a representative, tell them you want the video or DVD vacation planner that lists the benefits and costs of the various packages. Ask them to address the package to your child: he or she will love getting surprise mail.

2. **THE DISNEY CRUISE LINE BROCHURE AND DVD** This brochure provides details on vacation packages that combine a cruise on the Disney Cruise Line with a stay at Disney World. Disney Cruise Line also offers a free DVD that tells all you need to know about Disney cruises and then some. To obtain a copy, call ☎ 800-951-3532 or order at **www.disneycruise line.com**

3. **THE UNOFFICIAL GUIDE TO WALT DISNEY WORLD WEB SITE** Our Web site, **www.touringplans.com**, offers a free online trip organizer, 50 different touring plans, and updates on changes at Walt Disney World, among other features. The site is described more fully later in this chapter.

Bob

Request information as far in advance as possible and allow six weeks for delivery. Make a checklist of information you request, and follow up if you haven't received your materials within six weeks.

4. ORLANDO MAGICARD If you're considering lodging outside Disney World or if you think you might patronize out-of-the-World attractions and restaurants, obtain an Orlando Magicard, a Vacation Planner, and the *Orlando Official Accommodations Guide* (all free) from the Orlando Visitors Center. The Magicard entitles you to discounts for hotels, restaurants, ground transportation, shopping malls, dinner theaters, and non-Disney theme parks and attractions. The Orlando Magicard can be conveniently downloaded from **www.orlandoinfo.com/magicard.** To order the accommodations guide, call ☎ 800-643-9492. For additional information and materials, call ☎ 407-363-5872 weekdays during business hours. Allow four weeks for delivery by mail.

5. FLORIDA TRAVELER DISCOUNT GUIDE Another good source of discounts on lodging, restaurants, and attractions statewide is the *Florida Traveler Discount Guide,* published by Exit Information Guide. The guide is free, but you pay $3 for handling ($5 if shipped to Canada). Call ☎ 352-371-3948, Monday–Friday, 8 a.m.–5 p.m. EST, or go to **www.travelerdiscount guide.com** and order online. To order by mail, write to 4205 NW Sixth Street, Gainesville, FL 32609. Similar guides to other states are available at the same number. Also, print hotel coupons free from their **www.room saver.com** Web site.

6. KISSIMMEE–ST. CLOUD TOUR AND TRAVEL SALES GUIDE This full-color directory of hotels and attractions is one of the most complete available and is of particular interest to those who intend to lodge outside Disney World. It also lists rental houses, time-shares, and condominiums. For a copy, call the Kissimmee–St. Cloud Convention and Visitors Bureau at ☎ 800-327-9159 or 407-944-2400; or access **www.floridakiss.com.**

7. GUIDEBOOK FOR GUESTS WITH DISABILITIES Each park's *Guidebook for Guests with Disabilities* is available online at **www.disneyworld.com.**

8. PASSPORTER'S WALT DISNEY WORLD FOR YOUR SPECIAL NEEDS ($22.95) covers everything from ADHD to motion sensitivity to allergies and asthma. Search **www.passporter.com** for more information.

Recommended Web Sites

The *Unofficial Guide* data-collection director, Len Testa, has combed the Web, looking for the best Disney sites. Here are Len's picks:

BEST OFFICIAL THEME-PARK SITE The official Walt Disney World Web site (**www.disneyworld.com**) contains information on ticket options, park hours, attraction height requirements, disabled guest access, and the like. On the minus side, however, Disney's Web site is bogged down by too much high-tech gimmickry (music clips and animation that start up without asking), causing the pages to load slower than Space Mountain's standby line in July. (Wait, maybe they're just conditioning you!) In addition, the site is often needlessly complicated. For example, it takes at least 12 mouse clicks just to get the theme parks' basic operating hours for most visits, and more if you want to know parade and show times. Even so, this site gets the nod over the official Universal Studios site (**www.universalorlando.com**) and the official SeaWorld Web site (**www.seaworld.com**).

BEST GENERAL UNOFFICIAL SITES *The Walt Disney World Information Guide* (**www.allearsnet.com**) is the first Web site we recommend to friends interested in going to Disney World. It contains information on virtually every hotel, restaurant, and activity in the World. Want to know what the rooms look like at Disney resorts before you book one? This site has photos—sometimes for each floor of a resort. The Web site is updated several times per week and includes menus from Disney restaurants, ticketing information, maps, driving directions, and more.

We also read **www.mouseplanet.com** on a weekly basis. Besides timely information, MousePlanct delivers detailed, multipart stories on a wide range of Disney theme-park subjects, including restaurants, resorts, and transportation. The site hosts a lively set of discussion boards featuring a wide range of theme-park topics, and their "updates" section is the most comprehensive available.

UNOFFICIAL GUIDE WEB SITES *The Unofficial Guide to Walt Disney World* Web site can be found at **www.touringplans.com.** The official Web site of the *Unofficial Guide* Travel and Lifestyle Series, providing in-depth information on all the *Unofficial Guides* in print, is at **www.theunofficialguides.com.**

The official Web site for this guide, **www.touringplans.com,** has quite a few useful features: the most recent additions include crowd-level projections for each Disney theme park for each day of the year, as well as recommendations for the best park to visit on a given day. Updated daily, the projections take more than three dozen variables into account.

Our Web site also features a comprehensive, free online trip planner that allows you to keep track of all your trip details, including packing checklists, flight information, ground transportation, lodging, budgets, and daily activities in each of the parks. Best of all, you can optionally share trip details with family, friends, and others. So, for example, your travel agent can update your organizer, and you'll be able to see the new information immediately.

BEST MONEY-SAVING SITE Mary Waring's **MouseSavers** (**www.mouse savers.com**) is the kind of Web site for which the Internet was invented. It keeps an updated list of discounts and reservation codes for use at Disney resorts. The codes are separated into categories such as "For the general public" and "For residents of certain states." Anyone who calls Disney's central reservations office (☎ 407-W-DISNEY) can use a current code and get the discounted rate. Savings can be considerable. We've used discount codes to pay about $89 per night for a room in the Casitas section of Coronado Springs Resort. The family two doors down paid the full rate of $180 per night for basically the same room, but they probably didn't sleep as well as we did. Two often-overlooked site features are the discount codes for rental cars and non-Disney hotels in the area.

No matter where you travel, do a Web search with the city name and the word coupon—for example, "Orlando coupon." You'll be surprised how many deals for discounts come up. Avoid deals connected to time-shares and coupons that are valid only if you buy something first. Also, at **www.squaremouth.com** you'll find an independent travel insurance agency with a Web program that will allow you to compare more than 100 travel-insurance options from a multitude of insurance companies.

BEST DISNEY DISCUSSION BOARDS The best online discussions of all things Disney can be found at **www.mousepad.mouseplanet.com** and **www.disboards.com.** With tens of thousands of members and millions of posts, they are the most active and popular discussion boards on the Web. For boards that feel more familiar than your neighborhood bar, try **www.disneyecho.emuck.com.**

BEST SITE FOR WDW LIVE ENTERTAINMENT SCHEDULES Orlando resident Steve Soares posts the daily performance schedule a week in advance for every live show in Walt Disney World. This information is invaluable if you're trying to integrate these shows into our touring plans. Visit **http://pages.prodigy.net/stevesoares** for details.

BEST ORLANDO WEATHER INFORMATION Printable 15-day forecasts for the Orlando area are available from **www.accuweather.com.** The site is especially useful in winter and spring, when temperatures can vary dramatically. During summer, the ultraviolet-index forecasts will help you choose between a tube and a keg of sunscreen.

BEST SAFETY SITE All children younger than 6 must be properly restrained when traveling by car. Check **www.buckleupflorida.com** to learn about Florida child-restraint requirements.

BEST WEB SITE FOR ORLANDO TRAFFIC, ROADWORK, AND CONSTRUCTION INFORMATION Visit **www.expresswayauthority.com** for the latest information on road work in the Orlando and Orange County areas. The site also contains detailed maps, directions, and toll-rate information for the most popular tourist destinations.

GOING HIGH-TECH WITH LILIANE

Podcasts

If you just can't make it through the year without the Mouse, don't despair. Sounds, images, and news from the World are available in abundance online. Here are some of our favorites.

WDW TODAY *Unofficial Guide* Research Director Len Testa cohosts three weekly Podcasts (Monday, Wednesday, and Friday) on all things

Disney had the media and the Diz faithful worked into a lather over an impending announcement in June 2006. New theme park? New headliner attraction? Mickey and Minnie getting married? Nope, none of the above. To quote the famous line from *Who's Afraid of Virginia Woolf?,* "The puff went poof." In the end it was nothing but another pack-'em-through-the-turnstiles marketing campaign following in the footsteps of Magical Gatherings (still perking along after more than two years), Mickey's Birthday Celebration, and most recently, Disneyland's 50th Anniversary. All lasted for at least a year, as will the new Year of a Million Dreams, that runs from October 1, 2006, until October 1, 2007.

The new campaign promises "unique experiences," distributed supposedly at random to Disney resort and theme-park guests. Plans call for families being plucked out of the crowd and being awarded these experiences—or "dreams," in DisneySpeak—in a promotion called the Disney Dreams Giveaway. These range from little perks, such as riding in the front of the monorail, to bigger things that involve monetary value, like free VIP hotel stays, complimentary ice-cream sundaes, a private dinner with a princess, lessons in how to speak like a pirate, backdoor attraction privileges for the day, free admissions, and more. One of the biggies is a day of "royal treatment" followed by an overnight stay in Cinderella's royal bedchamber (sans Cinderella) at the castle. Given that the Magic Kingdom after closing turns into a frenzy of vacuuming, painting, cleaning, garbage removal, and inventory restocking, we hope that said bedchamber has thick, soundproof windows. It remains to be seen whether sleeping in the castle carries enough prestige to get you a table at Cinderella's Royal Table character breakfast the next morning.

If Disney distributes a million dreams in the course of the yearlong event, that works out to 2,740 winners a day (if we may use so crass a term when discussing "dreams come true"). How can you improve your chances of being chosen? Simple: go to the parks as many days as you can. And that, folks, is the name of the game.

Disney. Subscriptions are available free through iTunes. These programs consistently rank among the top 10 iTunes travel Podcasts, drawing 8,000 to 10,000 listeners per show. Visit **www.wdwtoday.com.**

THE MEANDERING MOUSE Host Jeff Falvo (from Houston), who bills his show as "Consciousness from the Happiest Place on Earth," has lots to say about what's happening at the parks, both in Florida and California. Access the Podcast and the Podcast Network Forum at **www.meanderingmouse.com.**

WINDOW TO THE MAGIC   Paul Barrie, your smooth-voiced host, brings you all the magic with his weekly Podcast. The show includes a game called "Where in the Park?" and delivers sounds, pictures, prizes, and more. Check it out at **www.windowtothemagic.com/podcast.html**.

SOUNDS OF DISNEY   Every other Sunday you can join Jeff Davis, aka "The Sorcerer," as he delights his audience with music, news, and Disney songs right from the parks. In addition to the Podcast, Davis's Web site, **www.srsounds.com,** provides music, videos, pictures, and a message board.

Blogs

My all-time favorite blogger is Jim Hill, who has been writing about Disney for years at **www.jimhillmedia.com.** Although Jim undoubtedly loves the Mouse, he tempers his enthusiasm with the right dose of criticism and is perfectly attuned to what's going on behind the scenes.

Another fun place for the latest rumors is **www.thedisneyblog.com.** I especially like how easy it is to navigate the different categories. From A to Z, it's the way to go! The site is really on top of things, so much so that the *Orlando Sentinel* monitors it regularly and is even known to report on the posts.

IMPORTANT WALT DISNEY WORLD TELEPHONE NUMBERS

When you call the main information number, you'll be offered a menu of options for recorded information on operating hours, recreation areas, shopping, entertainment, tickets, reservations, and driving directions. If you're using a rotary telephone, your call will be forwarded to a representative. If you're using a touch-tone phone and have a question not covered by recorded information, press 8 at any time to speak to a representative.

ALLOCATING TIME

DURING WALT DISNEY WORLD'S FIRST DECADE, a family with a week's vacation could enjoy the Magic Kingdom and now-defunct River Country and still have several days for the beach or other local attractions. Since Epcot opened in 1982, however, Disney World has steadily been enlarging to monopolize the family's entire week. Today, with the addition of Blizzard Beach, Typhoon Lagoon, Disney-MGM Studios, the Animal Kingdom, and Downtown Disney, you should allocate six days for a whirlwind tour (seven to ten days if you're old-fashioned and insist on a little relaxation during your vacation). If you don't have six or more days, or think you might want to venture beyond the edge of "the World," be prepared to make some hard choices.

A seemingly obvious point lost on many families is that Walt Disney World is not going anywhere. There's no danger that it will be

Important WDW Phone Numbers

General Information	☎ 407-824-4321
General Information for the Hearing Impaired	☎ 407-827-5741
Accommodations/Reservations	☎ 407- W-DISNEY or 407-824-8000
Blizzard Beach Information	☎ 407-560-3400
Centracare	☎ 407-238-3000
The Crossroads	☎ 407-239-7777
Disney Main Gate	☎ 407-397-7032
Kissimmee	☎ 407-390-1888
Lake Buena Vista	☎ 407-934-2273
Dining Advance Reservations	☎ 407-WDW-DINE
Disabled Guests Special Requests	☎ 407-939-7807
DisneyQuest	☎ 407-828-4600
Disney's Wide World of Sports	☎ 407-939-4263
Golf Reservations and Information	☎ 407-WDW-GOLF or 407-939-4653
Guided Tour Information	☎ 407-WDW-TOUR or 407-939-8687
Lost and Found:	
Yesterday or before (all Disney parks)	☎ 407-824-4245
Yesterday or before (Downtown Disney)	☎ 407-828-3058
Today at the Magic Kingdom	☎ 407-824-4521
Today at Epcot	☎ 407-560-7500
Today at Disney-MGM	☎ 407-824-4245
Today at Animal Kingdom	☎ 407-938-2785
Outdoor Recreation Reservations and Information	☎ 407-WDW-PLAY or 407-939-7529
Pleasure Island Information	☎ 407-939-2648
Resort Dining and Recreational Information	☎ 407-WDW-DINE or 407-939-3463
Tennis Reservations/Lessons	☎ 407-939-7529
Ticket Inquiries	☎ 407-566-4985
Typhoon Lagoon Information	☎ 407-560-4141
Walt Disney Travel Company	☎ 407-828-3232
Weather Information	☎ 407-827-4545
Wrecker Service	☎ 407-824-0976

packed up and shipped to Iceland anytime soon. This means that you can come back if you don't see everything this year. Disney has planned it this way, of course, but that doesn't matter. It's infinitely more sane to resign yourself to the reality that seeing everything during one visit is impossible. We recommend, therefore, that you approach Walt Disney World the same way you would an eight-course Italian dinner: leisurely, with plenty of time between courses. The best way not to have fun is to cram too much into too little time.

WHEN TO GO TO WALT DISNEY WORLD

LET'S CUT TO THE ESSENCE: Walt Disney World between June 12 and August 18 is rough. You can count on large summer crowds as well as Florida's trademark heat and humidity. Avoid these dates if you can. Ditto for Memorial Day weekend at the beginning of the summer and Labor Day weekend at the end. Other holiday periods (Thanksgiving, Christmas, Easter, Halloween, spring break, and so on) are extremely crowded, but the heat is not as bad.

The best time of year to visit Walt Disney World is in the fall, especially November before Thanksgiving and December before Christmas. Excluding New Year's and other national holidays, January and February are also good, although the weather is generally not as nice as it is in the fall. March and April bring spring break and Easter crowds, though it is sometimes possible (depending on the school and liturgical calendars) to find certain weeks in this period that are not too busy. Late April and May as well as the beginning of June are pretty good crowd-wise, but are hot and often rainy. Crowds in late August are more tolerable than the heat.

So, parents, what to do? If your children are of preschool age, definitely go during a cooler, less-crowded time. If you have school-age children, look first for an anomaly in your school-year schedule: in other words, a time when your kids will be out of school when most other schools are in session. Anomalies are most often found at the beginning or end of the school year (for example, school starts late or lets out early), at Christmas, or at spring break. In the event that no such anomalies exist, and providing that your kids are good students, our recommendation is to ask permission to take your children out of school either just before or after the Thanksgiving holiday. Teachers can assign lessons that can be made up at home over the Thanksgiving holiday, either before or after your Walt Disney World vacation.

If none of the forgoing is workable for your family, consider visiting Walt Disney World the week immediately before school starts (excluding Labor Day weekend) or the week immediately after school lets out (excluding Memorial Day weekend). This strategy should remove you from the really big mob scenes by about a week or more.

The time that works best for kids is the last week before school ends. Because grades must be finalized earlier, there is often little going on at school during that week. Check far in advance with your child's teacher to determine if any special exams or projects will occur in that last week. If no major assignments are on the child's schedule, then go for it.

Incidentally, taking your kids out of school for more than a few days is problematic. We have received well-considered letters from parents and teachers who don't think taking kids out of school is such a hot idea. A Fairfax, Virginia, dad put it thus:

> My wife and I do not encourage families to take their children out of school in order to avoid the crowds at Walt Disney World during the summer months. My wife is an eighth-grade science teacher of chemistry and physics. She has parents pull their children, some honor-roll students, out of school for vacations only to discover when they return that the students are unable to comprehend the material. Several students have been so thoroughly lost in their assignments that they ask if they can be excused from the tests. Parental suspicions [about] the quality of their children's education should be raised when children go to school for six hours a day yet supposedly can complete this same instruction with "less than an hour of homework" each night.

Likewise, a high-school teacher from Louisville, Kentucky, didn't mince words on this subject:

> Teachers absolutely hate it when a kid misses school for a week because: (a) parents expect a neat little educational packet to take with them as if every minute can be planned—not practicable; (b) when the kid returns he is going to be behind, and it is difficult to make up classroom instruction [at the time] when the kid needs it.
>
> If a parent bothers to ask my opinion, I tell them bluntly it's their choice. If the student's grades go down, then they have to accept that as part of their family decision. I have a student out this entire week, skiing in Colorado. There's no way she can make up some of the class activities (and that's exactly what I told her mom).

 I took my son out of school for a vacation trip. First and foremost, it was a rare occasion. We coordinated his absence with his teacher. In addition to any work she assigned, I asked him to keep a diary of the trip and to write an essay about his experiences and what he learned. We decorated the diary and essay with pictures, drawings, and ticket stubs and turned them in to

Liliane

his teacher upon our return. Eventually we got the compositions back at the end of the year, and today they are wonderful souvenirs from our trip.

If you are left with the choice of going during the hot, busy summer or not going at all, take heart. You can still have a great time, but you will probably see less. If you elect to go this route, visit as early in June or as late in August as possible, avoiding July. Set up your touring itinerary to visit the parks early in the morning and late in the evening with swimming and napping in between.

If you must visit during the busy summer season, cut your visit short by one or two days so that you will have the weekend or a couple of vacation days remaining when you get home to recuperate.

Bob

Though we strongly recommend going to Walt Disney World at less busy times of year, you should know that there are trade-offs. The parks often open late and close early on fall, winter, and spring days. When they open as late as 10 a.m., everyone arrives about the same time, making it hard to beat the crowd. A late opening coupled with an early closing drastically reduces the hours available for touring. Even when crowds are small, it's difficult to see a big park like the Magic Kingdom or Epcot between 10 a.m. and 6 p.m. Early closing (before 8 p.m.) also usually means that evening parades or fireworks are eliminated. And, because these are slow times at Disney World, some rides and attractions may be closed for maintenance or renovation. Finally, central Florida temperatures fluctuate wildly during the late fall, winter, and early spring; daytime lows in the 40s are not uncommon.

HOLIDAYS AND SPECIAL EVENTS AT WALT DISNEY WORLD

YOU CAN'T BEAT THE HOLIDAYS FOR live entertainment, special events, parades, fireworks, and elaborate decorations at the theme parks and resort hotels. Unfortunately, you also can't beat holiday periods for crowds. A mom from Ogden, Utah, puts it this way:

Our family spends part of Christmas week at Walt Disney World every year. We know the lines will be outrageous, but the special shows, parades, and decorations more than make up for it. For first-timers who want to see the rides, Christmas is not ideal, but for us it's the most colorful and exciting time to go.

Here's a look at the larger special events and major holidays at Walt Disney World.

MARDI GRAS A Mardi Gras party is held at Pleasure Island from the Friday before Mardi Gras through Fat Tuesday. Admission is required. Pleasure Island is mobbed, but the rest of the World is largely unaffected.

BLACK HISTORY MONTH Celebrated throughout Walt Disney World in February. There is no extra charge for the activities (displays, artisans, storytellers, and entertainers), and the celebration's effect on crowd levels in negligible.

ST. PATRICK'S DAY Pleasure Island offers a St. Patrick's Day event each year. The outdoor celebration is free from 7 p.m. until 2 a.m. Enjoy Irish music, leprechauns, and all things green. Raglan Road, the Irish pub at Pleasure Island, opens at noon and features Irish music, storytelling, and step dancing. A cover charge of $15 per person applies as of 4 p.m. (other Pleasure Island nightclubs require a separate admission ticket).

EASTER School is out; therefore, all the parks will be crowded. By far the most interesting event of the day is the Easter Parade at the Magic Kingdom. Outstanding floats carry Mickey, Minnie, and the gang, all dressed in their Sunday best, in a special parade. Of course, the appearance of the Easter Bunny is guaranteed. If you're staying in Walt Disney World, ask at the front desk about special activities (such as egg hunts) at your hotel and other Disney resorts.

Easter-morning religious services are usually held at the Fantasia Ballroom of Disney's Contemporary Resort (Convention Center) at 8 a.m. and 10:15 a.m. (Catholic Mass) and at 9 a.m. (Protestant service). Services are open to all visitors.

This is also prime season for all restaurants, and special Easter menus are available. For dinner reservations, call ☎ 407-WDW-DINE. For dining options and actual menus, visit **www.allearsnet.com/din/dining.htm.**

EPCOT INTERNATIONAL FLOWER AND GARDEN FESTIVAL Even if you don't have a green thumb, the 20 million blooms will make your eyes pop. This outstanding event is all yours to enjoy, and best of all, it doesn't affect crowd levels at the parks. The festival is held annually during April and May.

STAR WARS WEEKENDS On several weekends, usually from mid-May to mid-June, Disney-MGM Studios becomes a mecca for *Star Wars* aficionados. It's characters, trivia games, and merchandise galore during these weekends, and kids can even sign up for a Jedi Training Academy and test their light-saber skills. Celebrities from the film series are available for autographs and appear in the *Star Wars* Celebrity Motorcade Parade.

If you want a celebrity autograph, you'll need to be fast—as in FASTPASS. Yes, you can use FASTPASS to get the autograph of your favorite *Star Wars* star without spending half of eternity in line. So if this is a priority, we suggest you get a FASTPASS as soon as you enter the park. Not surprisingly, the passes go fast, and once all the ones for a particular actor have been distributed, only a limited number of standby tickets are made available. Even then, a standby ticket doesn't guarantee an autograph: it's useful only if a given celebrity still has time to sign after all FASTPASS holders have received their autographs. Most years, FASTPASSes are distributed at the *Indiana Jones Epic Stunt Spectacular.* May the force be with you!

Is all this excitement justified? If you're into *Star Wars,* the answer is yes. Over the years, celebrities in attendance have included Carrie Fisher (Princess Leia), Jake Lloyd (young Anakin Skywalker), David Prowse (Darth Vader), Kenny Baker (R2D2), Peter Mayhew (Chewbacca), and Anthony Daniels (C3PO).

Disney, at least on these weekends, sends out many characters from the series to mingle with guests, including Luke Skywalker, Queen Amidala, Darth Vader, and various Ewoks and Jawas. Then, of course, there's the Star Tours ride. Even Mickey gets into the act, dressing up as a Jedi (as do many visitors young and old). Last but not least, all events are included in your regular Disney-MGM Studios admission. If *Star Wars* is your thing, join the other Obi-Wan Kenobi wannabes and go for it. And if not? Well, we suggest you opt for a galaxy far, far away.

GAY DAYS Since 1991, gay, lesbian, bisexual, and transgendered (GLBT) people from around the world have converged on and around the World in June for a long weekend of events centered around the theme parks. Today, Gay Days attracts more than 135,000 GLBT visitors and their families and friends. Universal, SeaWorld, and Busch Gardens also participate, so be prepared: it's going to be crowded. For more information, visit **www.gaydays.com.**

FOURTH OF JULY AT WALT DISNEY WORLD Keep in mind that this particular holiday at Walt Disney World basically means crowds, crowds, and more crowds. All parks are in a festive and patriotic mood, and the fireworks are incredible. A very special place to visit is *The Hall of Presidents* at the Magic Kingdom. We recommend leaving the parks prior to the evening fireworks and watching them—from afar—at the Polynesian Resort. Keep in mind that most parks will reach full capacity by 10 a.m., and no advance reservations will get you into a park once it is closed. So pick your park and be prepared to stay there all day. If partying is your thing, consider Downtown Disney, which throws a DJ dance party and a fireworks show of its own.

TOM JOYNER FAMILY REUNION Radio personality Tom Joyner hosts an extremely popular party at Walt Disney World. Usually held during Labor Day weekend, the Reunion typically features live musical performances, comedy acts, and family-oriented discussions. Events take place at the Magic Kingdom, Disney-MGM Studios, the Animal Kingdom, and Pleasure Island. Of special interest to the young crowd are Kids Night Out, a party for kids ages 4 to 12, and the Tween Dance Party for the 13-and-up set. Past entertainers have included Ashanti, Lionel Richie, Hammer, and Aretha Franklin, just to name a few. For more information, visit **www.blackamericaweb.com.**

NIGHT OF JOY Christian-music festival usually held the second weekend of September at the Magic Kingdom. Crowds are manageable, but there is an extra fee of about $43 a night and $72 for both nights. The lineup of artists in 2006 included MercyMe, Casting Crowns, Kirk Franklin, BarlowGirl, Rebecca St. James, Jeremy Camp, Todd Agnew, David Crowder Band, Smokie Norful, ZOEgirl, Building 429, Matthew West, and Vicky Beeching. For more information, visit **www.disneyworld.com/nightofjoy.**

EPCOT INTERNATIONAL FOOD AND WINE FESTIVAL From late September to mid-November, about 30 nations trot out their best cuisine, wine, and entertainment. Although many of the activities are included in the park admission fee, the best workshops and tastings are by reservation only. Call ☎ 407-WDW-DINE well in advance for details and reservations. Crowd conditions are affected only slightly.

HALLOWEEN AND MICKEY'S NOT-SO-SCARY HALLOWEEN PARTY Held each year on two dozen or so nights before Halloween and on Halloween night, the party runs from 7 p.m. to midnight at the Magic Kingdom. The event includes trick-or-treating, Mickey's Boo to You Parade (performed twice), several DJ parties throughout the park, storytelling with Merlin, and HalloWishes, a special spooky fireworks show. Several times that evening, Disney villains will put on a great show followed by a Villains' Mix and Mingle in front of Cinderella Castle. Aimed primarily at younger children, the party is happy and upbeat rather than spooky and scary.

The park will be crowded, so arrive early (we recommend getting there an hour before the beginning of the party, as Disney starts letting guests with party tickets inside the park around 6:30 p.m., sometimes much earlier). Proceed directly to the table where the wristbands identifying you as a party guest are obtained. Also, get the special map for the event with details and hours of all the happenings. Go straight to the rides that are on your must-do list, and after that just enjoy the party. If trick-or-treating is a priority, do that first thing after you arrive or toward the end of the night, when crowds thin out and there are no long lines in front of the trick-or-treating stations.

An absolute must-ride is **The Haunted Mansion,** which is especially spooky but only in the sweetest way. Look for the ghost in the garden of the mansion when queuing up. His hilarious tales and interaction with the guests will make you forget you are standing in line. Characters are out in force all over the park, and the Boo to You Parade is pretty amazing. Our two favorite parts of the parade are the Headless Horseman riding at full speed through the park and The Haunted Mansion's groundskeeper, with his dim lantern in one hand and his bloodhound followed by a large group of ghosts and gravediggers. The many special activities and the costumed kids and adults help you forget the crowds. So don't be shy: wear a costume—about 50% of all the adults will be wearing a getup of some kind.

In 2007, look for a Halloween party for older kids and adults at Disney-MGM Studios. Be forewarned that, unlike the Magic Kingdom version, the Studios party will be seriously scary—definitely not for the 10-and-under set. Prices have not been announced, but we expect them to be in line with those of Mickey's Not-So-Scary Halloween Party.

Both parties are by reservation only; admission is about $40 for adults and $32 for ages 3 to 9 if purchased in advance. Tickets at the gate, if still available, run $46 for adults and $39 for children ages 3 to 9. For reservations, call ☎ 407-W-DISNEY.

In addition to activities in the theme parks, Disney's **Fort Wilderness Resort and Campground** offers haunted hayrides. The wagon rides include a performer who tells the story of Ichabod Crane and the Headless Horseman from Washington Irving's story "The Legend of Sleepy Hollow." Tickets are available on the day of the ride at the Fort Wilderness kennel from 9 a.m. to 5 p.m.; be aware that they often sell out within the first half hour. For more information, call ☎ 407-824-2734. Tours run about every 20 minutes from 6:15 p.m. to 10:15 p.m. Prices are $15 for adults and $10 for children ages 3 to 9.

Teens and young adults looking for a non-Disney Halloween happening should check out the party at **Universal CityWalk.** And if you'd rather have a monster with a chain saw running after you, consider attending the Universal theme parks' **Halloween Horror Nights.** (*Note:* No costumes are allowed at the parks on these special nights.) For more information, visit **www.halloweenhorrornights.com.**

ABC SUPER SOAP WEEKEND Stars from ABC daytime dramas make appearances at Disney-MGM Studios, usually during the second weekend in November (November 10 and 11 in 2007). If your teen or young adult wants to interact with his or her favorite actors and actresses from *All My Children, One Life to Live,* and *General Hospital,* this event is for them. The weekend includes autograph sessions, a glamorous motorcade of stars, interviews, and talk-show tapings, just to name a few of the activities.

Of course, one-of-a-kind memorabilia from the shows will be available for purchase. Admission is included in the regular park admission.

A word about the autograph sessions: as with those for the *Star Wars* Weekends, special FASTPASSes are distributed at different locations. The distribution is on a first-come, first-serve basis when the park opens, and the passes are only good for an autograph session on that same day. ABC Super Soap Weekend is very popular, so Disney-MGM Studios will be packed. If possible, try to get your hands on a schedule of events before you get to the park. For more information, visit **abc.go.com/daytime/supersoap/wdw/index.html,** or call ☎ 407-397-6808. Is the event worth the fuss? Only a die-hard soap-opera fan can tell.

THANKSGIVING AT THE PARKS There are no special Thanksgiving events or decorations in the parks, so if you're looking for the equivalent of the Macy's Thanksgiving Parade, you're out of luck, although many of the Christmas decorations are normally in place the day after Thanksgiving. But if you think the lack of festivities translates to smaller crowds, think again—the kids are out of school, and this is the busiest travel weekend of the year. Your best bet for the least-crowded park will be Epcot.

Remember to make your dining arrangements long before your visit, especially if you want a traditional Thanksgiving meal. While there is plenty of food at the World, note that not all restaurants offer turkey with all the trimmings. Some that do include the **Liberty Tree Tavern** at the Magic Kingdom; the **50's Prime Time Cafe** at Disney-MGM Studios; and **'Ohana** (which means "family" in Hawaiian) at the Polynesian Resort, which is perfect for families with small children. For information and reservations, call ☎ 407-WDW-DINE.

MOUSEFEST Usually held the first week in December, Mousefest is a meeting of hundreds of Disney theme-park fans, unofficial Disney Web-site owners, and guidebook authors (including us). Dozens of activities are offered, from trivia contests to guided walks through the theme parks. For more information, visit **www.mousefest.org.** Because the event is held while school is still in session, crowds are manageable.

CELEBRATING CHRISTMAS AT WALT DISNEY WORLD If you're visiting during Christmas week, don't expect to see all the attractions in a single day of touring at any park. All parks, especially the Magic Kingdom, will be filled to capacity, and Disney will stop admitting visitors as early as 10 a.m. (Not to mention that women will have to wait up to 20 minutes to use the restrooms in the Magic Kingdom during Christmas week.) As you might have guessed by now, your only way in is getting there early. Be at the gates with admission passes in hand at least one hour before scheduled opening time. Most of all, bring along a humongous dose of patience and humor. The daily tree-lighting ceremonies and the parades are wonderful. Again, most parks will reach full capacity by 10 a.m., and no advance reservations will get you into the park once it is closed. So *pick your park* and be prepared to stay there all day.

Also, be sure to make dinner reservations long before your visit, especially if you are spending Christmas Eve and Christmas Day at the parks. Christmas festivities at Walt Disney World usually run from November 24 through December 30. From the Monday following Thanksgiving weekend until December 20 or so, you can enjoy the decorations and holiday events without the crowds. This between-holidays period is one of our favorite times of year at Walt Disney World.

The **Magic Kingdom** is home to a stunning display of holiday decorations, a **tree-lighting ceremony** on Main Street, and **Mickey's Very Merry Christmas Parade** on select days at 12:30 p.m. and 3:30 p.m. The Magic Kingdom is also the scene of **Mickey's Very Merry Christmas Party,** held from mid-November to mid-December, from 7 p.m. until midnight. Separate admission is required, and costs run from $41 to $49; call ☎ 407-W-DISNEY for dates, prices, and reservations. Admission includes holiday-themed stage shows, cookies and hot chocolate, performances of Mickey's Very Merry Christmas Parade, a magical snowfall on Main Street, Christmas carolers, a visit with Santa Claus, and a Holiday Hop DJ Dance Party and fireworks. We do not recommend the party for first-time visitors.

Epcot is a good option on Christmas Day, when the Magic Kingdom is totally mobbed, but this doesn't mean it's a desolate place forgotten by the crowds, just somewhat less crowded than the Magic Kingdom. Again, if your heart is set on touring a park on Christmas Day, you will have to get up early.

Epcot has a daily **tree-lighting ceremony** at 6 p.m. at the World Showcase Plaza and a breathtaking sound-and-light show, *The Lights of Winter*, over the World Showcase breezeway bridge. Not to be missed is the **Candlelight Processional**, featuring a celebrity narrator accompanied by a huge live choir and a full orchestra. The show takes place daily at 5 p.m., 6:45 p.m., and 8:15 p.m. at the America Gardens Theatre and is included with regular Epcot admission. Special lunch and dinner packages are available for an additional charge and include preferred seating for the processional (call ☎ 407-WDW-DINE for reservations). If you don't want to spring for one of the packages, we recommend lining up at least 60 minutes prior to the show of your choice. Guests with preferred seating are well advised not to come at the last minute, either—instead, arrive at the reserved-seating entrance half an hour before the beginning of the show. Seats within this section are available on a first-come, first-served basis and are opened to general admission 15 minutes before the beginning of the show.

The nightly fireworks, water, and laser show *Illuminations: Reflections of Earth* is always worth watching and has an extra-special holiday finale.

Our favorite Epcot holiday event, however, is **Holidays from Around the World.** While strolling from land to land, visitors can enjoy storytellers in each country. In **Canada,** Santa Claus explains how Christmas is celebrated by our neighbor to the north. At the **United Kingdom Pavilion,** Father Christmas tells of his country's holiday customs. **France** is the home of Père Noël, and in **Morocco,** Taariji explains the Feast of Ashoora. In **Japan,** the Daruma Seller talks about how Japanese celebrate the New Year. (*Daruma* dolls are symbols of the New Year and are said to bring good luck.)

At the **American Adventure Rotunda,** you can visit Santa's Bakeshop, a life-size Gingerbread House made with real gingerbread, candies, and icing. Santa himself is also on hand to tell Christmas stories. Special programs are held for Kwanzaa and Hanukkah as well. (To learn more about Kwanzaa, an African American celebration of family, community, and culture, visit **www.officialkwanzaawebsite.org/index.shtml.** Wikipedia offers a nice description of Hanukkah, the Jewish Festival of Lights, at **en.wikipedia.org/wiki/Hanukkah.**)

In **Italy,** meet La Befana, the good witch who brings gifts to children on Epiphany. (For more information on La Befana, check out **en.wikipedia.org/wiki/Befana.**) **Germany** honors St. Nicholas on December 6, and he welcomes visitors throughout the afternoon. (To find out more about the legend of St. Nicholas, visit **www.kids domain.com/holiday/xmas/around/stnicholas.html.**)

Visit **China** and listen to the funny stories of the Monkey King. In **Norway,** meet the Christmas elf Julenissen, who represents simplicity and peace. (To learn more about Norway's Santa Claus, visit **www.emb-orway.ca/facts/Traditions/Christmas/julenissen.htm.**) In **Mexico,** the Three Sage Kings (Los Tres Reyes Magos) make appearances throughout the afternoon telling the story of Epiphany.

At **Disney-MGM Studios,** the park is also dressed for the season, but the big attraction here is the **Osborne Family Spectacle of Lights.** Millions—yes, millions—of lights decorate the buildings on the Streets of America, and snow machines provide the perfect atmosphere. There is no additional fee to see the display, but be prepared for huge crowds. A little background: Jennings Osborne of Little Rock, Arkansas, began putting up Christmas lights on his house about ten years ago and expanded his display by buying the two houses next to his home. As his collection grew, so did the displeasure of his neighbors. Eventually the matter was brought to court, and in 1994 the Arkansas Supreme Court ruled that his houses, with their three million lights, were a public nuisance. The Walt Disney Company brought Osborne's Christmas lights to Disney-MGM Studios in 1995 and has a special agreement with him to keep the display.

At the **Animal Kingdom,** don't miss **Mickey's Jingle Jungle Parade.** The park has festive holiday decorations and a gigantic Christmas tree with carolers performing throughout the day. At Camp Minnie-Mickey, kids can meet "Santa Goofy" and other favorite Disney characters all dressed in their holiday finest. If you don't mind the lines, this is the perfect place for taking holiday photographs.

Downtown Disney features holiday décor and offers photo ops with Santa but is mainly about shopping. The atmosphere is festive, with special window dressings at shops and restaurants.

You thought we were done? No way—there's much more to see outside of the parks.

A word of advice for families with small children: reassure the kids that Santa knows where the family is on Christmas Day. You don't want your little ones to suddenly worry that Santa won't find them on Christmas because they're not at home. Consider shipping a
Liliane   small tree and holiday decorations to your hotel. Kids can decorate the window of your hotel room with their drawings.

The holiday decorations at the Walt Disney resorts are attractions in their own right. Generally speaking, each resort incorporates its theme into its holiday finery. At **Port Orleans Resort,** for example, expect Mardi Gras colors in the trees, while the **Yacht Club** has trees adorned with miniature sailboats. At the **Polynesian Resort,** kids will love the gingerbread workshop complete with Santa sleeping in a hammock and elves taking it easy under the sun. For the mother of all Christmas trees, make sure to visit the **Grand Floridian,** where a five-story tree dominates the lobby, flanked by a gingerbread dollhouse and a miniature railroad. At the **Beach Club,** poinsettias, artificial snow, and a gingerbread carousel are the big draw. For a more natural approach, visit the **Wilderness Lodge** and **Animal Kingdom Lodge.**

If you're staying at a Walt Disney resort over Christmas, check with the concierge to see what holiday event your particular resort might be offering. Happenings can range from carolers, brass bands, and country singers to Christmas-cookie decorating, visits with Santa, and readings of "The Night Before Christmas." Many hotels also offer free cookies and punch in their lobbies.

RINGING IN THE NEW YEAR WITH MICKEY AND FRIENDS If you're in the mood for a night of partying and live entertainment, there's no better place than **Pleasure Island** or **Universal CityWalk.** Both offer a choice of parties and midnight fireworks. The party at Pleasure Island, for guests 21 and older, starts at 8 p.m. and costs $89 plus tax. For more information, call ☎ 407-934-7639. For $169 plus tax, you get VIP access at Universal CityWalk, including food, entertainment, admission to all clubs, and an open bar at select locations. For more information, call ☎ 800-711-0080.

Though all parks with the exception of the Animal Kingdom have spectacular fireworks at midnight, here are a few different options for the last night of the year:

- **Cirque du Soleil** offers a special New Year's production of La Nouba. For more information, visit **www.cirquedusoleil.com.**

- Forget the rides—the lines will be long. Relax at the pool of your hotel and go out for a great dinner that night. If you have little children, get a babysitter. The trick is to arrive a day before New Year's, settle in, go to a water park, and start the touring after January 2, when crowds thin out.

- At **Epcot,** welcome the New Year several times. Try to have a drink just before 6 p.m. at the Biergarten in Germany. (When the clock strikes 6, it will be midnight in Germany.) Then go over to the Rose & Crown Pub in the United Kingdom and repeat the celebration at 7 p.m., as guests and staff alike will be welcoming the New Year in the United Kingdom. Best of all, you get to start all over again a few hours later when the clock finally strikes midnight at Epcot.

Did I mention that it's going to be packed? This is not a good time for first-time visitors, but fun can be had by all at the parks even at peak times. (I actually stayed at Walt Disney World Christmas Eve and Christmas Day of 2006 and loved it.) If all else fails, go to bed—tomorrow is another day at Walt Disney World, and you should be rolling out of bed early!

Liliane

HIGH-LOW, HIGH-LOW, IT'S OFF TO DISNEY WE GO

THOUGH WE RECOMMEND OFF-SEASON TOURING, we realize that it's not possible for many families. We want to make it clear, therefore, that you can have a wonderful experience regardless of when you go. Our advice, irrespective of season, is to arrive early at the parks and avoid the crowds by using one of our touring plans. If attendance is light, kick back and forget the touring plans.

Selecting the Day of the Week for Your Visit
We receive thousands of e-mails and letters from readers each year asking which park is the best bet on a particular day. Because there

are now so many variables (about 38) to consider when recommending a specific best park for a given date, we've created a computer program that weighs all the variables and provides the answer. The results are posted in a Crowd Condition Calendar posted on our Web site, **www.touringplans.com.** Once you've decided the dates of your visit to Walt Disney World, access the Web site and check out your dates on the Crowd Condition Calendar (no charge). The calendar will tell you the park to visit (and to avoid) for each day of your stay. If you don't have regular Internet access, the information is worth a trip to an Internet café or to your local library to obtain.

Extra Magic Hours

"Extra Magic Hours" is a perk for families staying at a Walt Disney World resort, including the Swan, Dolphin, and Shades of Green, and the Hilton in the Downtown Disney resort area. On selected days of the week, Disney resort guests will be able to enter a Disney theme park one hour earlier, or stay in a selected theme park up to three hours later, than the official park-operating hours. Theme park visitors not staying at a Disney resort may stay in the park for Extra Magic Hour evenings but cannot experience any rides, attractions, or shows. In other words, they can shop and eat.

You'll need to have a Park-Hopping option on your theme-park admission to take advantage of Extra Magic Hours at more than one park on the same day.

Bob

WHAT'S REQUIRED? A valid admission ticket is required to enter the park, and you must show your Disney Resort I.D. when entering. For evening Extra Magic Hours, you must pick up a wristband inside the park at least two hours before park closing if you want to experience any of the rides or attractions.

WHEN ARE EXTRA MAGIC HOURS OFFERED? The Extra Magic Hours schedule is subject to constant change, especially during holidays and other periods of peak attendance. Gone are the days when you could be certain which park was running Extra Magic Hours.

You can phone Walt Disney World Information at ☎ 407-824-4321 (press 0 for a live representative), or access **disneyworld.disney.go.com/ wdw/common/helpFAQ?id=HelpFAQThemeParkPage#q8,** an FAQ page, to check the schedule for the dates of your visit (you can tell by this URL how difficult it is to find the Extra Magic Hours schedule on the official Disney Web site). Scroll down to the question "When are the Extra Magic Hours at each theme park?" The answer will *provide the Extra Magic Hours Schedule for the current month. The same information, along with tips for avoiding crowds during your Walt Disney World vacation, is available at our Web site, **www.touringplans.com.**

We seriously hope that Disney will adopt a permanent schedule, but if it does not, use the information available from Walt Disney

World Information or the Web site listed above to discover any schedule changes that might affect you. To avoid the most crowded park, simply steer clear of the one(s) offering morning Extra Magic Hours, or access **www.touringplans.com** for guidance.

WHAT DO EXTRA MAGIC HOURS MEAN TO YOU? Crowds are likely to be larger when the theme parks host an Extra Magic Hours session. If you're not staying at a Disney resort, we suggest avoiding the park hosting Extra Magic Hours, if at all possible.

Extra Magic Hours draw more Disney resort guests to the host park, which results in longer lines than you would otherwise experience.

If you're staying at a Disney resort, there are a couple of strategies you can employ to cut down on your wait in lines. One strategy is to avoid the park hosting Extra Magic Hours entirely, if possible. If you can be at the park when it opens, a second strategy would be to visit the park offering a morning Extra Magic Hours session until lunchtime, then visit another, less-crowded park in the afternoon.

PLANNING *your* WALT DISNEY WORLD VACATION BUDGET

HOW MUCH YOU SPEND DEPENDS on how long you stay at Walt Disney World. But even if you only stop by for an afternoon, be prepared to drop a bundle. Later we'll show you how to save money on lodging. This section will give you some sense of what you can expect to pay for admissions and food. And we'll help you decide which admission option will best meet your needs.

WALT DISNEY WORLD ADMISSION OPTIONS

IN AN EFFORT TO ACCOMMODATE VACATIONS of various durations and activities, Disney offers a number of different admission options to its theme parks. These options range from the basic "One Day, One Park" ticket, good for a single entry into any one of Disney's theme parks, to the top of the line Premium Annual Pass, good for 365 days of admission into every theme and water park Disney operates, plus DisneyQuest and Pleasure Island.

We wrote a computer program to help you figure out which of the many Disney admission options is best for you. You can use the program by visiting our Web site at **www.touringplans.com.** All you have to do is answer a few simple questions about what you want to see, whether you intend to stay at a Disney or non-Disney hotel, and so on (nothing personal). The program will then identify the four least-expensive ticket options for your vacation.

Magic Your Way

In January 2005, Walt Disney World pretty much chunked its entire panoply of admission options and introduced a completely new array of theme-park tickets in a program called "Magic Your Way." The new scheme applies to both one-day and multiday passports and begins with a "Base Ticket" (also referred to in some Disney literature as a "Starter Pass"). Features that were previously bundled with certain tickets, such as the ability to visit more than one park per day ("park hopping"), or the inclusion of admission to Disney's minor venues (Typhoon Lagoon, Blizzard Beach, Pleasure Island, DisneyQuest, and such) are now available as individual add-ons to the Base Ticket.

As before, there is a volume discount. The more days of admission you purchase, the lower the cost per day. For example, if you buy an adult Five-Day Base Ticket for $219.39 (taxes included), each day will cost $43.87, as compared to $71.36 a day for a one-day pass. Base Tickets can be purchased from one to up to ten days. The Base Ticket admits you to exactly one Disney theme park per day. Unlike Disney's previous multiday tickets, you cannot use a Base Ticket to visit more than one park per day.

Under the old system, unused days on multiday passports were good indefinitely. Now passes expire 14 days from the first day of use.

Base Ticket Add-On Options

Navigating the Magic Your Way program is much like ordering dinner in an upscale restaurant where all menu selections are à la carte: lots of choices, mostly expensive, virtually all of which require some thought.

Three add-on options are offered with the Base Ticket, each at an additional cost:

PARK HOPPING Adding this feature to your Base Ticket allows you to visit more than one theme park per day. The cost is a flat $47.93 (tax included) on top of the Base Ticket price and covers the total number of days' admission you buy. It's an exorbitant price for one or two days but becomes more affordable the longer your stay.

NO EXPIRATION DATE Adding this option to your ticket means that unused admissions to the major theme parks and the swimming parks, as well as other minor venues, never expire. The No Expiration option ranges from $10.65 with tax for a two-day ticket to $165.08 for a 10-day ticket. This option is not available on one-day tickets.

Research indicates that less than one in ten admission passes with unused days are ever used. I can report, however, that I have successfully kept track of all the partially used tickets I've taken home over the years. The secret? I keep them in the same place all the time with my passport, insurance papers, and other travel documents. And one more thing: I always keep a copy of my credit card receipt documenting the purchase. I even make a photocopy because receipts fade as time goes by.

Liliane

Magic Your Way: Facts on WDW Prices

	1-day	2-day	3-day	4-day	5-day
BASE TICKET AGE 10 AND UP:					
	$71.36	$140.58	$204.48	$215.13	$219.39
COST PER DAY	$70.29	$68.16	$53.78	$43.88
BASE TICKET AGES 3–9:					
	$59.64	$117.15	$170.40	$178.92	$179.99
COST PER DAY	$58.58	$56.80	$44.73	$36.00
FOR PARK HOPPER, ADD:					
	$47.93	$47.93	$47.93	$47.93	$47.93
PARK HOPPER COST PER DAY:					
		$23.97	$15.98	$11.98	$9.59
FOR WATER PARK FUN AND MORE, ADD:					
	$53.25	$53.25	$53.25	$53.25	$53.25
NUMBER OF WPFAM VISITS:					
	3	3	3	4	4
FOR NO EXPIRATION, ADD:					
	n/a	$10.65	$15.98	$42.60	$58.58
EFFECTIVE COST PER DAY ADULT (BASE PRICE + NO EXPIRATION):					
		$80.94	$76.15	$67.98	$58.52

WATER PARK FUN AND MORE (WPFAM) With this third add-on option, you can bundle single admissions to one of Disney's water parks (Blizzard Beach and Typhoon Lagoon), DisneyQuest, Disney's Wide World of Sports, or Pleasure Island with your base ticket. The cost is a flat $53.25, and the number of WPFAM admissions per ticket is tied to the number of days' admission you buy. One-, two-, and three-day tickets come with three admissions; four- and five-day tickets get four admissions; six-day tickets merit five admissions; and six admissions are accorded seven- through ten-day tickets. The number of admissions is fixed. You cannot, for example, purchase a Ten-day Base Ticket with only three admissions or a Three-day Base Ticket with four admissions. You can, however, skip the Plus Pack entirely and buy an individual admission to any of these minor parks.

The forgoing add-ons are available for purchase in any combination (except for a No Expiration add-on on one-day tickets). If you buy a Base Ticket and decide later that you want one or more of the options, you can upgrade the Base Ticket to add the feature(s) you desire.

PREMIUM PASSES A Premium Pass is simply a Base Ticket bundled with the Park Hopping and Plus Pack features. The No Expiration add-on can also be purchased for Premium Passes.

Theme-park Ticket Options with 6.5% Sales Tax

	6-day	7-day	8-day	9-day	10-day
BASE TICKET AGE 10 AND UP:					
	$221.52	$223.65	$225.78	$227.91	$230.04
	$36.92	$31.95	$28.22	$25.32	$23.00
BASE TICKET AGES 3-9:					
	$182.12	$184.25	$186.38	$187.44	$188.51
	$30.35	$26.32	$23.30	$20.83	$18.85
FOR PARK HOPPER, ADD:					
	$47.93	$47.93	$47.93	$47.93	$47.93
PARK HOPPER COST PER DAY:					
	$7.99	$6.85	$5.99	$5.33	$4.79
FOR WATER PARK FUN AND MORE, ADD:					
	$53.25	$53.25	$53.25	$53.25	$53.25
NUMBER OF WPFAM VISITS:					
	5	6	6	6	6
FOR NO EXPIRATION, ADD:					
	$63.90	$95.85	$133.13	$159.75	$165.08
EFFECTIVE COST PER DAY ADULT:					
	$49.70	$47.93	$47.24	$45.29	$41.35

ANNUAL PASSPORTS First-time Annual Passports with tax included run $462.21 and $406.83 for adults and children, respectively. Renewals cost $419.61 and $359.56. Although annual passholders qualify for free parking, room discounts, and other perks, the annual passport saves money on admissions only if you spend more than 11 days a year at the theme parks. For about $130 more you can buy a Premium Annual Pass that includes admission to the water parks, DisneyQuest, and Pleasure Island.

Big Brother Is Watching

All Magic Your Way tickets are personalized, with the ticket holder's name and biometric information stored on the ticket. A quick and painless measurement of two fingers from your right hand—taken the first time you use the ticket—is now part of what it takes to get into the park. In our experiments, however, we found out that the bio data recorded appears not to be very exact, and none of our researchers had any difficulty with the scanner using someone else's pass. This leads us to conclude that the scanner is only capable of gross measurement, such as a finger width, as opposed to capturing fine data.

The one thing we can tell you with certainty, however, is that finger-scanning brings the admissions process to a crawl.

Most partially used passes purchased before January 2005 don't bear the buyer's photograph or signature—or even name—and guests have generally had no difficulty gaining admission with a partially used pass acquired from a friend or a relative. This makes the pass perfectly, though illegally, transferable.

Where to Buy Your Tickets

You can buy admission passes on arrival at Walt Disney World or purchase them in advance. Passes are available at Walt Disney Resorts,

Liliane

Stay clear of passes bought on the black market or offered on eBay.

some non-Disney hotels, and in Walt Disney stores. Disney offers some discounts on certain tickets if you buy them in advance from their Web site. Visit **www.disneyworld.com.**

For discounts, check **www.mousesavers.com** or try using an online ticket wholesaler; all tickets sold are brand new, and savings can range from $7 to $25.

Some suggested sources include the following:

Undercover Tourist	**www.undercovertourist.com**
Kissimmee Guest Services	**www.kgstickets.com**
Maple Leaf Tickets	**www.mapleleaftickets.com**
The Official Ticket Center	**www.officialticketcenter.com**

Active-duty and retired military, Department of Defense civilian employees, some civil service employees, and dependents of these groups can buy Disney multiday admissions at a 9% to 10% discount. At most military and DOD installations, the passes are available from the Morale, Welfare, and Recreation office. Military personnel can buy discounted tickets for nonmilitary guests as long as the military member accompanies the nonmilitary member.

Other various discounts are offered to Canadians purchasing their tickets at a Disney store in Canada, AAA members, Disney Vacation Club members, and Disney corporate sponsors.

So where are the really cheap tickets, or even better, the free passes? Heavily discounted tickcts or even free offers abound, but obtaining them generally requires you to attend a time-share sales presentation. While there is nothing intrinsically wrong with the time-share concept, we feel that giving up two to four hours of your vacation time to sit through a high-pressure sales pitch is not worth it. If you are truly interested in a time-share, do your homework ahead of time. Check out the sellers and their reputations, and make appointments to visit the properties just as you would when you acquire any real estate. We believe that your vacation with your kids is not the right time for such an endeavor.

Liliane

What do you do with the kid's pass you bought when your now six-foot teenager was less than 10 years of age? Go to Guest Services and ask them to change the pass into a regular admission pass for the amount of days left on it. If you are lucky, they will do so without asking you to pay the price difference, but if not you are still better off paying the difference and using the pass instead of wasting whatever value is left on it.

HOW MUCH DOES IT COST PER DAY AT WALT DISNEY WORLD?

A TYPICAL DAY WOULD COST $475.67, excluding lodging and transportation, for a family of four—Mom, Dad, 12-year-old Tim, and 8-year-old Sandy—driving their own car and staying outside the World. They plan to be in the area for a week, so they buy Five-Day Base Tickets with Park-Hopping Option. Here's a breakdown:

HOW MUCH DOES A DAY COST?

Breakfast for four at Denny's with tax and tip	$32.00
Epcot parking fee	9.00
One day's admission on a 5-Day Base Ticket with Park-Hopping Option	
Dad: Adult 5-Day with tax = $267 divided by five (days)	53.46
Mom: Adult 5-Day with tax = $267 divided by five (days)	53.46
Tim: Adult 5-Day with tax = $267 divided by five (days)	53.46
Sandy: Child 5-Day with tax = $202 divided by five (days)	44.79
Morning break (soda or coffee)	15.50
Fast-food lunch (sandwich or burger, fries, soda), no tip	35.00
Afternoon break (soda and popcorn)	22.00
Dinner at Italy (no alcoholic beverages) with tax and tip	118.00
Souvenirs (Mickey T-shirts for Tim and Sandy) with tax*	37.00
One-Day total (without lodging or transportation)	$475.67

* Cheer up; you won't have to buy souvenirs every day.

BABYSITTING

CHILD-CARE CENTERS Child care isn't available inside the theme parks, but each Magic Kingdom resort connected by monorail or boat, two Epcot resorts (Yacht and Beach Club resorts), and Animal Kingdom Lodge have a child-care center for potty-trained children older than 3 years. Services vary, but children generally can be left between 4:30 p.m. and midnight. Milk and cookies, and blankets and pillows are provided at all centers, and dinner is provided at most. Play is supervised but not

CHILD-CARE CLUBS*			
HOTEL	NAME OF PROGRAM	AGES	PHONE
Animal Kingdom Lodge	Simba's Cubhouse	4–12	☎ 407-938-4785
Buena Vista Palace	All About Kids	All	☎ 407-934-7000
Dolphin	Camp Dolphin	4–12	☎ 407-934-4241
Grand Floridian Beach Resort	Mouseketeer Club	4–12	☎ 407-824-1666
The Hilton	All About Kids	4–12	☎ 407-812-9300
Polynesian Resort	Neverland Club	4–12	☎ 407-824-2000
Swan	Camp Dolphin	4–12	☎ 407-934-1621
Wilderness Lodge & Villas	Cub's Den	4–12	☎ 407-824-1083
Yacht and Beach Club resorts	Sandcastle Club	4–12	☎ 407-934-7000

* Child-care clubs operate afternoons and evenings. Before 4 p.m., call the hotel rather than the number listed above.

organized, and toys, videos, and games are plentiful. Guests at any Disney resort or campground may use the services.

The most elaborate of the child-care centers (variously called "clubs" or "camps") is Neverland Club at the Polynesian Resort. The rate for ages 4 to 12 is $10 per hour per child.

All clubs accept reservations (some six months in advance!) with a credit-card guarantee. Call the club directly or reserve through Disney central reservations at ☎ 407-WDW-DINE. Most clubs require a 24-hour cancellation notice and levy a hefty penalty of $15 per child for no-shows. A limited number of walk-ins are usually accepted on a first-come, first-serve basis.

If you're staying in a Disney resort that doesn't offer a child-care club and you don't have a car, you're better off using in-room babysitting. Trying to take your child to a club in another hotel via Disney bus requires a 50- to 90-minute trip each way. By the time you have deposited your little one, it will almost be time to pick him up again.

Child-care clubs close at or before midnight. If you intend to stay out late, in-room babysitting is your best bet.

IN-ROOM BABYSITTING Three companies provide in-room sitting in Walt Disney World and surrounding tourist areas, including the International Drive/Orange County Convention Center area, the Universal Orlando area, and the Lake Buena Vista area. They are **Kid's Nite Out** (a Kinder-Care company), **All About Kids,** and the **Fairy Godmothers** (no kidding). Kid's Nite Out also serves hotels in the greater Orlando area, including downtown. All three provide sitters older than age 18 who are insured, bonded, and trained in CPR. Some sitters have advanced medical/first-aid training and/or education credentials. All sitters are screened, reference-checked, and

Babysitting Services

KID'S NITE OUT	**ALL ABOUT KIDS**	**FAIRY GODMOTHERS**
☎ 407-828-0920 or 800-696-8105 www.kidsniteout.com	☎ 407-812-9300 or 800-728-6506 www.all-about-kids.com	☎ 407-277-3724 or 407-275-7326
HOTELS SERVED All Orlando, WDW hotels, and WDW area hotels	HOTELS SERVED All WDW hotels and some outside WDW area	HOTELS SERVED All WDW hotels and all hotels in the general WDW area
SITTERS Male and female	SITTERS Male and female	SITTERS Mothers and grandmothers
MINIMUM CHARGES 4 hours	MINIMUM CHARGES 4 hours	MINIMUM CHARGES 4 hours
BASE HOURLY RATES 1 child $14 2 children $16.50 3 children $19 4 children $21.50	BASE HOURLY RATES 1 child $12 2 children $13 3 children $15 4 children $15	BASE HOURLY RATES 1 child $12 2 children $14 3 children $14 4 children $16
EXTRA CHARGES Transportation fee $10; starting after 9 p.m. +$2 per hour	EXTRA CHARGES Transportation fee $8; starting after 9 p.m. +$2 per hour	EXTRA CHARGES Transportation fee $12; starting after 10 p.m. +$2 per hour
CANCELLATION DEADLINE 24 hours prior to service when reservation is made	CANCELLATION DEADLINE 3 hours prior to service	CANCELLATION DEADLINE 3 hours prior to service
FORM OF PAYMENT AE, D, MC, V; gratuity in cash	FORM OF PAYMENT Cash or travelers checks for actual payment; gratuity in cash. Credit card to hold reservation	FORM OF PAYMENT Cash or travelers checks for actual payment; gratuity in cash
THINGS SITTERS WON'T DO Transport children in private vehicle; take children swimming; give baths	THINGS SITTERS WON'T DO Transport children; give baths	THINGS SITTERS WON'T DO Transport children; give baths. Swimming is at sitter's discretion.

police-checked. In addition to caring for your children in your guest room, the sitters will, if you direct (and pay), take your children to the theme parks or other venues. Many sitters arrive loaded with reading books, coloring books, and games. All three services offer bilingual sitters.

SPECIAL PROGRAMS FOR CHILDREN

SEVERAL PROGRAMS FOR CHILDREN are available, but they are somewhat lacking in educational focus.

GRAND ADVENTURES IN COOKING This experience originates at the Grand Floridian at Walt Disney World, where children cook treats and decorate a chef hat and apron. Tuesday–Friday, 10–11:45 a.m., $30 per child (ages 4–10). Limited space; reservations can be made up to 120 days in advance, ☎ 407-WDW-DINE.

LET THE KIDS PLAY PIRATE This program originates at the Grand Floridian and is open to all Walt Disney World resort guests ages 4–10. Children don bandannas and cruise to other resorts situated on Bay Lake and the Seven Seas Lagoon, following a treasure map and discovering clues along the way. At the final port of call, the kids gobble down a snack and locate the buried treasure (doubloons, beads, and rubber bugs!). The two-hour cruise operates Monday, Wednesday, Thursday, and Saturday; 9:30–11:30 a.m. and costs $30 per child. Reservations can be made up to 120 days in advance by calling ☎ 407-WDW-DINE.

WONDERLAND TEA PARTY Although the name of this enchanting soiree is enough to make most boys break out in hives, it is nevertheless available at the Grand Floridian on Monday through Friday afternoons at 1:30 p.m. for $30 per child (ages 4–10). The program consists of making cupcakes, arranging flower bouquets, and having lunch and tea with characters from Alice in Wonderland. Reservations can be made by calling ☎ 407-WDW-DINE up to 180 days in advance.

MY DISNEY GIRL'S PERFECTLY PRINCESS TEA PARTY If your daughter loves princesses and dressing up, then My Disney Girl's Perfectly Princess Tea Party at the Grand Floridian will give you a boost toward the Parent of the Year Award. Your own little princess can sip tea, listen to stories, and join in sing-alongs led by hostess Rose Petal, all while decked out in her favorite regal attire. Princess Aurora will drop by to visit all the junior royalty. Plus, your daughter goes home with a variety of souvenirs, including a tiara, a princess scrapbook, and a silver princess link bracelet. To receive the royal treatment, you'd better be prepared to pay a royal bill: $225 for one adult and one child (ages 3 to 11). A light lunch is included. Each additional adult costs an extra $75, each additional child an extra $150. Tea parties are on Sunday, Monday, and Wednesday through Friday from 10:30 a.m. to noon. Call ☎ 407-939-6397 for reservations or more information.

JR. FISHING EXCURSIONS One-hour fishing excursions on Bay Lake and Lake Buena Vista are available for children ages 6–12; the cost is $30 per child. A similar outing is available at Disney's BoardWalk and Disney's Yacht Club and Beach Club resorts for ages 6–12 at a tariff of $30 per child. Soft drinks and all fishing equipment are provided. No parents are allowed along. Dockside Outing offers cane-pole fishing daily 9 a.m.–5 p.m. at Fort Wilderness Resort and Campground, Port Orleans, and Coronado Springs; $3.75 per half hour, advance reservations not required. For reservations or additional information, call ☎ 407-WDW-PLAY.

In our opinion, the excursions are far too short for the hefty price tags. By the time the kids are loaded on the boat, travel to the fishing spot, get baited up and receive instruction, there's not much time left for fishing. If you wish to take a child fishing yourself, canoes and poles are available for rent at Disney's Fort Wilderness Campground at the Bike Barn, open daily.

MAGIC KINGDOM FAMILY MAGIC TOUR This is a two-hour guided tour of the Magic Kingdom for the entire family. Even children in strollers are welcome. The tour combines information about the Magic Kingdom with the gathering of clues that ultimately lead the group to a character greeting at the tour's end. Definitely not for the self-conscious, the tour involves skipping, hopping, and walking sideways

as you progress from land to land. There's usually a marginal plot such as saving Wendy from Captain Hook, in which case the character at the end of the tour is Wendy. You get the idea. The tour departs daily at 10 a.m. The cost is $25 per person plus a valid Magic Kingdom admission. The maximum group size is 18 persons. Reservations can be made up to one year in advance by calling ☎ 407-WDW-TOUR.

DISNEY'S THE MAGIC BEHIND OUR STEAM TRAINS You must be age 10 or older for this three-hour tour, presented every Monday, Thursday, and Saturday. Kicking off at 7:30 a.m., you join the crew of the Walt Disney World Railroad as they prepare their steam locomotives for the day. Cost is $40 per person plus a valid Magic Kingdom admission. Call ☎ 407-WDW-TOUR for additional information and reservations.

BIRTHDAYS AND SPECIAL OCCASIONS

IF SOMEONE IN YOUR FAMILY CELEBRATES A BIRTHDAY while you're at Disney World, don't keep it a secret. A Lombard, Illinois, mom put the word out and was glad she did:

> *My daughter was turning five while we were there, and I asked about special things that could be done. Our hotel asked me who her favorite character was and did the rest. We came back to our*

room on her birthday and there were helium balloons, a card, and a Cinderella 5x7 photo autographed in ink!! When we entered the Magic Kingdom, we received an "It's My Birthday Today" pin (FREE!), and at the restaurant she got a huge cupcake with whipped cream, sprinkles, and a candle. IT PAYS TO ASK!!

An Ohio mom celebrated her child's first haircut at the Magic Kingdom barber shop:

The barber shop at the entrance of MK makes a big deal with baby's first haircut—pixie dust, photos, a certificate, and "free" mouse ears hat! ($12 total).

PART THREE

WHERE *to* STAY

WHEN TRAVELING WITH CHILDREN, your hotel is your home away from home, your safe harbor, and your sanctuary. Staying in a hotel, an activity usually reserved for adults, is in itself a great adventure for children. They take in every detail and delight in such things as having a pool at their disposal and obtaining ice from a noisy machine. Of course, it is critical that your children feel safe and secure, but it adds immeasurably to the success of the vacation if they really like the hotel.

In truth, because of their youth and limited experience, kids are far less particular about hotels than adults tend to be. A spartan room and a small pool at a budget motel will make most kids happier than a beagle with a lamb chop. But kids' memories are like little steel traps, so once you establish a lodging standard, that's pretty much what they'll expect every time. A couple from Gary, Indiana, stayed at the pricey Yacht Club Resort at Walt Disney World because they heard that it offered a knockout swimming area (true). When they returned two years later and stayed at Disney's All-Star Resorts for about a third the price, their 10-year-old carped all week. If you're on a budget, it's better to begin with more modest accommodations and move up to better digs on subsequent trips as finances permit.

"You Can't Roller-skate in a Buffalo Herd"

THIS WAS A SONG TITLE FROM THE 1960s. If we wrote that song today, we'd call it "You Can't Have Fun at Disney World if You're Drop-dead Tired." Believe us, Walt Disney World is an easy place to be penny-wise and pound-foolish. Many families who cut lodging expenses by booking a budget hotel end up so far away from Walt Disney World that it is a major hassle to return to the hotel in the middle of the day for swimming and a nap. By trying to spend the whole day at the theme parks, however, they wear themselves out quickly, and the dream vacation suddenly disintegrates into short tempers and exhaustion. And don't confuse this advice with a sales

Bob

In our opinion, if you are traveling with a child age 12 or younger, one of your top priorities should be to book a hotel within easy striking distance of the parks.

pitch for Disney hotels. There are, you will find, dozens of hotels outside Walt Disney World that are as close or closer to certain Disney theme parks than some of the resorts inside the World. Our main point—in fact, our only point—is to make it easy on yourself to return to your hotel when the need arises.

SOME BASIC CONSIDERATIONS

COST

A NIGHT IN A HOTEL AT DISNEY WORLD or the surrounding area can run anywhere from $40 to $900. Clearly, if you are willing to sacrifice some luxury and don't mind a 10- to 25-minute commute, you can really cut your lodging costs by staying outside Walt Disney

COSTS PER NIGHT OF DISNEY RESORT HOTEL ROOMS	
Grand Floridian Resort & Spa	$359–$890
Polynesian Resort	$315–$780
Swan (Westin)	$259–$405
Dolphin (Sheraton)	$259–$405
Beach Club Resort	$305–$695
Beach Club Villas	$305–$1,070
Yacht Club Resort	$305–$695
BoardWalk Inn	$305–$710
BoardWalk Villas	$305–$2,020
Wilderness Lodge	$205–$500
Wilderness Lodge Villas	$295–$1,040
Saratoga Springs Resort & Spa	$269–$1,545
Old Key West Resort	$269–$1,545
Contemporary Resort	$249–$725
Fort Wilderness Resort & Campground	$239–$349
Animal Kingdom Lodge	$205–$620
Coronado Springs Resort	$139–$215
Caribbean Beach Resort	$139–$215
Port Orleans Resort	$139–$215
All-Star Resorts	$79–$137
Pop Century Resort	$79–$137

World. Hotels in Walt Disney World tend to be the most expensive, but they also offer some of the highest quality as well as a number of perks not enjoyed by guests who stay outside of Walt Disney World.

BoardWalk Villas, Wilderness Lodge Villas, Old Key West Resort, Saratoga Springs Resort & Spa, and Beach Club Villas offer condo-type accommodations with one-, two-, and (at Saratoga Springs, BoardWalk Villas, and Old Key West) three-bedroom units with kitchens, living rooms, VCRs, and washers and dryers. Prices range from about $269 per night for a studio suite at Saratoga Springs to more than $2,000 per night for a three-bedroom villa at BoardWalk Villas. Fully-equipped cabins at Fort Wilderness Resort & Campground cost $239 to $349 per night. A limited number of suites are available at the more expensive Disney resorts, but they don't have kitchens.

Also at Disney World are the seven hotels of the Downtown Disney Resort Area (DDRA), also known as the Disney Village Hotel Plaza. Accommodations range from fairly luxurious to Holiday Inn quality. Though not typically good candidates for bargains, these hotels surprised us with some great deals during 2006. While the DDRA is technically part of Disney World, staying there is like visiting a colony rather than the motherland. Free parking at theme parks isn't offered—nor is early entry, with one exception, the Hilton—and hotels operate their own buses rather than use Disney transportation.

WHAT IT COSTS TO STAY IN THE DOWNTOWN DISNEY RESORT AREA	
Best Western Lake Buena Vista Resort Hotel	$109–$199
Buena Vista Palace	$199–$236
DoubleTree Guest Suites	$199–$229
Grosvenor Resort	$90–$199
Hilton Walt Disney World	$194–$324
Holiday Inn at Walt Disney World	$99–$180
Hotel Royal Plaza	$199–$229

LOCATION AND TRANSPORTATION OPTIONS

ONCE YOU HAVE DETERMINED YOUR BUDGET, think about what you want to do at Walt Disney World. Will you go to all four theme parks, or will you concentrate on one or two? If you intend to use your own car, the location of your Disney hotel isn't especially important unless you plan to spend most of your time at the Magic Kingdom. (Disney transportation is always more efficient than your car in this case because it bypasses the Transportation and Ticket Center and deposits you at the theme park entrance.)

Most convenient to the Magic Kingdom are the monorail hotels, the Grand Floridian, the Contemporary, and the Polynesian resorts. Linked by direct boat to the Magic Kingdom is the Wilderness Lodge.

Most convenient to Epcot and Disney-MGM Studios are the BoardWalk Inn and Villas, Yacht and Beach Club Resorts, and Swan and Dolphin. Though all are within easy walking distance of Epcot's International Gateway, boat service is also available. Vessels also connect Epcot hotels to Disney-MGM Studios. Epcot hotels are best for guests planning to spend most of their time at Epcot and/or Disney-MGM Studios.

For the record, the resorts within walking distance of the International Gateway (the back door, so to speak) of Epcot are expensive and are a long, long walk from Future World, the section of Epcot where families tend to spend most of their time.

Liliane

If you plan to use Disney transportation and intend to visit all four major parks and one or more of the swimming theme parks, book a centrally located resort with good transportation connections. The Epcot resorts and the Polynesian, Caribbean Beach, and Port Orleans resorts fill the bill.

Though not centrally located, the All-Star, Animal Kingdom Lodge, and Coronado Springs resorts have very good bus service to all Walt Disney World destinations and are closest to the Animal Kingdom. Independent hotels on US 192 near the entrance to Walt Disney World are also just a few minutes from the Animal Kingdom. Wilderness Lodge and Fort Wilderness Campground have the most convoluted and inconvenient transportation service of the Disney hotels. The Old Key West Resort is also transportationally challenged—that is, buses run less frequently than at other Disney resorts.

COMMUTING TO AND FROM THE THEME PARKS

FOR VISITORS LODGING INSIDE WALT DISNEY WORLD With three important exceptions, the fastest way to commute from your hotel to the theme parks and back is in your own car. And although many Walt Disney World guests use the Disney Transportation System and appreciate not having to drive, in the final analysis, based on timed comparisons, it is almost always less time-consuming to drive. The exceptions are these: (1) commuting to the Magic Kingdom from the hotels on the monorail (Grand Floridian, Polynesian, and Contemporary Resorts); (2) commuting to the Magic Kingdom from any Disney hotel by bus or boat; and (3) commuting to Epcot on the monorail from the Polynesian Resort via the Transportation and Ticket Center.

If you stay at the Polynesian Resort, you can catch a direct monorail to the Magic Kingdom, and by walking 100 yards or so to the Transportation and Ticket Center, you can catch a direct monorail to Epcot. Located at the nexus of the monorail system, the Polynesian is indisputably the most convenient of all hotels. From either the

Magic Kingdom or Epcot, you can return to your hotel quickly and easily whenever you desire. Sound good? It is, but it costs between $315 and $780 per night.

Second to the Polynesian in terms of convenience are the Grand Floridian and Contemporary resorts, also on the Magic Kingdom monorail, but they cost as much as or more than the Polynesian. Less expensive Disney hotels transport you to the Magic Kingdom by bus or boat. For reasons described below, this is more efficient than driving your own car.

DRIVING TIME TO THE THEME PARKS FOR VISITORS LODGING OUTSIDE WALT DISNEY WORLD For vacationers staying outside Walt Disney World, we've calculated the approximate commuting time to the major theme parks' parking lots from several off-World lodging areas. Add a few minutes to our times to pay your parking fee and park. Once parked at the Transportation and Ticket Center (Magic Kingdom parking lot), it takes an average of 20 to 30 more minutes to reach the Magic Kingdom. To reach Epcot from its parking lot, add 7 to 10 minutes. At Disney-MGM Studios and the Animal Kingdom, the lot-to-gate transit time is 5 to 10 minutes. If you haven't purchased your theme park admission in advance, tack on another 10 to 20 minutes.

DRIVING TIME TO THE THEME PARKS				
MINUTES TO: FROM	MAGIC KINGDOM PARKING LOT	EPCOT PARKING LOT	DISNEY- MGM STUDIOS PARKING LOT	ANIMAL KINGDOM PARKING LOT
Downtown Orlando	35	31	33	37
North International Drive and Universal Studios	24	21	22	26
Central International Drive–Sand Lake Road	26	23	24	27
South International Drive and SeaWorld	18	15	16	20
FL 535	12	9	10	13
US 192, north of I-4	10–15	7–12	5–10	5–10
US 192, south of I-4	10–18	7–15	5–13	5–12

SHUTTLE SERVICE FROM HOTELS OUTSIDE WALT DISNEY WORLD Many hotels in the Walt Disney World area provide shuttle service to the theme parks. They represent a fairly carefree alternative for getting to and from the parks, letting you off near the entrance (except for the

Magic Kingdom), and saving you the cost of parking. The rub is that they might not get you there as early as you desire (a critical point if you take our touring advice) or be available at the time you wish to return to your lodging. Also, be forewarned that most shuttle services do not add vehicles at park opening or closing times. In the morning, your biggest problem is that you might not get a seat. At closing time, however, and sometimes following a hard rain, you can expect a lot of competition for standing space on the bus. If there's not room for everyone, you might have to wait 30 minutes to an hour for the next shuttle.

CONVENIENCE CONVENIENTLY DEFINED Conceptually, it's easy to grasp that a hotel that is closer is more convenient than one that is far away. But nothing is that simple at Walt Disney World, so we'd better tell you exactly what you're in for. If you stay at a Walt Disney World resort and use the Disney transportation system, you'll have a five- to ten-minute walk to the bus stop, monorail station, or dock (whichever applies). Once there, buses, trains, or boats generally run about every 15 to 25 minutes, so you might have to wait a short time for your transportation to arrive. Once you're on board, most conveyances make additional stops en route to your destination, and many take a less-than-direct route. Upon arrival, however, they deposit you fairly close to the entrance of the theme park. Returning to your hotel is the same process in reverse and takes about the same amount of time.

Regardless of whether or not you stay in Walt Disney World, if you use your own car, here's how your commute shakes out. After a one- to five-minute walk from your room to your car, you drive to the theme park, stopping to pay a parking fee or showing your Disney ID for free parking (if you are a Disney resort guest). Disney cast members then direct you to a parking space. If you arrive early, your space may be close enough to the park entrance (Magic Kingdom excepted) to walk. If you park farther afield, a Disney tram will come along every five minutes to collect you and transport you to the entrance.

At the Magic Kingdom, the entrance to the theme park is away-and-gone, separated from the parking lot by the Transportation and Ticket Center (TTC) and the Seven Seas Lagoon. After parking at the Magic Kingdom lot, you take a tram to the TTC and there board a ferry or monorail (your choice) for the trip across the lagoon to the theme park. All this is fairly time consuming and is to be avoided if possible. The only way to avoid it, however, is to lodge in a Disney hotel and commute directly to the Magic Kingdom entrance via Disney bus, boat, or monorail. Happily, all of the other theme parks are situated adjacent to their parking lots.

Because families with children tend to spend more time on average at the Magic Kingdom than at the other parks, and because it's so important to return to your hotel for rest, the business of getting around the lagoon can be a major consideration when choosing a place to stay;

the extra hassle of crossing the lagoon (to get back to your car) makes coming and going much more difficult. The half hour it takes to commute to your hotel via car from the Animal Kingdom, Disney-MGM Studios, or Epcot takes an hour or longer from the Magic Kingdom. If you stay in a Disney hotel and use the Disney transportation system, you may have to wait 5 to 25 minutes for your bus, boat, or monorail, but it will take you directly from the Magic Kingdom entrance to your hotel, bypassing the lagoon and the TTC.

DINING

DINING FIGURES INTO THE DISCUSSION of where to stay only if you don't plan to have a car at your disposal. If you have a car, you can go eat wherever you want. Alternatively, if you plan on using the Disney Transportation System (for Disney hotel guests) or the courtesy shuttle of your non-Disney hotel, you will either have to dine at the theme park or at or near your hotel. If your hotel offers a lot of choice or if there are other restaurants within walking distance, then there's no problem. If your hotel is somewhat isolated and offers limited selection, you'll feel like the people on a canoe trip the author once took who ate northern pike at every meal for a week because that's all they could catch.

At Walt Disney World, although it's relatively quick and efficient to commute from your Disney hotel or campground to the theme parks, it's a long, arduous process requiring transfers to travel from hotel to hotel. Disney hotels that are somewhat isolated and that offer limited dining choices include the Old Key West, Caribbean Beach, All-Star, Pop Century, Animal Kingdom Lodge, Coronado Springs, and Wilderness Lodge resorts as well as the Fort Wilderness Campground and most of the Saratoga Springs Resort.

If you want a condo-type accommodation so that you have more flexibility for meal preparation than eating out of a cooler, the best deals in Walt Disney World are the Wilderness Cabins (prefab log cabins) at the Fort Wilderness Campground. Other Disney lodgings with kitchens are available at the BoardWalk Villas, Old Key West, Saratoga Springs, Wilderness Lodge Villas, and the Beach Club Villas, but all are much more expensive than the cabins at the campground. Outside Walt Disney World, there are an ever-increasing number of condos available, and some are very good deals. See our discussion of lodging outside of Walt Disney World later in this chapter.

The most cost-efficient lodging in Walt Disney World for groups of five or six people are the cabins at Fort Wilderness Campground. Both sleep six adults plus a child or toddler in a crib.

Bob

THE SIZE OF YOUR GROUP

LARGER FAMILIES AND GROUPS may be interested in how many people can stay in a Disney resort room, but only Lilli-

HOTEL	MAXIMUM OCCUPANCY PER ROOM
All-Star Resorts	4 people plus child in crib
Animal Kingdom Lodge	2 to 5 people plus child in crib
Beach Club Resort	5 people plus child in crib
Beach Club Villas	Studio: 4 people; 2-bedroom, 8 people Grand Villa: 12 people; all plus child in crib
BoardWalk Inn	4 people plus child in crib
BoardWalk Villas	Studio: 4 people; 2-bedroom, 8 people Grand Villa: 12 people; all plus child in crib
Caribbean Beach Resort	4 people plus child in crib
Contemporary Resort	5 people plus child in crib
Coronado Springs Resort	4 people plus child in crib
Dolphin (Sheraton)	4 people
Fort Wilderness Homes	6 people plus child in crib
Grand Floridian Beach Resort	4 or 5 people plus child in crib
Old Key West Resort	Studio: 4 people; 2-bedroom, 8 people Grand Villa: 12 people; all plus child in crib
Polynesian Resort	5 people plus child in crib
Pop Century Resort	4 people plus child in crib
Port Orleans French Quarter	4 people plus child in crib
Port Orleans Riverside	4 people plus child in crib or trundle bed
Saratoga Springs	Studio: 4 people, 2-bedroom, 8 people Grand Villa: 12 people; all plus child in crib
Swan (Westin)	4 people
Wilderness Lodge	4 people plus child in crib; junior suites with bunk beds accommodate 6 people
Wilderness Lodge Villas	Studio: 4 people; 2-bedroom, 8 people Grand Villa: 12 people; all plus child in crib
Yacht Club Resort	5 people plus child in crib

putians would be comfortable in a room filled to capacity. Groups requiring two or more rooms should consider condo/suite/villa accommodations, either in or out of Walt Disney World. If there are more than six in your party, you will need either two hotel rooms, a suite (see Wilderness Lodge above), or a condo.

STAYING IN OR OUT OF THE WORLD: WEIGHING THE PROS AND CONS

I. COST If cost is your primary consideration, you'll lodge much less expensively outside Walt Disney World.

Liliane

If you share a room with your children, you all need to hit the sack at the same time. Establish a single compromise bedtime, probably a little early for you and a bit later than the children's usual weekend bedtime. Observe any nightly rituals you practice at home, such as reading a book before lights out.

2. EASE OF ACCESS Even if you stay in Walt Disney World, you're dependent on some mode of transportation. It may be less stressful to use Disney transportation, but with the single exception of commuting to the Magic Kingdom, the fastest, most efficient, and most flexible way to get around usually is a car. If you're at Epcot, for example, and want to take the kids back to Disney's Grand Floridian Beach Resort for a nap, forget the monorail. You'll get back much faster in your own car.

A reader from Raynham, Massachusetts, who stayed at the Caribbean Beach Resort (and liked it very much) writes this:

> Even though the resort is on the Disney bus line, I recommend renting a car if it [fits] one's budget. The buses do not go directly to many destinations, and often you have to switch at the Transportation and Ticket Center. Getting a [bus] seat in the morning is no problem [because] they allow standees. Getting a bus back to the hotel after a hard day can mean a long wait in line."

It must be said that the Disney Transportation System is about as efficient as is humanly possible. No matter where you're going, you rarely wait more than 15 to 20 minutes for a bus, monorail, or boat. It is only for the use and benefit of Disney guests, nevertheless it is public transportation, and users must expect the inconveniences inherent in any transportation system: conveyances that arrive and depart on their schedule, not yours; the occasional need to transfer; multiple stops; time lost loading and unloading large numbers of passengers; and, generally, the challenge of understanding and using a complex transportation network.

3. YOUNG CHILDREN Although the hassle of commuting to most non-World hotels is only slightly (if at all) greater than that of commuting to Disney hotels, a definite peace of mind results from staying in the World. Regardless of where you stay, make sure you get your young children back to the hotel for a nap each day.

4. SPLITTING UP If your party will likely split up to tour (as frequently happens in families with children of widely varying ages), staying in the World offers more transportation options, thus more independence. Mom and Dad can take the car and return to the hotel for a relaxed dinner and early bedtime, while the teens remain in the park for evening parades and fireworks.

5. SLOPPING THE PIGS If you have a large crew that chows down like pigs at the trough, you may do better staying outside the World, where food is far less expensive.

6. VISITING OTHER ORLANDO-AREA ATTRACTIONS If you plan to visit SeaWorld, Kennedy Space Center, the Universal theme parks, or other area attractions, it may be more convenient to stay outside the World. Don't, however, book a hotel halfway to Orlando because you think you might run over to Universal or SeaWorld for a day. Remember the Number One Rule: "Stay close enough to Walt Disney World to return to your hotel for rest in the middle of the day."

WALT DISNEY WORLD LODGING

BENEFITS OF STAYING IN WALT DISNEY WORLD

IN ADDITION TO PROXIMITY—especially easy access to the Magic Kingdom—Walt Disney World resort hotel and campground guests are accorded other privileges and amenities unavailable to those staying outside the World. Though some of these perks are only advertising gimmicks, others are potentially quite valuable. Here are the benefits and what they mean:

1. EXTRA MAGIC HOURS AT THE THEME PARKS Disney World lodging guests (excluding guests at the independent hotels of Downtown Disney Resort Area, except for the Hilton) are invited to enter a designated park one hour earlier than the general public each day or to enjoy a designated theme park for three hours after it closes to the general public in the evening. Disney guests are also offered specials on admission, including discount tickets to the water parks. These benefits are subject to change without notice.

Early entry can be quite valuable if you know how to use it. It can also land you in gridlock.

2. THEME All of the Disney hotels are themed, in pointed contrast to non-Disney hotels, which are, well, mostly just hotels. Each Disney hotel is designed to make you feel you're in a special place or period of history. See page 81 for a chart depicting the various hotels and their respective themes.

Theming is a huge attraction for children, firing their imaginations and really making the hotel an adventure and a memorable place. Some resorts carry off their themes better than others, and some themes are more exciting. **The Wilderness Lodge,** for example, is extraordinary. The lobby opens eight stories to a timbered ceiling supported by giant columns of bundled logs. One look eases you into the Northwest wilderness theme. Romantic and isolated, the lodge is heaven for children.

The **Animal Kingdom Lodge** replicates the grand safari lodges of Kenya and Tanzania and overlooks its own private African game preserve. By far the most exotic of the Disney resorts, it's made to order for families with children.

The **Polynesian Resort,** also dramatic, conveys the feeling of the Pacific islands. It's great for families. Waterfront rooms in the Moorea building offer a perfect view of the Cinderella Castle and the Magic Kingdom fireworks across Seven Seas Lagoon. Kids don't know Polynesia from amnesia, but they like those cool "lodge" buildings and all the torches at night.

Grandeur, nostalgia, and privilege are central to the **Grand Floridian, Yacht and Beach Club Resorts, Beach Club Villas, Saratoga Springs Resort,** and the **BoardWalk Inn and Villas.** Although modeled after eastern seaboard hotels of different eras, the resorts are amazingly similar. Thematic distinctions are subtle and are lost on many guests. Children appreciate the creative swimming facilities of these resorts but are relatively neutral toward the themes.

The **Port Orleans Resort** lacks the real mystery and sultriness of the New Orleans French Quarter, but it's hard to replicate the Big Easy in a sanitized Disney version. The Riverside section of Port Orleans, however, hits the mark with its antebellum Mississippi River theme, as does **Old Key West Resort** with its Florida Keys theme. The **Caribbean Beach Resort**'s theme is much more effective at night, thanks to creative lighting. By day, the resort looks like a Miami condo development. Children like each of these resorts, even though the themes are a bit removed from their frame of reference. All three resorts are more spread out and the buildings built to a more human (two- or three-story) scale.

Coronado Springs Resort offers several styles of Mexican and Southwestern American architecture. Though the lake setting is lovely and the resort is attractive and inviting, the theme (with the exception of the main swimming area) isn't particularly stimulating. Coronado Springs feels more like a Scottsdale, Arizona, country club than a Disney resort.

The **All-Star Resorts** encompass 30 three-story, T-shaped hotels with almost 6,000 guest rooms. There are 15 themed areas: five celebrate sports (surfing, basketball, tennis, football, and baseball), five recall Hollywood movie themes, and five have musical motifs. The resorts' design, with entrances shaped like musical notes, Coke cups, and footballs, is somewhat adolescent, sacrificing grace and beauty for energy and novelty. Guest rooms are small, with décor reminiscent of a teenage boy's bedroom. Despite the themes, the All-Star Resorts lack sports, movies, and music. For children, staying at the All-Star Resorts is like being a permanent resident at a miniature golf course. They can't get enough of the giant footballs, dalmatians, and guitars. On a more subjective level, kids intuit that the All-Star Resorts are pretty close to what you'd get all the time if Disney had 12-year-olds designing their hotels. They're cool, and the kids feel right at home.

WALT DISNEY WORLD RESORT HOTEL THEMES

HOTEL	THEME
All-Star Resorts	Sports, movies, and music
Animal Kingdom Lodge	East African game preserve lodge
Beach Club Resort and Villas	New England beach club of the 1870s
BoardWalk Inn	East Coast boardwalk hotel of the early 1900s
BoardWalk Villas	East Coast beach cottage of the early 1900s
Caribbean Beach Resort	Caribbean islands
Contemporary Resort	The future as perceived by past and present generations
Coronado Springs Resort	Northern Mexico and the American Southwest
Dolphin (Sheraton)	Modern Florida resort
Grand Floridian Beach Resort	Turn-of-the-20th-century luxury hotel
Old Key West Resort	Key West
Polynesian Resort	Hawaii/South Sea islands
Pop Century	Icons from various decades of the last century
Port Orleans French Quarter	Turn-of-the-20th-century New Orleans and Mardi Gras
Port Orleans Riverside	Old South plantation and bayou theme
Saratoga Springs	Upstate NY lakeside resort
Swan (Westin)	Modern Florida resort
Wilderness Lodge	National park grand lodge of the early 1900s in the American Northwest
Yacht Club Resort	New England seashore hotel of the 1880s

The **Pop Century Resort** is almost a perfect clone of the All-Star Resorts, that is, three-story, motel-style buildings built around a central pool, food court, and registration area. Aside from location, the only differences between the All-Star and Pop Century resorts are the decorative touches. Where the All-Star Resorts are distinguished (if you can call it that) by larger-than-life icons from sports, music, and movies, Pop Century draws its icons from various decades of the 20th century. Look for such oddities as building-size Big Wheel tricycles, hula hoops, and the like.

Pretense aside, the **Contemporary, Swan,** and **Dolphin** are essentially themeless but architecturally interesting. The Contemporary is a 15-story, A-frame building with monorails running through the middle. Views from guest rooms in the Contemporary Tower are among the best at Walt Disney World. The Swan and Dolphin resorts are massive yet whimsical. Designed by Michael Graves, they're excellent examples of "entertainment architecture." Children are blown away by the giant sea creature and swans atop the Dolphin and Swan and love the idea of the monorail running through the middle of the Contemporary.

Liliane

Just in case your luggage is delayed or your room isn't ready, always pack a change of clothes and bathing suits for all family members in your carry-on luggage.

3. GREAT SWIMMING AREAS Walt Disney World resorts offer some of the most imaginative swimming facilities that you are likely to encounter anywhere. Exotically themed, beautifully landscaped, and equipped with slides, fountains, and smaller pools for toddlers, Disney resort swimming complexes are a quantum leap removed from the typical, rectangular, hotel swimming pool. Some resorts, like the Grand Floridian and the Polynesian, even offer a sand beach on the Seven Seas Lagoon in addition to swimming pools. Others, like the Caribbean Beach and Port Orleans resorts, have provided elaborate themed playgrounds near their swimming areas. Incidentally, lest there be any confusion, we are talking about Disney hotel swimming areas and not the Disney paid-admission water theme parks (Typhoon Lagoon and Blizzard Beach).

WALT DISNEY WORLD RESORT SWIMMING POOLS RATED AND RANKED

Hotel	Pool Rating
1. Yacht and Beach Club resorts (shared complex)	★★★★★
2. Port Orleans	★★★★½
3. Saratoga Springs	★★★★½
4. Wilderness Lodge and Villas	★★★★½
5. Animal Kingdom Lodge	★★★★
6. Coronado Springs Resort	★★★★
7. Dolphin and Swan	★★★★
8. Polynesian Resort	★★★★
9. Contemporary Resort	★★★½
10. BoardWalk Inn and Villas	★★★½
11. Grand Floridian Resort	★★★½
12. All-Star Resorts	★★★
13. Caribbean Beach Resort	★★★
14. Fort Wilderness Resort and Campground	★★★
15. Old Key West Resort	★★★
16. Pop Century Resort	★★★
17. Shades of Green	★★★

4. DISNEY'S MAGICAL EXPRESS SERVICE Checked baggage for those arriving in Orlando by commercial airliner are collected by Disney and sent via bus directly to your Walt Disney World resort, allowing you to bypass baggage claim. There's also a bus waiting to transport you to your hotel. This service (complimentary in 2007) still has a lot of kinks to be worked out, and your bus may stop at other Disney resorts before you're deposited at your hotel, but you can't beat the price.

When it's time to go home, you can check your baggage and receive your boarding pass at the front desk of your Disney resort. This service is available to all Disney resort guests, even those who don't use the Magical Express service (folks who have rental cars, for example). Resort check-in counters are open from 5 a.m. until 1 p.m., and you must check in no later than three hours before your flight. At press time the following airlines participated in the program: American, Continental, Delta, JetBlue, TED, Alaska Airlines, Northwest, and United. Southwest Airlines doesn't participate, but the resort front desk or concierge will check you in online, using your reservation number, and print a boarding pass for you. If you have bags to check, you'll have to do that at the Southwest counter at the airport.

5. BABYSITTING AND CHILD-CARE OPTIONS A number of options for babysitting, child-care, and children's programs are offered to Disney hotel and campground guests. All the resort hotels connected by the monorail, as well as several other Disney hotels, offer "clubs," or themed child-care centers, where potty-trained children ages 4 to 12 can stay while their adults go out.

Though somewhat expensive, the clubs do a great job and are highly regarded by children and parents. On the negative side, they're open only in the evening, and not all Disney hotels have them. If you're staying at a Disney hotel that doesn't have a child-care club, you're better off using one of the private in-room babysitting services such as Fairy Godmothers or Kid's Nite Out (see page 65). In-room babysitting is also available at hotels outside Walt Disney World.

6. GUARANTEED THEME PARK ADMISSIONS On days of unusually heavy attendance, Disney resort guests are guaranteed admission to the theme parks. In practice, no guest is ever turned away until a theme park's parking lot is full. When this happens, that park most certainly will be packed to the point of absolute gridlock. Under such conditions, you would have to possess the common sense of an amoeba to exercise your guaranteed-admission privilege. The privilege, by the way, doesn't extend to the swimming parks, Blizzard Beach and Typhoon Lagoon.

7. CHILDREN SHARING A ROOM WITH THEIR PARENTS There is no extra charge per night for children younger than age 18 sharing a room with their parents. Many hotels outside Walt Disney World also observe this practice.

8. FREE PARKING Disney resort guests with cars don't have to pay for parking in the theme park lots, which saves about $9 per day.

WALT DISNEY WORLD HOTELS:
Strengths and Weaknesses for Families

FOR THE SAKE OF ORIENTATION, we've grouped the Disney resorts, as well as the Swan and Dolphin resorts, by location. Closest to the Magic Kingdom are the Grand Floridian, the Polynesian, and the Contemporary resorts, all on the monorail; the Wilderness Lodge and Villas and Fort Wilderness Campground, which are connected to the Magic Kingdom by boat; and the U.S. military resort, Shades of Green, served exclusively by bus.

Close to Epcot are the Yacht Club and Beach Club resorts, the Beach Club Villas, the BoardWalk Inn and Villas; and the non-Disney-owned Swan and Dolphin resorts.

Closer to Downtown Disney and Bonnet Creek are the Old Key West, Saratoga Springs, Port Orleans, Caribbean Beach, and Pop Century resorts. Also nearby are the seven independent hotels of the Downtown Disney Resort Area.

MAGIC KINGDOM RESORTS
Grand Floridian Resort & Spa

GRAND FLORIDIAN RESORT & SPA	
STRENGTHS	**WEAKNESSES**
On Magic Kingdom monorail	Somewhat formal
Children's programs and character meals	Overly large physical layout
	Children don't get theme
Excellent children's pool	Only one on-site restaurant suitable for younger children
Beach	
Recreational options	Imposing, rather formal public areas
Restaurant selection via monorail	Distant guest self-parking
Child-care facility on-site	

The Grand Floridian has a lot to offer: a white sand beach, a spa and fitness center, tennis courts, elaborate theatrical dining from high tea to personal butler service, and so on. But the tone strikes some people as rather hoity-toity; the music in the lobby can be disconcertingly loud, the rooms are not so expansive or good-looking as the public spaces, and the complex is frequently crowded with sightseers and plantation nostalgics waving fat cigars. Also, since the Wedding Chapel is located on the grounds of the Grand Floridian, there are frequently receptions, photo sessions, and tizzies—which, depending on your outlook, add charm or are inconveniences.

Polynesian Resort

POLYNESIAN RESORT	
STRENGTHS	Beach and marina
Relaxed and casual	Excellent swimming complex
Exotic theme that children love	Recreational options
On Magic Kingdom monorail	Restaurant selection via monorail
Epcot monorail within easy walking distance	WDW's best child-care facility on-site
Transportation and Ticket Center adjoins resort	Easily accessible self-parking
Newly redecorated rooms among the nicest at WDW	**WEAKNESSES**
	Overly large and confusing layout
Children's programs and character meals	Walkways exposed to rain

The Polynesian is arrayed along the Seven Seas Lagoon facing the Magic Kingdom. It's a huge complex, but the hotel buildings, laid out like a South Sea island village surrounding a great ceremonial house, are of a decidedly human scale compared to the hulking Grand Floridian or Contemporary resorts. From the tiki torches at night to the bleached sand beach, kids love the Polynesian. The resort's location at WDW's transportation nexus makes it the most convenient resort for those without a car.

Contemporary Resort

CONTEMPORARY RESORT	
STRENGTHS	Recreational options including super games arcade
On Magic Kingdom monorail	Restaurant selection via monorail
Ten-minute walk to Magic Kingdom	Child-care facility on-site
Interesting architecture	Good restaurant on-site
Nicest rooms at WDW	
Super views of the Magic Kingdom or Bay Lake	**WEAKNESSES**
Children's programs and character meals	Sterility of theme and décor in public areas
Excellent children's pool	Monorail aside, theme leaves children cold
Marina	

The Contemporary Resort has finally shed its 1950s neo-Aztec/Tex-Mex décor and the mariachi band in the lobby for a sleeker, almost Asian look, although the pyramid structure itself is a period piece, of course. And it has lots to offer the active family: six lighted tennis courts, three swimming pools, a health club, volleyball courts, a beach, and a marina that rents out sailboats of various sizes—you have to be at least 18 years old, which helps limit the traffic a little—and offers parasailing and waterskiing. Guest rooms were completely refurbished in 2006 and are now the nicest to be found at Walt Disney World. There's no compelling theme, but then show me a child who isn't wowed by monorails tearing though the inside of a hotel.

Wilderness Lodge Resort

WILDERNESS LODGE RESORT	
STRENGTHS	Child-care facility on-site
Magnificently rendered theme that children can't get enough of	Convenient self-parking
Good on-site dining	**WEAKNESSES**
Great views from guest rooms	Boat service only to Magic Kingdom
Extensive recreational options	No direct bus to many destinations
Romantic setting and interesting architecture	No character meals
Elaborate swimming complex	Rooms sleep only four people (plus child in crib)
Health and fitness center	Must take boat or bus to access off-site dining options

This deluxe resort is inspired by national-park lodges of the early 20th century. The Wilderness Lodge and Villas ranks with Animal Kingdom Lodge as one of the most impressively themed and meticulously detailed Disney resorts. It's also by far the hands-down favorite hotel of children. You won't have any trouble convincing the kids to abandon the parks for rest and a swim if you stay at the Wilderness Lodge.

Situated on the shore of Bay Lake, the lodge consists of an eight-story central building flanked by two seven-story guest wings and a new wing of studio and one- and two-bedroom condominiums. The hotel features exposed timber columns, log cabin–style facades, and dormer windows. The grounds are landscaped with evergreen pines and pampas grass. The lobby boasts an 87-foot-tall stone fireplace and two 55-foot Pacific Northwest totem poles. Timber pillars, giant tepee chandeliers, and stone-, wood-, and marble-inlaid floors accentuate the lobby's rustic luxury. Although the resort isn't on vast acreage, it does have a beach and a delightful pool modeled on a mountain stream complete with waterfall and geyser. Adjoining the Wilderness Lodge is the Wilderness Lodge Villas, a Disney Vacation Club property offering condo accommodations.

Shades of Green

SHADES OF GREEN	
STRENGTHS	Video arcade
Large guest rooms	Game rooms with pool
Informality	Ice-cream shop
Quiet setting	
Views of golf course from guest rooms	**WEAKNESSES**
Convenient self-parking	No interesting theme
Swimming complex	Limited on-site dining
Fitness center	Limited bus service

This deluxe resort is owned and operated by the U.S. Armed Forces and is available only to U.S. military personnel (including members of the National Guard and reserves, retired military, and employees of the U.S. Public Health Service and the Department of Defense). Shades of Green consists of one three-story building nestled among three golf courses. Tastefully nondescript, Shades of Green is at the same time pure peace and quiet. There's no beach or lake, but there are several pools, including one shaped like Mickey's head. Surrounding golf courses are open to all Disney guests. If you qualify to stay here, don't even think about staying anywhere else.

FORT WILDERNESS CAMPGROUND	
STRENGTHS	Convenient self-parking
Informality	**WEAKNESSES**
Children's play areas	Isolated location
Best selection of recreational options at WDW	Complicated bus service
Special day and evening programs	Confusing campground layout
Campsite amenities	Lack of privacy
Number of showers and toilets	Very limited on-site dining options
Limited automobile traffic	Extreme distance to store and restaurant facilities from many campsites
Hoop-Dee-Doo Revue musical dinner show	Crowding at beaches and pools
Off-site dining options via boat at Magic Kingdom resorts	Small baths in cabins

Fort Wilderness Campground

If camping is one of your hobbies, you can rough it in beautiful territory at Fort Wilderness for as little as $38 per campsite. Either set up a tent and use the restrooms, showers, and Laundromat down the lane, or borrow your parents' RV. With the accessibility of two markets on-site, most visitors here choose to do their own cooking; do so and this becomes the absolute rock-bottom priced Disney World vacation.

FORT WILDERNESS CAMPGROUND

784 campsites	$38–$89 per night	boat/bus service
408 wilderness homes and cabins (sleep 4–6)	$234–$339 per night	boat/bus service

Fort Wilderness is ideal for nature lovers. For the less active, there are also electric carts for rent. Also available are pools, a marina and beach, a lot of outdoor games such as basketball and volleyball, shuffleboard, fishing and canoeing, biking, even tennis and horseback riding. If you really get into the mood, you can sit around the evening campfire and watch a movie with the other happy campers. The campgrounds are the only accommodations that allow you to have pets (not running loose, of course).

Here's what you cannot do: drive anywhere within the campground, not even from your campsite back to the trading post. You must take the bus, bike, or golf cart (both are for rent), or walk (it's not far, fortunately). And bus or boat transportation to the theme parks can be laborious.

Obviously, Fort Wilderness draws a lot of families (did we mention the petting farm and the hay rides?), and in hot weather, a lot of bugs and thunderstorms. If you want things a little more comfortable, ask for a full-service hookup and get water, electricity, an outdoor grill, sanitary disposal, and even a cable TV connection. If you want super privacy and even more amenities, rent one of the prefab log cabins, which get you a full kitchen, housekeeping services, air-conditioning, a daily newspaper, voice mail, and, yes, cable TV. It'll cost you from about $240 to $340 a night, but it's pretty much having your cake and eating it, too.

Bob

When booking, tent campers should request a site on loop 1500, Cottontail Curl, or on loop 2000, Spanish Moss Lane. The better loops for RVers are loops 300, 200, 700, and 1400. All loops have a comfort station with showers, toilets, phones, an ice machine, and a coin laundry. "

For tent and RV campers, there's a fairly stark trade-off between sites convenient to pools, restaurant, trading posts, and other amenities, and those that are most scenic, shady, and quiet. RVers who prefer to be near Guest Services, the marina, the beach, and the restaurant and tavern should go for loops 100, 200, 700, and 400 (in that order). Loops near the campground's secondary facility area with pool, trading post, bike and golf-cart rentals, and campfire program are 1400, 1300, 600, 1000, and 1500, in order of preference. If you're looking for a tranquil, scenic setting among mature trees, we recommend loops 1800, 1900, 1700, and 1600, in that order, and the backside sites on the 700 loop. The best loop of all, and the only one to offer both a lovely setting and proximity to key amenities, is loop 300. The best loops for tents and pop-up campers are loops 1500 and 2000, with 1500 being nearest a pool, convenience store, and the campfire program.

EPCOT RESORTS
Yacht & Beach Club Resorts and Beach Club Villas

YACHT & BEACH CLUB RESORTS AND BEACH CLUB VILLAS	
STRENGTHS	Ten-minute walk to BoardWalk
Fun and nautical New England theme	Best swimming complex at WDW
Attractive guest rooms	Health and fitness center
Good on-site dining	View from waterside guest rooms
Children's programs and character meals	Child-care facility on-site
Excellent selection of nearby off-site dining	**WEAKNESSES**
Boat service to Disney-MGM Studios and Epcot	No transportation to Epcot main entrance, except by taxi
Ten-minute walk to rear entrance of Epcot	

Situated on Crescent Lake across from Disney's BoardWalk, the Yacht and Beach Club resorts are connected and share a boardwalk, marina, and swimming complex. The Yacht Club Resort has a breezy Nantucket and Cape Cod atmosphere with its own lighthouse and boardwalks, lots of polished wood, and burnished brass (and boxes of chess or checkers pieces available for your room on request). Its sibling resort, the Beach Club, shares most of the facilities but is a little sportier and more casual in atmosphere. The Disney Vacation Club Villas at the Beach Club are available for rental, have their own small pool, and may offer more privacy. The resorts offer a shared mini–water park, Stormalong Bay, with a white-sand beach and marina, and an unusual number of sports facilities, such as croquet, tennis, and volleyball, plus fitness rooms, and so on. Many of the rooms have balconies with views looking out across the lagoon toward the BoardWalk.

BoardWalk Inn and Villas
On Crescent Lake across from the Yacht and Beach Club resorts, the BoardWalk Inn is another of the Walt Disney World deluxe resorts.

BOARDWALK INN AND VILLAS

STRENGTHS

Lively seaside and amusement pier theme

Attractive guest rooms

Ten-minute walk to Epcot rear entrance

Boat service to Disney-MGM Studios and Epcot

Modest but well-themed swimming complex

Three-minute walk to BoardWalk midway and nightlife

Selection of off-site dining within walking distance

Health and fitness center

View from waterside guest rooms

Child-care facility on-site

WEAKNESSES

No restaurants in hotel

Limited children's activities and no character meals

No restaurants within easy walking distance suitable for younger children

No transportation to Epcot main entrance

Distant guest self-parking

The complex is a detailed replica of an early-20th-century Atlantic coast boardwalk. Facades of hotels, diners, and shops create an inviting and exciting waterfront skyline. In reality, behind the facades, the BoardWalk Inn and Villas are a single integrated structure. Restaurants and shops occupy the boardwalk level, while accommodations rise up to six stories above. Painted bright red and yellow along with weathered pastel greens and blues, the BoardWalk resorts are the only Disney hotels that use neon signage as architectural detail. The complex shares one pool having an old-fashioned amusement-park theme.

The BoardWalk Inn and Villas have a lot to offer in terms of entertainment, in that the ESPN Club, the carnival midway, street performers, and for adults, BoardWalk nightspots, are all literally at your feet. But think about what that will mean when you're ready to call it quits; the sound can come right up through the building, and odd lights are glaring at all hours.

Walt Disney World Swan and Dolphin Resorts

The Walt Disney World Swan and Dolphin resorts were not designed by Disney Imagineers, though you might certainly think they were. They were the playgrounds of postmodern architect Michael Graves; in fact, they are not Disney-owned properties at all, though guests have most of the perks. The Swan and Dolphin are patronized by business types and adult travelers rather than families, and their theme runs more to the surrealistic rather than to the whimsical. That having been said, a quick glance at the Swan and Dolphin's strength's will verify that they have as much or more to offer families than the Disney resorts.

WALT DISNEY WORLD SWAN AND DOLPHIN RESORTS

STRENGTHS

Exotic architecture

Extremely nice guest rooms

Good on-site and nearby dining

Excellent beach and swimming complex

Health and fitness center

Child-care facilities on-site

Children's programs and character meals

Varied recreational offerings

View from guest rooms

Ten-minute walk to BoardWalk nightlife

Boat service to Disney-MGM Studios and Epcot

Qualify for Extra Magic Hours program

WEAKNESSES

Primarily adult convention and business clientele

No transportation to Epcot main entrance

Distant guest self-parking

Do not qualify for Disney's Magical Express service

BONNET CREEK/DOWNTOWN DISNEY AREA RESORTS

Caribbean Beach Resort

CARIBBEAN BEACH RESORT

STRENGTHS

Attractive Caribbean theme

Children's play areas

Convenient self-parking

Walking, jogging, biking

Lakefront setting

WEAKNESSES

Lackluster dining on-site

No easily accessible off-site dining

No character meals

Extreme distance of many guest rooms around the lake from dining and services

Occasionally poor bus service

Large, confusing layout

The huge Caribbean Beach Resort occupies 200 acres surrounding a 45-acre lake called Barefoot Bay. This midpriced resort, modeled after resorts in the Caribbean, consists of the registration area ("Custom House") and five two-story "villages" named after Caribbean islands. Each village has its own pool, laundry room, and beach. The Caribbean motif is maintained with red-tile roofs, widow's walks, and wooden-railed porches. The atmosphere is cheerful, with buildings painted blue, lime green, and sherbet orange. In addition to the five village pools, the resort's main swimming pool is themed as an old Spanish fort, complete with slides and water cannons.

Port Orleans French Quarter and Riverside Resort

PORT ORLEANS FRENCH QUARTER AND RIVERSIDE RESORT	
STRENGTHS	**WEAKNESSES**
Extremely creative swimming areas	Insufficient on-site dining
Nice guest rooms, especially in the French Quarter	No easily accessible off-site dining
Pleasant setting along Bonnet Creek	Extreme distance of many guest rooms from dining and services
Food courts	Large, confusing layout
Convenient self-parking	No character meals
Children's play areas	Congested bus-loading areas
Varied recreational offerings	
Boat service to Downtown Disney	

Port Orleans's Riverside and French Quarter Resorts are good-looking, lower-cost hotel alternatives that combine steamboat-era Southern décor and fairly easy access to Downtown Disney, and they're pretty popular among families, too.

The 1,008-room French Quarter section is a sanitized Disney version of the New Orleans French Quarter. Consisting of seven three-story guest-room buildings next to Bonnet Creek, the resort suggests what New Orleans would look like if its buildings were painted every year and garbage collectors never went on strike. There are prim pink-and-blue guest buildings with wrought-iron filigree, shuttered windows, and old-fashioned iron lampposts. In keeping with the Crescent City theme, the French Quarter is landscaped with magnolia trees and overgrown vines. The centrally located "Mint" contains the registration area and food court and is a reproduction of a turn-of-the-19th-century building where Mississippi Delta farmers sold their harvests. The registration desk features a vibrant Mardi Gras mural and old-fashioned bank-teller windows. The section's "Doubloon Lagoon" swimming complex surrounds a colorful fiberglass creation depicting Neptune riding a sea serpent.

Port Orleans's Riverside Resort draws on the lifestyle and architecture of Mississippi River communities in antebellum Louisiana. Spread along Bonnet Creek, which encircles "Ol' Man Island" (the section's main swimming area), Riverside is subdivided into two more themed areas: the "mansion" area, which features plantation-style architecture, and the "bayou" area, with tin-roofed rustic (imitation) wooden buildings. Mansions are three stories tall, while bayou guesthouses are a story shorter. The river-life theme is augmented by groves of azalea and juniper. Riverside's food court houses a working cotton press powered by a 32-foot waterwheel.

Disney's Old Key West Resort

DISNEY'S OLD KEY WEST RESORT	
STRENGTHS	**WEAKNESSES**
Extremely nice studios and villas	Old Key West theme meaningless to children
Full kitchens in villas	
Quiet, lushly landscaped setting	Large, confusing layout
Convenient self-parking	Substandard bus service
Small, more private swimming pools in each accommodations cluster	Limited on-site dining
	No easily accessible off-site dining
Recreation options	Extreme distance of many guest rooms from dining and services
Boat service to Downtown Disney	
	No character meals

This was the first Disney Vacation Club property. Although the resort is a time-share property, units not being used by owners are rented on a nightly basis. Old Key West is a large aggregation of two- to three-story buildings modeled after Caribbean residences and guesthouses of the Florida Keys. Arranged subdivision-style around a golf course and along Bonnet Creek, the buildings are in small neighborhood-like clusters. They feature pastel facades, white trim, and shuttered windows. The registration area is in Conch Flats Community Hall, along with a full-service restaurant, modest fitness center, marina, and sundries shop. Each cluster of accommodations has a quiet pool; a larger pool is at the community hall. A new waterslide in the shape of a giant sandcastle is the primary kid pleaser at the main pool.

Saratoga Springs Resort

SARATOGA SPRINGS RESORT	
STRENGTHS	**WEAKNESSES**
Extremely nice studio rooms and villas	Adult theme and atmosphere
Lushly landscaped setting	Very limited dining options
Best fitness center at Walt Disney World	Traffic congestion at resort's southeast exit
Convenient self-parking	Noise from Downtown Disney
Close to Downtown Disney	Distance of some accommodations from dining and services
Best spa at Walt Disney World	
Golf on property	No character meals
Excellent themed swimming complex	Most distant of all Disney resorts from the theme parks
Hiking, jogging, and water recreation	

The Saratoga Springs complex will eventually be the largest Vacation Club resort, with well over 800 units. It's expanding toward the Downtown Disney shopping area (across the lake) via a path and a pedestrian bridge. There is boat as well as bus service at the facility, although the boats are prohibited from running if lightning threatens. The resort's décor plays on the history and retro-Victorian style of the upstate New York racing resort, with traditional horse-country prints and drawings, horsey details in the lighting fixtures, paints in the summery gazebo palette (sand, cream, mint green), and stable boy uniforms for the bellmen, and so on. The spa, probably Disney's best, has a new fitness center attached, and the swimming complex is one of Walt Disney World's most appealling (it will remind you of the Wilderness Lodge pool much beloved by kids). The Downtown Disney fireworks are visible from some areas.

Pop Century Resort

POP CENTURY RESORT	
STRENGTHS	**WEAKNESSES**
Kid-friendly theme	Small guest rooms
Low (for Disney) rates	No full-service dining
Large swimming pools	Large, confusing layout
Food courts	Long lines to check in
Convenient self-parking	No character meals
	Limited recreation options

Located on Victory Way near Disney's Wide World of Sports, the Pop Century is the newest Disney value resort. It's to be completed in phases, but the first section, scheduled to open in December 2001, actually opened in early 2004. The second phase, which would complete the planned 5,760 guest rooms, is still in limbo.

Pop Century is an economy resort; rooms run about $79 to $137 per night. In terms of layout, architecture, and facilities, Pop Century is almost a clone of the All-Star Resorts (that is, four-story, motel-style buildings built around a central pool, food court, and registration area). Decorative touches make the difference. Where the All-Star Resorts display larger-than-life icons from sports, music, and movies, Pop Century draws its icons from decades of the 20th century. Look for such oddities as building-sized

The All-Star, Pop Century, and Caribbean Beach resorts are infamous for long lines at check-in time, which is usually 3 or 4 p.m. To avoid the lines, check in between 11 a.m. and 1 p.m. Your room might not be ready for occupancy, but odds are they'll check you in and issue your room keys. If you have luggage, you can check it with bell services and have it delivered or pick it up later.

Bob

Big Wheels, hula hoops, and the like, punctuated by silhouettes of people dancing the decade's fad dance.

The public areas at Pop Century are marginally more sophisticated than the ones at the All-Star Resorts, with 20th-century period furniture and décor rolled up in a saccharine, those-were-the-days theme. Food courts, bars, playgrounds, pools, and so on emulate the All-Star Resorts model in size and location. A Pop Century departure from the All-Star precedent has merchandise retailers thrown in with the fast-food concessions in a combination dining and shopping area. This apparently is what happens when a giant corporation tries to combine selling pizza with hawking Goofy hats. (You just know the word "synergy" was used like cheap cologne in those design meetings.) As at the All-Star Resorts, there is no full-service restaurant. The resort is connected to the rest of Walt Disney World by bus, but because of the limited dining options, we recommend having a car.

If you're considering one of the Disney "value" resorts, this reader from Dublin, Georgia, thinks Pop Century beats the All-Star Resorts hands-down.

> *Pop Century is now my favorite. 1. It is far superior to the All-Stars but the same price. 2. There is a lake at a value resort and a view of fireworks. 3. The courtyards have Twister games, neat pools, and a Goofy "surprise fountain" for little children. 4. The memorabilia is interesting to us over 18 years old. 5. I love the gift shop, food court, and bar combo. 6. There are frozen Cokes in the refillable-mug section. 7. Bus transportation is better than anywhere else, including Grand Floridian! 8. You can rent surrey bikes. 9. The rooms have real soap instead of the All-Stars' yucky globby stuff. 10. The layout is more convenient to the food court. 11. I never hear construction noise, and the noise from neighbors is not worse than anywhere else. 12. Where else do the [cast members] do the shag to oldies? Also, the shrimp lo mein is the best bargain and among the best food anywhere.*

ANIMAL KINGDOM AREA RESORTS

ANIMAL KINGDOM LODGE	
STRENGTHS	On-site nature programs and story-telling
Exotic theme	
Uniquely appointed guest rooms	Health and fitness center
Most rooms have private balconies	Child-care center on-site
View of savanna and animals from guest rooms	Proximity to non-Disney restaurants on US 192
Themed swimming area	
Excellent on-site dining, including a buffet	**WEAKNESSES**
	Remote location

Animal Kingdom Lodge

The Animal Kingdom Lodge is a snazzy take on safari chic, with balcony views of wildlife that alone may be worth the tabs ($205 to $620 per night), but its distance from the other parks may be a drawback for those planning to explore all of Walt Disney World. On the other hand, if you have a car, it's the closest resort to all of the affordable family restaurants lining US 192 (Irlo Bronson Parkway). By far the most exotic Disney resort, it's made to order for families with children.

Designed by Peter Dominick of Disney's Wilderness Lodge fame, Animal Kingdom Lodge fuses African tribal architecture with the exotic, rugged style of grand East African national-park lodges. Five-story, thatched-roof guest-room wings fan out from a vast central rotunda housing the lobby and featuring a huge mud fireplace. Public areas and about half of the rooms offer panoramic views of a private 33-acre plain punctuated with streams and elevated kopje (rock outcroppings) and populated with 200 free-roaming animals and 130 birds. Most of the 1,293 guest rooms are 344 square feet and boast hand-carved furnishings and richly colored soft goods. Almost all have full balconies.

Coronado Springs Resort

CORONADO SPRINGS RESORT	
STRENGTHS	**WEAKNESSES**
Nice guest rooms	Insufficient on-site dining
View from waterside guest rooms	*Extreme* distance of many guest rooms from dining and services
Food court	
Mayan-themed swimming area with water slides	No character meals
Fitness center	
Convenient self-parking	

If you'd like to save a little money without giving up services, consider the Coronado Springs Resort, a rich, Old Mexico–style complex with courtyards, fountains, stucco and terra-cotta buildings, a few Mayan ruins here and there, several swimming pools, a mini-water park, a white-sand beach, a fitness center, a walking path circling a 15-acre lake, and so on. Because it is also used as a convention hotel, expect a high percentage of guests to be business travelers. Coronado Springs has particularly good access to the Animal Kingdom and Blizzard Beach. Rooms start at about $139.

All-Star Resorts

Disney's version of a budget resort features three distinct themes executed in the same hyperbolic style. Spread over a vast expanse, the

ALL-STAR RESORTS	
STRENGTHS	**WEAKNESSES**
Super kid-friendly theme	Remote location
Low (for Disney) rates	Small guest rooms (except family suites)
Large swimming pools	No full-service dining
Food courts	Large, confusing layout
Convenient self-parking	Long lines to check in
Close to McDonald's	Congested bus-loading areas
	No character meals
	Limited recreation options
	Close to McDonald's (joke)

resorts comprise almost 35 three-story motel-style guest-room buildings. Although the three resorts are neighbors, each has its own lobby, food court, and registration area. All-Star Sports Resort features huge sports icons: bright football helmets, tennis rackets, and baseball bats—all taller than the buildings they adorn. Similarly, All-Star Music Resort features 40-foot guitars, maracas, and saxophones, while All-Star Movies Resort showcases giant popcorn boxes and icons from Disney films. Lobbies of all are loud (in both decibels and brightness) and cartoonish, with checkerboard walls and photographs of famous athletes, musicians, and film stars. At 260 square feet, guest rooms at the All-Star Resorts are very small. They're so small that a family of four attempting to stay in one room might redefine family values by week's end. Definitely a family resort, young children exercising their lungs make the All-Stars the noisiest Disney resorts, though guest rooms are well soundproofed and quiet.

To the rejoicing of parents everywhere, Disney opened the first 50 of a planned 192 family suites at its All-Star Music Resort in 2006. Located in the Jazz and Calypso buildings, these suites measure roughly 520 square feet, slightly larger than the cabins at Fort Wilderness. Each suite, formed from the combination of two formerly separate rooms, includes a kitchenette with mini-refrigerator, microwave, and coffeemaker. Sleeping accommodations include a queen bed in the bedroom, plus a pullout sleeper sofa and two chairs that convert to beds in the family room.

We get more reader mail about the All-Star Resorts than about all the other Disney hotels combined. The following comments are pretty representative. First from a Baltimore family that had a very positive experience:

We decided early on that we'd rather spend more money on food than lodging. We love to eat and figured that we wouldn't spend that

Hotel Information Chart

All-Star Resorts ★★★
Walt Disney World
1701–1901 W. Buena Vista Drive
Orlando 32830
☎ 407-934-7639
www.waltdisneyworld.com

LOCATION	WDW
ROOM RATING	73
COST ($ = $50)	$$+

COMMUTING TIMES TO PARKS (in minutes):

MAGIC KINGDOM	6:15
EPCOT	5:45
DISNEY-MGM	5:15
ANIMAL KINGDOM	4:15

Animal Kingdom Lodge
★★★★
Walt Disney World
2901 Osceola Parkway
Bay Lake 32830
☎ 407-938-3000
FAX 407-938-4799
www.waltdisneyworld.com

LOCATION	WDW
ROOM RATING	89
COST ($ = $50)	$$$$$$

COMMUTING TIMES TO PARKS (in minutes):

MAGIC KINGDOM	8:15
EPCOT	6:15
DISNEY-MGM	6:00
ANIMAL KINGDOM	2:15

Beach Club Resort ★★★★½
Walt Disney World
1800 Epcot Resort Blvd.
Lake Buena Vista 32830
☎ 407-934-8000
FAX 407-934-3850
www.waltdisneyworld.com

LOCATION	WDW
ROOM RATING	90
COST ($ = $50)	$$$$$$$$+

COMMUTING TIMES TO PARKS (in minutes):

MAGIC KINGDOM	7:15
EPCOT	5:15
DISNEY-MGM	4:00
ANIMAL KINGDOM	6:45

Caribbean Beach Resort
★★★½
Walt Disney World
900 Cayman Way
Orlando 32830
☎ 407-934-3400
FAX 407-934-3288
www.waltdisneyworld.com

LOCATION	WDW
ROOM RATING	80
COST ($ = $50)	$$$$–

COMMUTING TIMES TO PARKS (in minutes):

MAGIC KINGDOM	8:00
EPCOT	6:00
DISNEY-MGM	4:15
ANIMAL KINGDOM	7:15

Contemporary Resort
★★★★½
Walt Disney World
4600 N. World Drive
Orlando 32830
☎ 407-934-7639
FAX 407-824-3539
www.waltdisneyworld.com

LOCATION	WDW
ROOM RATING	93
COST ($ = $50)	$$$$$$$–

COMMUTING TIMES TO PARKS (in minutes):

MAGIC KINGDOM	on monorail
EPCOT	11:00
DISNEY-MGM	14:15
ANIMAL KINGDOM	17:15

Coronado Springs Resort
★★★★
Walt Disney World
1000 W. Buena Vista Drive
Orlando 32830
☎ 407-939-1000
FAX 407-939-1001
www.waltdisneyworld.com

LOCATION	WDW
ROOM RATING	83
COST ($ = $50)	$$$$–

COMMUTING TIMES TO PARKS (in minutes):

MAGIC KINGDOM	5:30
EPCOT	4:00
DISNEY-MGM	4:45
ANIMAL KINGDOM	4:45

Old Key West Resort ★★★★½
Walt Disney World
1510 N. Cove Road
Orlando 32830
☎ 407-827-7700
FAX 407-827-7710
www.waltdisneyworld.com

LOCATION	WDW
ROOM RATING	90
COST ($ = $50)	$$$$$$

COMMUTING TIMES TO PARKS (in minutes):

MAGIC KINGDOM	10:45
EPCOT	6:00
DISNEY-MGM	10:30
ANIMAL KINGDOM	14:30

Polynesian Isles Resort ★★★★
3045 Polynesian Isles Blvd.
Kissimmee 34746
☎ 407-396-1622
FAX 407-396-1744
www.polynesianisle.com

LOCATION	3
ROOM RATING	83
COST ($ = $50)	$$$–

COMMUTING TIMES TO PARKS (in minutes):

MAGIC KINGDOM	14:30
EPCOT	14:15
DISNEY-MGM	14:00
ANIMAL KINGDOM	12:30

Pop Century Resort ★★★
Walt Disney World
1050 Century Drive
Orlando 32830
☎ 407-938-4000
FAX 407-938-4040
www.waltdisneyworld.com

LOCATION	WDW
ROOM RATING	71
COST ($ = $50)	$$+

COMMUTING TIMES TO PARKS (in minutes):

MAGIC KINGDOM	8:30
EPCOT	6:30
DISNEY-MGM	5:00
ANIMAL KINGDOM	6:15

Beach Club Villas ★★★★½
Walt Disney World
1900 Epcot Resort Blvd.
Lake Buena Vista 32830
☎ 407-934-2175
FAX 407-934-3850
www.waltdisneyworld.com

LOCATION	WDW
ROOM RATING	90
COST ($ = $50)	$$$$$$$$+

COMMUTING TIMES TO PARKS (in minutes):

MAGIC KINGDOM	7:15
EPCOT	5:15
DISNEY-MGM	4:00
ANIMAL KINGDOM	6:45

BoardWalk Inn ★★★★
Walt Disney World
2101 Epcot Resort Blvd.
Orlando 32830
☎ 407-939-5100
FAX 407-939-5150
www.waltdisneyworld.com

LOCATION	WDW
ROOM RATING	89
COST ($ = $50)	$$$$$$$$+

COMMUTING TIMES TO PARKS (in minutes):

MAGIC KINGDOM	7:15
EPCOT	5:30
DISNEY-MGM	3:00
ANIMAL KINGDOM	7:00

BoardWalk Villas ★★★★½
Walt Disney World
2101 Epcot Resort Blvd.
Orlando 32830
☎ 407-939-5100
FAX 407-939-5150
www.waltdisneyworld.com

LOCATION	WDW
ROOM RATING	90
COST ($ = $50)	$$$$$$$$+

COMMUTING TIMES TO PARKS (in minutes):

MAGIC KINGDOM	7:15
EPCOT	5:30
DISNEY-MGM	3:00
ANIMAL KINGDOM	7:00

Dolphin ★★★★
Walt Disney World
1500 Epcot Resort Blvd.
Lake Buena Vista 32830
☎ 407-934-7639
FAX 407-934-4884
www.swandolphin.com

LOCATION	WDW
ROOM RATING	87
COST ($ = $50)	$$$$$$$

COMMUTING TIMES TO PARKS (in minutes):

MAGIC KINGDOM	6:45
EPCOT	5:00
DISNEY-MGM	4:00
ANIMAL KINGDOM	6:15

Fort Wilderness Resort
(cabins) ★★★★
Walt Disney World
4510 N. Fort Wilderness Trail
Orlando 32830
☎ 407-824-2900
FAX 407-824-3508
www.waltdisneyworld.com

LOCATION	WDW
ROOM RATING	86
COST ($ = $50)	$$$$$$+

COMMUTING TIMES TO PARKS (in minutes):

MAGIC KINGDOM	13:15
EPCOT	8:30
DISNEY-MGM	14:00
ANIMAL KINGDOM	20:00

Grand Floridian Resort & Spa
★★★★½
Walt Disney World
4401 Grand Floridian
Orlando 32830
☎ 407-824-3000
www.waltdisneyworld.com

LOCATION	WDW
ROOM RATING	93
COST ($ = $50)	$$$$$$$$$+

COMMUTING TIMES TO PARKS (in minutes):

MAGIC KINGDOM	on monorail
EPCOT	4:45
DISNEY-MGM	6:45
ANIMAL KINGDOM	11:45

Port Orleans Resort
(French Quarter) ★★★★
Walt Disney World
2201 Orleans Drive
Lake Buena Vista 32830
☎ 407-934-5000
FAX 407-934-5353
www.waltdisneyworld.com

LOCATION	WDW
ROOM RATING	84
COST ($ = $50)	$$$$–

COMMUTING TIMES TO PARKS (in minutes):

MAGIC KINGDOM	12:00
EPCOT	8:00
DISNEY-MGM	12:30
ANIMAL KINGDOM	16:15

Port Orleans Resort
(Riverside) ★★★★
Walt Disney World
1251 Riverside Drive
Lake Buena Vista 32830
☎ 407-934-6000
FAX 407-934-5777
www.waltdisneyworld.com

LOCATION	WDW
ROOM RATING	83
COST ($ = $50)	$$$$–

COMMUTING TIMES TO PARKS (in minutes):

MAGIC KINGDOM	12:00
EPCOT	8:00
DISNEY-MGM	12:30
ANIMAL KINGDOM	16:15

Saratoga Springs Resort & Spa
★★★★½
Walt Disney World
1901 E. Buena Vista Drive
Lake Buena Vista 32830
☎ 407-827-1100
www.waltdisneyworld.com

LOCATION	WDW
ROOM RATING	90
COST ($ = $50)	$$$$$$$

COMMUTING TIMES TO PARKS (in minutes):

MAGIC KINGDOM	14:45
EPCOT	8:45
DISNEY-MGM	14:30
ANIMAL KINGDOM	18:15

Hotel Information Chart (continued)

Shades of Green ★★★★½
Walt Disney World
1950 W. Magnolia Palm Drive
Lake Buena Vista 32830
☎ 407-824-3400
FAX 407-824-3665
www.shadesofgreen.org

LOCATION	WDW
ROOM RATING	91
COST ($ = $50)	$$

COMMUTING TIMES TO PARKS (in minutes):

MAGIC KINGDOM	3:30
EPCOT	4:45
DISNEY-MGM	6:15
ANIMAL KINGDOM	9:30

Swan ★★★★½
Walt Disney World
1500 Epcot Resort Blvd.
Lake Buena Vista 32830
☎ 407-934-3000
FAX 407-934-4499
www.swandolphin.com

LOCATION	WDW
ROOM RATING	91
COST ($ = $50)	$$$$$$$

COMMUTING TIMES TO PARKS (in minutes):

MAGIC KINGDOM	6:30
EPCOT	4:45
DISNEY-MGM	4:00
ANIMAL KINGDOM	6:15

Wilderness Lodge ★★★★
Walt Disney World
901 Timberline Drive
Orlando 32830
☎ 407-824-3200
FAX 407-824-3232
www.waltdisneyworld.com

LOCATION	WDW
ROOM RATING	86
COST ($ = $50)	$$$$$$

COMMUTING TIMES TO PARKS (in minutes):

MAGIC KINGDOM	n/a
EPCOT	10:00
DISNEY-MGM	13:30
ANIMAL KINGDOM	15:15

Wilderness Lodge Villas
★★★★½
Walt Disney World
901 Timberline Drive
Orlando 32830
☎ 407-824-3200
FAX 407-824-3232
www.waltdisneyworld.com

LOCATION	WDW
ROOM RATING	90
COST ($ = $50)	$$$$$$$$

COMMUTING TIMES TO PARKS (in minutes):

MAGIC KINGDOM	n/a
EPCOT	10:00
DISNEY-MGM	13:30
ANIMAL KINGDOM	15:15

Yacht Club Resort ★★★★
Walt Disney World
1700 Epcot Resort Blvd.
Orlando 32830
☎ 407-934-7000
FAX 407-934-3450
www.waltdisneyworld.com

LOCATION	WDW
ROOM RATING	89
COST ($ = $50)	$$$$$$$$+

COMMUTING TIMES TO PARKS (in minutes):

MAGIC KINGDOM	7:15
EPCOT	5:15
DISNEY-MGM	4:00
ANIMAL KINGDOM	6:45

much time in the room, so we picked the All-Star Movies Resort. We were pleasantly surprised. Yes, the rooms are small. But the overall magic there is amazing. The lobby played Disney movies, which is perfect if you get up early and the buses aren't running yet. There are great photo ops everywhere (Donald and Daisy were awesome). It's heaven for fans of Fantasia 2000. Everyone seems to bust on the food court, which—let's face it—is crap . . . except for the refrigerator cases where you can buy fresh-tasting (albeit expensive) fruit, water, healthy snacks, and great chicken-salad sandwiches. Further, despite forewarnings of loud children, we were in the Love Bug building and found it very quiet. The express-checkout service was also a godsend.

Amenities at Downtown Disney Resort Area Hotels

RESORT	PROGRAMS	DINING	KID-FRIENDLY	POOLS	RECREATION
Best Western LBV Resort	–	★★½	★★★	★★½	★★
Buena Vista Palace	★★★★	★★★★	★★★½	★★★★	★★★★
DoubleTree Guest Suites	–	★★	★★★	★★½	★★½
Grosvenor Resort	★★½	★★½	★★★	★★★½	★★★
Hilton WDW	–	★★★½	★★½	★★★	★★½
Holiday Inn at WDW	–	★★½	★★½	★★★	★★½
Hotel Royal Plaza	★★½	★★	★★½	★★½	★★★

But a Massachusetts family of four had this to say:

I would never recommend the All-Star for a family. It was like dormitory living. Our room was about one mile from the bus stop, and the food court got old very quickly. Buses were great, but the room was tiny. I'm in the hotel business, and it was one of the smallest [rooms] I've been in. You needed to step into the bathroom, shut the door, then step around the toilet that blocked half the tub.

INDEPENDENT HOTELS OF THE DOWNTOWN DISNEY RESORT AREA

THE SEVEN HOTELS OF THE DOWNTOWN Disney Resort Area (DDRA) were created in the days when Disney had far fewer of its own resorts. The hotels—the Holiday Inn at Walt Disney World, DoubleTree Guest Suites, Grosvenor Resort, Hilton, Hotel Royal Plaza, Best Western Lake Buena Vista Resort, and Buena Vista Palace—are chain-style hotels with minimal or nonexistent theming, though the Buena Vista Palace, especially, is pretty upscale.

The main advantage to staying in the DDRA is being in Disney World and proximal to Downtown Disney. Guests at the Hilton, Grosvenor Resort, Buena Vista Palace, and Holiday Inn at Walt Disney World are an easy 5- to 15-minute walk from Disney Marketplace on the east side of Downtown Disney. Guests at the Hotel Royal Plaza, Best Western Lake Buena Vista Resort, or DoubleTree Guest Suites are about ten minutes farther by foot. Disney transportation can be accessed at Downtown Disney, though the Disney buses take a notoriously long time to leave due to the number of stops throughout the shopping and entertainment complex. Although all DDRA hotels offer shuttle buses to the theme parks, the service is provided by private contractors and is somewhat inferior to Disney Transportation in frequency of service, number of buses, and hours of operation. Get firm details in advance about shuttle service from any DDRA hotel you're considering. All these hotels are easily accessible by car and are only marginally farther from the Disney parks than several of the Disney resorts (and DDRA hotels are quite close to Typhoon Lagoon water park).

All DDRA hotels try to appeal to families, even the business and meeting hotels. Some have pool complexes that rival those at any Disney resort, whereas others offer a food court or all-suite rooms. A few sponsor Disney character meals and organized children's activities; all have counters for buying Disney tickets, and most have Disney gift shops. In addition, we've seen some real room deals in the DDRA, especially in the off-season. To help you decide if the DDRA is right for you, take a peek at the combined Web site for the DDRA hotels at **www.down towndisneyhotels.com.** Finally, check the comparative chart above.

HOW TO GET DISCOUNTS ON LODGING AT WALT DISNEY WORLD

If all you need is a room, booking through Disney Central Reservations is better than booking online or through the Walt Disney Travel Company because Central Reservations offers better terms for cancellation and payment dates.

Bob

THERE ARE SO MANY GUEST ROOMS in and around Walt Disney World that competition is brisk, and everyone, including Disney, wheels and deals to keep them filled. This has led to a more flexible discount policy for Walt Disney World hotels. Here are tips for getting price breaks:

1. SEASONAL SAVINGS You can save $15 to $50 per night on a Walt Disney World hotel room by scheduling your visit during the slower times of the year.

2. ASK ABOUT SPECIALS When you talk to Disney reservationists, ask specifically about specials. For example, "What special rates or discounts are available at Disney hotels during the time of our visit?" Being specific and assertive paid off for an Illinois reader:

I called Disney's reservations number and asked for availability and rates. . . . [Because] of the Unofficial Guide *warning about Disney reservationists answering only the questions posed, I specifically asked, "Are there any special rates or discounts for that room during the month of October?" She replied, "Yes, we have that room available at a special price. . . ." [For] the price of one phone call, I saved $440.*

Similarly, a Warren, New Jersey, dad reports:

Your tip about asking Disney employees about discounts was invaluable. They will not volunteer this information, but by asking we saved almost $500 on our hotel room using a AAA discount.

3. KNOW THE SECRET CODE The folks at **www.mousesavers.com** keep an updated list of discounts and reservation codes for Disney resorts. The codes are separated into categories such as "For anyone," "For residents of certain states," and "For Annual Pass holders." For example, the site once listed code CVZ, published in an ad in some Spanish-language newspapers and magazines, offering a rate of $65 per night for Disney's All-Star Resorts from April 22 to August 8. Dozens of discounts are usually listed on the site, covering most Disney hotels. Anyone calling the Disney Reservations Center at ☎ 407-W-DISNEY can use a current code and get the discounted rate.

You should be aware that Disney is shying away from room-only codes that anyone can use. Instead, Disney is targeting people with pin codes in e-mails and direct mailings. Pin-code discounts are offered to specific individuals and are correlated with that person's name and address. Pin-code offers are nontransferable. When you try to make a reservation using the code, Disney will verify that the street or e-mail address to which the pin code was sent is yours.

To get your name in the Disney system, call the Disney Reservation Center at ☎ 407-824-8000 and request that written info or the free trip-planning DVD/video be sent to you. If you've been to Walt Disney World previously, your name and address will of course already be on record, but you won't be as likely to receive a pin-code offer as you would by calling and requesting to be sent information. On the Web, go to the official site, **www.waltdisneyworld.com,** and sign up to automatically be sent offers and news at your e-mail address.

Two other sites, **www.allearsnet.com** and **www.wdwinfo.com,** have discount codes we've used to get up to 50% off rack rates at the Swan and Dolphin resorts.

4. INTERNET SELLERS Online travel sellers Expedia (**www.expedia.com**), Travelocity (**www.travelocity.com**), and One Travel (**www.onetravel.com**) discount Disney hotels. Most breaks are in the 7% to 25% range, but they can go as deep as 40%.

5. RENTING DISNEY VACATION CLUB POINTS The Disney Vacation Club (DVC) is Disney's time-share condominium program. DVC resorts at Walt Disney World include Old Key West, Saratoga Springs Resort & Spa, the Beach Club Villas, Villas at Wilderness Lodge, and the BoardWalk Villas. Each resort offers studios and one- and two-bedroom villas (some resorts also offer three-bedroom villas). All accommodations are roomy and luxurious. The studios are equipped with wet bars and fridges, and the villas come with full kitchens. Most accommodations have patios or balconies.

DVC members receive a number of "points" annually that they use to pay for their Disney accommodations. Sometimes members elect to "rent" (sell) their points instead of using them in a given year. Though Disney is not involved in the transaction, it allows DVC members to make these points available to the general public. The going rental rate is usually in the range of $10 per point. A studio for a week at the BoardWalk Villas would run you $2,303 plus tax for regular season if you booked through the Disney Reservation Center. The same studio costs the DVC member 123 points for a week. If you rented his points at $10 per point, the BoardWalk Villas studio would cost you $1,230—that is, more than $1,000 less.

When you rent points, you deal with the selling DVC member and pay him or her directly. The DVC member makes a reservation in your name and pays Disney the requisite number of points. Arrangements vary widely, but some trust is required from both parties. Usually your reservation is documented by a confirmation sent from Disney to the owner, and then passed along to you. Though the deal you cut is strictly up to you and the owner, you should always insist on receiving the afore-mentioned confirmation before making more than a one-night deposit.

Disboards, **www.disboards.com,** the popular Disney discussion boards site, has a specific board that deals with DVC rentals, and the unofficial discount Web site, **www.mousesavers.com,** has a page with tips on renting DVC points: see **www.mousesavers.com/disney resorts.html#rentpoints.**

6. TRAVEL AGENTS Travel agents are active players and particularly good sources of information on limited-time programs and dis-counts. We believe a good travel agent is the best friend a traveler can have. And though we at the *Unofficial Guide* know a thing or two about the travel industry, we always give our agent a chance to beat any deal we find. If she can't beat it, we let her book it anyway if it's commissionable. We nurture a relationship that gives her plenty of incentive to roll up her sleeves and work on our behalf.

As you might expect, there are travel agents and agencies that spe-cialize, sometimes exclusively, in selling Walt Disney World. These agents have spent an incredible amount of time at Walt Disney World and have completed extensive Disney education programs. They are usually the most Disney-knowledgeable agents in the travel industry. Most of these specialists and their agencies display the "Earmarked" logo stating that they are an authorized Disney vacation planner.

These Disney specialists are so good we use them ourselves. The needs of our research team are many, and our schedules are compli-cated. When we work with an authorized Disney vacation planner we know we're dealing with someone who knows Disney inside and out, including where to find the deals and how to use all tricks of the trade that keep our research budget under control. Simply stated, they save us time and money, sometimes lots of both.

The best of the best include Sue Pisaturo, whom we've used many times and who is a contributor to this guide (**sue@wdwvacations.com**); Sue Ellen Soto-Rios (**disneytravelagent@gmail.com**); Lynne Amodeo (**lynnetravel@verizon.net**); Steve Schrohe (**steve@ittravel.com**); and Josephine Raccuia (**sandnshore@optonline.net**).

There are good Disney specialists throughout the country, however, if you prefer to work with someone close to home.

7. ORGANIZATIONS AND AUTO CLUBS Disney has developed time-limited programs with some auto clubs and organizations. Recently, for example, AAA members were offered 10% to 20% savings on Disney hotels, preferred parking at the theme parks, and discounts on Disney package vacations. Such deals come and go, but the market suggests there will be more. If you're a member of AARP, AAA, or any travel or auto club, ask whether the group has a program before shopping elsewhere.

LODGING *outside*
WALT DISNEY WORLD

AT THIS POINT YOU'RE PROBABLY WONDERING HOW, as mentioned above, a hotel outside Walt Disney World could be as convenient as one inside Walt Disney World? Well, Mabel, Walt Disney World is a *muy largo* place, but like any city or state, it has borders. By way of analogy, let's say you want to stay in a hotel in Cincinnati, Ohio, but can't find one you can afford. Would you rather book a hotel in Toledo or Cleveland, which are both still in Ohio but pretty darn far away, or would you be willing to leave Ohio and stay just across the river from Cincinnati in Covington, Kentucky?

Just west of Walt Disney World on US 192 are a bunch of hotels and condos, some great bargains, that are closer to the Animal Kingdom and the Disney-MGM Studios than are many hotels in Walt Disney World. Similarly, there are hotels along Disney's east border, FL 535, that are exceptionally convenient if you plan to use your own car.

Lodging costs outside Walt Disney World vary incredibly. If you shop around, you can find a clean motel with a pool within a few minutes of the World for as low as $40 a night. You also can find luxurious, expensive hotels. Because of hot competition, discounts abound.

SELECTING AND BOOKING A HOTEL
OUTSIDE WALT DISNEY WORLD

THERE ARE THREE PRIMARY out-of-the-World areas to consider:

1. INTERNATIONAL DRIVE AREA This area, about 15 to 20 minutes east of Walt Disney World, parallels I-4 on its southern side and offers a wide selection of both hotels and restaurants. Accommodations range from $40 to $320 per night. The chief drawbacks of the International Drive area are its terribly congested roads, countless traffic signals, and inadequate access to westbound I-4. While the biggest bottleneck is the intersection with Sand Lake Road, the mile of International Drive between Kirkman Road and Sand Lake Road stays in near-continuous gridlock. It's common to lose 25 to 35 minutes trying to navigate this one-mile stretch.

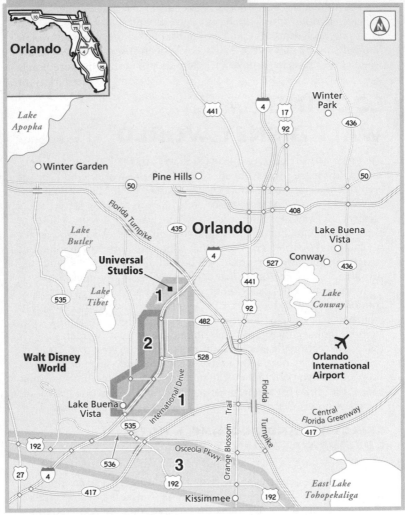

hotel concentrations around walt disney world

Hotels in the International Drive area are listed in the *Orlando Official Accommodations Guide,* published by the Orlando/ Orange County Convention and Visitors Bureau. For a copy, call ☎ 800-255-5786 or 407-363-5872.

2. LAKE BUENA VISTA AND THE I-4 CORRIDOR A number of hotels are situated along FL 535 and north of I-4 between Walt Disney World and I-4's intersection with the Florida Turnpike. These properties are easily reached from the interstate and are near a large number of restaurants, including those on International Drive. Most hotels in this area are listed in the *Orlando Official Accommodations Guide*.

3. US 192 (IRLO BRONSON MEMORIAL HIGHWAY) This is the highway to Kissimmee, southeast of Walt Disney World. In addition to a number of large, full-service hotels are many small, privately owned motels that are often a good value. Several dozen properties on US 192 are closer to the Disney theme parks than are the more expensive hotels in the Downtown Disney Resort Area. The number and variety of restaurants on US 192 has increased markedly in the past several years, easing the area's primary shortcoming.

Hotels on US 192 and in Kissimmee can be found in the *Kissimmee– St. Cloud Visitor's Guide;* call ☎ 800-327-9159 or check **www.florida kiss.com.**

THE BEST HOTELS FOR FAMILIES OUTSIDE WALT DISNEY WORLD

WHAT MAKES A SUPER FAMILY HOTEL? Roomy accommodations, in-room fridge, great pool, free breakfast, child-care options, and programs for kids are but a few of the things the *Unofficial* hotel team checked out to select the top hotels for families from among hundreds of properties in the Walt Disney World area. You can be assured that these hotels understand the needs of a family. Though all the hotels listed below offer some type of shuttle service to the theme parks, some offer very limited service. Call the hotel before you book to find out what the shuttle schedule will be during your visit. Since families, like individuals, have different wants and needs, we have not ranked the following properties; they are listed geographically by zone and alphabetically.

ZONE 1: INTERNATIONAL DRIVE

Doubletree Castle Hotel

8629 International Drive, Orlando; ☎ **407-345-1511 or 800-952-2785; www.doubletreecastle.com**

Rate per night $150. **Pool** ★★★; (No separate kiddie pool). **Fridge in room** Yes. **Maximum persons per room** 4. **Shuttle to parks** Yes (Disney, Universal, SeaWorld).

COMMENTS You can't miss this one—it's the only castle on I-Drive. Inside you'll find royal colors (purple dominates), opulent fixtures, and Renaissance music. Add $20 to the room rate and up to four people receive continental breakfast; two signature chocolate chip cookies come with every room.

Hard Rock Hotel

5800 Universal Boulevard, Orlando; ☎ **407-503-ROCK or 888-273-1311; www.universalorlando.com**

Rate per night $300. **Pool** ★★★★ **Fridge in room** $15 per day; microwave available for $15 a day. **Maximum persons per room** 4. **Shuttle to parks** Yes (Universal, SeaWorld, Wet 'n Wild).

COMMENTS Located on the Universal property, the 650-room Hard Rock Hotel is nirvana for any kid interested in music, as rock memorabilia is displayed throughout the hotel. Guests are entitled to special privileges at Universal, such as early theme-park admission on select days and all-day access to the Universal Express line-breaking program, plus delivery of packages to their hotel room and priority seating at select restaurants.

A supervised activity center, Camp Lil' Rock, serves kids ages 4 to 14. Pet-friendly rooms are available.

Nickelodeon Family Suites by Holiday Inn
14500 Continental Gateway Orlando; ☎ 407-387-5437 or 866-GO2-NICK; www.nickhotel.com

Rate per night $180–$370. **Pools** ★★★★★ **Fridge in room** Yes. **Maximum persons per room** 7. **Shuttle to parks** Yes (Disney only). **Special comments** Daily character breakfast.

COMMENTS This resort is as kid-friendly as they come. Decked out in all themes Nickelodeon, the hotel is sure to please any fan of TV shows the likes of *Rugrats*. Nickelodeon characters from the channel's many shows hang out in the resort's lobby and mall area. Guests can choose from one-, two-, and three-bedroom Kid Suites executed in a number of different themes—all very brightly and creatively decorated. The resort's two pools, Oasis and Lagoon, feature a water park complete with water cannons, rope ladders, geysers, and dump buckets, as well as two hot tubs for adults and a smaller play area for younger kids.

Portofino Bay Hotel
5601 Universal Boulevard, Orlando; ☎ 407-503-1000 or 888-273-1311; www.loewshotels.com/hotels/orlando_portofino_bay

Rate per night $395. **Pools** ★★★★ **Fridge in room** Minibar; fridge available for $15 per day. **Maximum persons per room** 4. **Shuttle to parks** Yes (Universal, SeaWorld, Wet 'n Wild). **Special comments** Character dinner on Friday.

COMMENTS Also located in Universal, the 750-room Portofino Bay Hotel is themed like a seaside village on the Italian Riviera. Like at the Hard Rock Hotel, Portofino guests receive special theme-park privileges. Campo Portofino offers supervised activities from 5 p.m. to midnight on Fridays and Saturdays for children ages 4–14. Cost is $12 per hour per child.

Renaissance Orlando Resort
6677 Sea Harbor Drive, Orlando; ☎ 407-351-5555 or 800-327-6677; www.marriott.com.

Rate per night $200. **Pool** ★★★★ **Fridge in room** Yes. **Maximum persons per room** 4. **Shuttle to parks** Yes (Disney, Universal, and SeaWorld).

COMMENTS The Renaissance Orlando Resort does a lot of convention business. However, its large size and convenience to SeaWorld and Universal make it an acceptable alternative for families. Babysitting and child-care services are available, and pets are permitted.

Rosen Shingle Creek
9939 Universal Boulevard, Orlando; ☎ 407-996-9939 or 866-996-9939; www.rosenshinglecreek.com

Rate per night $375–$425. **Pools ★ ★ ★ ★. Fridge in room** Yes. **Maximum persons per room** 4. **Shuttle to parks** Yes (Universal, Wet 'n Wild, and SeaWorld only).

COMMENTS Beautiful rooms (those facing east have great views) and excellent restaurants distinguish this mostly meeting-and-convention resort. Swimming options include a lap pool, a family pool, and a kiddie wading pool. There's an 18-hole golf course on-site, as well as a superior spa, a decent fitness center, and even a horseshoe pitch. The Kids Swamp Club provides both activities and child care. Though a state-of-the-art video arcade will gobble up your kids' pocket change, the real kicker, especially for the 8-years-and up-crowd, is a natural area encompassing lily ponds, grassy wetlands, Shingle Creek, and an adjacent cypress swamp. Running through the area is a nature trail complete with signs to help you identify wildlife. Blue herons, wood storks, coots, egrets, mallards, anhingas, and ospreys are common, as are sliders (turtles), chameleons, and skinks (lizards). Oh yeah, there are alligators and snakes, too—real ones, but that's part of the fun. If you stay at Shingle Creek and plan to visit the theme parks, you'll want to take a car: shuttle service is limited, departing and picking up at rather inconvenient times and stopping at three other hotels before delivering you to your destination.

Sheraton Studio City
5905 International Drive, Orlando; ☎ 407-351-2100 or 800-327-1366; www.sheratonstudiocity.com

Rate per night $130. **Pool ★ ★ ★ Fridge in room** No. **Maximum persons per room** 4. **Shuttle to parks** Yes (Universal, SeaWorld, Wet 'n Wild).

COMMENTS It's not for little ones, but preteens and teens will love the hip atmosphere at Sheraton Studio City. And movie buffs will appreciate the theme—a tribute to feature films of the 1940s and 1950s. The hotel is across from Wet 'n Wild.

Sheraton World Resort
10100 International Drive, Orlando; ☎ 407-352-1100 or 800-327-0363; www.sheratonworld.com

Rate per night $130–$160. **Pools ★ ★ ★ ½ Fridge in room** Yes. **Maximum persons per room** 4. **Shuttle to parks** Yes (Disney only).

COMMENTS A good option if you're visiting nearby SeaWorld, the 28-acre Sheraton World Resort offers plenty of room for kids to roam. And with three heated pools, two kiddie pools, a small playground, an arcade, and a complimentary mini-golf course (very mini, indeed), this resort offers more than enough kid-friendly diversions.

ZONE 2: LAKE BUENA VISTA AND I-4 CORRIDOR

Hilton Walt Disney World

1751 Hotel Plaza Boulevard, Lake Buena Vista; ☎ 407-827-4000 or 800-782-4414; www.hilton-wdwv.com

Rate per night $189. **Pools** ★★★½ **Fridge in room** Minibar. **Maximum persons per room** 4. **Shuttle to parks** Yes (Disney theme and water parks only).

COMMENTS Located in the Disney Village, the Hilton is an official Walt Disney World hotel and participates in the Extra Magic Hours program. One big family amenity offered by the Hilton is its character breakfast, on Sundays only from 8:30 to 11 a.m. Other important family amenities include babysitting services, an arcade, and a kiddie pool.

Idan

When I was little we stayed at the Holiday Inn SunSpree Resort. I loved being tucked in by Max, the mascot of the hotel. A reservation is required, but the service is absolutely free.

Holiday Inn SunSpree Resort

13351 FL 535, Lake Buena Vista; ☎ 407-239-4500 or 800-366-6299; www.kidsuites.com

Rate per night $124. **Pool** ★★★ **Fridge in room** Yes. **Maximum persons per room** 4–6. **Shuttle to parks** Yes (Disney only).

COMMENTS Put on your sunglasses—you'll know you're there when the multicolored exterior comes into view. Once inside, kids get into the action at their own check-in counter, where they'll receive a free goody bag. Max and Maxine, the character mascots here, come out to play with the kids at scheduled times during the day. But the big lures are the Kidsuites, which are 405-square-foot rooms with a separate themed play area for kids.

Hyatt Regency Grand Cypress

One Grand Cypress Boulevard, Lake Buena Vista; ☎ 407-239-1234; www.grandcypress.hyatt.com

Rate per night $269. **Pool** ★★★★★ **Fridge in room** Minibar; fridge available on request. **Maximum persons per room** 4. **Shuttle to parks** Yes (Disney only).

COMMENTS There are myriad reasons to stay at this 1,500-acre resort, but the pool ranks number one. It's a sprawling, 800,000-gallon tropical paradise with a 125-foot water slide, ubiquitous waterfalls, caves and grottoes, and a suspension bridge. The Hyatt is also a golfer's paradise, with a 45-hole championship Jack Nicklaus–designed course, an 18-hole course, a 9-hole pitch-and-putt course, and a golf academy.

Camp Hyatt (also Camp Gator) provides supervised programs for kids ages 5 to 12 as well as in-room babysitting. If outdoor recreation is high on your family's list, Hyatt is an excellent high-end choice.

Marriott Village at Lake Buena Vista Isle
8623 Vineland Avenue, Lake Buena Vista; ☎ 407-938-9001 or 877-682-8552; www.marriottvillage.com

Rate per night $129–$149. **Pools** ★★★ **Fridge in room** Yes. **Maximum persons per room** 4. **Shuttle to parks** Yes (Disney, Universal, SeaWorld, Wet 'n Wild). **Special comments** Fairfield Inn and Spring Hill Suites provide free continental breakfast.

COMMENTS This fully gated community includes a 388-room Fairfield Inn, a 400-suite Spring Hill Suites, and 312-room Courtyard. Whatever your budget, you'll find a room to fit it here. Each hotel features its own Kids Club. For kids ages 4 to 8, the themed clubs (backyard, tree house, and library) feature big-screen TVs, computer stations, and educational centers (for math and science, reading, and creative activities). Open approximately six hours per day, they have a staff member on duty at all times. The Kids Club is free!

   Marriott Village also offers a supervised Kid's Night Out program (ages 4 to 10) from 6 p.m. to 10 p.m. on select nights. The cost is $35 per child, which includes activities and dinner.

Sheraton Safari Hotel
12205 South Apopka-Vineland Road, Lake Buena Vista; ☎ 407-239-0444 or 800-423-3297; www.sheratonsafari.com

Rate per night $159. **Pool** ★★★ **Fridge in room** Safari suites only. **Maximum persons per room** 4–6. **Shuttle to parks** Yes (Disney complimentary; other parks for a fee).

COMMENTS A safari theme is nicely executed throughout this property—from the lobby dotted with African artifacts and native décor to the 79-foot python water slide dominating the pool. On-site amenities include a restaurant (children's menu available), deli, lounge, arcade, and fitness center. Should you want to escape for a night of strictly adult fun, babysitting services are available.

Sheraton Vistana Resort
8800 Vistana Center Drive, Lake Buena Vista; ☎ 407-239-3100; www.starwoodvo.com

Rate per night $189. **Pool** ★★★½ **Fridge in room** Minibar. **Maximum persons per room** 4. **Shuttle to parks** Yes (Disney complimentary; other parks for a fee).

COMMENTS The Sheraton Vistana is deceptively large, stretching as it does across either side of Vistana Center Drive. Though actually time-shares, the villas are rented nightly as well. If you want to have a very serene retreat from your days in the theme parks, this is an excellent home base.

   Grounds offer seven swimming pools, four playgrounds, game rooms, fitness centers, a mini-golf course, sports equipment rental (including bikes), and courts for basketball, volleyball, tennis, and shuffleboard. There's a mind-boggling array of activities for kids (and adults) ranging from crafts to games and sports tournaments. Of special note: Vistana is highly secure, with locked gates bordering all guest areas, so children can have the run of the place without parents worrying about them wandering off.

Wyndham Palace

1900 Buena Vista Drive, Lake Buena Vista; ☎ 407-827-2727 or 800-WYNDHAM; www.wyndham.com

Rate per night $150. **Pools** ★★★★ **Fridge in room** Minibar. **Maximum persons per room** 4. **Shuttle to parks** Yes (Disney only).

COMMENTS Located in the Disney Village, the Wyndham Palace is an upscale and convenient lodging choice. On Sunday, the Wyndham offers a character breakfast at the Watercress Cafe. Cost is $23 for adults and $13 for children. In-room babysitting is available.

ZONE 3: US 192

Comfort Suites Maingate Resort

7888 West US Irlo Bronson Memorial Highway, Kissimmee; ☎ 407-390-9888; www.comfortsuiteskissimmee.com

Rate per night $159. **Pool** ★★★★ **Fridge in room** Yes. **Maximum persons per room** 6. **Shuttle to parks** Yes (Disney, Universal, SeaWorld, Wet 'n Wild).

COMMENTS This property has 150 spacious one-room suites with double sofa bed, microwave, fridge, coffeemaker, TV, hair dryer, and safe. The big plus for this place is its location—right next door to a shopping center with just about everything a traveling family could possibly need, including a walk-in medical clinic.

Gaylord Palms Resort

6000 West Osceola Parkway, Kissimmee; ☎ 407-586-0000; www.gaylordpalms.com

Rate per night $200. **Pool** ★★★ **Fridge in room** Yes. **Maximum persons per room** 4. **Shuttle to parks** Yes (Disney).

COMMENTS Though it strongly caters to a business clientele, the Gaylord Palms is still a nice (if pricey) family resort. The hotel wings are defined by the three themed, glass-roofed atriums: Key West, the Everglades, and St. Augustine. Children will enjoy wandering the themed areas, playing in the family pool (complete with giant water-squirting octopus), or participating in the La Petite Academy Kids Station, which organizes a range of games and activities for wee ones.

Howard Johnson EnchantedLand

4985 West US 192, Kissimmee; ☎ 407-396-4343 or 888-753-4343

Rate per night $125–$150. **Pool** ★★ **Fridge in room** Yes. **Maximum persons per room** 4. **Shuttle to parks** Yes (Disney, Universal, SeaWorld).

COMMENTS Fairies, dragons, and superheroes have invaded the HoJo. If you stay here, be sure you book what they call a Family Value Room: a standard room that has been transformed into a kids' suite. Suites offer TV and VCR, microwave, fridge, coffeemaker, and safe. There's also a complimentary ice cream party nightly 7–7:30 pm.; Kids Theater each Friday and Saturday 7:30–9 p.m. with free popcorn; and arts, crafts, and children's activities in Granny's playroom.

Radisson Resort Parkway

2900 Parkway Boulevard, Kissimmee; ☎ 407-396-7000 or 800-634-4774; www.radisson.com

Rate per night $177. **Pool** ★★★★½ **Fridge in room** Minibar. **Maximum persons per room** 4. **Shuttle to parks** Yes (Disney, Universal, SeaWorld).

COMMENTS The pool alone is worth a stay here, with a waterfall and water slide surrounded by lush palms and flowering plants, plus an additional smaller heated pool, two whirlpools, and a kiddie pool. But the Radisson Resort gets high marks in all areas, save the absence of an organized children's program. Dining options include Parkway Deli & Diner, with breakfast, lunch, and dinner buffets; a 1950s-style diner serving burgers, sandwiches, and shakes; and Pizza Hut pizza.

GETTING A GOOD DEAL ON A ROOM OUTSIDE WALT DISNEY WORLD

HOTEL DEVELOPMENT AT WALT DISNEY WORLD has sharpened the competition among lodgings throughout the Orlando/Kissimmee area. Hotels outside Walt Disney World, in particular, struggle to fill

www.mousesavers.com	Best site for hotels in Disney World
www.dreamsunlimitedtravel.com	Excellent for both Disney and non-Disney hotels
www.2000orlando-florida.com	Comprehensive hotel site
www.valuetrips.com	Specializes in budget accommodations
www.travelocity.com	Multidestination travel superstore
www.roomsaver.com	Provides discount coupons for hotels
www.floridakiss.com	Primarily US 192–Kissimmee area hotels
www.orlandoinfo.com	Good info; not user-friendly for booking
www.orlandovacation.com	Great rates for a small number of properties, including condos and home rentals
www.expedia.com	Largest of the multidestination travel sites
www.hotels.com	Largest Internet hotel-booking service; many other sites link to hotels.com and their subsidiary, www.hoteldiscounts.com

their guest rooms. Unable to compete with Disney resorts for convenience or perks, off-World hotels lure patrons in with bargain rates. The extent of the bargain depends on the season, day of the week, and local events. Here are tips and strategies for getting a good deal on a room outside Walt Disney World.

1. ORLANDO MAGICARD Orlando MagiCard is a discount program sponsored by the Orlando/Orange County Convention and Visitors Bureau. Cardholders are eligible for discounts of 20–50% at approximately 50 participating hotels. The MagiCard is also good for discounts at area attractions, including SeaWorld, the Universal parks, several dinner theaters, and Disney's Pleasure Island. Valid for up to six persons, the card isn't available for groups or conventions.

To obtain an Orlando MagiCard and a list of participating hotels and attractions, call ☎ 800-255-5786 or 407-363-5874. On the Internet, go to **www.orlandoinfo.com/magicard;** the MagiCard and accompanying brochure can be printed from a personal computer.

Anyone older than 18 is eligible, and the card is free. If you miss getting a card before you leave home, you can get one at the Convention and Visitors Bureau at 8723 International Drive in Orlando. When you call for a MagiCard, also request the *Orlando Official Accommodations Guide* and the *Orlando Vacation Planner*.

2. EXIT INFORMATION GUIDE Exit Information Guide publishes a book of discount coupons for bargain rates at hotels statewide. The book is free in many restaurants and motels on main highways leading to Florida. Because most travelers make reservations before leaving home, picking up the coupon book en route doesn't help much. If you call and use a credit card, EIG will send the guide first class for $3 ($5 U.S. for Canadian delivery). Contact:

Exit Information Guide
4205 N.W. Sixth Street
Gainesville, FL 32609
☎ 352-371-3948 or 800-332-3948
www.travelsdiscountguide.com

3. HOTEL SHOPPING ON THE INTERNET Web sites we've found most dependable for Walt Disney Area hotel discounts are:

The secret to shopping on the Internet is . . . shopping. When we're really looking for a deal, we check all the above sites. Flexibility on dates and location are helpful, and we always give our travel agent the opportunity to beat any deal we find.

We recommend choosing a hotel based on location, room quality, price, commuting time to the parks, plus any features important to you. Next, check each of the applicable sites above. You'll be able to ferret out the best Internet deal in about 30 minutes. Then call the hotel to see if you can save more by booking directly. Start by asking the hotel for specials. If their response doesn't beat the Internet deal, tell them what you've found and ask if they can do better.

Another tool in the hotel-hunting arsenal is **www.travelaxe.com.** Travelaxe offers free software you can download on your PC (won't run on Macs) that will scan an assortment of the better hotel discount sites and find the cheapest rate (from among the sites scanned) for each of more than 200 Disney-area hotels. The site offers various filters such as price, quality rating, and proximity to a specific location (Walt Disney World, SeaWorld, the convention center, airport, and such) to allow you to more narrowly define your search. As you'll see when you visit the Travelaxe site, the same software scans for best rates in cities throughout the United States and around the world.

4. IF YOU MAKE YOUR OWN RESERVATION
Reservationists at the toll-free number are often unaware of local specials. Always phone the hotel directly and ask about specials before you inquire about corporate rates. Don't hesitate to bargain, but do it before you check in. If you're buying a ho-

Bob

Always call the hotel in question, not the hotel chain's national 800 number.

tel's weekend package, for example, and want to extend your stay, you can often obtain at least the corporate rate for the extra days.

OUT-OF-THE-WORLD CHILDREN'S PROGRAMS

MANY LARGE NON-DISNEY HOTELS offer supervised programs for children, some complimentary, some with fees. If you decide to take advantage of the kids' programs, call ahead to find out about specific children's events that are scheduled during your vacation. Ask about cost and the ages that can participate; the best programs divide children into age groups. Make reservations for activities your child might want to participate in. You can always cancel after arrival.

After checking in, visit with the kids' program staff. Ask about the counselor-child ratio and whether the counselors are trained in first aid and CPR. Briefly introduce your children to the staff and setting, which typically will leave them wanting more, thereby easing the separation anxiety.

CONDOMINIUMS AND VACATION HOMES

VACATION HOMES ARE FREE-STANDING, while condominiums are essentially one- to three-bedroom accommodations in a larger building housing a number of similar units. Because condos tend to be part of large developments (frequently time-shares), amenities such as swimming pools, playgrounds, game arcades, and fitness centers often rival those found in the best hotels.

In a vacation home, all the amenities are contained in the home (though in planned developments there may be community amenities available as well). Depending on the specific home, you might find a small swimming pool, hot tub, two-car garage, family room, game room, and even a home theater. Features found in both condos and vacation homes include full kitchens, laundry rooms, TVs, DVD players/VCRs, and frequently stereos. Interestingly, though almost all free-standing vacation homes have private pools, very few have back-yards. This means that, except for swimming, the kids are pretty much relegated to playing in the house or front yard.

Time-share condos are clones when it comes to furniture and décor, but single-owner condos and vacation homes are furnished and decorated in a style that reflects the taste of the owner. Vacation homes, usually one- to two-story houses located in a subdivision, very rarely afford interesting views (though some overlook lakes or natural areas), while condos, especially the high-rise variety, some-times offer exceptional ones.

The Price Is Nice

The best deals in lodging in the Walt Disney World area are vacation homes and single-owner condos. Prices range from about $65 a night for two-bedroom condos and townhomes to $200 to $500 a night for three- to seven-bedroom vacation homes. Forgetting about taxes to keep the comparison simple, let's compare renting a vacation home to staying at one of Disney's Value Resorts. A family of two parents, two teens, and two grandparents would need three hotel rooms at Disney's Pop Century Resort. At the lowest rate obtainable, that would run you $79 per night per room, or $237 total per night. Rooms are 260 square feet each, so you'd have a total of 780 square feet. Each room has a private bath and a television.

Renting at the same time of year from All Star Vacation Homes (no relation to Disney's All-Star Resorts), you can rent a 2,053-square-foot, four-bedroom, three-bath vacation home with a private pool three miles from Walt Disney World for $219—a savings of $18 per night over the Disney Value Resort rate. With four bedrooms, each of the teens can have his or her own room. Further, for the dates we checked, All Star Vacation Homes was running a special in which they threw in a free rental car with a one-week home rental.

But that's not all—the home comes with the following features and amenities: a big-screen TV with PlayStation, DVD player, and VCR (assorted games and DVDs available for complimentary check-out at the rental office); a CD player; a heatable private pool; five additional TVs (one in each bedroom and one in the family room); a fully equipped kitchen; a two-car garage; a hot tub; a laundry room with full-size washer and dryer; a fully furnished private patio; and a child-safety fence.

The home is in a community with a 24-hour gated entrance. Available at the community center are a large swimming pool; a whirlpool; tennis, volleyball, and half-court basketball courts; a children's play-ground; a gym and exercise room; a convenience store; and a 58-seat cinema.

Location, Location, Location

The best vacation home is one that is within easy commuting distance of the theme parks. If you plan to spend some time at SeaWorld and the Universal parks, you'll want something just to the northeast of Walt Disney World (between the World and Orlando). If you plan to spend most of your time in the World, the best selection of vacation homes is along US 192 to the south of the park.

To get the most from a vacation home, you need to be close enough to commute in 20 minutes or less to your Walt Disney World destination. This will allow for naps, quiet time, swimming, and dollar-saving meals you prepare yourself. Though traffic and road conditions are as important as the distance from a vacation home to your Disney destination, we recommend a home no farther than 5 miles away in areas northeast of Walt Disney World and no farther than 4.5 miles away in areas south of the park.

The only practical way to shop for a rental home is on the Web. This makes it relatively easy to compare different properties and rental companies. On the downside, there are so many owners, rental companies, and individual homes to choose from that you could research yourself into a stupor. There are three main types of Web sites in the home-rental game: those for property-management companies, which showcase a given company's homes and are set up for direct bookings; individual owner sites; and third-party listings sites, which advertise properties available through different owners and sometimes management companies as well. Sites in the last category will usually refer prospective renters to an owner's or management company's site for reservations.

The best Web sites provide the following:

- Numerous photos and in-depth descriptions of individual homes to make comparisons quick and easy
- Overview maps or text descriptions that reflect how distant specific homes or developments are from Walt Disney World
- The ability to book the specific individual rental home of your choice on the site
- A prominently displayed phone number for non-Internet bookings and questions

The best sites are also easy to navigate, let you see what you're interested in without logging in or giving personal information, and list memberships in such organizations as the Better Business Bureau and the Central Florida Property Management Association (log on to **www.cfpma.org** for the association's code of ethics and a list of members).

Recommended Web Sites

After checking out dozens upon dozens of sites, here are the ones we recommend. All of them meet the criteria listed above. If you're stunned that there are so few of them, well, so were we. (For the record, we elected not to list some sites that met our criteria but whose homes are too far away from Walt Disney World.)

All Star Vacation Homes (**www.allstarvacationhomes.com**) is easily the best of the management-company sites, with easily accessible photos and plenty of details about featured homes. All the company's rental properties are within either four miles of Walt Disney World or three miles of Universal Studios.

The Web site for the **Orlando/Orange County Convention and Visitors Bureau** (**www.orlandoinfo.com**) is the place to go if you're interested in a condo at one of the many time-share developments (click on "Accommodations" at the home page). You can call the developments directly, but going through this site allows you to bypass sales departments and escape their high-pressure invitations to sit through sales presentations. The site also lists hotels and vacation homes.

Vacation Rental by Owner (**www.vrbo.com**) is a nationwide listings service that puts prospective renters in direct contact with owners. The site is straightforward and always lists a large number of rental properties in Celebration, Disney's planned community situated about eight to ten minutes from the theme parks. Two similar listings services with good Web sites are **Vacation Rentals 411** (**www.vacation rentals411.com**) and **Last Minute Villas** (**www.lastminutevillas.net**).

VillaDirect Florida (**www.villadirect.com**) manages more than 600 rental homes and condos in the greater Walt Disney World area. Though some of their properties are too far from the World for our taste, they offer a lot to choose from, and their Web site is a snap to navigate.

Once you've found a vacation home you like, check around the Web site for a Frequently Asked Questions (FAQ) page. This should provide answers to most of the questions you have.

We frequently receive letters from readers extolling the virtues of renting a condo or vacation home. This endorsement by a family from Ellington, Connecticut, is typical:

Our choice to stay outside Disney was based on cost and sanity. We've found over the last couple of years that our children can't share the same bed. We have also gotten tired of having to turn off the lights at 8 p.m. and lie quietly in the dark waiting for our children to fall asleep. With this in mind, we needed a kind of condo/suite layout. Anything in Disney offering this option [for example, BoardWalk Villas, Beach Club Villas, and Old Key West] was going to cost approximately $400 to $500 a night. This was not built into our Disney budget. We decided on the Sheraton Vistana Resort. We had a two-bedroom villa with full kitchen, living room, three TVs, and washer/dryer. I packed for half the trip and did laundry almost every night. The facilities offered a daily children's program and several pools, kiddie pools, and "playscapes." Located

on FL 535, we had a five- to ten-minute drive to most attractions,
including SeaWorld, Disney, and Universal.

A St. Joe, Indiana, family also had a good experience:

We rented a home in Kissimmee this time, and we'll never stay in a ho-
tel at WDW again. It was by far the nicest, most relaxing time we've
ever had down there. Our rental home was within 10 to 15 minutes of
all the Disney parks and 25 minutes from SeaWorld. We had three bed-
rooms, two baths, and an in-ground pool in a screened enclosure out
back. We paid $90 per night for the whole shootin' match. We did
spring for the pool heating, $25 per night extra [in February].

HOW *to* CHILDPROOF
a HOTEL ROOM

TODDLERS AND SMALL CHILDREN up to 3 years of age (and sometimes older) can wreak mayhem if not outright disaster in a hotel
room. They're mobile, curious, and amazingly fast, and they have a
penchant for turning the most seemingly innocuous furnishing or
decoration into a lethal weapon. Chances are you're pretty experienced when it comes to spotting potential dangers, but just in case
you need a refresher course, here's what to look for.

Always begin by checking the room for hazards that you cannot
neutralize, like balconies, chipping paint, cracked walls, sharp surfaces, shag carpeting, and windows that can't be secured shut. If you
encounter anything that you don't like or is too much of a hassle to
fix, ask for another room.

If you use a crib supplied by the hotel, make sure that the mattress
is firm and covers the entire bottom of the crib. If there is a mattress
cover, it should fit tightly. Slats should be 2⅜ inch (about the width
of a soda can) or less apart. Test the drop sides to ensure that they
work properly and that your child cannot release them accidentally.
Examine the crib from all angles (including from underneath) to
make sure it has been assembled correctly and that there are no sharp
edges. Check for chipping paint and other potentially toxic sub-
stances that your child might ingest. Wipe down surfaces your child
might touch or mouth to diminish the potential of infection trans-
mitted from a previous occupant. Finally, position the crib away from
drape cords, heaters, wall sockets, and air conditioners.

If your infant can turn over, we recommend changing him or her on
a pad on the floor. Likewise, if you have a child seat of any sort, place
it where it cannot be knocked over, and always strap your child in.

If your child can roll, crawl, or walk, you should bring about eight electrical outlet covers and some cord to tie cabinets shut and to bind drape cords and the like out of reach. Check for appliances, lamps, ashtrays, ice buckets, and anything else that your child might pull down on him- or herself. Have the hotel remove coffee tables with sharp edges, and both real and artificial plants that are within your child's reach. Round up items from table and counter tops such as matchbooks, courtesy toiletries, and drinking glasses and store them out of reach.

If the bathroom door can be accidentally locked, cover the locking mechanism with duct tape or a doorknob cover. Use the security chain or upper latch on the room's entrance door to ensure that your child doesn't open it without your knowledge.

Inspect the floor and remove pins, coins, and other foreign objects that your child might find. Don't forget to check under beds and furniture. One of the best tips we've heard came from a Fort Lauderdale, Florida, mother who crawls around the room on her hands and knees in order to see possible hazards from her child's perspective.

If you rent a suite or a condo, you'll have more territory to childproof and will have to deal with the possible presence of cleaning supplies, a stove, a refrigerator, cooking utensils, and low cabinet doors, among other things. Sometimes the best option is to seal off the kitchen with a folding safety gate.

PART FOUR

DINING

DINING OPTIONS ABOUND BOTH IN AND OUT of Walt Disney World, and if you're so inclined, there are a lot of ways to save big bucks while keeping your crew nourished and happy.

EATING *outside* WALT DISNEY WORLD

1. **A CAR HELPS** Access to restaurants outside of Walt Disney World can really cut the cost of your overall vacation, but you've got to have wheels. If you eat only your evening meal outside the World, the savings will more than pay for the car.

2. **PLENTY OF CHOICES** Eating outside of Walt Disney World doesn't relegate you to dining in lackluster restaurants. The range of choices is quite broad and includes elegant dining options as well as familiar chain restaurants and local family eateries.

3. **DISCOUNTS ARE EVERYWHERE** Visitor magazines and booklets containing discount coupons to dozens of out-of-the-World restaurants are available everywhere except in Walt Disney World. The coupons are good at a broad selection of eateries ranging from burger joints to some of the best restaurants in the area. Though coupon booklets and freebie visitor mags are pretty much everywhere, the mother lode can be found at the Orlando/Orange County Official Visitors Center at 8723 International Drive, at the corner of Austrian Row, open 8 a.m. to 7 p.m.; ☎ 407-363-5872 or **www.info@orlandocvb.com.** Here you'll find copies of every magazine and booklet available. The center also sells slightly discounted tickets to the theme parks.

4. **WHEN YOU DON'T HAVE A CAR** If you're staying in a hotel outside Disney World, Take Out Express (7111 Grand National Drive; ☎ 407-352-1170) will deliver a meal from your choice of among 20 restaurants, including

T.G.I. Fridays, Toojay's Deli, Passage to India, Sweet Basil, Bella Roma, Taste of Hong Kong, Ocean Grill, Houlihan's, and Sizzler. The delivery charge is $4.99 per restaurant, with a minimum $15 order. Gratuity is added to the bill. Cash, traveler's checks, MasterCard, VISA, American Express, and Discover are accepted. Hours are 4:30 p.m. until 11 p.m.

BUFFETS AND MEAL DEALS OUTSIDE WALT DISNEY WORLD

BUFFETS, RESTAURANT SPECIALS, AND DISCOUNT DINING abound in the area surrounding Walt Disney World, especially on US 192 (locally known as the Irlo Bronson Memorial Highway) and along International Drive. For a family trying to economize on meals, some of the come-ons are mighty attractive. But are these places any good? Is the food fresh, tasty, and appealing? Are the restaurants clean and inviting?

Buffets

GENERAL BUFFETS Two buffets, the **Las Vegas Buffet** (5269 West US 192; ☎ 407-397-1288) and **Bill Wong's** (5668 International Drive; ☎ 407-352-5373), offer fair value. The Las Vegas Buffet, the better of the two, features a carving station with prime rib, ham, turkey, and sometimes lamb. Bill Wong's represents itself as a Chinese buffet but shores up its Chinese selections with peel-and-eat shrimp, prime rib, and a nice selection of hot and cold vegetables.

SEAFOOD AND LOBSTER BUFFETS These affairs do not exactly fall under the category of inexpensive dining. Prices range from $20 to $27.95 for early birds (4 p.m. until 6 p.m.) and $29.95 to $32.95 after 6 p.m. The main draw (no pun intended) is all the lobster you can eat. The problem is that lobsters don't wear well on a steam table. After a few minutes on the buffet line, they make better tennis balls than dinner. If, however, you have someone in the kitchen who knows how to steam a lobster, and if you grab your lobster immediately after a fresh batch has been brought out, it will probably be fine. There are three lobster buffets on US 192 and another two on International Drive. Although all five do a reasonable job, we prefer **Boston Lobster Feast** (6071 West Irlo Bronson [US 192]; ☎ 407-396-2606; and 8731 International Drive, five blocks north of the Convention Center; ☎ 407-248-8606; **www.bostonlobsterfeast.com**). Both locations are distinguished by a vast variety of seafood in addition to the lobster. The International Drive location is cavernous and insanely noisy, so we prefer the Irlo Bronson location, where you can actually have a conversation over dinner. There's ample parking at the International Drive location, while parking places are in short supply at the Irlo Bronson restaurant. At about $33 after 6 p.m., dining is expensive at both locations.

BREAKFAST BUFFETS AND ENTREE BUFFETS Entree buffets are offered by most of the area chain steak houses such as **Ponderosa, Sizzler, Western Steer,** and **Golden Corral.** Among them, there are 18 locations in the Walt Disney World area. All serve breakfast, lunch, and dinner. At lunch and dinner, you get the buffet when you buy an entree, usually a steak. Generally speaking, the buffets are less elaborate than a stand-alone buffet and considerably more varied than a salad bar. Breakfast service is a straightforward buffet (that is, there is no obligation to buy an entree). Concerning the food, it's chain-restaurant quality but pretty decent all the same. Prices are a bargain, and you can get in and out at lightning speed—important at breakfast when you're trying to get to the theme parks early. Some locations offer lunch and dinner buffets at a set price without buying an entree.

Though you can argue about which chain serves the best steak, Golden Corral wins the buffet contest hands down, with at least twice as many offerings as its three competitors. Where buffets at Golden Corral, Western Steer, and Ponderosa are pretty consistent from location to location, the buffets at the various Sizzlers vary a good deal. The pick of the Sizzlers is the 4006 West US 192 location. In addition to the steak houses, area **Shoney's** also offer breakfast, lunch, and dinner buffets. Local freebie visitor magazines are full of discount coupons for all of the above.

CHINESE BUFFETS   Many Chinese dishes simply do not work on a buffet. The exception might be a busy local Chinese lunch spot where buffet items are replenished every five or so minutes. Even then, however, the food doesn't measure up to dishes that are cooked to order and served fresh out of the wok. At the so-called Chinese super buffets, the food often sits a long time. We tried all the buffets advertised in the visitor magazines (and a few that were not), and while a number of them had great eye appeal, the food was often lackluster. A notable exception is **Asian Harbor Chinese and Japanese Super Buffet** (in Lake Buena Vista at the intersection of FL 535 and FL 536 next to the CVS drugstore; ☎ 407-238-9998). The restaurant features Chinese dishes, Japanese seafood, and an Oriental grill bar. Items on the buffet are replenished frequently to ensure freshness. The best Chinese buffet in the International Drive area is **Mei Asian Bistro** (8255 International Drive, in the shopping center just north of Mercado; ☎ 407-352-0867).

INDIAN BUFFETS   Indian food works much better on a buffet than Chinese food. The mainstay of Indian buffets is curries. Curry, you may be surprised to know, is essentially the Indian word for any mix of spices. In India, each curry is prepared with a different spice combination, and no self-respecting cook would dream of using an off-the-shelf mix like the so-called curry powder sold in American groceries. The salient point about Indian buffets is that curries, unlike stir-frys, actually improve with a little aging. If you've ever heated a leftover stew at home and commented that it tasted better than when originally served, it's because the flavors and ingredients continued to marry during the storage period, making it richer and tastier.

In the Walt Disney World area, most Indian restaurants offer a buffet at lunch only—not too convenient if you plan on spending your day at the theme parks. If you're out shopping or taking a day off, here are some Indian buffets worth trying:

- **Aashirwad** 5748 International Drive, at the corner of International Drive and Kirkman Road; ☎ 407-370-9830

- **Punjab Indian Restaurant** 7451 International Drive; ☎ 407-352-7887

- **Spice Cafe** 7536 Dr. Phillips Boulevard, in the Market Place complex at Sand Lake Road and Dr. Phillips Boulevard; ☎ 407-264-0205

BRAZILIAN BUFFETS A number of budget Brazilian buffets have sprung up along International Drive. The best of these is **Vittorio's** (5159 International Drive, near the outlet malls at the northern end of International Drive; ☎ 407-352-1255).

There are a number of buffets and family service meals offered by Walt Disney World restaurants. The quality and selection usually (but not always) surpass the bulk loaders in the nether regions, but so in a totally major way do the prices.

Meal Deals

Discount coupons are available for a wide range of restaurants, including some wonderful upscale ethnic places like **Mings Court** (Chinese; 9188 International Drive, ☎ 407-351-9988). For those who crave both beef and a bargain, try **JT's Prime Time Restaurant & Bar** (16299 W. Irlo Bronson; ☎ 407-239-6555). JT's serves all-you-can-eat prime rib on Wednesday nights for $18.99. They slice it a little thin but are very attentive in regard to bringing you additional helpings. Other prime rib specials can be found at **Cattleman's Steakhouse,** with locations at 8801 International Drive a quarter of a mile north of the convention center (☎ 407-354-9888) and on US 192 at FL 535 (2948 Vineland Road; ☎ 407-397-1888). Our favorite prime rib option is **Wild Jack's Steaks & BBQ** (7364 International Drive; ☎ 407-352-4407). The décor is strictly cowboy modern, but the beef is some of the best in town, and the price is right. The best steak deal in the Disney World area is the $9.99, ten-ounce New York strip at the **Black Angus Steak House.** The beef is served with salad, choice of vegetables or potato, and bread, and is available at all three locations convenient to Disney: 7516 West Irlo Bronson (US 192), ☎ 407-390-4548; 12399 FL 535, ☎ 407-239-4144; and 6231 International Drive, ☎ 407-354-3333. Another meat eater's delight is the Feast for Four at **Sonny's Real Pit Bar-B-Q,** a Florida chain that turns out good barbecue. For $34 per family of four, you get sliced pork or beef, plus chicken, ribs, beans, slaw, fries, garlic bread, and soft drinks or tea, all served family-style. Locations include 3189 South John Young Parkway, ☎ 407-847-8889; and US 192 at 4475 13th Street, ☎ 407-892-2285. No coupons are needed or available for JT's or Sonny's, but coupons are available for the other "meateries."

DINING *in* WALT DISNEY WORLD

A FEW YEARS AGO, you could have joked that a chapter about dining in Walt Disney World was an oxymoron. Whatever else it was (and it was many wonderful things), Disney World was no gourmet paradise. For the most part, in fact, the restaurants were as much "entertainment" as the rest of Disney World: the fast-food joints feature character décor, and the international pavilions sport native costumes.

Not that Walt Disney World has been transformed overnight into a gourmet paradise. Some restaurants still seem to be mere commercial extensions of the theme parks, like the Rainforest Cafes in Animal Kingdom and at the Downtown Disney Marketplace, which have their own audio-animatronic elephants (among others). Sometimes it's even harder to tell the live entertainment and the dinner apart—for example, at the Coral Reef restaurant in The Seas pavilion at Epcot, where some 6,000 sea creatures, including close relatives of those on the menu, are swimming around the glass wall of the dining room, trying to make you feel guilty.

Nevertheless, in the past few years, Disney's food and beverage department has vastly expanded, and they have succeeded in launching a remarkable upgrade of the full-service restaurants around the World. Now there are nine or ten first-class restaurants and perhaps an equal number of B+ establishments. The wine lists have been seriously improved and expanded—there is even a full-fledged wine bar at the Yacht and Beach Club, Martha's Vineyard.

Of course, if the average parents roaming the Walt Disney World parks were primarily concerned with pleasing their palates, the hottest dinner ticket at the park would not be the *Hoop-Dee-Doo Revue.* In fact, if you want to know what Disney World visitors really like, look at the numbers: Every year, they consume 1.6 million smoked turkey legs, nearly 10 million hamburgers, 7.7 million hot dogs, 46 million sodas, and 5 million bags of popcorn.

One thing parents should be aware of is that both full- and counter-service restaurants at Walt Disney World serve very substantial portions. You can easily put aside parts of dinners for lunches the next day (if you have a refrigerator in your room), split an entrée, or load up at lunch and go light on dinner.

Liliane

So, for many families, food is a secondary consideration, but if you do care more about dining out on your vacation or would like to experiment with different cuisines, *The Unofficial Guide to Walt Disney World,* referred to in the Introduction, includes more detailed reviews not only of the sit-down establishments in Disney World itself but also some of the better restaurants outside the World.

DISNEY DINING 101

Advance Reservations—What's in a Name

Once called Priority Seating, Disney restaurant reservations are now called, somewhat redundantly, "Advance Reservations." The new system, however, is exactly the same as the old one except in name. Previously, under Priority Seating, guests thought they had a reservation when all they actually had was a promise to be seated ahead of walk-ins. Under the Advance Reservation system, nothing has changed except that Disney now says you have an Advance Reservation. In reality, however, you have a Priority Seating, because you're still only guaranteed to be accorded priority over walk-ins. Now if all this makes sense to you, please write and explain it to us.

When you call ☎ 407-WDW-DINE, your name and essential information are taken as if you were making a "real" reservation. The Disney representative then tells you that you have Advance Reservations for the restaurant on the date and time you requested and usually explains that Advance Reservations mean you will be seated ahead of walk-ins, that is, those without Advance Reservations.

Even though no seats are reserved for walk-ins, it's easy to get a walk-in seat during slower times of the year (with the exception of Cinderella's Royal Table). During high season, it's tougher to get seated as a walk-in, but by no means impossible. You can land a seat in the event of no-shows, but you can also get in if the tables turn over more rapidly than usual. Needless to say, scoring a table as a walk-in is more difficult if your family resembles the Children's Crusade, but if you can fit at a table for four or six persons, your chances are good.

The no-show rate in January, a slow month, is about 33%, while in July it's less than 10%.

Bob

With Advance Reservations, your wait will almost always be less than 20 minutes during peak hours, and often less than ten minutes. If you just walk in, especially during busier seasons, expect to wait 40 to 75 minutes. Disney offers a dining program as an add-on to vacation packages. Unlike previous dining programs, Magic Your Way Dining can save money for certain guests (see description starting on page 155).

Getting Your Act Together

If you want to patronize any of the Walt Disney World Resort full-service restaurants, buffets, character meals, or dinner shows, you should make Advance Reservations. On the following page is a listing of how far ahead of time you can make Advance Reservations.

For most full-service restaurants, buffets, and character meals, you can make advance reservations 180 days ahead of time.

If you fail to make Advance Reservations before you leave home, or if you want to make your dining decisions spontaneously while at Walt Disney World, your chances of getting a table at the restaurant

You can make reservations up to 365 days in advance for:

Mickey's Backyard Barbeque at Fort Wilderness

You can make reservations up to 180 days in advance for:

Afternoon tea and children's programs at the Grand Floridian

All Disney table-service restaurants except Bistro de Paris at Epcot

Downtown Disney's Fulton's Crab House, House of Blues, **and** Portobello Yacht Club

Fantasmic! dinner package at Disney-MGM Studios

Hoop-Dee-Doo Revue at Fort Wilderness

Spirit of Aloha Polynesian luau at the Polynesian Resort

Victoria & Albert's at the Grand Floridian (Chef's Table only)

Wolfgang Puck Cafe at Downtown Disney

You can make reservations up to 90 days in advance for:

Cirque de Soleil's *La Nouba* at Downtown Disney

You can make reservations up to 30 days in advance for:

Bistro de Paris (dinner only) at Epcot

of your choice are pretty good but not a slam dunk. The *Hoop-Dee-Doo Revue* and Cinderella's Royal Table character meals will almost certainly be sold out, as will several of the other more popular character meals. If, however, you visit Walt Disney World during a busier time of year, it's to your advantage to make Advance Reservations before you leave home. Except for Cinderella's Royal Table breakfast and lunch, the *Hoop-Dee-Doo Revue,* and Victoria & Albert's, don't worry about calling the maximum number of days in advance. It will suffice to call three to five weeks before you leave home, by which time you will have sorted out your dining preferences. If you change your mind once you arrive, you can try to change your Advance Reservations by calling ☎ 407-WDW-DINE.

Disney resort guests can call 180 days ahead of their *check-in date* and make reservations for up to ten additional days in advance, which effectively gives them a 190-day window.

Liliane

If you poop out in the theme park and you don't feel like using your Advance Reservations that night, be aware that some restaurants have penalties for being a no-show and will charge you a cancellation fee. Note that you must pay in full at the time of booking for all meals at Cinderella's Royal Table, the *Hoop-Dee-Doo Revue, Spirit of Aloha,* and *Mickey's Backyard Barbeque.* If you're a no-show, you lose the entire amount, so be sure to get the exact cancellation policy at the time you book your meal. Incidentally, if you're asked for a credit card to secure a seating, be aware that it's a real reservation as opposed to an Advance Reservation. Also be aware that if you're a no-show for a particular reservation, it will not affect any other Advance Reservations you may have made.

Bob

For Advance Reservations, make sure you bring your confirmation number to the restaurant.

If you have an Advance Reservation for a theme-park restaurant at a time prior to opening, simply proceed to the turnstiles and inform a cast member, who will admit you to the park.

Liliane

Disney Kids' Meals are now for ages 3 to 9; the cutoff used to be age 11.

Dress

Dress is informal at all theme-park restaurants. Some of its resort restaurants, however, have a "business casual" dress code: dress slacks (or dress shorts) with a collared shirt for men, and skirts or dress shorts with a blouse or sweater (or a dress) for women. Restaurants with this dress code are **Jiko—The Cooking Place** at Disney's Animal Kingdom Lodge; the **Flying Fish Cafe** at Disney's BoardWalk; the **California Grill** at Disney's Contemporary Resort; **Cítricos** at Disney's Grand Floridian Resort & Spa; **Narcoossee's** at the Grand Floridian; **Artist Point** at Disney's Wilderness Lodge; and **Yachtsman Steakhouse** at Disney's Yacht and Beach Club Resorts.

Food Allergies and Special Requests

If you have food allergies or observe some specific type of diet, like eating kosher, make your needs known when you make your Advance Reservations. Does it work? Well, a Phillipsburg, New Jersey, mom reports her family's experience:

> My 6-year-old has many food allergies, and we often have to bring food with us to restaurants when we go out to eat. I was able to make reservations at the Disney restaurants in advance and indicate these allergies to the reservation clerk. When we arrived at the restaurants, the staff was already aware of my child's allergies and assigned our table a chef who double-checked the list of allergies with us. Each member of the waitstaff was also informed of the allergies. The chefs were very nice and made my son feel very special (to the point where my other family members felt a little jealous).

A Few Caveats

Before you begin eating your way through the World, you need to know these things:

1. However creative and enticing the menu descriptions, avoid fancy food, especially at full-service restaurants in the Magic Kingdom and Disney-

MGM Studios. Order dishes the kitchen is unlikely to botch. An exception to this caveat is the excellent Hollywood Brown Derby restaurant at the Studios.

2. Don't order baked, broiled, poached, or grilled seafood unless the restaurant specializes in seafood or rates at least 3.5 stars on our restaurant chart.

3. Theme-park restaurants rush their customers in order to make room for the next group of diners. Dining at high speed may appeal if you have young, restless children, but if you want to relax, it's more like eating in a pressure chamber than fine dining.

4. If you're dining in a theme park and cost is an issue, make lunch your main meal. Entrees are similar to those on the dinner menu, but prices are significantly lower.

Walt Disney World Restaurant Categories

In general, food and beverage offerings at Walt Disney World are defined by service, price, and convenience:

FULL-SERVICE RESTAURANTS Full-service restaurants are in all Disney resorts, except the All-Star and Pop Century, and all major theme parks, Downtown Disney Marketplace, Pleasure Island, and Disney's West Side. Disney operates most of the restaurants in the theme parks and its hotels. Contractors or franchisees operate the restaurants in hotels of the Downtown Disney Resort Area (DDRA), the Swan and Dolphin resorts, Pleasure Island, Disney's West Side, and some in Epcot, the Marketplace, and the BoardWalk. Advance Reservations (explained above), arranged in advance, are recommended for all full-service restaurants except those in the DDRA. The restaurants accept VISA, MasterCard, American Express, Discover, Diners Club, and the Disney Credit Card.

BUFFETS AND FAMILY-STYLE RESTAURANTS There has been an explosion of buffets at Disney World during recent years. Many have Disney characters in attendance, and most have a separate children's menu featuring hot dogs, burgers, chicken nuggets, pizza, macaroni and cheese, and spaghetti and meatballs. In addition to the buffets, several restaurants serve a family-style, all-you-can-eat, fixed-price meal. Advance Reservations arrangements are required for character buffets and recommended for all other buffets and family-style restaurants. Most major credit cards are accepted.

If you want to eat a lot but don't feel like standing in another line, consider one of the all-you-can-eat family-style or fixed-menu restaurants. The former features platters of food brought to your table in courses, the latter extra helpings on request delivered by your wait person. You can sample everything on the menu and eat as much as you like. You can even have a favorite appetizer after you finish the main course. The food tends to be a little better than you'll find on a buffet line.

Walt Disney World Buffets, Family-style, and Fixed-menu Restaurants

LOCATION	RESTAURANT	CUISINE	MEALS SERVED	DISNEY CHARACTERS PRESENT
Magic Kingdom	Cinderella's Royal Table	American	B*, L, D	Yes
Magic Kingdom	Crystal Palace	American	B, L, D	Yes
Magic Kingdom	Liberty Tree Tavern	American	D	Yes
Epcot	Akershus Royal Banquet Hall	Scandinavian	B, L, D	Yes
Epcot	Biergarten	German	L, D	No
Epcot	Garden Grill	American	L, D	Yes
Disney-MGM Studios	Hollywood and Vine	American	B, L, D	Yes (B, L)
Animal Kingdom	Restaurantosaurus	American	B, L, D, S	Yes (B)
Contemporary Resort	Chef Mickey's	American	B, D	Yes
Polynesian	'Ohana	Pan-Asian	B, D	Yes (B)
Coronado Springs	Maya Grill	American	B	No
Beach Club Resort	Cape May Cafe	Clambake (D)	B, D	Yes (B)
Grand Floridian	1900 Park Fare	American (B)	B, D	Yes
Animal Kingdom Lodge	Boma	African (D), American (B)	B, D	No
Wilderness Lodge	Whispering Canyon	American	B, L, D	No
Fort Wilderness	Settlement Pavilion	American	D	Yes
Fort Wilderness	Trail's End	American	B, L, D	No
Swan	Garden Grove Cafe	American	B, L	Yes (B weekends)
Swan	Gulliver's Grill	American	D	No
Dolphin	Fresh Mediterranean Market	Mediterranean	B, L	No

Cinderella's Royal Table serves family-style meals only at breakfast.

Family-style and fixed-menu, all-you-can-eat service is available at the **Liberty Tree Tavern** and **Cinderella's Royal Table** in the Magic Kingdom, at the **Garden Grill** in the Land Pavilion in Epcot (all with character dining), or at **'Ohana** in the Polynesian Resort and **Whispering Canyon Cafe** in the Wilderness Lodge (diners at Whispering Canyon also have the option of ordering from a standard menu).

The table lists buffets and family-style restaurants where you can belly up for bulk loading at Walt Disney World.

CAFETERIAS AND FOOD COURTS Cafeterias in all the major theme parks offer a middle ground between full-service and counter-service dining. Food courts, featuring a collection of counter-service eateries under one roof, are found at the theme parks and at the moderate (Coronado Springs, Caribbean Beach, Port Orleans) and budget (All-Star and Pop Century) Disney resorts. No Advance Reservation is required or available at cafeterias or food courts.

COUNTER SERVICE Counter-service fast food is available in all theme parks and at Downtown Disney Marketplace, Pleasure Island, Disney's BoardWalk, and Disney's West Side. The food compares in quality with McDonald's, Captain D's, or Taco Bell but is more expensive, though often served in larger portions.

FAST CASUAL Somewhere between burgers and formal dining are the establishments in Disney's new "fast casual" category. Initially launched with two restaurants (**Sunshine Season Food Fair** in Epcot and **Backlot Express** at the Studios), fast-casual restaurants feature

THE COST OF COUNTER-SERVICE FOOD

To help you develop your dining budget, here are prices of common counter-service items. Sales tax isn't included.

Food item	Price
Bagel or muffin	$2.29–$2.50
Brownie	$2.39–$2.79
Cake or pie	$2.79–$4.29
Cereal with milk	$2.69–$2.99
Cheeseburger with fries	$5.89–$6.50
Chicken-breast sandwich (grilled)	$5.19–$7.95
Children's meals	$4.29–$5.49
Chips	$1.29–$2.50
Cookies	$1.59–$2.09
Fish basket (fried) with fries	$6.49–$6.89
French fries	$1.89
Fried-chicken strips with fries	$6.69
Fruit (whole piece)	$0.99–$1.99
Fruit cup/fruit salad	$2.59–$3.49
Hot dogs	$3.99–$5.79 (basket)
Ice-cream bars	$2.39
Nachos with cheese	$2.99–$4.59

THE COST OF COUNTER-SERVICE FOOD (CONTINUED)

PB&J sandwich	$2.29–$4.29
Pizza	$5.59–$6.29
Popcorn	$2.29–$3.49
Pretzel	$3.29–$3.79
Salad (entree)	$6.39–$7.59
Salad (side)	$2.59
Smoked turkey leg	$5.19
Soup/chili	$2.49–$3.50
Sub/deli sandwich	$4.99–$7.09
Taco salad	$4.79–$7.99
Tacos (2) with beans and salsa	$4.79–$4.99
Veggie burger	$4.19–$6.19

Drinks	Small	Large
Beer (not available in the Magic Kingdom)	$3.50	$8.25
Bottled water	$1.25	$2.00
Bottled water (in glass bottle)	$3.25	$6.50
Cappuccino/espresso	$3.19	$4.19
Coffee	$1.69	$1.89
Floats/milk shakes/sundaes	$2.99	$4.99
Fruit juice	$1.49	$2.39
Milk	$1.29	$1.99
Soft drinks, iced tea, and lemonade	$1.99	$2.29–$4.99
Refillable souvenir mug ($12 to buy)	$3.79	$3.99
Hot tea and cocoa	$1.69	$1.99

menu choices a cut above what you'd normally see at a typical counter-service location. At Sunshine Season, chefs will prepare grilled salmon on an open cooking surface while you watch, or you can choose from grilled beef, tasty noodle bowls, or large sandwiches made with artisanal breads. The three initial locations all feature Asian or Mediterranean cuisine, something previously lacking inside the parks. Entrees cost about $2 more on average than traditional counter service, but the variety and the food quality more than make up for the difference.

VENDOR FOOD Vendors abound at the theme parks, Downtown Disney Marketplace, Pleasure Island, Disney's West Side, and Disney's BoardWalk. Offerings include popcorn, ice-cream bars, churros

(Mexican pastries), soft drinks, bottled water, and (in theme parks) fresh fruit. Prices include tax, and payment must be in cash.

Hard Choices

Dining choices will definitely affect your Walt Disney World experience. If you're short on time and you want to see the theme parks, avoid full-service restaurants. Ditto if you're short on funds. If you want to try a Disney full-service restaurant, arrange Advance Reservations ahead of time—this won't reserve you a table, but it will minimize your wait.

Integrating Meals into the *Unofficial Guide* Touring Plans

Arrive before the park of your choice opens. Tour expeditiously, using your chosen plan (taking as few breaks as possible), until about 11 to 11:30 a.m. Once the park becomes crowded around midday, meals and other breaks won't affect the plan's efficiency. If you intend to stay in the park for evening parades, fireworks, or other events, eat dinner early enough to be finished in time for the festivities.

Fast Food in the Theme Parks

Because most meals during a Disney World vacation are consumed on the run while touring, we'll tackle counter-service and vendor foods first. Plentiful in all theme parks are hot dogs, hamburgers, chicken sandwiches, green salads, and pizza. They're augmented by special items that relate to the park's theme or the part of the park you're touring. In Epcot's Germany, for example, counter-service bratwurst and beer are sold. In Frontierland in the Magic Kingdom, vendors sell smoked turkey legs. Counter-service prices are fairly consistent from park to park. Expect to pay the same for your coffee or hot dog at the Animal Kingdom as at Disney-MGM Studios.

Getting your act together in regard to counter-service restaurants in the parks is more a matter of courtesy than necessity. Rude guests rank fifth among reader complaints. A mother from Fort Wayne, Indiana, points out that indecision can be as maddening as outright discourtesy, especially when you're hungry:

> *Every fast-food restaurant has menu signs the size of billboards, but do you think anybody reads them? People waiting in line spend enough time in front of these signs to memorize them, and still don't have a clue what they want when they finally get to the order taker. If by some miracle they've managed to choose between the hot dog and the hamburger, they then fiddle around another ten minutes deciding what size Coke to order. Tell your readers PULEEEZ get their orders together ahead of time!*

Cutting Your Dining Time at the Theme Parks

Even if you confine your meals to vendor and counter-service fast food, you lose a lot of time getting food in the theme parks. At Walt Disney World, everything begins with a line and ends with a cash register. When it comes to fast food, "fast" may apply to the time you spend eating it, not the time invested in obtaining it.

Here are suggestions for minimizing the time you spend hunting and gathering food:

1. **Eat breakfast before arriving.** Don't waste touring time eating breakfast at the parks. Besides, restaurants outside the World offer some outstanding breakfast specials. Some hotels furnish small refrigerators in their guest rooms, or rent them. If you can get by on cold cereal, rolls, fruit, and juice, having a fridge in your room will save a ton of time. If you can't get a fridge, bring a cooler.

2. **After a good breakfast,** buy snacks from vendors in the parks as you tour, or stuff some snacks in a hip pack. This is very important if you're on a tight schedule and can't spend a lot of time waiting in line for food.

3. **All theme-park restaurants are busiest** between 11:30 a.m. and 2:15 p.m. for lunch and 6 p.m. and 8:15 p.m. for dinner. For shorter lines and faster service, don't eat during these hours, especially 12:30 p.m. to 1:30 p.m.

4. **Many counter-service restaurants sell cold sandwiches.** Buy a cold lunch (except for drinks) before 11:30 a.m. and carry it until you're ready to eat. Ditto for dinner. Bring small plastic bags in which to pack the food. Purchase drinks at the appropriate time from any convenient vendor.

5. **Most fast-food eateries have more than one service window.** Regardless of time of day, check the lines at all windows before queuing. Sometimes a window that's manned but out of the way will have a much shorter line or none at all. Note, however, that some windows may not offer all items.

6. **If you're short on time** and the park closes early, stay until closing and eat dinner outside Disney World before returning to your hotel. If the park

stays open late, eat dinner about 4 or 4:30 p.m. at the restaurant of your choice. You should miss the last wave of lunchers and sneak in just ahead of the dinner crowd.

Tips for Saving Money on Food

Every time you buy a soda at the theme parks it's going to set you back about $2.50, and everything else from hot dogs to salad is comparably high. You can say, "Oh well, we're on vacation," and pay the exorbitant prices, or you can plan ahead and save big bucks. For comparison purposes, let's say that a family of two adults and two young teens arrives at Walt Disney World on Sunday afternoon and departs for home the following Saturday after breakfast. During that period the family eats six breakfasts, five lunches, and six dinners. What those meals cost, of course, depends on where and what they eat. It is possible for them to rent a condo and prepare all of their own meals, but they didn't travel all the way to Walt Disney World to cook. So, let's be realistic and assume that they will eat their evening meals out (this is what most families do, because, among other reasons, they're too tired to think about cooking). It may be just burgers or pizza, but they eat dinner in a restaurant.

That leaves breakfast and lunch to contend with. Here, basically, are the options. Needless to say, there are dozens of other various combinations. They could eat all of their meals in full-service restaurants, for example, but the bottom line is that most people don't, so we'll just keep this relatively simple.

1. Eat breakfast in their room out of their cooler or fridge and prepare sandwiches and snacks to take to the theme parks in their hip packs. Carry water bottles or rely on drinking fountains for water. Cost: $121 for family of four for six days (does not include dinners or food purchased on travel days)

2. Eat breakfast in their room out of their cooler or fridge, carry snacks in their hip packs, and buy lunch at Disney counter-service restaurants. Cost: $288 for family of four for six days (does not include dinners or food purchased on travel days)

3. Eat breakfast at their hotel restaurant, buy snacks from vendors, and eat lunch at Disney counter-service restaurants. Cost: $532 for family of four for six days (does not include dinners or food purchased on travel days)

In case you're wondering, these are the foods on which we've based our grocery costs for those options where breakfast, lunch, and/or snacks are prepared from the cooler:

BREAKFAST Cold cereal (choice of two), breakfast pastries, bananas, orange juice, milk, and coffee.

LUNCH Cold cuts or peanut butter and jelly sandwiches, condiments (mayo, mustard, and such), boxed juice, apples.

SNACKS Packaged cheese or peanut butter crackers, boxed juice, and trail mix (combination of M&Ms, nuts, raisins, and so on).

If you opt to buy groceries, you can stock up on food for your cooler at the Publix Supermarket on the corner of FL 535 and Vineland Road. A second, more upscale (and pricier) store is the Goodings Supermarket in the Disney-owned Crossroads Shopping Center on FL 535 opposite the entrance to the Disney Hotel Plaza and Downtown Disney. Finally, there's a Winn Dixie about a mile north of the Crossroads Center on FL 535.

Projected costs for snacks purchased at the theme parks are based on drinks (coffee or sodas) twice a day and popcorn once each day. Counter-service meal costs assume basic meals (hot dogs, burgers, fries, and soda or coffee). Hotel breakfast expense assumes eggs, bacon, and toast, or pancakes with bacon, and juice, milk, or coffee to drink.

If you are an Entertainment Club member, don't forget to take your card and coupons for Orlando. Publix currently offers $5 off any purchase over $50.

Liliane

Readers love to share tips for economizing on food. A Missouri mom offers a comprehensive plan:

I have shared our very successful meal plan with many families. We stayed six nights and arrived at WDW after some days on the beach south of Sarasota. We shopped there and arrived with our steel Coleman cooler well stocked with milk and sandwich fixings. I froze a block of ice in a milk bottle, and we replenished it daily with ice from the resort ice machine. I also froze small packages of deli-type meats for later in the week. We ate cereal, milk, and fruit each morning, with boxed juices. I also had a hot pot to boil water for instant coffee, oatmeal, and soup.

Each child had a belt bag of his own, which he filled from a special box of "goodies" each day. I made a great mystery of filling that box in the weeks before the trip. Some things were actual food, like packages of crackers and cheese, packets of peanuts, and raisins. Some were worthless junk, like candy and gum. They grazed from their belt bags at will throughout the day, with no interference from Mom and Dad. Each also had a small, rectangular plastic water bottle that could hang on the belt. We filled these at water fountains before getting into lines and were the envy of many.

We left the park before noon, ate sandwiches, chips, and soda in the room, and napped. We purchased our evening meal in the park, at a counter-service eatery. We budgeted for both morning and evening snacks from a vendor but often did not need them. It made the occasional treat all the more special. Our cooler had been pretty much emptied by the end of the week, but the block of ice was still there.

We interviewed one woman who brought a huge picnic for her family of five packed in a large diaper/baby paraphernalia bag. She stowed the bag in a locker under the Main Street Station and retrieved it when the family was hungry.

A mom from Whiteland, Indiana, who purchases drinks in the parks, offers this suggestion:

One "must-take" item if you're traveling with younger kids is a supply of small paper or plastic cups to split drinks, which are both huge and expensive.

DISNEY DINING SUGGESTIONS

BELOW ARE SUGGESTIONS FOR DINING at each of the major theme parks. If you are interested in trying a theme-park full-service restaurant, be aware that the restaurants continue to serve after the park's official closing time. We showed up at the Hollywood Brown Derby just as Disney-MGM Studios closed at 8 p.m. We were seated almost immediately and enjoyed a leisurely dinner while the crowds cleared out. Don't worry if you are depending on Disney transportation: buses, boats, and monorails run two to three hours after the parks close.

The Magic Kingdom

Food at the Magic Kingdom has improved noticeably over the past several years. The **Crystal Palace** at the end of Main Street offers a good (albeit pricey) buffet chaperoned by Disney characters, while the **Liberty Tree Tavern** in Liberty Square features hearty family-style dining, also with Disney characters in attendance. **Cinderella's Royal Table,** a fixed-price full-service restaurant on the second floor of the castle features characters at breakfast and lunch.

Authors' Favorite Counter-service Restaurants

Cosmic Ray's (serves kosher food) Tomorrowland

Pecos Bill's Tall Tale Inn & Cafe Frontierland

Fast food at the Magic Kingdom is, well, fast food. It's more expensive, of course, than what you would pay at McDonald's, but what do you expect? It's like dining at an airport—you're a captive audience. On the positive side, portions are large, usually large enough for children to share. Overall, the variety of fast food offerings provides a lot of choice, though the number of selections at any specific eatery remains quite limited.

Epcot

From the beginning, dining has been an integral component of Epcot's entertainment product. The importance of dining is reflected in the number of restaurants and in their ability to serve consistently interesting and well-prepared meals. This is in stark contrast to the

The Top Ten Snacks at Walt Disney World

Following is a top-ten list of particularly decadent or unusual snacks available at WDW. We've omitted the usual funnel cakes, popcorn, and ice cream available anywhere. Also absent are the truly bizarre snacks, such as the squid treats sold at the Mitsukoshi Department Store in the Japan Pavilion at Epcot's World Showcase. These are the goodies worth scouring the parks and resorts for, in ascending order:

10. **Kaki Gori at the Japan Pavilion, Epcot World Showcase** A little on the sweet side but lighter than ice cream, the shaved ice at this small stand comes in such unique flavors as honeydew melon, strawberry, and tangerine. And at $2.25, it's a bargain.

9. **Turkey legs** Available at every theme park, these must come from 85-pound turkeys, because they're huge, not to mention extra-juicy and flavorful. Grab some napkins and go primal on one of these bad boys, and don't worry about the stares you might attract—they're all just jealous.

8. **Twinkie tiramisù at Disney's Pop Century Resort** A retro spin on a classic dessert.

7. **Main Street Bakery at the Magic Kingdom** Homemade goodies, including some sugar-free offerings. Try the blueberry loaf, hot French-toast loaf, and Mickey Bundt cakes (but probably not all at once). Also check out the assortment of Mickey Mouse Rice Krispie treats, available plain, dipped in chocolate, and with sprinkles.

6. **Cadbury chocolate bars at the U.K. Pavilion, Epcot World Showcase** If you've never had an English Cadbury bar, you just don't know what you're missing.

Magic Kingdom, where, until recently, food service was seemingly an afterthought, with quality and selection a distant runner-up to logistical efficiency.

For the most part, Epcot's restaurants have always served decent food, though the World Showcase restaurants have occasionally been timid about delivering an honest representation of the host nation's cuisine. While these eateries have struggled with authenticity and have sometimes shied away from challenging the meat-and-potatoes palate of the average tourist, they are bolder now, encouraged by America's exponentially expanding appreciation of ethnic dining. True, the less adventuresome can still find sanitized and homogenized meals, but the same kitchens will serve up the real thing for anyone with a spark of curiosity and daring.

Authors' Favorite Counter-service Restaurants

Kringla Bakeri og Kafé **Norway**

5. **Milk shakes from Beaches & Cream at the Beach Club Resort** Hand dipped, thick, and creamy. When was the last time you sported a milk-shake mustache? For large crowds, or large appetites, try the Kitchen Sink: a huge sundae consisting of mountains of ice cream and toppings that is actually served in a kitchen sink.

4. **Selma's cookies at the BoardWalk** Oddly enough, these are available at the candy store, Seashore Sweets, rather than at the BoardWalk Bakery (go figure), but they're worth tracking down for their rich, buttery, homemade taste.

3. **Ghirardelli Soda Fountain and Chocolate Shop at Downtown Disney Marketplace** Everything is good, and the atmosphere has a sophisticated ice-cream-shop–plus–coffee-bar vibe. *Very* San Fran.

2. **Zebra Domes at Animal Kingdom Lodge** Offered as a dessert on the Boma buffet, they're also available at the Mara food court, on the lower level of the resort near the pool. They consist of a layer of sponge cake topped with chocolate mousse, then covered in white- and dark-chocolate ganache stripes. Fun and yum rolled into one!

And the number-one snack at the Walt Disney World Resort is . . .

1. **Two words: Dole Whip!** Available in Adventureland at the Magic Kingdom, a Dole Whip is a soft-serve pineapple–ice-cream dream. Adding to the ecstasy, Dole Whips are also paired with pineapple juice in Dole Floats. Heavenly!

Liliane

There's another goody that even trumps the Dole Whip, but Bob says we can't tell you. Maybe if you behave we can slip it in at the end of the chapter.

Sommerfest Germany

Sunshine Season Food Fair The Land

Yakitori House Japan

Many Epcot restaurants are overpriced, most conspicuously **Nine Dragons Restaurant** (China) and the **Coral Reef** (The Seas). Representing relatively good value through the combination of ambience and well-prepared food are **Akershus Royal Banquet Hall** (Norway), **Biergarten** (Germany), and **Restaurant Marrakesh** (Morocco). The Biergarten and the Marrakesh also have entertainment.

If you want to sample the ethnic foods of World Showcase without eating in restaurants requiring Advance Reservations, we recommend these counter-service specialties:

France Boulangerie Pâtisserie, for French pastries

Germany Sommerfest, for bratwurst and Beck's beer

Full-service Restaurants in Epcot

FUTURE WORLD

Coral Reef	The Seas
The Garden Grill Restaurant	The Land

WORLD SHOWCASE

Akershus Royal Banquet Hall	Norway
Biergarten	Germany
Bistro de Paris	France
Le Cellier Steakhouse	Canada
Les Chefs de France	France
Mitsukoshi Teppanyaki Dining Room	Japan
Nine Dragons Restaurant	China
L'Originale Alfredo di Roma Ristorante	Italy
Restaurant Marrakesh	Morocco
Rose & Crown Dining Room	United Kingdom
San Angel Inn Restaurante	Mexico
Tempura Kiku	Japan

Japan Yakitori House, for yakitori (meat or vegetables on skewers)

Norway Kringla Bakeri og Kafé, for pastries, open-face sandwiches, and Ringnes beer (our favorite)

United Kingdom Rose & Crown Pub, for Guinness, Harp, and Bass beers and ales

Disney-MGM Studios

Dining at Disney-MGM Studios is more interesting than in the Magic Kingdom and less ethnic than at Epcot. Disney-MGM has five restaurants where Advance Reservations are recommended: the **Hollywood Brown Derby, 50's Prime Time Cafe, Sci-Fi Dine-In Theater Restaurant, Mama Melrose's Ristorante Italiano,** and the **Hollywood & Vine** cafeteria. The upscale Brown Derby is by far the best restaurant at the Studios. For simple Italian food, including pizza, Mama Melrose's is fine. Just don't expect anything fancy. At the Sci-Fi Dine-In, you eat in little cars at a simulated drive-in movie of the 1950s. Though you won't find a more entertaining restaurant in Walt Disney World, the food is quite disappointing. Somewhat better is the 50's Prime Time Cafe, where you sit in Mom's kitchen of the 1950s and scarf down meat loaf while watching clips of vintage TV sitcoms. The 50's Prime Time Cafe is fun, and the food is a step up. The best way to experience either restaurant is to stop in for dessert or a drink between 2:30 and 4:30 p.m. Hollywood & Vine features singing and dancing characters from Playhouse Disney during lunch and dinner.

Authors' Favorite Counter-service Restaurants

ABC Commissary Backlot

Backlot Express Backlot

Toluca Legs Turkey Co. Sunset Boulevard

Toy Story Pizza Planet Backlot

Animal Kingdom

Because touring the Animal Kingdom takes less than a day, crowds are heaviest from 9:30 a.m. until about 3:30 p.m. Expect a mob at lunch and thinner crowds at dinner. We recommend you tour early after a good breakfast, then eat a very late lunch or graze on vendor

Although grilled meats are available, don't expect a broad choice of exotic dishes in the Animal Kingdom.

Bob

food. If you tour later in the day, eat lunch before you arrive, then enjoy dinner in or out of the theme park.

The Animal Kingdom mostly offers counter-service fast food. Most Animal Kingdom eateries serve up traditional Disney theme-park fare: hot dogs, hamburgers, deli sandwiches, and the like. Even so, we found Animal Kingdom fast food to be a cut above the average Disney fare. **Flame Tree Barbecue** in Discovery Island is our pick of the litter, both in terms of food quality and atmosphere. For a quiet refuge away from the crowds, you can't beat Flame Tree Barbecue's waterfront dining pavilions.

Authors' Favorite Counter-service Restaurant

Flame Tree Barbecue Discovery Island

The only full-service restaurant in the Animal Kingdom is the **Rainforest Cafe,** with entrances both inside and outside the theme park (you don't have to purchase theme-park admission, in other words, to eat at the restaurant). Unlike the Rainforest Cafe at the Downtown Disney Marketplace, the Animal Kingdom branch accepts Advance Reservations.

READERS' COMMENTS ABOUT
WALT DISNEY WORLD DINING

EATING IS A POPULAR TOPIC AMONG *Unofficial Guide* readers. In addition to participating in our annual restaurant survey, many readers share their thoughts. The following comments are representative.

A reader from Glendale, Illinois, had a positive experience with Disney food, writing:

> On the food: in general, we were pleasantly surprised. I expected it
> to be overpriced, generally bad, and certainly unhealthy. There were
> a lot of options—and almost all restaurants (including counter ser-
> vice) had generally good food and some healthy options. It is not the

place to expect fine cuisine—and is certainly overpriced—but if you understand the parameters, you can eat quite well. One thing I appreciated was having a children's menu that did not consist only of hot dogs and fries. My children ate well, and we were able to get them a good variety of food—with plenty of fruits and vegetables.

A family of five loved Whispering Canyon at the Wilderness Lodge:

Our best experience for dining was at the Whispering Canyon. My girls (ages 6, 10, and 11) thought the servers were great. They joked with each other, shouted, and laughed with the kids. They had wooden-pony races around the restaurant for the kids. Our waiter even sat down with our kids and helped my oldest "finish" her salad and showed my youngest how to eat whipped cream off her nose. Out of all the places we ate, this was my kids' (and Mom's and Dad's) favorite. Oh, and the food was pretty good too.

We've received consistent raves for Boma:

Boma (the African Buffet at the Animal Kingdom Lodge) is terrific!

A Lombard, Illinois, mom underscores the need to make Advance Reservations:

Please stress that if you want a "normal" dining hour at a specific restaurant, call them 90 or 60 days in advance—IT IS WORTH IT! One reservation I wanted to change about two weeks before our arrival date, and I had a choice of dinner times of either 7:45 or 9 p.m. (not feasible with little ones).

A Greenwood, Indiana, family had this to say:

The food was certainly expensive, but contrary to many of the views expressed in the Unofficial Guide, *we all thought the quality was excellent. Everything we had, from chicken strips and hot dogs in the parks to dinner at the Coral Reef, tasted great and seemed very fresh.*

A family from Youngsville, Louisiana, got a leg up on other guests:

The best thing we ate were the smoked turkey legs.

A mom from Aberdeen, South Dakota, writes:

When we want great food, we'll be on a different vacation. Who wants to waste fun time with the kids at a sit-down restaurant when you know the food will be mediocre anyway?

A woman from Verona, Wisconsin, offers this:

We think the character meals are underrated in all guidebooks. These meals are in pleasant settings and provide an easy, efficient way for little kids to interact with characters while providing adults with an opportunity to relax. For value and good food, we especially like the breakfasts. Yes, they're a little pricey, but you get more than food. Probably our favorite is at the Garden Grill at The Land at Epcot. This year, they even gave us souvenir hats.

A mother of three from Jamaica, New York, waited two hours and 40 minutes for a table at the Rainforest Cafe and still had a good time:

The Rainforest Cafe was an absolute delight. Our 6-year-old sat right next to a gorilla that ranted every few minutes; our 10-month-old loved the huge fish tanks; and they loved the food. Our wait for a table was two hours, so we went back to the hotel and returned two hours later. We still had to wait 40 minutes, but it was worth it. The gorilla room had more of a jungle feel than the elephant room.

But a Richardson, Texas, family weighed in with this:

A terrible dining experience. It was wild, wet, and loud, and the service was the worst in WDW.

A Lehi, Utah, woman also had a rough time:

Rainforest Cafe was awful!!! It was so loud we couldn't even hear our waitress or each other. The service was unorganized, and the food wasn't worth the price we paid.

We should note that most negative reader comments concerning the Rainforest Cafe pertain to the Downtown Disney location and not to the Animal Kingdom location.

On the topic of saving money, a Seattle woman offered the following:

For those wanting to save a few bucks (or in some cases several bucks) we definitely suggest eating outside WDW for as many meals as possible. To keep down our costs, we ate a large breakfast before leaving the hotel, had a fast-food lunch in the park, a snack later to hold us over, and then ate a good dinner outside the park. Several good restaurants in the area have excellent food at reasonable prices, notably Cafe Tu Tu Tango and Ming [Court], both on International Drive. We also obtained the "Entertainment Book" for Orlando, which offers 50% off meals all over town.

COUNTER-SERVICE RESTAURANT MINI-PROFILES

TO HELP YOU FIND PALATABLE FAST-SERVICE FOOD that suits your taste, we have developed mini-profiles of Walt Disney World theme-park counter-service restaurants. The restaurants are listed alphabetically by theme park.

The restaurants profiled below are rated for quality and portion size (self-explanatory), as well as for value. The value rating ranges from A to F as follows:

A	=	Exceptional value, a real bargain
B	=	Good value
C	=	Fair value, you get exactly what you pay for
D	=	Somewhat overpriced
F	=	Extremely overpriced

MAGIC KINGDOM

Aunt Polly's Dockside Inn
(Seasonal)

QUALITY Good	VALUE B	PORTION Medium	LOCATION Tom Sawyer Island

Selections Desserts, ice-cream cones, floats, sundaes, and apple pie.
Comments Open seasonally. Scenic and off the beaten path. Closes at dusk.

Casey's Corner

QUALITY Good	VALUE B	PORTION Medium	LOCATION Main Street, U.S.A.

Selections Quarter-pound hot dogs, fries, and brownies.
Comments A little pricey on the dogs and very crowded—keep walking.

Columbia Harbour House

QUALITY Fair	VALUE C+	PORTION Medium	LOCATION Liberty Square

Selections Fried fish and chicken strips; hummus, ham-and-cheese, veggie, and tuna-salad sandwiches; child's plate with macaroni and cheese or grilled chicken with grapes and child's beverage; New England clam chowder (in bread bowl) and vegetable chili; coleslaw; chips; fries; garden salad; and chocolate cake.
Comments Fried items aren't appetizing, but the soups and sandwiches are a nice change from the usual pizza and burger fare. Tables are usually available upstairs. It's the quickest service within spitting distance of Fantasyland.

Cosmic Ray's Starlight Cafe

QUALITY Good	VALUE B	PORTION Large	LOCATION Tomorrowland

Selections Something for everyone at this quick-service location: rotisserie chicken and ribs; turkey-bacon wrap and grilled-chicken sandwiches; hot dogs, hamburgers, including veggie burgers; Caesar salad with chicken, chicken-noodle soup, and vegetable soup; carrot cake and brownies for dessert. Kosher choices include a burger, chicken strips, and corned beef on rye.
Comments Big place. Tables inside usually available. Out-of-this-world entertainment on stage. This is the place if everybody in your party is picky—you'll have plenty of options. Nice burger-fixin' bar. Cosmic Ray's was the first Disney counter-service restaurant to offer kosher food.

El Pirata y el Perico *(Seasonal)*

QUALITY Fair	VALUE B	PORTION Medium to large	LOCATION Adventureland

Selections Nachos, taco salad, tacos, beef empanada with black beans and rice, churros, and ice-cream bars.

Comments Large, shaded eating area. Open seasonally and sometimes overlooked.

The Lunching Pad

QUALITY Good	VALUE B–	PORTION Medium	LOCATION Tomorrowland

Selections Smoked turkey legs, pretzels, and frozen sodas.

Comments Smack in the middle of Tomorrowland, The Lunching Pad is good for a quick snack or for waiting for people on nearby rides.

Mrs. Potts' Cupboard

QUALITY Good	VALUE B	PORTION Medium	LOCATION Fantasyland

Selections Sundaes, including fudge brownie and strawberry shortcake; floats, shakes; cookies; drinks.

Comments An ice-cream stop. Good options, decent value.

Pecos Bill's Tall Tale Inn & Cafe

QUALITY Good	VALUE B	PORTION Medium to large	LOCATION Frontierland

Selections Cheeseburgers; chicken wraps; chicken salad; chili; child's plate with hot dog or grilled chicken and child's beverage; fries and chili-cheese fries; peanut-butter mousse.

Comments Use the great fixin's station to garnish your burger. Combos come with fries or carrots.

The Pinocchio Village Haus

QUALITY Fair	VALUE C	PORTION Medium	LOCATION Fantasyland

Selections Personal pizzas; chicken strips; turkey-and-bacon panini; Italian subs; antipasto salad; kids' meals of mac and cheese or PB&J; fries plain or with toppings; salads; milk shakes.

Comments Almost always crowded, and with several cash registers open, the Village Haus is a place where it's possible to have your food but no place to sit and eat it. The panini isn't as good as it sounds, and pizza isn't something Disney does well anywhere. Antipasto is our favorite item on the menu here, but consider Columbia Harbour House and Pecos Bill's, both only a few minutes' walk away.

Scuttle's Landing

QUALITY Fair to good	VALUE B	PORTION Medium	LOCATION Fantasyland

Selections Frozen Cokes, soft pretzels, chips.

Comments Essentially a snack bar, but not a bad place to grab a drink.

Tomorrowland Terrace Café

QUALITY Fair	VALUE C	PORTION Large	LOCATION Tomorrowland

Selections The buffet features seafood and chicken stir-fries as well as barbecue strip loin.

Comments The food tastes better than it looks. Though most reader comments have been unfavorable, consider that the Terrace Cafe is still troubleshooting a brand-new menu. Look for improvements in the future.

EPCOT

Boulangerie Pâtisserie

QUALITY Good	VALUE B	PORTION Small to medium	LOCATION France

Selections Coffee, croissants, pastries, chocolate mousse, sandwiches, baguettes, cheese plate, ham-and-cheese croissant, quiche Lorraine, and cake of the day.

Comments OK for a light meal, better for a snack. A few outside tables. Tucked away in the corner, a little hard to find.

Cantina de San Angel

QUALITY Fair to good	VALUE C+	PORTION Medium	LOCATION Mexico

Selections Tacos; burritos; quesadillas; ensalada Mexicana; child's plate with burrito, chips, and child's beverage; nachos; churros; draft beer and frozen margaritas.

Comments Most meals are served with refried beans and salsa. Tables are outdoors.

Crêpes des Chefs de France

QUALITY Good	VALUE B+	PORTION Medium	LOCATION France

Selections Crêpes with chocolate, strawberry, marmalade, or sugar; vanilla and chocolate ice cream; specialty beer (Kronenbourg 1664); espresso.

Comments Kiosk treats made while you watch.

Electric Umbrella Restaurant

QUALITY Fair to good	VALUE B–	PORTION Medium	LOCATION Innoventions East

Selections Cheese-omelet meal, French-toast sticks, cereal, bagel breakfast sandwich, sausage, bacon; burgers and chicken strips with fries; roast beef–and–provolone cheese sandwich; whole-wheat turkey wrap; island chicken salad; vegetarian chili; child's plate with macaroni and cheese, chicken nuggets, or turkey-and-cheese pinwheels; fruit cups; cookies; cheesecake; Coors and Miller Lite.

Comments Many items are served with fries. Shaded outdoor seating; topping bar.

Kringla Bakeri og Kafé

QUALITY Good to excellent	VALUE B	PORTION Small to medium	LOCATION Norway

Selections Pastries; no-sugar-added chocolate mousse; *lefse* (traditional potato bread); cakes and cookies; rice cream; open-faced sandwiches (smoked ham, smoked turkey, smoked salmon); green salad; fruit cup; sweet pretzels with raisins and almonds; cinnamon rolls; waffles; wine and imported beers (Carlsberg beer for $7).

Comments Good but pricey. Shaded outdoor seating.

Liberty Inn

QUALITY Fair	VALUE C	PORTION Medium	LOCATION United States

Selections Bacon double cheeseburger; hot dogs; smoked-turkey-breast sandwich (with cheese and chipotle mayo on an everything bagel); chicken strips; Southwest chicken salad with creamy ancho dressing; vegetarian salad with low-fat vinaigrette; barbecue-pork sandwich; child's plate of grilled chicken over romaine lettuce, chicken nuggets with fries, or PB&J served with applesauce.

Comments A menu upgrade offers more than dogs and burgers. Kosher items also available. Still, too many interesting options in World Showcase to dine here unless you're just craving all-American food.

Lotus Blossom Cafe

QUALITY Fair	VALUE C	PORTION Medium	LOCATION China

Selections Beef and chicken rice bowls; vegetable lo mein; egg rolls; beef-fried rice; chicken salad; ginger ice cream, red-bean ice cream, smoothies, bubble tea (tea with tapioca balls), fruit, almond cookies, fortune cookies; child's plate with egg roll and beef fried rice; and Chinese beer and wine.

Comments Marginal Chinese food at fancy prices. Nothing terrible, nothing amazing.

Refreshment Outpost

QUALITY Good	VALUE B–	PORTION Small	LOCATION Between Germany and China

Selections Gourmet ice cream (waffle cones or dish); snacks; fresh fruit; frozen slushes (frozen soda); coffee, hot cocoa, or tea; bottled or draft Michelob beer (20-ounce for $5.75).

Comments Mainly prepackaged food for a quick drink or snack.

Refreshment Port

QUALITY Good	VALUE B	PORTION Medium
LOCATION Between World Showcase and Future World		

Selections Chicken nuggets, fries, McFlurry dessert.

Comments Though now a thinly disguised McDonald's, it's still a convenient place for a snack.

Rose & Crown Pub

QUALITY Good	VALUE C	PORTION Medium	LOCATION United Kingdom

Selections Seasonal salads; smoked salmon; lamb-and-barley soup; shortbread; fruit-and-cheese plate; spicy pork pastry; Guinness, Harp, and Bass beers and ales, as well as other spirits.

Comments The attraction here is the pub atmosphere and the draft beer. Note that the restaurant requires Advance Reservations while the pub does not. Order food at the bar to get anything to go or as a quick sit-down alternative. Outside the pub is Yorkshire County Fish Shop serving food to go. Also see the full-service restaurant profile for the Rose & Crown Dining Room later in this chapter.

Sommerfest

QUALITY Good	VALUE B–	PORTION Medium	LOCATION Germany

Selections Bratwurst and frankfurter sandwiches with kraut; soft pretzels; apple strudel and Black Forest cake; German wine and beer (Löwenbrau, Franziskaner Weissbier, and Spaten Optimator).

Comments Tucked in the entrance to the Biergarten restaurant, Sommerfest is hard to find from the street. There is very limited seating. It's not a place for kids who are picky eaters.

Sunshine Season Food Fair

QUALITY Excellent	VALUE A	PORTION Medium	LOCATION The Land Pavilion

Selections Includes the following four areas: (1) wood-fired grills and rotisseries, with selections like beef or chicken flatbread sandwiches and wood-grilled Atlantic salmon with mashed potatoes and kalamata olive pesto; (2) sandwich shop, with made-to-order sandwiches like grilled vegetable, Cuban and Black Forest ham, and salami grinders; (3) Asian shop, with noodle bowls and various stir-fry combos; (4) salad shop, with soups made daily and unusual creations like seared tuna on mixed greens with sesame–rice wine vinaigrette and roasted-beet-and-goat-cheese salad with cilantro-lime vinaigrette.

Comments This is the next generation of Disney quick service. No fried food or pizza, no burgers—everything is prepared as you watch.

Tangierine Cafe

QUALITY Good	VALUE B	PORTION Medium	LOCATION Morocco

Selections Chicken and lamb *shawarma;* hummus; tabbouleh; lentil salad; chicken with couscous; chicken and tabbouleh wraps; olives; child's meal of pizza, hamburger, or chicken tenders with fries and small beverage; Moroccan wine and beer; baklava.

Comments You won't get the belly dancers that entertain inside the pavilion at Restaurant Marrakesh, but the food here is good with an authentic flavor. The best seating is at the outdoor tables. Sufficient shade under umbrellas and trees.

Yakitori House

QUALITY Excellent	VALUE B	PORTION Small to medium	LOCATION Japan

Selections Shogun combo meal with beef and chicken teriyaki, vegetables, and rice (adult and child versions); beef curry; shrimp and vegetable tempura; side salad; sushi; miso soup; ginger green tea; chestnut cake with chocolate icing; Kirin beer, sake, and plum wine.

Comments A great place for a light meal. Nice cultural detailing. Limited seating.

Yorkshire County Fish Shop

QUALITY Good	VALUE B+	PORTION Medium	LOCATION United Kingdom

Selections Fish and chips, child's PB&J sandwich with applesauce and carrots, crisps (English potato chips), shortbread, Bass Ale draft.
Comments A convenient fast-food window attached to Rose & Crown Pub.

DISNEY-MGM STUDIOS

ABC Commissary

QUALITY Good	VALUE B+	PORTION Medium to large	LOCATION Backlot

Selections Tabbouleh wrap, Cuban sandwich, chicken curry, black-bean salad, cheeseburgers, fries, vegetable-noodle stir-fry, fish 'n' chips, child's chicken-nugget or fish-'n'-chips plate, ice-cream bars, pie, beer.
Comments Indoors, centrally located, air-conditioned, and usually not too crowded. Also offers a great traditional breakfast (seasonal). Hard to find. Kosher food available.

Backlot Express

QUALITY Fair	VALUE C	PORTION Medium to large	LOCATION Backlot

Selections Burgers and fries or fruit, sesame chicken salad, grilled turkey and cheese, chicken strips, hot dogs, grilled-vegetable sandwich, salad, desserts. For children, chicken nuggets or chicken strips with vegetables. Frozen soft drinks, beer.
Comments Often overlooked. Great burger-fixin' bar. Indoor and outdoor seating.

Catalina Eddie's

QUALITY Fair	VALUE B	PORTION Medium to large	LOCATION Sunset Boulevard

Selections Cheese, pepperoni, barbecue-chicken pizzas; salads; apple pie, chocolate cake.
Comments Seldom crowded.

Min and Bill's Dockside Diner

QUALITY Fair	VALUE C	PORTION Small to medium	LOCATION Echo Lake

Selections Shakes and beverages, beer; chips and cookies; variety of pretzels, including spicy cheese-stuffed and apple-cinnamon.
Comments Limited outdoor seating.

Rosie's All American Cafe

QUALITY Fair	VALUE C	PORTION Medium	LOCATION Sunset Boulevard

Selections Cheeseburgers, veggie burgers, chicken strips, soups, side salads, fries, chips, child's mac and cheese with grapes or chicken nuggets with fries and grapes, apple pie, chocolate cake.

Comments Sandwiches are premade. Backlot Express is a better option for the same fare.

Starring Rolls Cafe

QUALITY Good	VALUE B	PORTION Small to medium	LOCATION Sunset Boulevard

Selections Brown Derby Cobb salad, deli sandwiches, salads, pastries, desserts, chocolates, coffee. Gourmet.
Comments Open for breakfast on some mornings. Slowest service of any counter-service eatery.

Studios Catering Co. *(Seasonal)*

QUALITY Good	VALUE B	PORTION Small to medium	LOCATION Backlot

Selections Flatbread sandwiches including cumin-spiced lamb *kefta* with baba ghanoush and harissa sauce; tandoori chicken with tomato-and-cucumber raita; gyro-style steak sandwich with roasted-red-pepper hummus and tomato-and-onion relish.
Comments Ice cream has separate service lines. Good place for a break while your kids enjoy the *Honey, I Shrunk the Kids* playground. Shady outside seating.

Toluca Legs Turkey Co.

QUALITY Good	VALUE B	PORTION Medium to large	LOCATION Sunset Boulevard

Selections Smoked turkey legs, hot dogs; coffee, tea, hot chocolate, and bottled soda.
Comments For fans of the giant turkey legs.

Toy Story Pizza Planet

QUALITY Good	VALUE B+	PORTION Medium	LOCATION Backlot

Selections Cheese, pepperoni, or veggie pizzas; salads; cookies and crisped-rice treats.
Comments The place for pizza at the Studios. Fresh ingredients. Gets good marks from readers. Combo meals are not a good deal (same price as buying separately).

ANIMAL KINGDOM

Flame Tree Barbecue

QUALITY Good	VALUE B-	PORTION Large	LOCATION Discovery Island

Selections Half slab St. Louis–style ribs; smoked half chicken; smoked beef, pork, and chicken sandwiches; barbecue chicken salad; combination barbecue platters; crisp green salad with barbecued chicken; child's plate of baked chicken wings or mini–hot dogs; steak fries (with or without cheese), coleslaw, onion rings; chocolate cake; Safari Amber, Budweiser.
Comments Queues very long at lunchtime, but seating is ample and well shaded. One of our favorites for lunch. Try the covered gazebo overlooking the water. Be sure to pick up lots of napkins.

Pizzafari

| QUALITY Good | VALUE B | PORTION Medium | LOCATION Discovery Island |

Selections Cheese and pepperoni personal pizzas, chicken Parmesan sandwich, grilled chicken Caesar salad, bread sticks, Italian deli sandwich, child's PB&J or cheese quesadilla with marinara sauce, apple tart, frozen strawberry lemonade, Budweiser and Safari Amber beer.

Comments A favorite with children. Hectic at peak mealtimes. The pizza is pretty unimpressive—toppings resemble those on a cheap frozen pizza. Kosher menu available.

Restaurantosaurus

| QUALITY Good | VALUE B+ | PORTION Medium to large | LOCATION Dinoland U.S.A. |

Selections Hamburgers, cheeseburgers, hot dogs; McDonald's Chicken McNuggets and Happy Meals; Mandarin chicken salad; veggie burger; fries; brownies, strawberry shortcake, and cookies; espresso products, coffee, tea, cocoa; apple and orange juice; and beer.

Comments Picky children might enjoy Restaurantosaurus. Topping bar available. Character breakfast every day.

Royal Anandapur Tea Company

| QUALITY Good | VALUE B | PORTION Medium | LOCATION Asia |

Selections Wide variety of hot and iced teas; lattes; coffee, espresso, and cappuccino; fruit and cheese Danish; cookies.

Comments Located halfway between Expedition Everest and Kali River Rapids, this is the kind of small, eclectic food stand unique to the Animal Kingdom that you wish could be found at other parks. Offers about a dozen loose-leaf teas from Asia and Africa, many of which can be made either hot or iced. Pastries violate the "never eat anything larger than your head" rule, but everyone knows that doesn't apply when you're on vacation.

Tamu Tamu

| QUALITY Good | VALUE C | PORTION Large | LOCATION Africa |

Selections Various flavors of yogurt or ice cream, available in cones or as sundaes; ice-cream floats; smoothies. Sugar-free options.

Comments Seating is behind building and could easily be overlooked.

Tusker House Restaurant

| QUALITY VERY GOOD | VALUE B- | PORTION MEDIUM TO LARGE | LOCATION AFRICA |

Selections Half rotisserie chicken; grilled salmon; fried-chicken sandwich; turkey wraps; veggie focaccia; chicken salad; child's plate with macaroni and cheese or chicken drumstick with applesauce and mashed potatoes; cheesecake, chocolate, or carrot cake. Beer: Bud Light and Safari Amber.

Comments Good selections for health-conscious diners. Salads are refreshing. Separate line for bakery items. Also serves a nice sit-down breakfast.

DISNEY'S FULL-SERVICE RESTAURANTS: A QUICK ROMP AROUND THE WORLD

DISNEY RESTAURANTS OFFER AN EXCELLENT (though expensive) opportunity to introduce young children to the variety and excitement of ethnic food. No matter how formal a restaurant appears, the staff is accustomed to wiggling, impatient, and often boisterous children. **Les Chefs de France** at Epcot, for example, may be the nation's only French restaurant where most patrons wear shorts and T-shirts and at least two dozen young diners are attired in basic black . . . mouse ears.

Bottom line: young children are the rule, not the exception, at Disney restaurants.

Liliane

Almost all Disney restaurants offer children's menus, and all have booster seats and high chairs. They understand how tough it may be for children to sit for an extended period of time, and waiters will supply little ones with crackers and rolls and serve your dinner much faster than in comparable restaurants elsewhere. Letters from readers suggest that being served too quickly is much more common than having a long wait.

In **Epcot,** preschoolers most enjoy the **Biergarten** in Germany, **San Angel Inn** in Mexico, and **Coral Reef** in the Seas Pavilion in Future World. The Biergarten combines a rollicking and noisy atmosphere with good basic food, including roast chicken; a German oompah band entertains. Children often have the opportunity to participate in Bavarian dancing. San Angel Inn is in the Mexican village marketplace. From the table, children can watch boats on Gran Fiesta Tour drift beneath a smoking volcano. With a choice of chips, tacos, and other familiar items, picky children usually have no difficulty finding something to eat. Be aware that the service is sometimes glacially slow. The Coral Reef, with tables beside windows looking into The Seas' aquarium, offers a satisfying mealtime diversion for all ages. If your kids don't eat fish, Coral Reef also serves beef and chicken. The Biergarten offers reasonable value, plus good food. The Coral Reef and San Angel Inn are overpriced, though the food is palatable.

Cinderella's Royal Table in Cinderella Castle is the big draw in the **Magic Kingdom.** Interestingly, other Magic Kingdom full-service restaurants hold little appeal for children. For the best combination of food and entertainment, book a character meal at the **Liberty Tree Tavern** or **The Crystal Palace.**

At **Disney-MGM Studios,** all ages enjoy the atmosphere and entertainment at the **Sci-Fi Dine-In Theater Restaurant** and the **50's Prime Time Cafe.** Unfortunately, the Sci-Fi's food is close to dismal except for dessert, and the Prime Time's is uneven. Theme aside, children enjoy the character meals at Hollywood and Vine, and the pizza at **Mama Melrose's** never fails to please.

The only full-service restaurant at the **Animal Kingdom** is the **Rainforest Cafe,** which is a great favorite of children. Coming soon, however, is **Ying and Yak,** a new 300-seat table-service restaurant next to Expedition Everest.

As you've undoubtedly noticed by now, Disney World is a trend-savvy place, and every market share has its niche. So if you've become habituated to wood-fired pizza (the **California Grill** atop the Contemporary Resort, **Mama Melrose's** at MGM Studios, **Spoodles** on the Boardwalk, **Portobello Yacht Club** at Pleasure Island), sushi (California Grill, **Matsu No Ma Lounge** on the Japan showcase, **Kimono's** in the Swan, the **Wolfgang Puck Cafe** on the West Side, and for breakfast at the **Grand Floridian Cafe**), big steaks (**Shula's** in the Dolphin, **Le Cellier of Canada,** the **Yachtsman Steakhouse** at the Yacht Club, or the **Concourse Steakhouse** at the Contemporary), espresso (the **Starring Rolls Bakery** at MGM Studios, **Kusafiri Coffee Shop** in Harambe, **Forty-Thirst Street** on the West Side, and the **Fountain View** at Epcot), or all-you-can-eat (**'Ohana** at the Polynesian, **Chef Mickey's** in the Contemporary, the **Crystal Palace** at the Magic Kingdom, **Cape May Café** at the Beach Club, **1900 Park Fare** in the Grand Floridian), you can find a home here.

But Disney World is also about stars, about fantasies, and about meeting characters; the restaurant lineup is beginning to sound as much like a movie cast as the character meals at Cinderella's Royal Table.

The **Planet Hollywood** at Pleasure Island (teens love it) famously belongs to and has memorabilia from the likes of Demi Moore, Bruce Willis, and Sylvester Stallone (and, since this branch of the chain really looks like a planet, it becomes the "globe" entrance that matches Epcot's Spaceship Earth, which just goes to show you how big an attraction it is). The West Side has two other celebrity-connected restaurant-nightclubs: the **House of Blues,** a New Orleans–style nightspot partly owned by surviving Blues Brother Dan Aykroyd and James Belushi; and **Bongos,** a Cuban-flavored cafe created by Gloria Estefan and her husband, Emilio. The Wide World of Sports complex has a branch of the **Official All-Star Café** chain, whose owner roster includes Andre Agassi, Monica Seles, Wayne Gretzky, Ken Griffey Jr., and Shaquille O'Neal—who, it should be remembered in this promo-happy World, starred as the genial genie in Disney's *Kazaam!* Unfortunately, you'd think the jocks were running the kitchen: the food is among the most lackluster at Walt Disney World.

Not only film and sports stars, but Food Network and food-magazine stars have been enlisted in the Disney World parade. Paul Bocuse was one of the eponymous **Chefs de France** who designed the menu for that restaurant and the **Bistro de Paris** in Epcot (and now that the building actually has a kitchen rather than hauling in food from outside commissaries, it does them much more credit). Boston star chef Todd English created **bluezoo** for the Dolphin. California's Wolfgang Puck is so celebrity-kitchen conscious that the TV monitors at his cafe-plex in the West Side show not sports or movies but the cooks at work (a fad English has also adopted).

Celebrity status notwithstanding, neither Wolfgang Puck's Café nor the Estefans' Bongos have drawn much praise from diners, though bluezoo is very good (but also quite adult). The House of Blues, surprisingly enough, has done much better with its New Orleans–style jambalayas and gospel brunch.

There are not one but two super-trendy Rainforest Cafe branches, one at the renovated Disney Village Marketplace and a super-theatrical version at the entrance to Animal Kingdom, where the décor and audio-animatronic elephants make it fit right into the scenery there. Not surprisingly in a place where the sky "rains" and the stars flicker overhead, more thought went into naming the dishes than perfecting the recipes.

In fact, although Disney's "official" guides to Walt Disney World describe various restaurants as "delicious," "delectable," or "delightful"—George Gershwin, call your agent—the truth is that only perhaps a dozen of the nearly 100 full-service establishments are first-rate. And some of the most disappointing restaurants in general are the often attractive but commissary-bland ethnic kitchens.

Though a blessing in disguise to many children and picky eaters of all ages, most of the "ethnic" food at Walt Disney World is Americanized, or rather homogenized, especially at Epcot, where visitors from so many countries, as well as the United States, tend to have preconceived notions of egg rolls and enchiladas. **The Teppanyaki Dining Room** in the Japan Pavilion happens to be one of the better restaurants in the World, with pretty good teppanyaki (and good tempura next door)—but it specializes in a particularly Westernized form of Japanese cuisine, first produced in New York only about 30 years ago. **The Nine Dragons** restaurant in the China Pavilion has been seriously reconceived and now features not only quite satisfying dim sum but handmade noodles (taffy-pulled out in the dining room), a respectable Peking duck, and really crisp vegetables. Both the restaurant in the Italian Pavilion, **L'Originale Alfredo di Roma,** and that in the Mexican Pavilion, the **San Angel Inn,** are associated with famous family establishments—the DeLilio family of Florence (reputed inventors of fettuccine Alfredo) and the Deblers of Mexico City, respectively. And the **Chefs de France/Bistro Paris,** with executive chefs Paul Bocuse, Gaston LeNotre, and Roger Verge, is now a fairly serious destination—one with an Old-Worldly view.

The buffet at Norway's Akershus isn't bad, but it's stodgy, smoky, and cheese- and mayonnaise-heavy. (Frankly, if smoked meats are your thing, the smoked turkey legs from the carts, which are enough for at least two people and only $4, are far better.)

Among the places the culinary staff actually recommends (off the record) are the classic-continental prix-fixe **Victoria and Albert's** at the Grand Floridian, where you pay $100 a head to have every waitress introduce herself as Vicky and all the waiters as Al; the **Flying Fish Cafe;**

Artist Point; Jiko; Cítricos; and the **California Grill,** which has one of only seven ultra-chic Tom Shandley soufflé ovens in the United States. All of the above are best reserved for a parents' night out.

Another thing: a lot of the food at Disney World, particularly the fast food, is not what you'd describe as healthy. (Funnel cakes? Happy Meals?) But this is an area that the parks have started to address. **The Artist Palette** at Saratoga Springs Resort, and **Sunshine Seasons** in The Land Pavilion at Epcot have been reconceived as "fast casual" spots, where the food is prepared fresh, often when you order it, but can be carried out or taken to nearby tables. At Sunshine Seasons, there are four different fully staffed kitchens, one preparing entree salads with seared tuna, roasted beets with goat cheese, and soups du jour; another stir-frying veggies and preparing Asian noodle soup; a third wood-grilling chicken and beef to be wrapped in grilled flat-bread or salmon with pesto; and a fourth preparing deluxe focaccia sandwiches. Artist Palette offers everything from French toast to individual wood-grilled pizzas to gourmet-prepared entrees for carryout. (See the nice **Turf Club** bar next door.)

Beyond that, there are fruit stands and juice bars scattered around, veggie sandwiches and chili, wraps, rotisscrie chicken, soft pretzels as well as the deceptively simple popcorn, baked potatoes (not, frankly, prepared with the apparent care of the turkey legs, but about one-tenth the calories and salt), as well as the frozen fruit bars in the ice-cream freezers, and frozen yogurt or smoothies at the ice-cream shops. Yes, it's hard, especially with all those fudge and cookie stands blasting chocolate at you, but stick to your guns. Look for the fruit markets in Liberty Square and Mickey's Toontown Fair in the Magic Kingdom, on Sunset Boulevard in the MGM Studios, and in the Harambe marketplace at Animal Kingdom.

 And yes, OK, because you've been good, I'll tell you the one junk food to blow your calorie budget on: as you cross the bridge between Future World and the World Showcase in Epcot, there's a little wagon just to the right, toward Canada, that sells cones of glazed pecans called "sticky beavers." Don't say we never spoiled you.

MAGIC YOUR WAY DINING PLAN

DISNEY HAS A DINING PLAN to accompany its Magic Your Way ticket system. Called the Magic Your Way Package Plus Dining, it's available to all Disney resort guests except those staying at the Swan, Dolphin, and Shades of Green, none of which are Disney owned or operated. Guests must purchase a Magic Your Way Package including admission tickets and lodging to qualify for the dining plan add-on. The dining plan's cost is determined by the number of nights you stay at a Disney resort. For guests ages 10 and up, the price is $38 per night, and for guests ages 3 to 9, the price is $11 per night, tax included. Children younger than age 3 eat free.

How It Works

For each member of your group, for each night of your stay, the dining plan provides one counter-service meal, one full-service meal, and one snack at participating Disney dining locations and restaurants (view the entire list at **www.wdwvacations.com/magicyourwaydining locations.htm**).

The counter-service meal includes a main course (sandwich, dinner salad, pizza, and the like), dessert, and nonalcoholic drink, or a complete combo meal (a main course and a side dish—think burger and fries), dessert, and nonalcoholic drink, including tax. The full-service sit-down meals include an appetizer, a main course, dessert, a nonalcoholic drink, tax, and tip. If you're dining at a buffet, the full-service meal includes the buffet and a nonalcoholic drink, tax, and tip. The snack includes items normally sold from carts or small stands throughout the parks and resorts: ice-cream bars, popcorn, soft drinks, or a piece of fruit, a single-serving bag of chips, or apple juice.

For instance, if you're staying for three nights, each member of your party will be credited with three counter-service meals, three full-service meals, and three snacks. All those meals will be put into an individual "meal account" for each person in your group. Meals in your account can be used on any combination of days, so you're not required to eat every meal every day. Thus, you can skip a full-service meal one day and have two on another day.

Disney's top-of-the-line restaurants, dubbed "Disney Signature" restaurants in the plan, and all the dinner shows count as two full-service meals. If you choose to eat at one of these locations, two full-service meals will be deducted from your meal account for each person dining.

In addition to the above, the new dining plan comes with several other important rules:

- Everyone staying in the same resort room has to participate in the plan.
- Children ages 3 to 9 must order from the kids' menu, if one is available.
- Room service, pizza delivery, in-room minibars, and refillable mugs are not included in the plan.
- A full-service meal can be breakfast, lunch, or dinner. You realize the greatest savings when you use your full-service meal allocations for dinner.
- The meal plan expires at midnight on the day you check out of the Disney resort. Unused meals are nonrefundable. Extra meals cannot be purchased unless you extend your stay at the Disney resort.

Things to Consider When Evaluating the Dining Plan

If you prefer to always dine at counter-service restaurants, you're better off without the plan. Adults who are light eaters or split portions when dining out and those whose largest meal comes at breakfast should skip the plan as well. Poor candidates for the plan also include finicky eaters and families who can't agree on restaurants.

The dining plan costs $38 a day for adults and $11 a day for children ages 3 to 9. Combining two of your table-service options, you can eat one meal higher on the hog at Disney's more upscale eateries. Maximizing the value of the dining plan requires research and planning, but the money you can save is worth the time and effort. The average counter-service meal runs $8 to $10 for an adult, and the price of the more expensive menu items at many Disney restaurants can total more than the $38 daily cost of the dining plan.

The flexibility of the plan, however, coupled with the number of good-quality participating restaurants, means that you can get some fairly substantial savings. The greatest savings are realized by ordering the higher-priced items on the menu at dinner at full-service restaurants. Those who typically order the least-expensive menu items fare the worst. Those ordering from the middle end of the menu save around 13%, and the gourmands make out like bandits.

How to Get the Most Out of the Plan

1. A car allows you to easily access all the participating restaurants. Using the Disney transportation system, dining at the various Disney resort restaurants can be a logistical nightmare.

2. Make Advance Reservations for the full-service restaurants as soon as possible.

CHARACTER DINING

ALL THE RAGE AT WALT DISNEY WORLD for more than a decade, character dining combines a meal with meeting the characters. The characters circulate throughout the meal, stopping at each table to sign autographs, pose for photos, and lavish attention on mostly adoring (but sometimes stupefied) children. For a detailed description of this Disney ritual, see pages 227–239.

WALT DISNEY WORLD RESTAURANTS: RATED AND RANKED

STAR RATING The star rating represents the entire dining experience: style, service, and ambience, in addition to taste, presentation, and quality of food. Five stars is the highest rating and indicates that the restaurant offers the best of everything. Four-star restaurants are above average, and three-star restaurants offer good, though not necessarily memorable, meals. Two-star restaurants serve mediocre fare, and one-star restaurants are below average. Our star ratings don't correspond to ratings awarded by AAA, Mobil, Zagat, or other restaurant reviewers.

★★★★★	Exceptional value, a real bargain
★★★★	Good value
★★★	Fair value, you get exactly what you pay for
★★	Somewhat overpriced
★	Significantly overpriced

COST RANGE The next rating tells how much a complete meal will cost. We include a main dish with vegetable or side dish, and a choice of soup or salad. Appetizers, desserts, drinks, and tips aren't included. We've rated the cost as inexpensive, moderate, or expensive.

Inexpensive	$12 or less per person
Moderate	$13 to $23 per person
Expensive	More than $23 per person

QUALITY RATING The food quality is rated on a scale of one to five stars, five being the best rating attainable. The quality rating is based on the taste, freshness of ingredients, preparation, presentation, and creativity of food served. There is no consideration of price. If you are a person who wants the best food available and cost is not an issue, you need look no further than the quality ratings.

VALUE RATING If, on the other hand, you are looking for both quality and value, then you should check the value rating, expressed as stars.

Walt Disney World Restaurants by Cuisine

CUISINE	LOCATION	OVERALL RATING	COST	QUALITY RATING	VALUE RATING
AFRICAN					
Jiko—The Cooking Place	Animal Kingdom Lodge	★★★★½	Exp	★★★★ ½	★★★½
Boma	Animal Kingdom Lodge	★★★★	Mod	★★★★	★★★★½
AMERICAN					
California Grill	Contemporary	★★★★½	Exp	★★★★½	★★★½
The Hollywood Brown Derby	Disney-MGM	★★★★	Exp	★★★★	★★★
Artist Point	Wilderness Lodge	★★★½	Mod	★★★★	★★★
Whispering Canyon Cafe	Wilderness Lodge	★★★	Mod	★★★½	★★★★
Yacht Club Galley	Yacht Club	★★★	Mod	★★★½	★★★
50's Prime Time Cafe	Disney-MGM	★★★	Mod	★★★	★★★
The Garden Grill Restaurant	Epcot	★★★	Mod	★★★	★★★
Planet Hollywood	Pleasure Island	★★★	Mod	★★★	★★★
Cinderella's Royal Table	Magic Kingdom	★★★	Exp	★★★	★★
All-Star Cafe	Wide World of Sports	★★½	Mod	★★★	★★★
ESPN Club	BoardWalk	★★½	Mod	★★★	★★★
Hollywood & Vine	Disney-MGM	★★½	Inexp	★★★	★★★
Liberty Tree Tavern	Magic Kingdom	★★½	Mod	★★★	★★★
Boatwright's Dining Hall	Port Orleans	★★½	Mod	★★★	★★
Grand Floridian Cafe	Grand Floridian	★★½	Mod	★★★	★★
Beaches & Cream	Beach Club	★★½	Inexp	★★	★★
Rainforest Cafe	Downtown Disney and Animal Kingdom	★★½	Mod	★★	★★
House of Blues	West Side	★★	Mod	★★★½	★★★
Gulliver's Grill	Swan	★★	Exp	★★★	★★
Olivia's Cafe	Old Key West	★★	Mod	★★½	★★★
Wolfgang Puck Cafe	West Side	★★	Exp	★★½	★★½
Sci-Fi Dine-In Theater Restaurant	Disney-MGM	★★	Mod	★★½	★★
Baskervilles	Grosvenor Resort	★★	Mod	★★	★★★
Big River Grille & Brewing Works	BoardWalk	★★	Mod	★★	★★

WDW Restaurants by Cuisine (continued)

CUISINE	LOCATION	OVERALL RATING	COST	QUALITY RATING	VALUE RATING
AMERICAN (CONTINUED)					
The Fountain	Dolphin	★★	Inexp	★★	★★
The Plaza Restaurant	Magic Kingdom	★★	Mod	★★	★
BUFFET					
Boma	Animal Kingdom Lodge	★★★★	Mod	★★★★	★★★★½
Cape May Cafe	Beach Club	★★★½	Mod	★★★½	★★★★
Akershus Royal Banquet Hall	Epcot	★★★½	Mod	★★★	★★★★
Biergarten	Epcot	★★★½	Mod	★★★	★★★★
The Crystal Palace	Magic Kingdom	★★★	Mod	★★★½	★★★
Chef Mickey's	Contemporary	★★½	Mod	★★★	★★★
Hollywood & Vine	Disney-MGM	★★½	Mod	★★★	★★★
1900 Park Fare	Grand Floridian	★★½	Mod	★★★	★★★
CHINESE					
Nine Dragons Restaurant	Epcot	★★½	Exp	★★★	★★
CUBAN					
Bongos Cuban Cafe	West Side	★★	Mod	★★	★★
ENGLISH					
Rose & Crown Dining Room	Epcot	★★★	Mod	★★★½	★★
FRENCH					
Bistro de Paris	Epcot	★★★	Exp	★★★½	★★
Les Chefs de France	Epcot	★★★	Mod	★★★	★★★
GERMAN					
Biergarten	Epcot	★★★½	Mod	★★★	★★★★
GOURMET					
Victoria & Albert's	Grand Floridian	★★★★★	Exp	★★★★★	★★★★
IRISH					
Raglan Road	Pleasure Island	★★★★	Mod	★★★½	★★★
ITALIAN					
Andiamo Italian Bistro & Grille	Hilton	★★★	Mod	★★★	★★★
Portobello Yacht Club	Pleasure Island	★★★	Exp	★★★	★★

CUISINE	LOCATION	OVERALL RATING	COST	QUALITY RATING	VALUE RATING
ITALIAN (CONTINUED)					
L'Originale Alfredo di Roma Ristorante	Epcot	★★½	Exp	★★★	★★½
Mama Melrose's Ristorante Italiano	Disney-MGM	★★½	Mod	★★★	★★
Tony's Town Square Restaurant	Magic Kingdom	★★½	Mod	★★★	★★
JAPANESE					
Kimonos	Swan	★★★★	Mod	★★★★½	★★★
Mitsukoshi Teppanyaki Dining Room*	Epcot	★★★½	Exp	★★★★	★★★
Tempura Kiku	Epcot	★★★	Mod	★★★★	★★★
Benihana— Steakhouse & Sushi	Hilton	★★★	Mod	★★★½	★★★
MEDITERRANEAN					
Cítricos	Grand Floridian	★★★½	Exp	★★★★½	★★★
Spoodles	BoardWalk	★★★	Mod	★★★★	★★★
Fresh Mediterranean Market	Dolphin	★★½	Mod	★★½	★★
MEXICAN					
San Angel Inn	Epcot	★★★	Exp	★★★	★★
Maya Grill	Coronado Springs	★	Exp	★	★
MOROCCAN					
Restaurant Marrakesh	Epcot	★★★	Mod	★★★½	★★★
NORWEGIAN					
Akershus Royal Banquet Hall	Epcot	★★★½	Mod	★★★	★★★★
POLYNESIAN/PAN-ASIAN					
'Ohana	Polynesian	★★★	Mod	★★★½	★★★
Kona Cafe	Polynesian	★★★	Mod	★★★	★★★★
SEAFOOD					
Flying Fish Cafe	BoardWalk	★★★★	Exp	★★★★	★★★
Artist Point	Wilderness Lodge	★★★½	Mod	★★★★	★★★
Narcoossee's	Grand Floridian	★★★½	Exp	★★★½	★★

Scheduled to reopen June 1, 2007 after renovation

WDW Restaurants by Cuisine (continued)

CUISINE	LOCATION	OVERALL RATING	COST	QUALITY RATING	VALUE RATING
SEAFOOD (CONTINUED)					
bluezoo	**Dolphin**	★★★	Exp	★★★	★★
Fulton's Crab House	**Pleasure Island**	★★½	Exp	★★★½	★★
Coral Reef	**Epcot**	★★½	Exp	★★½	★★
Cap'n Jack's	**Downtown Disney**	★★½	Mod	★★	★★
Shutters at Old Port Royale	**Caribbean Beach**	★★	Mod	★★½	★★
STEAK					
Shula's Steak House	**Dolphin**	★★★★	Exp	★★★★	★★
Le Cellier Steakhouse	**Epcot**	★★★½	Mod	★★★½	★★★
Yachtsman Steakhouse	**Yacht Club**	★★★	Exp	★★★½	★★
The Outback	**Wyndham Palace**	★★	Exp	★★★	★★
Shutters at Old Port Royale	**Caribbean Beach**	★★	Mod	★★½	★★
Concourse Steakhouse	**Contemporary**	★★	Mod	★★	★★

PART FIVE

DISNEY BOOT CAMP:
Basic Training for World-bound Families

THE BRUTAL TRUTH *about* FAMILY VACATIONS

IT HAS BEEN SUGGESTED THAT THE PHRASE *family vacation* is a bit of an oxymoron. This is because you can never take a vacation from the responsibilities of parenting if your children are traveling with you. Though you leave work and normal routine far behind, your children require as much attention, if not more, when traveling as they do at home.

Parenting on the road is an art. It requires imagination and organization. Think about it: you have to do all the usual stuff (feed, dress, bathe, supervise, teach, comfort, discipline, put to bed, and so on) in an atmosphere where your children are hyperstimulated, without the familiarity of place and the resources you take for granted at home. Although it's not impossible—and can even be fun—parenting on the road is not something you want to learn on the fly, particularly at Walt Disney World.

The point we want to drive home is that preparation, or the lack thereof, can make or break your Walt Disney World vacation. Believe us, you do *not* want to leave the success of your expensive Disney vacation to chance. But don't confuse chance with good luck. Chance is what happens when you fail to prepare. Good luck is when preparation meets opportunity.

Your preparation can be organized into several categories, all of which we will help you undertake. Broadly speaking, you need to prepare yourself and your children mentally, emotionally, physically, organizationally, and logistically. You also need a basic understanding of Walt Disney World and a well-considered plan for how to go about seeing it.

MENTAL *and* EMOTIONAL PREPARATION

THIS IS A SUBJECT THAT WE WILL TOUCH on here and return to many times in this book. Mental preparation begins with realistic expectations about your Disney vacation and consideration of what each adult and child in your party most wants and needs from their Walt Disney World experience. Getting in touch with this aspect of planning requires a lot of introspection and good, open family communication.

DIVISION OF LABOR

TALK ABOUT WHAT YOU AND YOUR PARTNER NEED and what you expect to happen on the vacation. This discussion alone can preempt some unpleasant surprises midtrip. If you are a two-parent (or two-adult) family, do you have a clear understanding of how the parenting workload is to be distributed? We have seen some distinctly disruptive misunderstandings in two-parent households where one parent is (pardon the legalese) the primary caregiver. Often, the other parent expects the primary caregiver to function on vacation as she (or he) does at home. The primary caregiver, on the other hand, is ready for a break. She expects her partner to either shoulder the load equally or perhaps even assume the lion's share so she can have a *real* vacation. However you divide the responsibility, of course, is up to you. Just make sure you negotiate a clear understanding *before* you leave home.

TOGETHERNESS

ANOTHER DIMENSION TO CONSIDER is how much "togetherness" seems appropriate to you. For some parents, a vacation represents a rare opportunity to really connect with their children, to talk, exchange ideas, and get reacquainted. For others, a vacation affords the time to get a little distance, to enjoy a round of golf while the kids are participating in a program organized by the resort.

At Walt Disney World you can orchestrate your vacation to spend as much or as little time with your children as you desire, but more about that later. The point here is to think about your and your children's preferences and needs concerning your time together. A typical day at a Disney theme park provides the structure of experiencing attractions together, punctuated by periods of waiting in line, eating, and so on, which facilitate conversation and sharing. Most attractions can be enjoyed together by the whole family, regardless of age ranges. This allows for more consensus and less dissent when it comes to deciding what to see and do. For many parents and children, however, the rhythms of a Walt Disney World day seem to consist of passive entertainment experiences alternated with endless discussions of where to go and what to do next. As a mother from Winston-Salem, North Carolina, reported, "Our family mostly talked about what to do next with very little sharing or discussion about what we had seen. [The conversation] was pretty task-oriented."

Two observations: First, fighting the crowds and keeping the family moving along can easily escalate into a pressure-driven outing. Having an advance plan or itinerary eliminates moment-to-moment guesswork and decision making, thus creating more time for savoring and connecting. Second, external variables such as crowd size, noise, and heat, among others, can be so distracting as to preclude any meaningful togetherness. These negative impacts can be moderated, as previously discussed (pages 46–48), by your being selective concerning the time of year, day of the week, and time of day you visit the theme parks. The bottom line is that you can achieve the degree of connection and togetherness you desire with a little advance planning and a realistic awareness of the distractions you will encounter.

LIGHTEN UP

PREPARE YOURSELF MENTALLY to be a little less compulsive on vacation about correcting small behavioral deviations and pounding home the lessons of life. Certainly, little Mildred will have to learn eventually that it's very un-Disney-like to take off her top at the pool. But there's plenty of time for that later. So what if Matt eats hamburgers for breakfast, lunch, and dinner every day? You can make him eat peas and broccoli when you get home and are in charge of meal preparation again. Roll with the little stuff, and remember when your children act out that they are wired to the max. At least some of that adrenaline is bound to spill out in undesirable ways. Coming down hard will send an already frayed little nervous system into orbit.

Try to schedule some time alone with each of your children, if not each day, then at least a couple of times during the trip.

Liliane

SOMETHING FOR EVERYONE

IF YOU TRAVEL WITH AN INFANT, TODDLER, or any child who requires a lot of special attention, make sure that you have some energy and time remaining for your other children. In the course of your planning, invite each child to name something special to do or see at Walt Disney World with mom or dad alone. Work these special activities into your trip itinerary. Whatever else, if you commit, write it down so that you don't forget. Remember, a casually expressed willingness to do this or that may be perceived as a promise by your children.

WHOSE IDEA WAS THIS, ANYWAY?

THE DISCORD THAT MANY VACATIONING FAMILIES experience arises from the kids being on a completely different wavelength from mom and dad. Parents and grandparents are often worse than children when it comes to conjuring up fantasy scenarios of what a Walt Disney World vacation will be like. A Disney vacation can be many things, but believe us when we tell you that there's a lot more to it than just riding Dumbo and seeing Mickey.

In our experience, most parents and nearly all grandparents expect children to enter a state of rapture at Walt Disney World, bouncing from attraction to attraction in wide-eyed wonder, appreciative beyond words to their adult benefactors. What they get, more often than not, is not even in the same ballpark. Preschoolers will, without a doubt, be wide-eyed, often with delight but also with a general sense of being overwhelmed by noise, crowds, and Disney characters as big as tool sheds. We have substantiated through thousands of interviews and surveys that the best part of a Disney vacation for a preschooler is the hotel swimming pool. With some grade-schoolers and pre-driving-age teens you get near-manic hyperactivity coupled with periods of studied nonchalance. This last, which relates to the importance of being "cool at all costs," translates into a maddening display of boredom and a "been there, done that" attitude. Older teens are frequently the exponential version of the younger teens and grade-schoolers, except without the manic behavior.

As a function of probability, you may escape many—but most likely not all—of the above behaviors. Even in the event that they are all visited on you, however, take heart, there are antidotes.

For preschoolers you can keep things light and happy by limiting the time you spend in the theme parks. The most critical point is that the overstimulation of the parks must be balanced by adequate rest and more mellow activities. For grade-schoolers and early teens, you can moderate the hyperactivity and false apathy by enlisting their help in planning the vacation, especially by allowing them to take a leading role in determining the itinerary for days at the theme parks. Being in charge of specific responsibilities that focus on the happiness of other family members also works well. One reader, for example, turned a 12-year-old liability into an asset by asking him to help guard against attractions that might frighten his 5-year-old sister.

Short forays to the parks interspersed with naps, swimming, and quiet activities such as reading to your children will go a long way toward keeping things on an even keel.

Liliane

Knowledge enhances anticipation and at the same time affords a level of comfort and control that helps kids understand the big picture. The more they feel in control, the less they will act out of control.

The more information your children have before arriving at Walt Disney World, the less likely they will be to act out.

Liliane

DISNEY, KIDS, AND SCARY STUFF

DISNEY ATTRACTIONS, BOTH RIDES AND SHOWS, are adventures. They focus on themes common to adventures: good and evil, life and death, beauty and the grotesque, fellowship and enmity. As you sample the attractions at Walt Disney World, you transcend the spinning and bouncing of midway rides to thought-provoking and emotionally powerful entertainment. All of the endings are happy, but the adventures' impact, given Disney's gift for special effects, often intimidates and occasionally frightens young children.

My first roller coaster experience was with my mom. We rode Goofy's Barnstormer [a coaster for the under-7 crowd]—and she screamed my ears off. Next she took a ride with you know who: Bob. He somehow managed to get her on The Hulk at Universal's Islands of Adventure. I can't begin to imagine what she must have said to him [*Editor's Note:* Bob is still deaf in one ear].

Idan

There are rides with menacing witches, burning towns, and ghouls popping out of their graves, all done with a sense of humor, provided you're old enough to understand the joke. And bones. There are bones everywhere: human bones, cattle bones, dinosaur bones, even whole skeletons. There's a stack of skulls at the headhunter's camp on the Jungle Cruise, a platoon of skeletons sailing ghost ships in Pirates of the Caribbean, and a haunting assemblage of skulls and skeletons in The Haunted Mansion. Skulls, skeletons, and bones punctuate Snow White's Scary Adventures, Peter Pan's Flight, and Big Thunder Mountain Railroad. In the Animal Kingdom, there's an entire children's playground made up exclusively of giant bones and skeletons.

Monsters and special effects at Disney-MGM Studios are more real and sinister than those in the other theme parks. If your child has difficulty coping with the witch in Snow White's Scary Adventures, think twice about exposing him or her to machine-gun battles, earthquakes, and the creature from *Alien* at the Studios.

One reader tells of taking his preschool children on Star Tours:

We took a 4-year-old and a 5-year-old, and they had the *^%#! scared out of them at Star Tours. We did this first thing in the morning, and it took hours of Tom Sawyer Island and Small World to get back to normal.

Our kids were the youngest by far in Star Tours. I assume that other adults had more sense or were not such avid readers of your book. Preschoolers should start with Dumbo and work up to the Jungle Cruise in late morning, after being revved up and before getting hungry, thirsty, or tired. Pirates of the Caribbean is out for preschoolers. You get the idea.

At Walt Disney World, anticipate the almost inevitable emotional overload of your young children. Be sensitive, alert, and prepared for practically anything, even behavior that is out of character for your child at home. Most young children take Disney's macabre trappings in stride, and others are easily comforted by an arm around the shoulder or a squeeze of the hand. Parents who know that their children tend to become upset should take it slow and easy, sampling more benign adventures, gauging reactions, and discussing with the children how they felt about what they saw.

Before lining up for any attraction, be it a ride or a theater presentation, check out our description of it and see our Fright Factor list on the following page.

Bob

Some Tips

1. START SLOW AND WARM UP Although each major theme park offers several fairly unintimidating attractions that you can sample to determine your child's relative sensitivity, the Magic Kingdom is probably the best testing ground. At the Magic Kingdom, try Buzz Lightyear's Space Ranger Spin in Tomorrowland, Peter Pan in Fantasyland, and the Jungle Cruise in Adventureland to measure your child's reaction to unfamiliar sights and sounds. If your child takes these in stride, try Pirates of the Caribbean. Try the Astro Orbiter in Tomorrowland, the Mad Tea Party in Fantasyland, or Goofy's Barnstormer in Mickey's Toontown Fair to observe how your child tolerates certain ride speeds and motions.

Do not assume that because an attraction is a theater presentation it will not frighten your child. Trust us on this one. An attraction does not have to be moving to trigger unmitigated, panic-induced hysteria. Rides like the Big Thunder Mountain Railroad and Splash Mountain may look scary, but they do not have even one-fiftieth the potential for terrorizing children as do theater attractions like *Stitch's Great Escape*.

You know I scream a lot on roller coasters, but did you know that I don't leave my feet on the floor during the *It's Tough to Be a Bug!* 3-D show at the Animal Kingdom? Well, now you know I do not like bugs, and they sting too; they do, they do.

Liliane

2. BE ATTUNED TO PEER AND PARENT PRESSURE Sometimes young children will rise above their anxiety in an effort to please parents or siblings. This doesn't necessarily indicate a mastery of fear, much less enjoyment. If children leave a ride in apparently good shape, ask if they would like to go on it again (not necessarily now, but sometime). The response usually will indicate how much they actually enjoyed the experience. There's a big difference between having a good time and just mustering the courage to get through.

3. ENCOURAGE AND EMPATHIZE Evaluating a child's capacity to handle the visual and tactile effects of Walt Disney World requires patience, understanding, and experimentation. Each of us, after all, has our own demons. If a child balks at or is frightened by a ride, respond constructively. Let your children know that lots of people, adults and children, are scared by what they see and feel. Help them understand that it's OK if they get frightened and that their fear doesn't lessen your love or respect. Take pains not to compound the discomfort by making a child feel inadequate; try not to undermine self-esteem, impugn courage, or ridicule. Most of all, don't induce guilt by suggesting the child's trepidation might be ruining the family's fun. It is also sometimes necessary to restrain older siblings' taunting or teasing.

A visit to Walt Disney World is more than just an outing or an adventure for a young child. It's a testing experience, a sort of controlled rite of passage. If you help your little one work through the challenges, the time can be immeasurably rewarding and a bonding experience for you both.

The Fright Factor

Of course, each youngster is different, but there are eight attraction elements that alone or combined can push a child's buttons:

1. NAME OF THE ATTRACTION Young children will naturally be apprehensive about something called "The Haunted Mansion" or "The Tower of Terror."

2. VISUAL IMPACT OF THE ATTRACTION FROM OUTSIDE Big Thunder Mountain Railroad and Splash Mountain look scary enough to give even adults second thoughts, and they visually terrify many young children.

3. VISUAL IMPACT OF THE INDOOR QUEUING AREA Pirates of the Caribbean's caves and dungeons and The Haunted Mansion's "stretch rooms" can frighten kids even before they board the ride.

4. INTENSITY OF THE ATTRACTION Some attractions are overwhelming, inundating the senses with sights, sounds, movement, and even smell. Epcot's *Honey, I Shrunk the Audience* and *It's Tough to Be a Bug!* in the Animal Kingdom (no pun intended), for example, combine loud sounds, lasers, lights, and 3-D cinematography to create a total sensory experience. For some preschoolers, this is two or three senses too many.

5. VISUAL IMPACT OF THE ATTRACTION ITSELF Sights in various attractions range from falling boulders to lurking buzzards, from grazing dinosaurs to attacking white blood cells. What one child calmly absorbs may scare the bejeebers out of another.

6. DARK Many Disney World attractions operate indoors in the dark. For some children, darkness alone triggers fear. A child who is frightened on one dark ride (Snow White's Scary Adventures, for example) may be unwilling to try other indoor rides.

7. THE RIDE ITSELF; THE TACTILE EXPERIENCE Some rides are wild enough to cause motion sickness, to wrench backs, and to discombobulate patrons of any age.

Small-child Fright-potential Chart

This is a quick reference to identify attractions to be wary of, and why. The chart represents a generalization, and all kids are different. It relates specifically to kids ages 3 to 7. On average, children at the younger end of the range are more likely to be frightened than children in their sixth or seventh year.

Magic Kingdom

MAIN STREET, U.S.A.

Main Street Vehicles Not frightening in any respect.

Walt Disney World Railroad Not frightening in any respect.

ADVENTURELAND

Enchanted Tiki Room A thunderstorm, loud volume level, and simulated explosions frighten some preschoolers.

Jungle Cruise Moderately intense, some macabre sights. A good test attraction for little ones.

Magic Carpets of Aladdin Much like Dumbo. A favorite of most younger children.

Pirates of the Caribbean Slightly intimidating queuing area; intense boat ride with gruesome (though humorously presented) sights and a short, unexpected slide down a flume.

Swiss Family Treehouse Not frightening in any respect.

FRONTIERLAND

Big Thunder Mountain Railroad Visually intimidating from outside, with moderately intense visual effects. The roller coaster is wild enough to frighten many adults, particularly seniors. Switching-off option provided (page 220).

Country Bear Jamboree Not frightening in any respect.

Frontierland Shootin' Arcade Not frightening in any respect.

Splash Mountain Visually intimidating from outside, with moderately intense visual effects. The ride, culminating in a 52-foot plunge down a steep chute, is somewhat hair-raising for all ages. Switching-off option provided (page 220).

Tom Sawyer Island Some very young children are intimidated by dark, walk-through tunnels that can be easily avoided.

LIBERTY SQUARE

The Hall of Presidents Not frightening, but boring for young ones.

The Haunted Mansion Name raises anxiety, as do sounds and sights of waiting area. Intense attraction with humorously presented macabre sights. The ride itself is gentle.

Liberty Belle Riverboat Not frightening in any respect.

FANTASYLAND

Cinderella's Golden Carousel Not frightening in any respect.

Dumbo the Flying Elephant A tame midway ride; a great favorite of most young children.

It's a Small World Not frightening in any respect.

Mad Tea Party Midway-type ride can induce motion sickness in all ages.

The Many Adventures of Winnie the Pooh Frightens a small percentage of preschoolers.

Peter Pan's Flight Not frightening in any respect.

Snow White's Scary Adventures Moderately intense spook-house-genre attraction with some grim characters. Absolutely terrifies many preschoolers.

MICKEY'S TOONTOWN FAIR

All attractions except roller coaster Not frightening in any respect.

The Barnstormer at Goofy's Wiseacres Farm (children's roller coaster) May frighten some preschoolers.

TOMORROWLAND

Astro Orbiter Visually intimidating from the waiting area, but the ride is relatively tame.

Buzz Lightyear's Space Ranger Spin Dark ride with cartoonlike aliens may frighten some preschoolers.

The Laugh Floor Comedy Club May frighten a small percentage of preschoolers.

Space Mountain Very intense roller coaster in the dark; the Magic Kingdom's wildest ride and a scary roller coaster by any standard. Switching-off option provided (page 220).

Stitch's Great Escape Very intense. May frighten children age 9 and younger. Switching-off option provided (page 220).

Tomorrowland Speedway Noise of waiting area slightly intimidates preschoolers; otherwise, not frightening.

Tomorrowland Transit Authority Not frightening in any respect.

Walt Disney's *Carousel of Progress* (open seasonally) Not frightening in any respect.

Epcot

FUTURE WORLD

Innovations East and West Not frightening in any respect.

Journey into Imagination—*Honey, I Shrunk the Audience* Extremely intense visual effects and loudness frighten many young children.

Journey into Imagination with Figment Loud noises and unexpected flashing lights startle younger children.

The Land—*Circle of Life* **Theater** Not frightening in any respect.

The Land—*Living with the Land* Not frightening in any respect.

The Land—Soarin' May frighten children age 7 and younger. Really a very mellow ride.

Mission: Space Extremely intense space-simulation ride that has been known to frighten guests of all ages. Switching-off option provided (page 220).

The Seas—The Seas with Nemo and Friends Very sweet but may frighten some toddlers.

Small-child Fright-potential Chart *(continued)*

Epcot *(continued)*

FUTURE WORLD (CONTINUED)

The Seas—Sea Base Alpha Exhibits Not frightening in any respect.

The Seas—*Turtle Talk with Crush* Not frightening in any respect.

Spaceship Earth Dark, imposing presentation intimidates a few preschoolers.

Test Track Intense thrill ride may frighten any age. Switching-off option provided (page 220).

Universe of Energy Dinosaur segment frightens some preschoolers; visually intense, with some intimidating effects.

Wonders of Life—*Body Wars* (open seasonally) Very intense, with frightening visual effects. Ride causes motion sickness in riders of all ages. Switching-off option provided (page 220).

Wonders of Life—*Cranium Command* (open seasonally) Not frightening in any respect.

Wonders of Life—*The Making of Me* (open seasonally) Not frightening in any respect.

WORLD SHOWCASE

The American Adventure Not frightening in any respect.

Canada—*O Canada!* Not frightening in any respect, but audience must stand.

China—*Reflections of China* Not frightening in any respect.

France—*Impressions de France* Not frightening in any respect.

Germany Not frightening in any respect.

Italy Not frightening in any respect.

Japan Not frightening in any respect.

Mexico—*Gran Fiesta Tour* Not frightening in any respect.

Morocco Not frightening in any respect.

Norway—*Maelstrom* Visually intense in parts. Ride ends with a plunge down a 20-foot flume. A few preschoolers are frightened.

United Kingdom Not frightening in any respect.

Disney-MGM Studios

Backstage Walking Tours Not frightening in any respect.

Disney-MGM Studios Backlot Tour Sedate and nonintimidating except for "Catastrophe Canyon," where an earthquake and a flash flood are simulated. Prepare younger children for this part of the tour.

Fantasmic! Terrifies some preschoolers.

The Great Movie Ride Intense in parts, with very realistic special effects and some visually intimidating sights. Frightens many preschoolers.

Honey, I Shrunk the Kids **Movie Set Adventure** Not scary (though oversized).

Indiana Jones Epic Stunt Spectacular! An intense show with powerful special effects, including explosions, but young children generally handle it well.

Jim Henson's MuppetVision 3-D Intense and loud, but not frightening.

Lights! Motors! Action! Extreme Stunt Show Super stunt spectacular; intense with loud noises and explosions, but not threatening in any way.

The Magic of Disney Animation Not frightening in any respect.

Playhouse Disney: Live on Stage Not frightening in any respect.

Rock 'n' Roller Coaster The wildest coaster at Walt Disney World. May frighten guests of any age. Switching-off option provided (page 220).

Sounds Dangerous Noises in the dark frighten children as old as 8.

Star Tours Extremely intense visually for all ages. Not as likely to cause motion sickness as Body Wars at Epcot. Switching-off option provided (page 220).

The Twilight Zone **Tower of Terror** Visually intimidating to young children; contains intense and realistic special effects. The plummeting elevator at the ride's end frightens many adults as well as kids. Switching-off option provided (page 220).

Voyage of the Little Mermaid Not frightening in any respect.

Walt Disney: One Man's Dream Not frightening in any respect.

Animal Kingdom

The Boneyard Not frightening in any respect.

Dinosaur High-tech thrill ride rattles riders of all ages. Switching-off option provided (page 220).

Expedition Everest Frightening to guests of all ages.

Festival of the Lion King A bit loud, but otherwise not frightening in any respect.

Finding Nemo: The Musical Not frightening in any respect, but loud.

Flights of Wonder Swooping birds alarm a few small children.

It's Tough to Be a Bug! Very intense and loud with special effects that startle viewers of all ages and potentially terrify young children.

Kali River Rapids Potentially frightening and certainly wet for guests of all ages. Switching-off option provided (page 220).

Kilimanjaro Safaris A "collapsing" bridge and the proximity of real animals make a few young children anxious.

Maharaja Jungle Trek Some children may balk at the bat exhibit.

The Oasis Not frightening in any respect.

Pangani Forest Exploration Trail Not frightening in any respect.

Pocahontas and Her Forest Friends Not frightening in any respect.

Primeval Whirl A beginner roller coaster. Most children age 7 and older will take it in stride.

Rafiki's Planet Watch Not frightening in any respect.

TriceraTop Spin A midway-type ride that will frighten only a small percentage of younger children.

Wildlife Express Train Not frightening in any respect.

8. LOUD The sound levels in some attractions and live shows are so loud that younger children flip out even though the general content of the presentation is quite benign. For toddlers and preschoolers especially, it's good to have a pair of earplugs handy.

While there is no certain way to know what will scare your kids or what will garner a big smile, many rides are so intense that they can even eat adults. I make a huge detour around *The Twilight Zone* Tower of Terror or Space Mountain, but I can't get enough of Star Tours, Mission: Space, and the Kali River Rapids—and I have survived the Mad Tea Party and Expedition Everest. Parents know their children best. I do remember braving *The Twilight Zone* Tower of Terror once because I felt that I could not deprive my 10-year-old just because I was a chicken. I didn't let on that this was not my cup of tea. My prayers to exit the attraction were answered when he asked me shyly if we could ask a cast member to get out. The request was granted instantly by both me and the cast member.

Liliane

Disney Orientation Course

We receive many tips from parents telling how they prepared their young children for the Disney experience. A common strategy is to acquaint children with the characters and stories behind the attractions by reading Disney books and watching Disney videos at home. A more direct approach is to watch Walt Disney World travel videos that show the attractions. Of the latter, a father from Arlington, Virginia, reports:

> *My kids both loved The Haunted Mansion, with appropriate preparation. We rented a tape before going so they could see it, and then I told them it was all "Mickey Mouse Magic" and that Mickey was just "joking you," to put it in their terms, and that there weren't any real ghosts, and that Mickey wouldn't let anyone actually get hurt.*

A Teaneck, New Jersey, mother adds:

> *I rented movies to make my 5-year-old more comfortable with rides (Star Wars; Indiana Jones; Honey, I Shrunk the Kids). If kids are afraid of rides in the dark (like ours), buy a light-up toy and let them take it on the ride.*

If your video store doesn't rent Disney travel videos, you can order the free Walt Disney World Holiday Planning Video/DVD by calling Disney reservations at ☎ 407-824-8000, or log on to **disneyworld .disney.go.com/wdw/index** and click on "Vacation Planning Kit" to order or view online. Ignore all prompts, and the phone system will assume you're on a rotary phone and patch you through to a live person (though you may be on hold a couple minutes). This video/DVD isn't as comprehensive as travelogues you might rent, but it's adequate for giving your kids a sense of what they'll see.

A MAGICAL TIME FOR MOM AND DAD

OK, LILIANE WRITING HERE. Because Bob's idea of a romantic evening is watching Monday night football on the sofa with his honey instead of sitting in his La-Z-Boy, I'm going to tackle this subject solo. Let's face it: we all know that moms and dads deserve some special time. But the reality on the ground is that the kids come first. And when the day is over, mom and dad are way too tired to think about having a special evening alone. It is difficult enough to catch a movie or go out for a romantic dinner in our hometowns, so how realistic is a romantic parents' night out while on vacation at Walt Disney World?

The answer is: no planning, no romance! With a little magic and some advanced preparation, you can make it happen. Here are some suggestions:

Staying at a hotel that offers great kids' programs is a big plus. Consider signing up small children for a half-day program with lunch or dinner while you enjoy your resort. Go to the pool and read a book, and then have a meal in calm and peace. Rent a bike, a boat, or just take off outside the World. This is also a great opportunity to enjoy the thrill rides you passed up when you were busy worshipping at the altar of Dumbo.

Here are some tips for a romantic evening for "just the two of us":

- Plan that special day or evening before you leave home.
- Discuss with your partner what the ideal activity for that special evening would be. Decide whether you want to spend this time "with the Mouse" or take a break from nonstop Disney.
- Once you know where you want to dine, make an Advance Reservation (see page 126) before leaving home. For Walt Disney World dining call ☎ 407-WDW-DINE or 407-939-3463.
- Make arrangements for babysitting (see page 63).
- Tell the children in advance that on this day/evening, Mom and Dad are going out.
- Pick a day when the afternoon schedule is not too heavy and you return from the parks with enough time for a nap and some time with the kids in the pool before going out.
- Taking a break from your little ones may be a lot easier than getting away from everybody else's. For quiet romantic dining, avoid the theme-park restaurants. Exceptions are the Brown Derby at the Disney-MGM Studios, the terrace at the Rose & Crown (England), and the San Angel Inn (Mexico) at Epcot. If you can obtain an 8 or 8:15 p.m. Advanced Reservation for the Rose & Crown, you can watch IllumiNations from your table.
- Ouside the parks, a great place to have dinner is the California Grill atop the Contemporary Resort. Make sure you get a table with a good view of the nightly fireworks over the Magic Kingdom.

- Exotic food and atmosphere are always on the menu at Jiko in the Animal Kingdom Lodge. Come early to watch the animals graze on the savanna. Another great restaurant choice is Artist Point at the Wilderness Lodge overlooking Bay Lake. "Very adult, very romantic, and very good" describes Cítricos at the Grand Floridian and bluezoo at the Dolphin. For the best steak and prime rib in the World, try Shula's, also at the Dolphin. 'Ohana at the Polynesian Resort is another romantic place to go. The food is not as stellar as at the restaurants mentioned previously, but the South Pacific atmosphere makes up for it. After dinner, stroll the beach or watch the nightly Electrical Water Pageant or the Magic Kingdom fireworks from the Poly's dock.

- Romantic walks are in the offing at the Port Orleans Resort, where you can also catch a boat ride to Downtown Disney and dance the night away. Another lovely walk, at Disney's BoardWalk, takes you around Crescent Lake past the Yacht and Beach Club resorts. After your walk, drop in at the ever lively Jellyrolls nightspot with its dueling pianos.

- For the height of romance and a taste of grand splendor, there is always dinner at Victoria & Albert's at the Grand Floridian Resort and Spa, but be prepared to pay big bucks. Also at the Grand Floridian, waterfront dining is available at Narcoossee's.

And while there is nothing wrong with you enjoying Cinderella's carousel on your special night, here are some suggestions for an evening away from it all:

- Attending a performance of Cirque du Soleil's *La Nouba* is guaranteed to leave you in awe. We rate the show as the single best thing in all of Walt Disney World . . . a must see. Tickets range from $61 to $95 plus tax. For booking call ☎ 407-939-7328 or visit **www.cirquedusoleil.com.**

- Dine at Boheme, where an elegant, upscale setting and an eclectic menu await you. The restaurant is located at 325 South Orange Avenue in downtown Orlando. For more information, call ☎ 407-581-4700 or visit **www.grandbohemianhotel.com.**

- A relaxed atmosphere and excellent French preparations at affordable prices distinguish Le Coq au Vin, a perennial local favorite at 4800 South Orange Avenue in Orlando; ☎ 407-851-6980.

- If you enjoy Indian food, try Memories of India at 7625 Turkey Lake Road in Orlando; ☎ 407-370-3277. This quiet restaurant dishes up some of the best Indian cuisine in the area.

- For an authentic Italian restaurant in a lovely setting, book Bice at the Portofino Bay Hotel, Universal Orlando Resort, 5601 Universal Boulevard, Orlando; ☎ 407-503-3463. Though the bill will be hefty, you will be rewarded with authentic Italian cuisine and one of the best selections of Italian wines in Florida.

Should you have the luxury of a whole day away from the kids (thank God for Grandma or Grandpa), consider spending a day at Juniper Springs in the Ocala National Forest, just an hour and a half from Orlando. The seven-mile canoe trip from the Juniper Recreation Area to the FL 19 bridge will reward you with an exotic jungle setting complete with real birds, animals, turtles, and alligators. The canoe trip takes about 4½ hours. Canoe rentals and shuttle service are available at the recreation area. Phone ☎ 352- 625-2808 for more information.

And for the morning after—plan a fun day at one of the water parks!

PREPARING YOUR CHILDREN TO MEET THE CHARACTERS

ALMOST ALL DISNEY CHARACTERS ARE QUITE LARGE; several, like Brer Bear, are huge! Young children don't expect this and can be intimidated if not terrified. Discuss the characters with your children before you go. If there is a high school or college with a costumed mascot nearby, arrange to let your kids check it out. If not, then Santa Claus or the Easter Bunny will do.

On the first encounter at Walt Disney World, don't thrust your child at the character. Allow the little one to deal with this big thing from whatever distance feels safe to him or her. If two adults are present, one should stay near the youngster while the other approaches the character and demonstrates that it's safe and friendly. Some kids warm to the characters immediately; some never do. Most take a little time and several encounters.

Tell children in advance that headpiece characters don't talk.

Ian

At Walt Disney World there are two kinds of characters: those whose costume includes a face-covering headpiece (animal characters and such humanlike characters as Captain Hook) and "face characters," those who resemble the characters so no mask or headpiece is necessary. Face characters include Mary Poppins, Ariel, Jasmine, Aladdin, Cinderella, Belle, Snow White, Tarzan, Esmerelda, and Prince Charming.

Only face characters speak. Headpiece characters don't make noises of any kind. Because cast members couldn't possibly imitate the distinctive cinema voice of the character, Disney has determined that it's more effective to keep them silent. Lack of speech notwithstanding, headpiece characters are very warm and responsive, and communicate very effectively with gestures.

Some character costumes are cumbersome and give cast members very poor visibility. (Eye holes frequently are in the mouth of the costume or even on the neck or chest.) This means characters are somewhat clumsy and have limited sight. Children who approach the character from the back or side may not be noticed, even if the child touches the character. It's possible in this situation for the character to accidentally step on the child

If a character appears to be ignoring your child, pick up your child and hold him or her in front of the character until the character responds.

Liliane

or knock him or her down. It's best for a child to approach a character from the front, but occasionally not even this works. Duck characters (Donald, Daisy, Uncle Scrooge), for example, have to peer around their bills.

It's okay for your child to touch, pat, or hug the character. Understanding the unpredictability of children, the character will keep his feet very still, particularly refraining from moving backward or sideways. Most characters will sign autographs or pose for pictures.

> If your child wants to collect character autographs, it's a good idea to carry a pen the width of a magic marker. Costumes make it exceedingly difficult for characters to wield a pen, so the bigger the writing instrument, the better.

Another great way to show young kids how the characters appear in the parks is to rent or buy a Disney "Musical Adventure" video/DVD. Not unlike similar Barney videos, they are children's sing-along programs showing the costumed Disney characters interacting with real kids. At a minimum the shows will give your kids a sense of how big the Disney characters are. The best two are *Flik's Musical Adventure* at the Animal Kingdom and *Mickey's Campout* at Walt Disney World. *It's a Small World* (shot at Disneyland) is a third offering, but then there's THAT SONG. No sense turning your brain to mush before even leaving home.

ROLE-PLAYING

ESPECIALLY FOR YOUNGER CHILDREN, role-playing is a great way to inculcate vital lessons concerning safety, contingency situations, and potential danger. Play "what would you do if" for a variety of scenarios, including getting lost, being approached by strangers, getting help if mommy is sick, and so on. Children have incredible recall when it comes to role-playing with siblings and parents, and are much more likely to respond appropriately in an actual situation than they will if the same information is presented in a lecture.

PHYSICAL PREPARATION

YOU'LL FIND THAT SOME PHYSICAL CONDITIONING coupled with a realistic sense of the toll that Walt Disney World takes on your body will preclude falling apart in the middle of your vacation. As one of our readers put it, "If you pay attention to eat, heat, feet, and sleep, you'll be OK."

As you contemplate the stamina of your family, it's important to understand that somebody is going to run out of steam first, and when they do, the whole family will be affected. Sometimes a cold drink or a snack will revive the flagging member. Sometimes, however, no amount of cajoling or treats will work. In this situation it's crucial that you recognize that the child, grandparent, or spouse is at the end of his or her rope. The correct decision is to get them back to the hotel. Pushing the exhausted beyond their capacity will spoil the day for them—and you. Accept that stamina and energy levels vary and be prepared to administer to members of your family who poop out. One more thing: no guilt trips. "We've driven a thousand miles to take you to Disney World and now you're going to ruin everything!" is not an appropriate response.

THE AGONY OF THE FEET

HERE'S A LITTLE FACTOID TO CHEW ON: If you spend a day at Epcot and visit both sections of the park, you will walk five to nine miles! The walking, however, will be nothing like a five-mile hike in the woods. At Epcot (and the other Disney parks as well) you will be in direct sunlight most of the time, will have to navigate through huge jostling crowds, will be walking on hot pavement, and will have to endure waits in line between bursts of walking. The bottom line, if you haven't figured it out, is that Disney theme parks (especially in the summer) are not for wimps!

Though most children are active, their normal play usually doesn't condition them for the exertion of touring a Disney theme park. We recommend starting a program of family walks six weeks or more before your trip. A Pennsylvania mom who did just that offers the following:

We had our 6-year-old begin walking with us a bit every day one month before leaving—when we arrived [at Walt Disney World] her little legs could carry her and she had a lot of stamina.

The first thing you need to do, immediately after making your hotel reservation, is to get thee to a footery. Take the whole family to a shoe store and buy each member the best pair of walking, hiking, or running shoes you can afford. Wear exactly the kind of socks to try on the shoes as you will wear when using them to hike. Do not under any circumstances attempt to tour Walt Disney World shod in sandals, flip-flops, loafers, or any kind of high heel or platform shoe.

Good socks are as important as good shoes. When you walk, your feet sweat like a mule in a peat bog, and moisture increases friction. To minimize friction, wear a pair of Smart Wool or CoolMax hiking socks, available at most outdoor retail (camping equipment) stores. To further combat moisture, dust your feet with some anti-fungal talcum powder.

All right, now you've got some good shoes and socks. The next thing to do is to break the shoes in. You can accomplish this painlessly by wearing the shoes in the course of normal activities for about three weeks.

If your children (or you, for that matter) do not consider it cool to wear socks, get over it! Bare feet, whether encased in Nikes, Weejuns, Docksiders, or Birkenstocks, will turn into lumps of throbbing red meat if you tackle a Disney park without socks.

Once the shoes are broken in, it's time to start walking. The whole family will need to toughen up their feet and build endurance. As you begin, remember that little people have little strides, and though your 6-year-old may create the appearance of running circles around you, consider that (1) he won't have the stamina to go at that pace very long, and (2) more to the point, he probably has to take two strides or so to every one of yours to keep up when you walk together.

Start by taking short walks around the neighborhood, walking on pavement, and increasing the distance about a quarter of a mile on each outing. Older children will shape up quickly. Younger children should build endurance more slowly and incrementally. Increase distance until you can manage a six- or seven-mile hike without requiring CPR. And remember, you're not training to be able to walk six or seven miles just once; at Walt Disney World you will be hiking five to nine miles or more almost *every day*. So unless you plan to crash after the first day, you've got to prepare your feet to walk long distances for three to five consecutive days.

Be sure to give your kids adequate recovery time between training walks (48 hours will usually be enough), however, or you'll make the problem worse.

Let's be honest and admit up front that not all feet are created equal. Some folks are blessed with really tough feet, whereas the feet of others sprout blisters if you look at them sideways. Assuming that there's nothing wrong with either shoes or socks, a few brisk walks will clue you in to what kind of feet your family have. If you have a tenderfoot in your family, walks of incrementally increased distances will usually toughen up his or her feet to some extent. For those whose feet refuse to toughen, your only alternative is preventive care. After several walks, you will know where your tenderfoot tends to develop blisters. If you can anticipate where blisters will develop, you can cover sensitive spots in advance with moleskin, a friction-resistant adhesive dressing.

When you initiate your walking program, teach your children to tell you if they feel a "hot spot" on their feet. This is the warning that a blister is developing. If your kids are too young, too oblivious, too preoccupied, or don't understand the concept, your best bet is to make regular foot checks. Have your children remove their shoes and socks and present their feet for inspection. Look for red spots and blisters, and ask if they have any places on their feet that hurt.

During your conditioning, and also at Walt Disney World, carry a foot emergency kit in your daypack or hip pack. The kit should contain gauze, Betadine antibiotic ointment, moleskin and an assortment of Band-Aid Blister Bandages, scissors, a sewing needle or some such to drain blisters, as well as matches to sterilize the needle. An extra pair of dry socks and talc are optional.

If your child is age 8 or younger, we recommend regular feet inspections whether he or she understands the hot spot idea or not. Even the brightest and most well-intentioned child will fail to sound off when distracted.

Bob

If you discover a hot spot, dry the foot and cover the spot immediately with moleskin. Cut the covering large enough to cover the skin surrounding the hot spot. If you find that a blister has fully or partially developed, first air out and dry the foot. Next, using your sterile needle, drain the fluid but do not remove the top skin. Clean the area with your Betadine, and place a Band-Aid Blister Bandage over the blister. If you do not have moleskin or Band-Aid Blister Bandages, do not try to cover the hot spot or blister with regular Band-Aids. Regular Band-Aids slip and wad up.

unofficial **TIP**
If you have a child who will physically fit in a stroller, rent one, no matter how well conditioned your family is.

A stroller will provide the child the option of walking or riding, and, if he collapses, you won't have to carry him. Even if your child hardly uses the stroller at all, it serves as a convenient rolling depository for water bottles and other stuff you may not feel like carrying. Strollers at Walt Disney World are covered in detail on pages 239–241.

SLEEP, REST, AND RELAXATION

OK, WE KNOW THAT THIS SECTION is about physical preparation *before you go,* but this concept is so absolutely critical that we need to tattoo it on your brain right now.

Physical conditioning is important but is *not* a substitute for adequate rest. Even marathon runners need recovery time. If you push too hard and try to do too much, you'll either crash or, at a minimum, turn what should be fun into an ordeal. Rest means plenty of sleep at night, naps during the afternoon on most days, and planned breaks in your vacation itinerary. And don't forget that the brain needs rest and relaxation as well as the body. The stimulation inherent in touring a Disney theme park is enough to put many children and some adults into system overload. It is imperative that you remove your family from this unremitting assault on the senses, preferably for part of each day, and do something relaxing and quiet like swimming or reading.

If your kids are little and don't mind a hairdo change, consider getting them a short haircut before you leave home. Not only will they be cooler and more comfortable, but—especially with your girls—you'll save them (and yourselves) the hassle of tangles and about 20 minutes of foo-fooing a day. Don't try this with your confident teen or preteen though. Braids will do the trick for girls, and your Mick Jagger in the party will be grateful for the bandanna or sports headband unless of course the hair is meant to keep the monsters and dinosaurs out of sight!

Liliane

The theme parks are huge; don't try to see everything in one day. Tour in early morning and return to your hotel around 11:30 a.m. for lunch, a swim, and a nap. Even during off-season, when the crowds are smaller and the temperature more pleasant, the size of the major theme parks will exhaust most children under age 8 by lunchtime. Return to the park in late afternoon or early evening and continue touring. A family from Texas underlines the importance of naps and rest:

> *Despite not following any of your "tours," we did follow the theme of visiting a specific park in the morning, leaving midafternoon for either a nap back at the room or a trip to the Dixie Landings pool, and then returning to one of the parks in the evening. On the few occasions when we skipped your advice, I was muttering to myself by dinner. I can't tell you what I was muttering . . .*

When it comes to naps, this mom does not mince words:

> *One last thing for parents of small kids—take the book's advice and get out of the park and take the nap, take the nap, TAKE THE NAP! Never in my life have I seen so many parents screaming at, ridiculing, or slapping their kids. (What a vacation!) Walt Disney World is overwhelming for kids and adults. Even though the rental strollers recline for sleeping, we noticed that most of the toddlers and preschoolers didn't give up and sleep until 5 p.m., several hours after the fun had worn off, and right about the time their parents wanted them to be awake and polite in a restaurant.*

A mom from Rochester, New York, was equally adamant:

[You] absolutely must rest during the day. Kids went from 8 a.m. to 9 p.m. in the Magic Kingdom. Kids did great that day, but we were all completely worthless the next day. Definitely must pace yourself. Don't ever try to do two full days of park sightseeing in a row. Rest during the day. Go to a water park or sleep in every other day.

If you plan to return to your hotel in midday and would like your room made up, let housekeeping know.

DEVELOPING *a* GOOD PLAN

ALLOW YOUR CHILDREN TO PARTICIPATE in the planning of your time at Walt Disney World. Guide them diplomatically through the options, establishing advance decisions about what to do each day and how the day will be structured. Begin with your trip *to* Walt Disney World, deciding what time to depart, who sits by the window, whether to stop for meals or eat in the car, and so on. For the Walt Disney World part of your vacation, build consensus for wake-up call, bedtime, and building naps into the itinerary, and establish ground rules for eating, buying refreshments, and shopping. Determine the order for visiting the different theme parks and make a list of "must-see" attractions. To help you with filling in the blanks of your days, and especially to prevent you from spending most of your time standing in line, we offer a number of field-tested touring plans. The plans are designed to minimize your waiting time at each park by providing step-by-step itineraries that route you counter to the flow of traffic. The plans are explained in detail on pages 207–213.

Generally it's better to just sketch in the broad strokes on the master plan. The detail of what to do when you actually arrive at the park can be decided the night before you go, or with the help of one of our touring plans once you get there. Above all, be flexible. One important caveat, however: Make sure you keep any promises or agreements that you make when planning. They may not seem important to you, but they will to your children, who will remember for a long, long time that you let them down.

 To keep your thinking fresh and to adequately cover all bases, develop your plan in a series of family meetings no longer than 30 minutes each. You'll discover that all members of the family will devote a lot of thought to the plan both in and between meetings. Don't try to anticipate every conceivable contingency or you'll end up with something as detailed and unworkable as the tax code.

The more you can agree to and nail down in advance, the less potential you'll have for disagreement and confrontation once you arrive. Because children are more comfortable with the tangible than the conceptual, and also because they sometimes have short memories, we recommend typing up all of your decisions and agreements and providing a copy to each child. Create a fun document, not a legalistic one. You'll find that your children will review it in anticipation of all the things they will see and do, will consult it often, and will even read it to their younger siblings.

By now you're probably wondering what one of these documents looks like, so here's a sample. Incidentally, this itinerary reflects the preferences of its creators, the Shelton family, and is not meant to be offered as an example of an ideal itinerary. It does, however, incorporate many of our most basic and strongly held recommendations, such as setting limits and guidelines in advance, getting enough rest, getting to the theme parks early, touring the theme parks in shorter visits with naps and swimming in between, and saving time and money by having a cooler full of food for breakfast. As you will see, the Sheltons go pretty much full-tilt without much unstructured time and will probably be exhausted by the time they get home, but that's their choice. One more thing—the Sheltons visited Walt Disney World in late June, when all of the theme parks stay open late.

THE GREAT WALT DISNEY WORLD EXPEDITION

CO-CAPTAINS Mary and Jack Shelton

TEAM MEMBERS Lynn and Jimmy Shelton

EXPEDITION FUNDING The main Expedition Fund will cover everything except personal purchases. Each team member will receive $40 for souvenirs and personal purchases. Anything above $40 will be paid for by team members with their own money.

EXPEDITION GEAR Each team member will wear an official expedition T-shirt and carry a hip pack.

PRE-DEPARTURE Jack makes priority seating arrangements at Walt Disney World restaurants. Mary, Lynn, and Jimmy make up trail mix and other snacks for the hip packs.

Notice that the Sheltons' itinerary on pages 186–189 provides minimal structure and maximum flexibility. It specifies which park the family will tour each day without attempting to nail down exactly what the family will do there. No matter how detailed your itinerary is, be prepared for surprises at Walt Disney World, both good and bad. If an unforeseen event renders part of the plan useless or impractical, just roll with it. And always remember that it's your itinerary; you created it, and you can change it. Just try to make any changes the result of family discussion and be especially careful not to scrap an element of the plan that your children perceive as something you promised them.

Routines That Travel

If when at home you observe certain routines—for example, reading a book before bed or having a bath first thing in the morning—try to incorporate these familiar activities into your vacation schedule. They will provide your children with a sense of security and normalcy.

Maintaining a normal routine is especially important with toddlers, as a mother of two from Lawrenceville, Georgia, relates:

> *The first day, we tried an early start, so we woke the children (ages 2 & 4) and hurried them to get going. BAD IDEA with toddlers. This put them off schedule for naps and meals the rest of the day. It is best to let young ones stay on their regular schedule and see Disney at their own pace, and you'll have much more fun.*

We offer a Sleepy Head Touring Plan for each park, perfect for families like this reader's.

LOGISTIC PREPARATION

WHEN WE RECENTLY LAUNCHED into our spiel about good logistic preparation for a Walt Disney World vacation, a friend from Indianapolis said, "Wait, what's the big deal? You pack clothes, a few games for the car, then go!" So OK, I confess, that will work, but life can be sweeter and the vacation smoother (as well as less expensive) with the right gear.

CLOTHING

LET'S START WITH CLOTHES. We recommend springing for vacation uniforms. Buy for each child several sets of jeans (or shorts) and T-shirts, all matching, and all the same. For a one week trip, as an example, get each child three or so pairs of khaki shorts, three or so light yellow T-shirts, three pairs of Smart Wool or CoolMax hiking socks. What's the point? First, you don't have to play fashion designer, coordinating a week's worth of stylish combos. Each morning the kids put on their uniform. It's simple, it's time-saving, and there are no decisions to make or arguments about what to wear. Second, uniforms make your children easier to spot and keep together in the theme parks. Third, the uniforms give your family, as well as the vacation itself, some added identity. If you're like the Shelton family who created the sample itinerary in the section on organizational planning, you might go so far as to create a logo for the trip to be printed on the shirts.

Give your teens the job of coming up with the logo for your shirts. They will love being the family designer. —Liliane

When it comes to buying your uniforms, we have a few suggestions. Purchase well-made, durable shorts or jeans that will serve your children well beyond the vacation. Active children can never have too many pairs of shorts or jeans. As far as the T-shirts go, buy short-sleeve shirts in light colors for warm weather, or long-sleeve, darker-colored T-shirts for cooler weather. We suggest that you purchase your colored

Shelton Family Itinerary

DAY 1: FRIDAY

6:30 p.m.	Dinner
After dinner	Pack car
10 p.m.	Lights out

DAY 2: SATURDAY

7 a.m.	Wake up!
7:15 a.m.	Breakfast
8 a.m.	Depart Chicago for Hampton Inn, Chattanooga; Confirmation # DE56432; Lynn rides shotgun
About noon	Stop for lunch; Jimmy picks restaurant
7 p.m.	Dinner
9:30 p.m.	Lights out

DAY 3: SUNDAY

7 a.m.	Wake up!
7:30 a.m.	Breakfast
8:15 a.m.	Depart Chattanooga for Walt Disney World, Port Orleans Resort; Confirmation # L124532; Jimmy rides shotgun
About noon	Stop for lunch; Lynn picks restaurant
5 p.m.	Check in, buy park admissions, and unpack
6–7 p.m.	Mary and Jimmy shop for breakfast food for cooler
7:15 p.m.	Dinner at Boatwright's at Port Orleans
After dinner	Walk along Bonnet Creek
10 p.m.	Lights out

shirts from a local T-shirt printing company. Cleverly listed under "T-shirts" (sometimes under "Screen Printing") in the Yellow Pages, these firms will be happy to sell you either printed T-shirts or unprinted T-shirts (called "blanks") with long or short sleeves. You can select from a wide choice of colors not generally available in retail clothing stores and will not have to worry about finding the sizes you need. Plus, the shirts will cost a fraction of what a clothing retailer would charge. Most shirts come in the more durable 100% cotton or in the more wrinkle-resistant 50% cotton and 50% polyester (50/50s). The cotton shirts are a little cooler and more comfortable in hot, humid weather. The 50/50s dry a bit faster if they get wet.

DAY 4: MONDAY

7 a.m.	Wake up! Cold breakfast from cooler in room
8 a.m.	Depart room to catch bus for Epcot
Noon	Lunch at Epcot
1 p.m.	Return to hotel for swimming and a nap
5 p.m.	Return to Epcot for touring, dinner, and *IllumiNations*
9:30 p.m.	Return to hotel
10:30 p.m.	Lights out

DAY 5: TUESDAY

7 a.m.	Wake up! Cold breakfast from cooler in room
7:45 a.m.	Depart room to catch bus for Disney-MGM Studios
Noon	Lunch at Studios
2:30 p.m.	Return to hotel for swimming and a nap
6 p.m.	Drive to dinner at cafe at Wilderness Lodge
7:30 p.m.	Return to Studios via car for touring and *Fantasmic!*
10 p.m.	Return to hotel
11 p.m.	Lights out

LABELS A great idea, especially for younger children, is to attach labels with your family name, hometown, the name of your hotel, the dates of your stay, and your cell phone number inside the shirt, for example:

Carlton Family of Frankfort, KY; Port Orleans; May 5–12; 502-662-2108

Instruct your smaller children to show the label to an adult if they get separated from you. Elimination of the child's first name (which most children of talking age can articulate in any event) allows you to order labels that are all the same, that can be used by anyone in the family, and that can also be affixed to such easily lost items as caps, hats, jackets, hip packs, ponchos, and umbrellas. If fooling with labels sounds like too

Shelton Family Itinerary (continued)

DAY 6: WEDNESDAY

ZZZZZZ!	Lazy morning—sleep in!
10:30 a.m.	Late-morning swim
Noon	Lunch at Port Orleans food court
1 p.m.	Depart room to catch bus for Animal Kingdom. Tour until Animal Kingdom closes.
8 p.m.	Dinner at Rainforest Cafe at Animal Kingdom
9:15 p.m.	Return to hotel via bus
10:30 p.m.	Lights out

DAY 7: THURSDAY

6 a.m.	Wake up! Cold breakfast from cooler in room
6:45 a.m.	Depart via bus for early entry at Magic Kingdom
11:30 a.m.	Return to hotel for lunch, swimming, and a nap
4:45 p.m.	Drive to Contemporary for dinner at Chef Mickey's
6:15 p.m.	Walk from the Contemporary to the Magic Kingdom for more touring, fireworks, and parade
11 p.m.	Return to Contemporary via walkway or monorail; get car and return to hotel
11:45 p.m.	Lights out

Consider affixing labels to the clothing of young children to help in the event that they become separated from the family.

much of a hassle, check out "When Kids Get Lost" (pages 241–244) for some alternatives.

DRESSING FOR COOLER WEATHER
Central Florida experiences temperatures all over the scale from November through March, so it could be a bit chilly if you visit during those months. Our suggestion is to layer: for example, a breathable, waterproof or water-resistant Windbreaker over a light, long-sleeved polypro shirt over a long-sleeved T-shirt. As with the baffles of a sleeping bag or down coat, it is the air trapped between the layers that keeps you warm. If all the layers are thin, you won't be left with something bulky to cart around if you want to pull one or more off. Later in this section, we'll advo-

DAY 8: FRIDAY

8 a.m.	Wake up! Cold breakfast from cooler in room
8:40 a.m.	Drive to Blizzard Beach water park
Noon	Lunch at Blizzard Beach
1:30 p.m.	Return to hotel for nap and packing
4 p.m.	Revisit favorite park or do whatever we want
Dinner	When and where we decide
10 p.m.	Return to hotel
10:30 p.m.	Lights out

DAY 9: SATURDAY

7:30 a.m.	Wake up!
8:30 a.m.	After fast-food breakfast, depart for Executive Inn, Nashville; Confirmation # SD234; Lynn rides shotgun
About noon	Stop for lunch; Jimmy picks restaurant
7 p.m.	Dinner
10 p.m.	Lights out

DAY 10: SUNDAY

7 a.m.	Wake up!
7:45 a.m.	Depart for home after fast-food breakfast; Jimmy rides shotgun
About noon	Stop for lunch; Lynn picks restaurant for lunch
4:30 p.m.	Home Sweet Home!

cate wearing a hip pack. Each layer should be sufficiently compactible to fit easily in that hip pack along with whatever else is in it.

ACCESSORIES

I (BOB) WANTED TO CALL THIS PART "Belts and Stuff," but Liliane (who obviously spends a lot of time at Macy's) thought "Accessories" put a finer point on it. In any event, we recommend pants for your children with reinforced elastic waistbands that eliminate the need to wear a belt (one less thing to find when you're trying to leave). If your children like belts or want to carry an item suspended from their belts, buy them military-style 1½-inch-wide web belts at any army/navy surplus or camping equipment store. The belts weigh less than half as much as leather, are cooler, and are washable.

SUNGLASSES The Florida sun is so bright and the glare so blinding that we recommend sunglasses for each family member. For children and adults of all ages, a good accessory item is a polypro eyeglass strap for spectacles or sunglasses. The best models have a little device for adjusting the amount of slack in the strap. This allows your child to comfortably hang sunglasses from his or her neck when indoors or, alternately, to secure them fast to his or her head while experiencing a fast ride outdoors.

HIP PACKS AND WALLETS Unless you are touring with an infant or toddler, the largest thing anyone in your family should carry is a hip pack, or fanny pack. Each adult and child should have one. They should be large enough to carry at least a half-day's worth of snacks as well as other items deemed necessary (lip balm, bandanna, antibacterial hand gel, and so on) and still have enough room left to stash a hat, poncho, or light Windbreaker. We recommend buying full-sized hip packs at outdoor retailers as opposed to small, child-sized hip packs. The packs are light; can be made to fit any child large enough to tote a hip pack; have slip-resistant, comfortable, wide belting; and will last for years.

 Unless you advise the front desk to the contrary, all Disney resort room keys can be used for park admission and as credit cards. They are definitely something you don't want to lose. Our advice is to void the charge privileges on your preteen children's cards and then collect them and put them together someplace safe when not in use.

Do not carry billfolds or wallets, car keys, Disney Resort IDs, or room keys in your hip packs. We usually give this advice because hip packs are vulnerable to thieves (who snip them off and run), but pickpocketing and theft are not all that common at Walt Disney World. In this instance, the advice stems from a tendency of children to inadvertently drop their wallet in the process of rummaging around in their hip packs for snacks and other items.

You should weed through your billfold and remove to a safe place anything that you will not need on your vacation (family photos, local library card, department store credit cards, business cards, movie rental ID cards, and so on). In addition to having a lighter wallet to lug around, you will decrease your exposure in the event that your wallet is lost or stolen. When we are working at Walt Disney World, we carry a small profile billfold with a driver's license, a credit card, our Disney Resort room key, and a small amount of cash. Think about it: you don't need anything else.

DAY PACKS We see a lot of folks at Walt Disney World carrying day packs (that is, small, frameless backpacks) and/or water bottle belts that strap around your waist. Day packs might be a good choice if you plan to carry a lot of camera equipment or if you need to carry baby

supplies on your person. Otherwise, try to travel as light as possible. Packs are hot, cumbersome, not very secure, and must be removed every time you get on a ride or sit down for a show. Hip packs, by way of contrast, can simply be rotated around the waist from your back to your abdomen if you need to sit down. Additionally, our observation has been that the contents of one day pack can usually be redistributed to two or so hip packs (except in the case of camera equipment).

CAPS We do not recommend caps (or hats of any kind) for children unless they are especially sun sensitive. Simply put, kids pull caps on and off as they enter and exit attractions, restrooms, and restaurants, and . . . big surprise, they lose them. In fact, they lose them by the thousands. You could provide a ball cap for every Little Leaguer in America from the caps that are lost at Walt Disney World each summer.

If your children are partial to caps, there is a device sold at ski and camping supply stores that might increase the likelihood of the cap returning home with the child. Essentially, it's a short, light cord with little alligator clips on both ends. Hook one clip to the shirt collar and the other to the hat. It's a great little invention. Bob uses one when he skis in case his ball cap blows off.

Liliane

Equip each child with a big bandanna. Although bandannas come in handy for wiping noses, scouring ice cream from chins and mouths, and dabbing sweat from the forehead, they can also be tied around the neck to protect from sunburn.

RAIN GEAR Rain in central Florida is a fact of life, although persistent rain day after day is unusual (it is the Sunshine State, after all!). Our suggestion is to check out the Weather Channel or weather forecasts on the Internet for three or so days before you leave home to see if there are any major storm systems heading for central Florida. Weather forecasting has improved to the extent that predictions concerning systems and fronts four to seven days out are now pretty reliable. If it appears that you might see some rough weather during your visit, you're better off bringing rain gear from home. If, however, nothing big is on the horizon weatherwise, you can take your chances.

We at the *Unofficial Guide* usually do not bring rain gear. First, scattered thundershowers are more the norm than are prolonged periods of rain. Second, rain gear is pretty cheap at Walt Disney World, especially the ponchos for about $7 adults, $6 child, available in seemingly every retail shop. Third, in the theme parks, a surprising number of attractions and queuing areas are under cover. Fourth, we prefer to travel light.

If you do find yourself in a big storm, however, you'll want to have both a poncho and an umbrella. As one *Unofficial* reader put it, "Umbrellas make the rain much more bearable. When rain isn't beating down on your ponchoed head, it's easier to ignore."

An advantage of buying ponchos before you leave home is that you can choose the color. At Walt Disney World all the ponchos are clear, and it's quite a sight when 30,000 differently clad individuals suddenly transform themselves into what looks like an army of really big larvae. If your family is wearing blue ponchos, they'll be easier to spot.

And consider this tip from a Memphis, Tennessee, mom:

Scotchgard your shoes. The difference is unbelievable.

MISCELLANEOUS ITEMS

MEDICATION Some parents of hyperactive children on medication discontinue or decrease the child's normal dosage at the end of the school year. If you have such a child, be aware that Walt Disney World might overly stimulate him or her. Consult your physician before altering your child's medication regimen. Also, if your child has attention deficit disorder, remember that especially loud sounds can drive him or her right up the wall. Unfortunately, some Disney theater attractions are almost unbearably loud.

SUNSCREEN Overheating and sunburn are among the most common problems of younger children at Walt Disney World. Carry and use sunscreen of SPF 15 or higher. Be sure to put some on children in strollers, even if the stroller has a canopy. Some of the worst cases of sunburn we've seen were on the exposed foreheads and feet of toddlers and infants in strollers. Protect skin from overexposure. To avoid overheating, rest regularly in the shade or in an air-conditioned restaurant or show.

 Often little ones fall asleep in their strollers (hallelujah!). Bring a large lightweight cloth and drape it over the stroller to cover your child from the sun. A few clothespins will keep it in place.

Liliane

WATER BOTTLES Don't count on keeping young children hydrated with soft drinks and stops at water fountains. Long lines may hamper buying refreshments, and fountains may not be handy. Furthermore, excited children may not realize or tell you that they're thirsty or hot. We recommend renting a stroller for children ages 6 and younger and carrying plastic bottles of water. Plastic squeeze bottles with caps run about $3 in all major parks.

COOLERS AND MINI-FRIDGES If you drive to Walt Disney World, bring two coolers: a small one for drinks in the car, and a large one for the hotel room. If you fly and rent a car, stop and purchase a large Styrofoam cooler, which can be discarded at the end of the trip. If you will be without a car, rent a mini-fridge from your hotel. At Disney resorts, mini-refrigerators cost about $13 a day. Make sure you reserve one when you book your room. Refrigerators have either been placed or are in the process of being placed in all Disney Deluxe and Moderate resort rooms, free of charge to guests. If you arrive at your room and there is no refrigerator, call housekeeping and request one. Along with free fridges, coffeemakers have also been added in the rooms.

Coolers and mini-fridges allow you to have breakfast in your hotel room, store snacks and lunch supplies to take to the theme parks, and supplant expensive vending machines for snacks and beverages at the hotel. To keep the contents of your cooler cold, we suggest freezing a two-gallon milk jug full of water before you head out. In a good cooler, it will take the jug five or more days to thaw. If you buy a Styrofoam cooler in Florida, you can use bagged ice and ice from the ice machine at your hotel. Even if you have to rent a mini-fridge, you will save a bundle of cash as well as significant time by reducing dependence on restaurant meals and expensive snacks and drinks purchased from vendors.

FOOD PREP KIT If you plan to make sandwiches, bring along your favorite condiments and seasonings from home. A typical travel kit will include mayonnaise, ketchup, mustard, salt and pepper, and packets of sugar or artificial sweetener. Also throw in some plastic knives and spoons, paper napkins, plastic cups, and a box of zip-top plastic bags. For breakfast you will need some plastic bowls for cereal. Of course, you can buy this stuff in Florida, but you probably won't consume it all, so why waste the money? If you drink bottled beer or wine, bring a bottle opener and corkscrew.

Liliane

About two weeks before I arrive at WDW, I always ship a box to my hotel containing food, plastic cutlery, and toiletries, plus pretty much any other consumables that might come in handy during my stay. If you fly, this helps avoid overweight fees and problems with liquid restrictions for carry-on luggage.

ENERGY BOOSTERS Kids get cranky when they're hungry, and when that happens your entire group has a problem. Like many parents you might, for nutritional reasons, keep a tight rein on snacks available to your children at home. At Walt Disney World, however, maintaining energy and equanimity trumps between-meal snack discipline. For maximum zip and contentedness, give your kids snacks containing complex carbohydrates (fruits, crackers, nonfat energy bars, and the like) *before* they get hungry or show signs of exhaustion. You should avoid snacks that are high in fats and proteins because these foods take a long time to digest and will tend to unsettle your stomach if it's a hot day.

ELECTRONICS Regardless of your children's ages, always bring a night-light. Flashlights are also handy for finding stuff in a dark hotel room after the kids are asleep. If you are big coffee drinkers and if you drive, bring along a coffeemaker.

Walkmans and portable CD players with headphones as well as some electronic games are often controversial gear for a family outing. We recommend compromise. Headphones allow kids to create their own space even when they're with others, and that can be a safety valve. That said, try to agree before the trip on some headphone parameters, so you don't begin to feel as if they're being used to keep other family members and the trip itself at a distance. If you're traveling by car, take turns choosing the radio station, CD, or audio tape for part of the trip.

An increasing number of readers stay in touch while on vacation by using walkie-talkies. From a Roanoke, Virginia, family:

The single best purchase we made was to get the Motorola Talk-About walkie-talkies. They have a two-mile range and are about the size of a deck of cards. We first started using them at the airport when I was checking the bags and she took the kids off to the gate. At the parks, the kids would invariably have diverse interests. With the walkie-talkies, however, we easily could split up and simply communicate with each other when we wanted to meet back up. At least half-dozen times, exasperated parents asked where they could rent/buy the walkie-talkies.

If you go the walkie-talkie route, get a set that operates on multiple channels or opt for cell phones, as a Duluth, Georgia, family did:

I spoke with a woman who invested $100 in walkie-talkies. All day long all she could hear were other people's conversations as so many people are using them. My husband and I used our cell phones, and they worked beautifully. Even though I pay roaming charges on mine, there's no way I could use $100 worth!

DON'T FORGET THE TENT This is not a joke and has nothing to do with camping. When Bob's daughter was preschool age, he about went crazy trying to get her to sleep in a shared hotel room. She was accustomed to having her own room at home and was hyperstimulated whenever she traveled. Bob tried makeshift curtains and room dividers and even rearranged the furniture in a few hotel rooms to create the illusion of a more private, separate space for her. It was all for naught. It wasn't until she was around 4 years old and Bob took her camping that he seized on an idea that had some promise. She liked the cozy, secure, womb-like feel of a backpacking tent, and quieted down much more readily than she ever had in hotel rooms. So the next time the family stayed in a hotel, he pitched his backpacking tent in the corner of the room. In she went, nested for a bit, and fell asleep.

Since the time of Bob's daughter's childhood, there has been an astounding evolution in tent design. Responding to the needs of climbers and paddlers who often have to pitch tents on rocks (where it's impossible to drive stakes), tent manufacturers developed a broad range of tents with self-supporting frames that can be erected virtually anywhere without ropes or stakes. Affordable and sturdy, many are as simple to put up as opening an umbrella. So, if your child is too young for a room of his or her own, or you can't afford a second hotel room, try pitching a small tent. Modern tents are self-contained, with floors and an entrance that can be zipped up (or not) for privacy but cannot be locked. Kids appreciate having their own space and enjoy the adventure of being in a tent, even one set up in the corner of a hotel room. Sizes range from children's "play tents" with a two- to three-foot base to models large enough to sleep two or three husky teens. Light and compact when stored, a two-adult-size tent in its own storage bag (called a "stuffsack") will take up about one-tenth or less of a standard overhead bin on a commercial airliner. Another option for infants and toddlers is to drape a sheet over a portable crib or playpen to make a tent.

THE BOX Bob writing: On one memorable Walt Disney World excursion when my children were younger, we started each morning with an immensely annoying, involuntary scavenger hunt. Invariably, seconds before our scheduled departure to the theme park, we discovered that some combination of shoes, billfolds, sunglasses, hip packs, or other necessities were unaccountably missing. For the next 15 minutes we would root through the room like pigs hunting truffles in an attempt to locate the absent items. Now I don't know about your kids, but when my kids lost a shoe or something, they always searched where it was easiest to look, as opposed to where the lost article was most likely to be. I would be jammed under a bed feeling around while my children stood in the middle of the room intently inspecting the ceiling. As my friends will tell you, I'm as open to a novel theory as the next guy, but we never did find any shoes on the ceiling. Not once. Anyway, here's what I finally did: I swung by a

liquor store and mooched a big empty box. From then on, every time we returned to the room, I had the kids deposit shoes, hip packs, and other potentially wayward items in the box. After that the box was off limits until the next morning, when I doled out the contents.

PLASTIC GARBAGE BAGS There are two attractions, the Kali River Rapids raft ride in the Animal Kingdom and Splash Mountain in the Magic Kingdom, where you are certain to get wet and possibly soaked. If it's really hot and you don't care, then fine. But if it's cool or you're just not up for a soaking, bring a large plastic trash bag to the park. By cutting holes in the top and on the sides you can fashion a sack poncho that will keep your clothes from getting wet. On the raft ride, you will also get your feet wet. If you're not up for walking around in squishing, soaked shoes, bring a second, smaller plastic bag to wear over your feet while riding.

SUPPLIES FOR INFANTS AND TODDLERS

BASED ON RECOMMENDATIONS FROM HUNDREDS of *Unofficial Guide* readers, here's what we suggest you carry with you when touring with infants and toddlers:

- A disposable diaper for every hour you plan to be away from your hotel room
- A plastic (or vinyl) diaper wrap with Velcro closures

- A cloth diaper or kitchen towel to put over your shoulder for burping
- Two receiving blankets: one to wrap the baby, one to lay the baby on or to drape over you when you nurse
- Ointment for diaper rash
- Moistened towelettes such as Handi Wipes
- Prepared formula in bottles if you are not breast-feeding
- A washable bib, baby spoon, and baby food if your infant is eating solids
- For toddlers, a small toy for comfort and to keep them occupied during attractions

Baby Care Centers at the theme parks will sell you just about anything that you forget or run out of. Like all things Disney, prices will be higher than elsewhere, but at least you won't need to detour to a drug store in the middle of your touring day.

REMEMBERING *your* TRIP

1. Purchase a notebook for each child and spend some time each evening recording the events of the day. If your children have trouble getting motivated or don't know what to write about, start a discussion; otherwise, let them write or draw whatever they want to remember from the day's events.

2. Collect mementos along the way and create a treasure box in a small tin or cigar box. Months or years later, it's fun to look at postcards, pins, seashells, or ticket stubs to jump-start a memory.

3. Add inexpensive postcards to your photographs to create an album, then write a few words on each page to accompany the images.

4. Give each child a disposable camera to record his or her version of the trip. One 5-year-old snapped an entire series of photos that never showed anyone above the waist—his view of the world (and the photos were priceless).

5. Nowadays, many families travel with a camcorder, though we recommend using one sparingly—parents end up viewing the trip through the lens rather than being in the moment. If you must, take it along, but only record a few moments of major sights (too much is boring anyway). And let the kids tape and narrate. On the topic of narration, speak loudly so as to be heard over the not insignificant background noise of the parks. Make use of lockers at all of the parks when the camcorder becomes a burden or when you're going to experience an attraction that might damage it or get it wet. Unless you've got a camcorder designed for underwater shots, leave it behind on Splash Mountain, the Kali River Rapids, and any other ride where water is involved.

6. Another inexpensive way to record memories is a palm-size tape recorder. Let all family members describe their experiences. Hearing a small child's voice years later is so endearing, and those recorded descriptions will trigger an album's worth of memories, far more focused than what many novices capture with a camcorder.

Finally, when it comes to taking photos and collecting mementos, don't let the tail wag the dog. You are not going to Walt Disney World to build the biggest scrapbook in history. Or as this Houston mom put it:

Tell your readers to get a grip on the photography thing. We were so busy shooting pictures that we kind of lost the thread. We had to get our pictures developed when we got home to see what all we did [while on vacation].

TRIAL RUN

IF YOU GIVE THOUGHTFUL CONSIDERATION to all areas of mental, physical, organizational, and logistical preparation discussed in this chapter, what remains is to familiarize yourself with Walt Disney World itself, and of course, to conduct your field test. Yep, that's right, we want you to take the whole platoon on the road for a day to see if you are combat ready. No joke, this is important. You'll learn who poops out first, who is prone to developing blisters, who has to pee every 11 seconds, and given the proper forum, how compatible your family is in terms of what you like to see and do.

For the most informative trial run, choose a local venue that requires lots of walking, dealing with crowds, and making decisions on how to spend your time. Regional theme parks and state fairs are your best bets, followed by large zoos and museums. Devote the whole day. Kick off the morning with an early start, just like you will

"No, no, really, it's OK. It's just not what I was expecting."

at Walt Disney World, paying attention to who's organized and ready to go and who's dragging his or her butt and holding up the group. If you have to drive an hour or two to get to your test venue, no big deal. You'll have to do some commuting at Walt Disney World, too. Spend the whole day, eat a couple meals, stay late.

Don't bias the sample (that is, mess with the outcome) by telling everyone you are practicing for Walt Disney World. Everyone behaves differently when they know they are being tested or evaluated. Your objective is not to run a perfect drill but to find out as much as you can about how the individuals in your family, as well as the family as a group, respond to and deal with everything they experience during the day. Pay attention to who moves quickly and who is slow; to who is adventuresome and who is reticent; to who keeps going and who needs frequent rest breaks; to who sets the agenda and who is content to follow; to who is easily agitated and who stays cool; to who tends to dawdle or wander off; to who is curious and who is bored; to who is demanding and who is accepting. You get the idea.

Discuss the findings of the test run with your spouse the next day. Don't be discouraged if your test day wasn't perfect; few (if any) are. Distinguish between problems that are remediable and problems that are intrinsic to your family's emotional or physical makeup (no amount of hiking, for example, will toughen up some people's feet).

Establish a plan for addressing remediable problems (further conditioning, setting limits before you go, trying harder to achieve family consensus, whatever) and develop strategies for minimizing or working around problems that are a fact of life (waking sleepyheads 15 minutes early, placing moleskin on likely blister sites before setting out, packing familiar food for the toddler who balks at restaurant fare). If you are an attentive observer, a fair diagnostician, and a creative problem solver, you'll be able to work out a significant percentage of the problems you're likely to encounter at Walt Disney World before you ever leave home.

PART SIX

GET *in the* BOAT, MEN!

THE ABOVE IS NOT A *JEOPARDY!* ANSWER, but if it were, the question would be this: "What did George Washington say to his soldiers before they crossed the Delaware?" We share this interesting historic aside as our way of sounding the alarm, blowing the bugle, or whatever. It's time to move beyond preparation and practice and to leap into action. Walt Disney World here we come! Get in the boat, men!

READY, SET, TOUR!
Some Touring Considerations

HOW MUCH TIME IS REQUIRED TO SEE EACH PARK?

THE MAGIC KINGDOM AND EPCOT offer such a large number of attractions and special live entertainment options that it is impossible to see everything in a single day, with or without a midday break. For a reasonably thorough tour of each, allocate a minimum of one and a half days and preferably two days. The Animal Kingdom and the Disney-MGM Studios can each be seen in a day, although planning on a day and a half allows for a more relaxed visit.

WHICH PARK TO SEE FIRST?

THIS QUESTION IS LESS ACADEMIC than it appears. Children who see the Magic Kingdom first expect more of the same type of entertainment at the other parks. At Epcot, children are often disappointed by the educational orientation and more serious tone (as are many adults). Disney-MGM offers some pretty wild action, but the general presentation is educational and more mature. Though most children enjoy zoos, live animals can't be programmed to entertain. Thus, children may not find the Animal Kingdom as exciting as the Magic Kingdom or Disney-MGM.

First-time visitors should see Epcot first; you will be able to enjoy it fully without having been preconditioned to think of Disney entertainment as solely fantasy or adventure. Children will be more likely to enjoy Epcot on its own merits if they see it first, and they will be more relaxed and patient in their touring.

See the Animal Kingdom second. Like Epcot, it has an educational thrust, but it provides a change of pace because it features live animals. Next, see Disney-MGM Studios, which helps all ages make a fluid transition from the educational Epcot and Animal Kingdom to the fanciful Magic Kingdom. Also, because Disney-MGM Studios is smaller, you won't walk as much or stay as long. Save the Magic Kingdom for last.

OPERATING HOURS

DISNEY CAN'T BE ACCUSED of being inflexible regarding operating hours at the parks. They run a dozen or more schedules each year, making it advisable to call ☎ 407-824-4321 for the exact hours before you arrive. In the off-season, parks may be open for as few as eight hours (from 10 a.m. to 6 p.m.). By contrast, at busy times (particularly holidays), they may be open from 8 a.m. until 2 a.m. the next morning.

Usually, hours approximate the following: From September through mid-March, excluding holiday periods, the Magic Kingdom is open from 9 a.m. to 7, 8, or 9 p.m. During the same period, Epcot is open from 9 a.m. to 9 p.m., and Disney-MGM Studios is open from 9 a.m. to 7 or 8 p.m. The Animal Kingdom is open from 9 a.m. until 6 or 7 p.m. During summer, expect the Animal Kingdom to remain open until 8 p.m. Epcot and Disney-MGM Studios are normally open until 9 or 10 p.m., with the Magic Kingdom sometimes open as late as 1 a.m.

OFFICIAL OPENING VERSUS REAL OPENING

THE OPERATING HOURS YOU'RE QUOTED when you call are "official hours." The parks sometimes open earlier. Many visitors, relying on information disseminated by Disney Guest Relations, arrive at the official opening time and find the park packed with people. If the official hours are 9 a.m. to 9 p.m., for example, Main Street in the Magic Kingdom opens at 8 or 8:30 a.m. with the remainder of the park opening at 8:30 or 9 a.m. If the official opening for the Magic Kingdom is 8 a.m. and you're eligible for early entry (if you are staying in a Disney resort), you sometimes are able to enter the park as early as 6:30 a.m.

Disney publishes hours of operation well in advance but reserves the flexibility to react daily to gate conditions. Disney traffic controllers survey local hotel reservations, estimate how many visitors they should expect on a given day, and open the theme parks early to avoid bottlenecks at parking facilities and ticket windows and to absorb the crowds as they arrive.

If you're a Disney resort guest and want to take advantage of Extra Magic Hours early entry, arrive one hour and 20 minutes before the early-entry park is scheduled to open to the general public. Buses, boats, and monorails will initiate service to the early-entry park about two hours before it opens to the general public.

At day's end, rides and attractions shut down at approximately the official closing time. Main Street remains open 30 minutes to an hour after the rest of the Magic Kingdom has closed.

THE RULES

SUCCESSFUL TOURING OF THE MAGIC KINGDOM, the Animal Kingdom, Epcot, or Disney-MGM Studios hinges on five rules:

1. Determine in Advance What You Really Want to See

What rides and attractions appeal most to you? Which additional rides and attractions would you like to experience if you have some time left? What are you willing to forgo?

To help you set your touring priorities, we describe each theme park and their attractions later in this book. In each description, we include the author's evaluation of the attraction and the opinions of Walt Disney World guests expressed as star ratings. Five stars is the best possible rating.

Finally, because attractions range from midway-type rides and horse-drawn trolleys to colossal, high-tech extravaganzas, we have developed a hierarchy of categories to pinpoint attractions' magnitude:

SUPER HEADLINERS The best attractions the theme park has to offer. Mind-boggling in size, scope, and imagination. Represents the cutting edge of modern attraction technology and design.

HEADLINERS Full-blown, multimillion-dollar, full-scale themed adventures and theater presentations. Modern in technology and design and employing a complete range of special effects.

MAJOR ATTRACTIONS Themed adventures on a more modest scale, but incorporating state-of-the-art technologies. Or, larger-scale attractions of older design.

MINOR ATTRACTIONS Midway-type rides, small "dark" rides (cars on a track, zigzagging through the dark), small theater presentations, transportation rides, and elaborate walk-through attractions.

DIVERSIONS Exhibits, both passive and interactive. Includes playgrounds, video arcades, and street theater.

Though not every Walt Disney World attraction fits neatly into these descriptions, the categories provide a comparison of attractions' size and scope. Remember that bigger and more elaborate doesn't always mean better. Peter Pan's Flight, a minor attraction in the Magic Kingdom, continues to be one of the park's most beloved rides. Likewise, for many young children, no attraction, regardless of size, surpasses Dumbo.

2. Arrive Early! Arrive Early! Arrive Early!

This is the single most important key to efficient touring and avoiding long lines. There are no lines and fewer people first thing in the morning. The same four rides you can experience in one hour in early morning can take as long as three hours to see after 10:30 a.m. Have breakfast before you arrive so you won't waste prime touring time sitting in a restaurant.

The earlier a park opens, the greater the potential advantage. This is because most vacationers won't make the sacrifice to rise early and get to a theme park before it opens. Fewer people are willing to be on hand for an 8 a.m. opening than for a 9 a.m. opening. On those rare occasions when a park opens at 10 a.m., almost everyone arrives at the same time, so it's almost impossible to get a jump on the crowd. If you're a Disney resort guest and have early-entry privileges, arrive as early as early entry allows (6:30 a.m. if the park opens to the public at 8 a.m., or 7:30 a.m. if the park opens to the public at 9 a.m.). If you are visiting during midsummer, arrive at non-early-entry parks 30 minutes before the official opening time. During holiday periods, arrive at non-early-entry parks 40 minutes before the official opening.

3. Avoid Bottlenecks

Crowd concentrations and/or faulty crowd management cause bottlenecks. Avoiding bottlenecks involves being able to predict where, when, and why they occur. Concentrations of hungry people create bottlenecks at restaurants during lunch and dinner. Concentrations of people moving toward the exit at closing time create bottlenecks in gift shops en route to the gate. Concentrations of visitors at new and popular rides and at rides slow to load and unload create bottlenecks and long lines. To help you get a grip on which attractions cause bottlenecks, we have developed a Bottleneck Scale with a range of one to ten. If an attraction ranks high on the Bottleneck Scale, try to experience it during the first two hours the park is open. The scale is included in each attraction profile in Parts Seven through Eleven.

The best way to avoid bottlenecks, however, is to use one of our field-tested touring plans available in clip-out form complete with a map on pages 407–430. The plans will save you as much as 4½ hours of standing in line in a single day.

 If you can't calm them—dunk them. Whenever my son was too wound up to nap or go to bed at night, I took him to the pool—water works wonders.

Liliane

4. Go Back to Your Hotel for a Rest in the Middle of the Day

You may think we're beating the dead horse with this midday nap thing, but if you plug away all day at the theme parks, you'll understand

how the dead horse feels. No joke; resign yourself to going back to the hotel in the middle of the day for swimming, reading, and a snooze.

5. Let Off Steam

Time at a Disney theme park is extremely regimented for younger children. Often held close for fear of losing them, they are ushered from line to line and attraction to attraction throughout the day. After a couple of hours of being on such a short leash, it's not surprising that they're in need of some physical freedom and an opportunity to discharge that pent-up energy. As it happens, each of the major theme parks offers some sort of elaborate, creative playground perfect for such a release. At the Magic Kingdom it's Tom Sawyer Island, at the Animal Kingdom it's The Boneyard, and at the Disney-MGM Studios it's the *Honey, I Shrunk the Kids* Adventure Set. At Epcot the playground pickings are a little slim though there is a Viking ship–themed play area at the Norway Pavilion in the World Showcase section of the park. Because Epcot has such large pedestrian plazas, however, there are several places where children can cut loose without making nuisances of themselves. Be advised that each playground (or plaza) is fairly large, and it's pretty easy to misplace a child while they're exploring. All children's playgrounds, however, have only one exit, so although your kids might get lost within the playground, they cannot wander off into the rest of the park without passing through the single exit (usually staffed by a Disney cast member).

YOUR DAILY ITINERARY

PLAN EACH DAY IN THREE BLOCKS:

1. Early morning theme-park touring
2. Midday break
3. Late afternoon and evening theme-park touring

Choose the attractions that interest you most, and check their bottleneck ratings along with what time of day we recommend you visit. If your children are 8 years old or younger, review the attraction's fright potential rating. Use one of our touring plans or work out a step-by-step plan of your own and write it down. Experience attractions with a high bottleneck rating as early as possible, transitioning to attractions with bottleneck ratings of six to eight around midmorning. Plan on departing the park for your midday break by 11:30 a.m. or so.

For your late afternoon and evening touring block, you do not necessarily have to return to the same theme park. If you have purchased one of the Disney admission options that allow you to "park hop," that is, visit more than one theme park on a given day, you may opt to spend the afternoon/evening block somewhere different. In any event, as you start your afternoon/evening block, see attractions with low bottleneck ratings until about 5 p.m. After 5 p.m., any attraction with a rating of one to seven is fair game. If you stay into the evening, try attractions with ratings of eight to ten during the hour just before closing.

In addition to attractions, each theme park offers a broad range of special live entertainment events. In the morning block, concentrate on the attractions. For the record, we regard live shows that offer five or more daily performances a day (except for street entertainment) as attractions. Thus, *Indiana Jones* at the Disney-MGM Studios is an attraction, as is *Festival of the Lion King* at the Animal Kingdom. *IllumiNations* at Epcot or the parades at the Magic Kingdom, on the other hand, are live entertainment events. A schedule of live performances is listed on the handout park map available at the entrance of each park. When planning your day, also be aware that major live events draw large numbers of guests from the attraction lines. Thus, a good time to see an especially popular attraction is during a parade or other similar event.

> We strongly recommend deferring special parades, stage shows, and other productions until the afternoon/evening block.

Bob

TOURING PLANS

OUR TOURING PLANS ARE STEP-BY-STEP GUIDES for seeing as much as possible with a minimum of standing in line. They're designed to help you avoid crowds and bottlenecks on days of moderate-to-heavy attendance. On days of lighter attendance (see "When to Go to Walt Disney World," page 46), the plans will still save time, but they won't be as critical to successful touring.

> Don't get obsessed with the touring plans. It's your vacation, after all. You can amend or even scrap the plans if you want.

Liliane

What You Can Realistically Expect from the Touring Plans

The best way to see as much as possible with the least amount of waiting is to arrive early. Several of our touring plans require that you be on hand when the park opens. Because this is often difficult and sometimes impossible for families with young children or nocturnal teens, we've developed additional touring plans for families who get a late start. You won't see as much as with the early-morning plans, but you'll see significantly more than visitors without a plan.

Variables That Will Affect the Success of the Touring Plans

The plans' success will be affected by how quickly you move from ride to ride; when and how many refreshment and restroom breaks you take; when, where, and how you eat meals; and your ability (or lack thereof) to find your way around. Smaller groups almost always move faster than larger groups, and parties of adults generally cover more ground than families with young children. Switching off (page

220), also know as baby swapping or child swapping, among other things, inhibits families with little ones from moving expeditiously among attractions.

If you have young children in your party, be prepared for character encounters. The appearance of a Disney character usually stops a touring plan in its tracks. While some characters stroll the parks, it's equally common that they assemble in a specific venue (such as the Hall of Fame at Mickey's Toontown Fair) where families queue up for photos and autographs. Meeting characters, posing for photos, and collecting autographs can burn hours of touring time. If your kids collect character autographs, you need to anticipate these interruptions and negotiate some understanding with your children about when you will follow the plan and when you will collect autographs. Our advice is to go with the flow or set aside a specific morning or afternoon for photos and autographs. Note that queues for autographs, especially in Toontown at the Magic Kingdom and Camp Minnie-Mickey at the Animal Kingdom, are sometimes as long as the queues for major attractions. The only time-efficient way to collect autographs is to line up at the character-greeting areas first thing in the morning. Because this is also the best time to experience the popular attractions, you may have tough choices to make.

 Character meals are another way to collect autographs and might be something you could promise your avid collector in exchange for a full day of touring when the signature hunt is off.

Liliane

While we realize that following the plans isn't always easy, we nevertheless recommend continuous, expeditious touring until around noon. After noon, breaks and diversions won't affect the plans significantly.

What to Do if You Lose the Thread

Anything from a blister to a broken attraction can throw off a touring plan. If unforeseen events interrupt a plan:

1. Skip one step on the plan for every 20 minutes' delay. If, for example, you lose your billfold and spend an hour finding it, skip three steps and pick up from there.

2. Forget the plan and organize the remainder of your day using the bottleneck ratings in conjunction with the best-times-to-go suggestion in each attraction profile.

What to Expect When You Arrive at the Parks

Because most touring plans are based on being present when the theme park opens, you need to know about opening procedures. Disney transportation to the parks begins an hour and a half to two hours before official opening. The parking lots open at around the same time.

Each park has an entrance plaza outside the turnstiles. Usually, you're held there until 30 minutes before the official opening time, when you're admitted. What happens next depends on the season and the day's crowds.

1. **LOW SEASON** At slower times, you will usually be confined outside the turnstiles or in a small section of the park until the official opening time. At the Magic Kingdom you might be admitted to Main Street, U.S.A.; at Animal Kingdom, to The Oasis and sometimes to Discovery Island; at Epcot, to the fountain area around Spaceship Earth; and at Disney-MGM Studios, to Hollywood Boulevard. Rope barriers supervised by Disney cast members keep you there until the "rope drop," when the barrier is removed and the park and its attractions begin operating at the official opening time.

2. **HIGH-ATTENDANCE DAYS** When large crowds are expected, you will be admitted through the turnstiles 30 minutes before official opening, and the entire park will be operating.

3. **VARIATIONS** Sometimes Disney will run a variation of those two procedures. In this, you'll be permitted through the turnstiles and find that one or several specific attractions are open early. At Epcot, Spaceship Earth and sometimes Test Track or Soarin' will be operating. At Animal Kingdom, you may find Kilimanjaro Safaris and *It's Tough to Be a Bug!* running early. At Disney-MGM Studios, look for Tower of Terror and/or Rock 'n' Roller Coaster. The Magic Kingdom almost never runs a variation. Instead, you'll usually encounter plan number one described above, or occasionally plan two.

HOW TO FIND THE TOURING PLAN THAT'S BEST FOR YOU

THE DIFFERENT TOURING PLANS FOR EACH PARK are described in the chapter pertaining to that park. The descriptions will tell you for whom (for example, teens, parents with preschoolers, grandparents, and so on) or for what situation (such as sleeping late or enjoying the park at night) the plans are designed. *The actual touring plans are located on pages 407–430 at the back of the book.* Each plan includes a numbered map of the park in question to help you find your way around. Clip the plan of your choice out of the book by cutting along the line indicated, and take it with you to the park.

Will the Plans Continue to Work Once the Secret Is Out?

Yes! First, some of the plans require that a patron be there when a park opens. Many Disney World patrons simply won't get up early while on vacation. Second, less than 1% of any day's attendance has been exposed to the plans—too few to affect results. Last, most groups tailor the plans, skipping rides or shows according to taste.

How Frequently Are the Touring Plans Revised?

Because Disney is always adding new attractions and changing operations, we revise the plans every year. Most complaints we receive come from readers using out-of-date editions of the *Unofficial Guide*. Be prepared, however, for surprises. Opening procedures and show times may change, for example, and you can't predict when an attraction might break down.

"Bouncing Around"

Many readers object to crisscrossing a theme park, as our touring plans sometimes require. A lady from Decatur, Georgia, said she "got dizzy from all the bouncing around." We empathize, but here's the rub, park by park.

In the Magic Kingdom, the most popular attractions are positioned across the park from one another. This is no accident. It's a method of more equally distributing guests throughout the park. If you want to experience the most popular attractions in one day without long waits, you can arrive before the park fills and see those attractions first (which requires crisscrossing the park), or you can enjoy the main attractions on one side of the park first, then try the most popular attractions on the other side during the hour or so before closing, when crowds presumably have thinned. Using FAST-PASS lessens the time you wait in line but tends to increase the bouncing around because you must visit the same attraction twice: once to obtain your FASTPASS and again to use it.

The best way to minimize "bouncing around" at the Magic Kingdom is to do half the touring plan on one day and the other half on another. This makes for much more relaxing touring and facilitates returning to your hotel for rest and a swim. The Disney-MGM Studios is configured in a way that precludes an orderly approach to touring, or to a clockwise or counterclockwise rotation. Orderly touring is further confounded by live entertainment that prompts guests to interrupt their touring to head for whichever theater is about to crank up. At the Studios, therefore, you're stuck with "bouncing around" whether you use our plan or not. In our opinion, when it comes to Disney parks, it's best to have a plan.

The Animal Kingdom is arranged in a spoke-and-hub configuration like the Magic Kingdom, simplifying crisscrossing the park. Even so, the only way to catch various shows is to stop what you're doing and troop across the park to the next performance.

Touring Plans and the Obsessive-compulsive Reader

We suggest you follow the touring plans religiously, especially in the mornings, if you're visiting during busy times. The consequence of touring spontaneity in peak season is hours of standing in line. During quieter times, there's no need to be compulsive about following the plans.

Bob

We've revised the Epcot plans to eliminate most of the "bouncing around" and have added instructions to further minimize walking.

A mom in Atlanta, Georgia, suggests:

Emphasize perhaps not following [the touring plans] in off-season. There is no reason to crisscross the park when there are no lines.

A mother in Minneapolis advises:

Please let your readers know to stop along the way to various attractions to appreciate what else may be going on around them. We encountered many families using the Unofficial Guide *[who] became too serious about getting from one place to the next, missing the fun in between.*

What can we say? It's a lesser-of-two-evils situation. If you visit Walt Disney World at a busy time, you can either rise early and hustle around, or you can sleep in and see less.

When using the plans, however, relax and always be prepared for surprises and setbacks. When your type-A brain does cartwheels, reflect on the advice of a woman from Trappe, Pennsylvania:

You cannot emphasize enough the dangers of using your touring plans that were printed in the back of the book, especially if the person using them has a compulsive personality. I have a compulsive personality. I planned for this trip for two years, and researched it by use of guidebooks, computer programs, videotapes, and information received from WDW. I had a two-page itinerary for our one-week trip in addition to your touring plans of the theme parks. On night three of our trip, I ended up taking an unscheduled trip to the emergency room of Sand Lake Hospital in Lake Buena Vista. When the doctor asked what seemed to be the problem, I responded with "I don't know, but I can't stop shaking, and I can't stay here very long because I have to get up in a couple hours to go to MGM according to my itinerary." Diagnosis: an anxiety attack caused by my excessive itinerary. He gave me a shot of something, and I slept through the first four attractions the next morning. This was our third trip to WDW (not including one trip to Disneyland); on all previous trips I used only the Steve Birnbaum book, and I suffered no ill effects. I am not saying your book was not good. It was excellent! However, it should come with a warning label for people with compulsive personalities.

Touring-plan Rejection

Some folks don't respond well to the regimentation of a touring plan. If you encounter this problem with someone in your party, roll with the punches as this Maryland couple did:

The rest of the group was not receptive to the use of the touring plans. I think they all thought I was being a little too regimented about planning this vacation. Rather than argue, I left the touring plans behind as we ventured off for the parks. You can guess the outcome. We took our camcorder with us and watched the movies when we returned home. About every five minutes or so there is a shot of us all gathered around a park map trying to decide what to do next.

Finally, as a Connecticut woman alleges, the plans are incompatible with some readers' bladders and personalities:

I want to know if next year when you write those "day" schedules you could schedule bathroom breaks in there, too. You expect us to be at a certain ride at a certain time and with no stops in between. In one of the letters in your book, a guy writes, "You expect everyone to be theme-park commandos." When I read that, I thought there is a man who really knows what a problem the schedules are if you are a laid-back, slow-moving, careful detail noticer. What were you thinking when you made these schedules?

Touring Plans for Low-attendance Days

We receive a number of letters each year similar to this one from Lebanon, New Jersey:

The guide always assumed there would be large crowds. We had no lines. An alternate tour for low-traffic days would be helpful.

If attendance is low, you don't need a touring plan. Just go where your taste and instinct direct, and glory in the hassle-free touring. Having said that, however, there are attractions in each park that bottleneck even if attendance is low. These are Space Mountain, Splash Mountain, Dumbo, The Many Adventures of Winnie the Pooh, and Peter Pan's Flight in the Magic Kingdom; Test Track, and Soarin' at Epcot; Kilimanjaro Safaris and Expedition Everest at Animal Kingdom; and Tower of Terror and Rock 'n' Roller Coaster at Disney-MGM Studios. All are FASTPASS attractions. Experience them immediately after the parks open, or use FASTPASS. Remember that crowd size is relative and that large crowds can gather at certain attractions even during less-busy times. We recommend following a touring plan through the first five or six steps. If you're pretty much walking onto every attraction, feel free to scrap the remainder of the plan.

Extra Magic Hours and the Touring Plans

If you're a Disney resort guest and use your morning Extra Magic Hours privileges, complete your early-entry touring before the general public is admitted and position yourself to follow the touring plan. When the public is admitted, the park will suddenly be aswarm. A Wilmington, Delaware, mother advises:

The early-entry times went like clockwork. We were finishing up the Great Movie Ride when Disney-MGM opened [to the public], and [we] had to wait in line quite a while for Voyage of the Little Mermaid, which sort of screwed up everything thereafter. Early-opening attractions should be finished up well before regular opening time so you can be at the plan's first stop as early as possible.

In the Magic Kingdom, the early-entry attractions are in Fantasyland and Tomorrowland. At Epcot, they're in the Future World section. At Disney-MGM Studios, they're dispersed. Practically speaking, see any attractions on the touring plan that are open for early entry, crossing them off as you do. If you finish all early-entry attractions on the touring plan and have time left before the general public is admitted, sample early-entry attractions not included in the plan. Stop touring about ten minutes before the public is admitted and position yourself for the first attraction on the plan that wasn't open for early entry. During early entry in the Magic Kingdom, for example, you can usually experience Peter Pan's Flight and It's a Small World in Fantasyland, plus Space Mountain and *Stitch's Great Escape* in Tomorrowland. As official opening nears, go to the boundary between Fantasyland and Liberty Square, and be ready to blitz to Splash Mountain and Big Thunder Mountain according to the touring plan when the rest of the park opens.

Evening Extra Magic Hours, when a designated park remains open for Disney resort guests three hours beyond normal closing time, have less effect on the touring plans than early entry in the morning. Parks are almost never scheduled for both early entry and evening Extra Magic Hours on the same day. Thus a park offering evening Extra Magic Hours will enjoy a fairly normal morning and early afternoon. It's not until late afternoon, when park hoppers coming from the other theme parks descend, that the late-closing park will become especially crowded. By that time, you'll be well toward the end of your touring plan.

FASTPASS

IN 1999 DISNEY LAUNCHED A SYSTEM for moderating the wait at popular attractions. Called FASTPASS, it was originally tried at Animal Kingdom, then expanded to attractions at the other parks.

Here's how it works. Your handout park map and signage at attractions will tell you which attractions are included. Attractions operating FASTPASS will have a regular line and a FASTPASS line. A sign at the entrance will say how long the wait is in the regular line. If the wait is acceptable to you, hop in line. If it seems too long, insert your park admission pass into a FASTPASS machine and receive an appointment time (for later in the day) to return and ride. When you return at the designated time, you enter the FASTPASS line and proceed directly to the attraction's preshow or boarding area. Interestingly, this procedure was pioneered by Universal Studios Hollywood years ago and had been virtually ignored by theme parks since (Universal now has a reworked variation called Universal Express). The system works well, however, and can save a lot of waiting time. There's no extra charge to use FASTPASS.

FASTPASS is evolving, and attractions continue to be added and deleted from the lineup. Changes aside, here's an example of how to use FASTPASS. Say you have only one day to tour the Magic Kingdom. You arrive early and ride Space Mountain and Buzz Lightyear with minimal waits. Then you cross the park to Splash Mountain and find a substantial line. Because Splash Mountain is a FASTPASS attraction, you can insert your admission pass into the machine and receive an appointment to come back and ride, thus avoiding a long wait.

FASTPASS works remarkably well, mainly because FASTPASS holders get amazingly preferential treatment.

Bob

The effort to accommodate FASTPASS holders makes anyone in the regular line feel second class. And a telling indication of their status is that they're called "standby guests." Indeed, we watched people in regular lines despondently stand by and stand by, while dozens and sometimes hundreds of FASTPASS holders were ushered into the boarding area ahead of them. Disney is sending a message here: FASTPASS is heaven; anything else is limbo at best and probably purgatory. In any event, you'll think you've been in hell if you're stuck in the regular line during the hot, crowded part of the day.

Readers regularly send standby-line horror stories. Here's one from a Pequea, Pennsylvania, family:

> We, a group of four 12-year-olds and five adults, decided to ride Test Track when we arrived at Epcot at 11 a.m. FASTPASSes were being issued for [late that night] and the singles line was not open yet, so we decided to brave the 120-minute wait (at MK and MGM many waits ended up being less than the posted time). What a disaster! Once inside the building, the FASTPASS and singles line (which opened when we were very near the building) sped ahead while the standby line barely moved. After 3 hours and 20 minutes, we finally made it to the car! One man who was in the FASTPASS line said that he counted a 12:1 ratio between FASTPASSers and standby people being let into the [boarding] area. Disney needs to seriously reconsider their boarding policy!

FASTPASS doesn't eliminate the need to arrive early at a theme park. Because each park offers a limited number of FASTPASS attractions, you still need an early start if you want to see as much as possible in one day. Plus, there's a limited supply of FASTPASSes available for each attraction on any day. If you don't arrive until midafternoon, you might find that no more FASTPASSes are available. FASTPASS does make it possible to see more with less waiting, and it's a great benefit to those who like to sleep late or who choose an afternoon or evening at the parks on their arrival day. It also allows you to postpone wet rides, such as Kali River Rapids at Animal Kingdom or Splash Mountain at the Magic Kingdom, until a warmer time of day.

Understanding the FASTPASS System

The purpose of FASTPASS is to reduce the wait for designated attractions by distributing guests at those attractions throughout the day. This is accomplished by providing an incentive (a shorter wait) for guests willing to postpone experiencing the attraction until later in the day. The system also, in effect, imposes a penalty (standby status) on those who don't use it. However, spreading out guest arrivals sometimes also decreases the wait for standby guests.

When you insert your admission pass into a FASTPASS time clock, the machine spits out a slip of paper about two-thirds the size of a credit card—small enough to fit in your wallet but also small enough to lose easily. Printed on it is the attraction's name and a time window, for example 1:15 to 2:15 p.m., during which you can return to ride.

As a rule of thumb, the earlier in the day you secure a FASTPASS, the shorter the interval between time of issue and your one-hour return window.

Liliane

Returning to Ride

In practice, cast members are not very strict about enforcing the return window. They won't let you in before your window begins, but they'll usually admit you after your return window expires. We've used FASTPASSes more than three years old, and the worst we got was a snarky comment from the cast member minding the line. We'd estimate the probability of being denied entry at 10% or less—it's only happened a couple of times in many dozens of attempts.

At Disneyland in Anaheim the return window expiration time is ignored as a matter of policy, though Disneyland keeps this somewhat of a secret. In other words, a FASTPASS is good from the beginning of the return window until closing time. This is shaping up to be the actuality at Walt Disney World, even if not a matter of policy.

When you report back, you'll enter a line marked "FASTPASS Return" that routes you more or less directly to the boarding or preshow area. Each person in your party must have his own FASTPASS and be ready to show it at the entrance of the FASTPASS return line. Before you enter the boarding area or theater, another cast member will collect your FASTPASS.

Each person in your party must have his or her own FASTPASS.

Bob

Cast members are instructed to minimize waits for FASTPASS holders. Thus, if the FASTPASS return line is suddenly inundated (something that occurs by chance), cast members intervene to reduce the FASTPASS line. As many as 25 FASTPASS holders will be admitted for each standby guest until the FASTPASS line is reduced to an acceptable length. Although FASTPASS usually eliminates 80% or more of the wait you would experience in the regular line, you can still expect a short wait, usually less than 15 minutes and frequently under 10 minutes.

Obtaining a FASTPASS

You can ordinarily obtain a FASTPASS anytime after a park opens (some attractions are a little tardy getting their FASTPASS system up), but the FASTPASS return lines don't usually begin operating until 45 to 90 minutes after opening.

Whenever you obtain a FASTPASS, you can be assured of a period of time between when you receive your FASTPASS and when you report back. The interval can be as short as 15 minutes or as long as seven hours, depending on park attendance and the attraction's popularity and hourly capacity. Generally, the earlier in the day you obtain a FAST-PASS, the shorter the interval before your return window. If the park opens at 9 a.m. and you obtain a FASTPASS for Splash Mountain at 9:25 a.m., your appointment for returning to ride would be 10 to 11 a.m. or 10:10 to 11:10 a.m. The exact time will be determined by how many other guests have obtained FASTPASSes before you.

The fewer guests who obtain FASTPASSes for an attraction, the shorter the interval between receipt of your pass and the return window. Conversely, the more guests issued FASTPASSes, the longer the interval. If an attraction is exceptionally popular and/or its hourly capacity is relatively small, the return window might be pushed back almost to park closing time. When this happens the FASTPASS machines shut down and a sign is posted saying all FASTPASSes are gone for the day. It's not unusual, for example, for Test Track at Epcot or Winnie the Pooh at the Magic Kingdom to have distributed all available FASTPASSes by 1 p.m.

Rides routinely exhaust their daily FASTPASS supply, but shows almost never do. FASTPASS machines at theaters try to balance attendance at each show so that the audience for any given performance is divided about evenly between standby and FASTPASS guests. Consequently, standby guests for shows aren't discriminated against to the degree that standby guests for rides are. In practice, FASTPASS for shows also diminishes the wait for standby guests. With few exceptions, the standby line at theater attractions requires less waiting than using FASTPASS.

When to Use FASTPASS

Except as discussed below, there's no reason to use FASTPASS during the first 30 to 40 minutes a park is open. Lines for most attractions are manageable during this period, and this is the only time of day when FASTPASS attractions exclusively serve those in the regular line.

Using FASTPASS requires two trips to the same attraction: one to obtain the pass and another to use it. You must invest time to obtain the pass (sometimes FASTPASS machines have lines!), then interrupt your touring later to backtrack to use your FASTPASS. The additional time, effort, and touring modification are justified only if you can save more than 30 minutes. Don't forget: even the FASTPASS line requires some waiting.

Eight attractions build lines so quickly in the morning that failing to queue up within the first six or so minutes of operation will mean a long wait: Test Track, Soarin', and Mission: Space (Epcot); Kilimanjaro Safaris and Expedition Everest (Animal Kingdom); Space Mountain (Magic Kingdom); and Tower of Terror and Rock 'n' Roller Coaster (Disney-MGM Studios). With these, you should race directly to the attractions when the park opens or obtain a FASTPASS.

Another four FASTPASS attractions—Splash Mountain, Winnie the Pooh, Peter Pan's Flight, and Jungle Cruise in the Magic Kingdom—develop long lines within 30 to 50 minutes of park opening. If you can get to them before the wait becomes intolerable, great. Otherwise, your options are FASTPASS or a long wait.

Regardless of the time of day, if the wait in the regular line at a FASTPASS attraction is 25 to 30 minutes or less, join the regular line.

Bob

You can obtain a second FASTPASS at a time printed on the bottom of your most recent FASTPASS, usually two hours or less from the time the first was issued. Always check the posted return time before obtaining a FASTPASS. If the return time is hours away, forgo FASTPASS. Especially in the Magic Kingdom, there will be other FASTPASS attractions where the return time is only an hour or so away.

When obtaining FASTPASSes, it's quicker and more considerate if one person obtains passes for your entire party. This means entrusting one individual with your valuable park-admission passes and your FASTPASSes, so choose wisely.

Obtain FASTPASSes for all members of your party, including those who are too short, too young, or simply not interested in riding, as this family of four recommends:

Utilize the FASTPASSes of people in your group who don't want to ride. Our 6-year-old didn't want to ride anything rough. All four of us got FASTPASSes for each ride. [When] the 6-year-old didn't want to ride, my husband and I took turns riding with the 12-year-old. It was our version of the FASTPASS child swap, and the 12-year-old got double rides.

FASTPASS Guidelines

- Don't mess with FASTPASS unless it can save you 30 minutes or more.
- If you arrive after a park opens, obtain a FASTPASS for your preferred FASTPASS attraction first thing.
- Do not obtain a FASTPASS for a theater attraction until you have experienced all the FASTPASS rides on your itinerary. (Using FASTPASS at theater attractions usually requires more time than using the standby line.)
- Check the FASTPASS return time before obtaining a FASTPASS.
- Obtain FASTPASSes for Rock 'n' Roller Coaster at Disney-MGM Studios; Mission: Space, Soarin,' and Test Track at Epcot; Expedition Everest at the

> Animal Kingdom; and Winnie the Pooh, Peter Pan's Flight, Space Mountain, and Splash Mountain at the Magic Kingdom as early in the day as possible.

- Try to obtain FASTPASSes for rides not mentioned by 1 p.m.

- Don't depend on FASTPASSes being available after 2 p.m. during busier times.

- Make sure everyone in your party has his or her own FASTPASS.

- You can obtain a second FASTPASS at the time printed at the bottom of your first FASTPASS.

- Note your FASTPASS return slot, and plan activities accordingly.

A WORD ABOUT DISNEY THRILL RIDES

READERS OF ALL AGES SHOULD ATTEMPT to be open-minded about the so-called Disney "thrill rides." In comparison with rides at other theme parks, most Disney thrill attractions are quite tame, with more emphasis on sights, atmosphere, and special effects than on the motion, speed, or feel of the ride itself. While we suggest you take Disney's preride warnings seriously, we can tell you that guests of all ages report enjoying rides such as Tower of Terror, Big Thunder Mountain, and Splash Mountain.

A reader from Washington sums up the situation well:

> *Our boys and I are used to imagining typical amusement park rides when it comes to roller coasters. So, when we thought of Big Thunder Mountain and Space Mountain, what came to mind was gigantic hills, upside-down loops, huge vertical drops, etc. I actually hate roller coasters, especially the unpleasant sensation of a long drop, and I have never taken a ride that loops you upside down.*
>
> *In fact, the Disney [rides] are tame in comparison. There are never any long and steep hills (except Splash Mountain, and it is there for anyone to see, so you have informed consent going on the ride). I was able to build up courage to go on all of them, and the more I rode them the more I enjoyed them—the less you tense up expecting a big long drop, the more you enjoy the special effects and even swinging around curves. Swinging around curves is really the primary motion challenge of Disney roller coasters.*

Disney, recognizing that it needs more attractions that appeal to the youth and young adult markets, has added some roller coasters to its parks. The Rock 'n' Roller Coaster at the Disney-MGM Studios, and Expedition Everest at the Animal Kingdom, for example, incorporate at least some of the features our Washington reader seeks to avoid.

A WORD ABOUT HEIGHT REQUIREMENTS

A NUMBER OF ATTRACTIONS REQUIRE children to meet minimum height and age requirements. If you have children too short or too young to ride, you have several options, including switching off (described on page 220). Although the alternatives may resolve some practical and logistic issues, be forewarned that your smaller children might nonetheless be resentful of their older (or taller) siblings who qualify to ride. A mom from Virginia bumped into just such a situation, writing:

> You mention height requirements for rides but not the intense sibling jealousy this can generate. Frontierland was a real problem in that respect. Our very petite 5-year-old, to her outrage, was stuck hanging around while our 8-year-old went on Splash Mountain and [Big] Thunder Mountain with Grandma and Granddad, and the nearby alternatives weren't helpful [too long a line for rafts to Tom Sawyer Island, etc.]. If we had thought ahead, we would have left the younger kid back in Mickey's Toontown with one of the grown-ups for another roller coaster ride or two and then met up later at a designated point. The best areas had a playground or other quick attractions for short people near the rides with height requirements, like The Boneyard near the dinosaur ride at the Animal Kingdom.

The reader makes a valid point, though in practical terms splitting the group and meeting later can be more complicated that she might imagine. If you choose to split up, ask the Disney greeter at the entrance to the attraction(s) with height requirements how long the wait is. Tack five minutes for riding onto the anticipated wait, and then add five or so minutes to exit and reach the meeting point for an approximate sense of how long the younger kids (and their supervising adult) will have to do other stuff. Our guess is that even with a long line for the rafts, the reader would have had more than sufficient time to take her daughter to Tom Sawyer Island while the sibs rode Splash Mountain and Big Thunder Mountain with the grandparents. For sure she had time to tour the Swiss Family Treehouse in adjacent Adventureland.

WAITING-LINE STRATEGIES FOR ADULTS WITH YOUNG CHILDREN

CHILDREN HOLD UP BETTER THROUGH THE DAY if you minimize the time they spend in lines. Arriving early and using our touring plans immensely reduces waiting. Here are additional ways to reduce stress for children:

1. LINE GAMES Wise parents anticipate restlessness in line and plan activities to reduce the stress and boredom. In the morning, have waiting children discuss what they want to see and do during the day. Later, watch for and count Disney characters or play simple guessing games like 20 Questions. Lines move continuously, so games requiring pen and paper are impractical. The holding area of a theater attraction, however, is a different story. Here, tic-tac-toe, hangman, drawing, and coloring make the time fly by. As an alternative we've provided a trivia game for each park developed by Walt Disney World trivia guru Lou Mongello, author of the *Walt Disney World Trivia Book, Volumes 1 and 2*; see **www.intrepidtraveler.com.**

2. LAST-MINUTE ENTRY If an attraction can accommodate an unusually large number of people at once, it's often unnecessary to stand in line. The Magic Kingdom's *Liberty Belle* Riverboat is a good example. The boat holds about 450 people, usually more than are waiting in line. Instead of standing uncomfortably in a crowd, grab a snack and sit in the shade until the boat arrives and loading is under way. After the line is almost gone, join it.

At large-capacity theaters like that for Epcot's *The American Adventure,* ask the entrance greeter how long it will be until guests are admitted for the next show. If it's 15 minutes or more, take a restroom break or get a snack, returning a few minutes before the show starts. You aren't allowed to carry food or drink into the attraction, so make sure you have time to finish your snack.

ATTRACTIONS YOU CAN USUALLY ENTER AT THE LAST MINUTE	
Magic Kingdom	
Liberty Square	*The Hall of Presidents*
	Liberty Belle Riverboat
Epcot	
Future World	*The Circle of Life* (except during mealtimes)
World Showcase	*Reflections of China*
The American Adventure	*O Canada!*
Disney-MGM Studios	
Sounds Dangerous	Backlot Tour
Animal Kingdom	
Flights of Wonder	*Pocohontas and Her Forest Friends*

3. THE HAIL MARY PASS Certain lines are configured to allow you and your smaller children to pass under the rail to join your partner just before actual boarding or entry. This technique allows children and one adult to rest, snack, or go to the potty while another adult or older sibling stands in line. Other guests are very understanding about this strategy when used for young children. You're likely to meet hostile opposition, however, if you try to pass older children or more than one adult under the rail. To preempt hostility, tell the folks behind you in line what you are doing and why.

4. SWITCHING OFF (aka The Baby Swap) Several attractions have minimum height and/or age requirements, usually 40 to 48 inches tall to ride with an adult, or age 7 *and* 40 inches to ride alone. Some couples with children too small or too young forgo these attractions, while others take turns to ride. Missing some of Disney's best rides is an unnecessary sacrifice, and waiting in line twice for the same ride is a tremendous waste of time.

ATTRACTIONS WHERE YOU CAN USUALLY COMPLETE A HAIL MARY PASS	
Magic Kingdom	
Adventureland	Swiss Family Treehouse
Frontierland	*Country Bear Jamboree*
Fantasyland	Mad Tea Party
Snow White's Scary Adventures	Dumbo the Flying Elephant
Cinderella's Golden Carousel	Peter Pan's Flight
Epcot Future World	
Spaceship Earth	Living with the Land
Disney-MGM Studios	
Sounds Dangerous	*Indiana Jones Epic Stunt Spectacular!*
Animal Kingdom	
DinoLand U.S.A.	TriceraTop Spin

Instead, take advantage of the "switching off" option, also called "The Baby Swap." To switch off, there must be at least two adults. Everybody waits in line together, adults and children. When you reach an attendant (called a "greeter"), tell him or her that you want to switch off. The greeter will allow everyone, including the young children, to enter the attraction. When you reach the loading area, one adult rides while the other stays with the kids. Then the riding adult disembarks and takes charge of the children while the other adult rides. A third adult in the party can ride twice, once with each

ATTRACTIONS WHERE SWITCHING OFF IS COMMON	
Magic Kingdom	
Tomorrowland	Space Mountain
Frontierland	Splash Mountain
	Big Thunder Mountain Railroad
Epcot Future World	
Body Wars	Test Track
Mission: Space	Soarin'
Disney-MGM Studios	
Star Tours	*The Twilight Zone* Tower of Terror
Rock 'n' Roller Coaster	
Animal Kingdom	
DinoLand U.S.A.	Dinosaur
Asia	Expedition Everest
Kali River Rapids	Primeval Whirl

Attraction and Ride Restrictions

MAGIC KINGDOM

Big Thunder Mountain Railroad	40" minimum height
Goofy's Barnstormer	35" minimum height
Mickey's Toontown Fair playground attractions	40" maximum height
Space Mountain	44" minimum height
Splash Mountain	40" minimum height
Stitch's Great Escape	40" minimum height
Tomorrowland Indy Speedway	52" minimum height (to drive unassisted)

EPCOT

Body Wars	40" minimum height
Mission: Space	44" minimum height
Soarin'	40" minimum height
Test Track	40" minimum height

DISNEY-MGM STUDIOS

Honey, I Shrunk the Kids Movie Set Adventure	4 years minimum age
Rock 'n' Roller Coaster	48" minimum height
Star Tours	40" minimum height
Tower of Terror	40" minimum height

ANIMAL KINGDOM

Dinosaur	40" minimum height
Expedition Everest	44" minimum height
Kali River Rapids	38" minimum height

of the switching off adults, so that the switching off adults don't have to experience the attraction alone.

On many FASTPASS attractions, Disney handles switching off somewhat differently. When you tell the cast member that you want to switch off, he or she will issue you a special "rider exchange" FASTPASS good for three people. One parent and the nonriding child (or children) will at that point be asked to leave the line. When those riding reunite with the waiting adult, the waiting adult and two other persons from the party can ride using the special FASTPASS. This system eliminates confusion and congestion at the boarding area while sparing the nonriding adult and child the tedium and physical exertion of waiting in line.

Attractions at which switching off is practiced are oriented to more mature guests. Sometimes it takes a lot of courage for a child just to move through the queue holding dad's hand. In the boarding area, many children suddenly fear abandonment as one parent leaves to experience the attraction. Unless your children are prepared for switching

ANIMAL KINGDOM (CONTINUED)	
Primeval Whirl	48" minimum height
BLIZZARD BEACH WATER PARK	
Chair Lift	32" minimum height
Crush 'n' Gusher	48" minimum height
Downhill Double Dipper slide	48" minimum height
Slush Gusher slide	48" minimum height
Summit Plummet slide	48" minimum height
T-Bar (in Ski Patrol Training Camp)	48" maximum height
Tike's Peak children's area	48" maximum height
TYPHOON LAGOON WATER PARK	
Humunga Kowabunga slide	48" minimum height
Ketchakiddee Creek children's area	48" maximum height
Mayday Falls raft ride	48" minimum height
Shark Reef saltwater reef swim	10 years minimum age unless accompanied by an adult
Wave Pool	Adult supervision required
DISNEY QUEST	
Buzz Lightyear's AstroBlasters	51" minimum height
CyberSpace Mountain	51" minimum height
Mighty Ducks Pinball Slam	48" minimum height
Pirates of the Caribbean	35" minimum height

off, you might have an emotional crisis on your hands. A mom from Edison, New Jersey, advises:

> Once my son came to understand that the switch-off would not leave him abandoned, he did not seem to mind. I would recommend to your readers that they practice the switch off on some dry runs at home, so that their child is not concerned that he will be left behind. At the very least, the procedure could be explained in advance so that the little ones know what to expect.

Finally, a mother from Ada, Michigan, who discovered that the procedure for switching off varies from attraction to attraction, offered this suggestion:

> Parents need to tell the very first attendant they come to that they would like to switch off. Each attraction has a different procedure for this. Tell every other attendant too, because they forget quickly.

5. LAST-MINUTE COLD FEET If your young child gets cold feet just before boarding a ride where there is no age or height requirement, you usually can arrange with the loading attendant for a switch off. This is common at Pirates of the Caribbean, where children lose their courage while winding through the dungeon-like waiting area. Additionally, no law says you *have* to ride. If you reach the boarding area and someone is unhappy, tell an attendant you've changed your mind and you'll be shown the way out.

6. CATCH-22 AT TOMORROWLAND SPEEDWAY Though Tomorrowland Speedway is a great treat for young children, they're required to be 52 inches tall in order to drive unassisted. Few children ages 6 and younger measure up, so the ride is essentially withheld from the very age group that would most enjoy it. To resolve this catch-22, go on the ride with your small child. The attendants will assume that you will drive. After getting into the car, shift your child over behind the steering wheel. From your position, you will still be able to control the foot pedals. Children will feel like they're really driving, and because the car travels on a self-guiding track, there's no way they can make a mistake while steering.

CHARACTER ANALYSIS

THE LARGE AND FRIENDLY COSTUMED VERSIONS of Mickey, Minnie, Donald, Goofy, and others—known as "Disney characters"—provide a link between Disney animated films and the theme parks. To people emotionally invested, the characters in Disney films are as real as next-door neighbors, never mind that they're just drawings on plastic. In recent years, theme park personifications of the characters also have become real to us. It's not just a person in a mouse costume we see; it is Mickey himself. Similarly, meeting Goofy or Snow White in Fantasyland is an encounter with a celebrity, a memory to be treasured.

Liliane

When my son was 3 years old he was nuts to meet Cinderella. Like so many moms before me, I stood in line at Cinderella Castle to meet her [this was before you had to buy a meal to meet Cinderella]. The wait was long, and when it was finally our turn my boy had fallen asleep. Oh, the agony! Should I wake him? Should I leave the mission unaccomplished? Well, in the end Cinderella came to the rescue. She smiled and asked me to sit down for a chat. She signed my son's autograph book and said, "Tell him to look for me waving at him tonight at the evening parade." And wave she did. I am not even sure it was the same Cinderella but my son was convinced it was and believed that he had met Cinderella, albeit in his dreams.

While there are hundreds of Disney animated film characters, only about 250 have been brought to life in costume. Of these, a relatively small number (less than a fifth) are "greeters" (characters who mix with guests). The remaining characters perform in shows or parades. Originally confined to the Magic Kingdom, characters are now found in all the major theme parks and Disney hotels.

If your children can't enjoy things until they see Mickey, ask a cast member where to find him. If the cast member doesn't know right away, he or she can find out quickly. Cast members have a number they can call to learn exactly where the characters are at any time.

CHARACTER WATCHING

CHARACTER WATCHING HAS BECOME A PASTIME. Families once were content to meet characters only occasionally and by chance. They now pursue them relentlessly, armed with autograph books and cameras. Because some characters are only rarely seen, character watching has become character collecting. (To cash in on character collecting, Disney sells autograph books throughout the World.) Mickey, Minnie, and Goofy are a snap to bag; they seem to be everywhere. But Jiminy Cricket seldom comes out. Other characters appear regularly, but only in a location consistent with their starring role. Cinderella, predictably, reigns at Cinderella Castle in Fantasyland, while Brer Fox and Brer Bear frolic in Frontierland near Splash Mountain.

A Brooklyn dad thinks the character autograph–hunting craze has gotten out of hand, complaining:

> Whoever started the practice of collecting autographs from the characters should be subjected to Chinese water torture! We went to Walt Disney World 11 years ago, with an 8-year-old and an 11-year-old. We would bump into characters, take pictures, and that was it. After a while, our children noticed that some of the other children were getting autographs. We managed to avoid joining in during our first day at the Magic Kingdom and our first day at Epcot, but by day three our children were collecting autographs. However, it did not get too out of hand, since it was limited to accidental character meeting.
>
> This year when we took our youngest child (who is now age 8), he had already seen his siblings' collection and was determined to outdo them. However, rather than random meetings, the characters are now available practically all day long at different locations, according to a printed schedule, which our son was old enough to read. We spent more time standing in line for autographs than we did for the most popular rides!

A family from Birmingham, Alabama, found some benefit in their children's relentless pursuit of characters, writing:

> We had no idea we would be caught up in this madness, but after my daughters grabbed your guidebook to get Pocahontas to sign it (we

*had no blank paper), we quickly bought a Disney autograph book
and gave in. It was actually the highlight of their trip, and my son
even got into the act by helping get places in line for his sisters. They
LOVED looking for characters (I think it has all been planned by
Kodak to sell film). The possibility of seeing a new character revived
my 7-year-old's energy on many occasions. It was an amazing,
totally unexpected part of our visit.*

"THEN SOME CONFUSION HAPPENED" Young children sometimes
become lost at character encounters. Usually, there's a lot of activity
around a character, with both adults and children touching it or posing for pictures. Most commonly, mom and dad stay in the crowd
while Junior approaches to meet the character. In the excitement and
with people milling and the char-
acter moving around, Junior
heads off in the wrong direction
to look for mom and dad. In the
words of a Salt Lake City mom:
"Milo was shaking hands with
Dopey one minute, then some
confusion happened and [Milo]
was gone." Families with several young children and parents who are
busy with cameras can lose track of a youngster in a heartbeat.

> Our advice for parents
> with preschoolers is to
> stay with the kids when
> they meet characters,
> stepping back only to
> take a quick picture.

Bob

CHARACTER DINING: WHAT TO EXPECT

CHARACTER DINING HAS BECOME SO POPULAR that Disney offers
character breakfasts, brunches, lunches, and dinners where families can
dine in the presence of Mickey, Minnie, Goofy, and other costumed versions of animated celebrities. Besides grabbing customers from
Denny's and Hardee's, character meals provide a controlled setting in
which young children can warm to the characters. All meals are at-
tended by several characters. Adult prices apply to persons age 10 or
older, children's prices to kids ages 3 to 9. Children younger than 3
years eat free. For more information on character dining, call ☎ 407-
WDW-DINE (407-939-3463).

Because character dining is very popular, arrange Advance Reservations as early as possible by calling ☎ 407-WDW-DINE. Advance
Reservations aren't reservations, per se, only a commitment to seat
you ahead of walk-in patrons at the scheduled date and time. At very
popular character meals like the breakfast at Cinderella's Royal
Table, you are required to make a for-real reservation and to guarantee it with a for-real deposit.

Character meals are bustling affairs held in hotels' or theme
parks' largest full-service restaurants. Character breakfasts offer a
fixed menu served individually, family-style, or on a buffet. The typical breakfast includes scrambled eggs; bacon, sausage, and ham;
hash browns; waffles or French toast; biscuits, rolls, or pastries; and

fruit. With family-style service, the meal is served in large skillets or on platters at your table. Seconds (or thirds) are free at both family-service and fixed-menu character meals. Buffets offer much the same fare, but you fetch it yourself.

Character dinners range from a set menu served family-style to buffets or ordering off the menu. The character dinner at the Magic Kingdom's Liberty Tree Tavern, for example, is served family-style and consists of turkey, ham, marinated flank steak, salad, mashed potatoes, green vegetables, and, for kids, macaroni and cheese. Dessert is extra. Character dinner buffets, such as those at 1900 Park Fare at the Grand Floridian and Chef Mickey's at the Contemporary Resort, offer separate adults' and children's serving lines. Typically, the children's buffet includes hamburgers, hot dogs, pizza, fish sticks, fried chicken nuggets, macaroni and cheese, and peanut-butter-and-jelly sandwiches. Selections at the adult buffet usually include prime rib or other carved meat, baked or broiled Florida seafood, pasta, chicken, an ethnic dish or two, vegetables, potatoes, and salad.

At all meals characters circulate around the room while you eat. During your meal, each of the three to five characters present will visit your table, arriving one at a time to cuddle the kids (and sometimes the adults), pose for photos, and sign autographs. Keep autograph books (with pens) and loaded cameras handy. For the best photos, adults should sit across the table from their children. Seat the children where characters can easily reach them. If a table is against a wall, for example, adults should sit with their backs to the wall and children on the aisle.

At some larger restaurants, including 'Ohana at the Polynesian Resort and Chef Mickey's at the Contemporary, character meals involve impromptu parades of characters and children around the room, group singing, napkin waving, and other organized mayhem.

Servers don't rush you to leave after you've eaten—you can stay as long as you wish to enjoy the characters. Remember, however, that lots of eager kids and adults are waiting not so patiently to be admitted.

When to Go

Attending a character breakfast usually prevents you from arriving at the theme parks in time for opening. Because early morning is best for touring and you don't want to burn daylight lingering over breakfast, we suggest the following:

1. Go to a character dinner or lunch instead of breakfast; it won't conflict with your touring schedule.

2. Substitute a late character breakfast for lunch. Have a light breakfast early from room service or your cooler to tide you over. Then tour the theme park for an hour or two before breaking off around 10:15 a.m. to go to the character breakfast. Make a big brunch of your character breakfast and skip lunch. You should be fueled until dinner.

3. Go on your arrival or departure day. The day you arrive and check in is usually good for a character dinner. Settle at your hotel, swim, then dine with the characters. This strategy has the added benefit of exposing your children to the characters before chance encounters at the parks. Some children, moreover, won't settle down to enjoy the parks until they have seen Mickey. Departure day also is good for a character meal. Schedule a character breakfast on your check-out day before you head for the airport or begin your drive home.

4. Go on a rest day. If you plan to stay five or more days, you'll probably take a day or half day from touring to rest or do something else. These are perfect days for a character meal.

How to Choose a Character Meal

Many readers ask for advice about character meals. This question from a Waterloo, Iowa, mom is typical:

Are all character breakfasts pretty much the same, or are some better than others? How should I go about choosing one?

In fact, some are better, sometimes much better. When we evaluate character meals, we look for these things:

1. **THE CHARACTERS** The meals offer a diverse assortment of characters. Select a meal that features your kids' favorites. Check out our Character-meal Hit Parade chart (pages 230–231) to see which characters are assigned to each meal. With the exception of 1900 Park Fare at

"Casting? There's been a mistake. We were supposed to get the Assorted Character Package with one Mickey, one Goofy, one Donald . . . ."

Character-meal Hit Parade

1. CINDERELLA'S ROYAL TABLE

LOCATION	Magic Kingdom
MEALS SERVED	Breakfast/lunch/dinner
CHARACTERS	Cinderella, Snow White, Belle, Jasmine, Aladdin, the Fairy Godmother (dinner)
SERVED	Daily
SETTING	★★★★★
TYPE OF SERVICE	Family-style at breakfast; set menu (all you care to eat) at lunch and dinner
FOOD VARIETY AND QUALITY	★★★
NOISE LEVEL	Quiet
CHARACTER-TO-GUEST RATIO	1:26

2. AKERSHUS ROYAL BANQUET HALL

LOCATION	Epcot
MEALS SERVED	Breakfast/lunch/dinner
CHARACTERS	4–6 characters chosen from Belle, Mulan, Snow White, Sleeping Beauty, Esmeralda, Mary Poppins, Jasmine, Pocahontas
SERVED	Daily
SETTING	★★★★
TYPE OF SERVICE	Family-style and menu (all you care to eat)
FOOD VARIETY AND QUALITY	★★★½
NOISE LEVEL	Quiet
CHARACTER-TO-GUEST RATIO	1:54

3. CHEF MICKEY'S

LOCATION	Contemporary
MEALS SERVED	Breakfast/dinner
CHARACTERS	*Breakfast:* Minnie, Mickey, Chip, Pluto, Goofy *Dinner:* Mickey, Pluto, Chip, Dale, Goofy
SERVED	Daily
SETTING	★★★
TYPE OF SERVICE	Buffet
FOOD VARIETY AND QUALITY	★★★ (breakfast) ★★★ (dinner)
NOISE LEVEL	Loud
CHARACTER-TO-GUEST RATIO	1:56

7. LIBERTY TREE TAVERN

LOCATION	Magic Kingdom
MEALS SERVED	Dinner
CHARACTERS	Minnie, Pluto, Donald Duck, Meeko, Chip and/or Dale
SERVED	Daily
SETTING	★★★½
TYPE OF SERVICE	Family-style
FOOD VARIETY AND QUALITY	★★★
NOISE LEVEL	Moderate
CHARACTER-TO-GUEST RATIO	1:26

8. RESTAURANTOSAURUS

LOCATION	Animal Kingdom
MEALS SERVED	Breakfast
CHARACTERS	Mickey, Donald, Pluto, Goofy
SERVED	Daily
SETTING	★★★
TYPE OF SERVICE	Buffet
FOOD VARIETY AND QUALITY	★★★
NOISE LEVEL	Very loud
CHARACTER-TO-GUEST RATIO	1:112

9. CAPE MAY CAFE

LOCATION	Beach Club
MEALS SERVED	Breakfast
CHARACTERS	Goofy, Chip, Dale, Pluto
SERVED	Daily
SETTING	★★★
TYPE OF SERVICE	Buffet
FOOD VARIETY AND QUALITY	★★½
NOISE LEVEL	Moderate
CHARACTER-TO-GUEST RATIO	1:67

13. GARDEN GROVE CAFE

LOCATION	Swan
MEALS SERVED	Breakfast
CHARACTERS	Goofy and Pluto
SERVED	Saturday and Sunday
SETTING	★★★
TYPE OF SERVICE	Buffet/Menu
FOOD VARIETY AND QUALITY	★★★½
NOISE LEVEL	Moderate
CHARACTER-TO-GUEST RATIO	1:198

4. CRYSTAL PALACE

LOCATION	Magic Kingdom
MEALS SERVED	Breakfast/lunch/dinner
CHARACTERS	*Breakfast:* Pooh, Tigger, Eeyore, Piglet
	Dinner: Pooh, Tigger, Eeyore
SERVED	Daily
SETTING	★★★
TYPE OF SERVICE	Buffet
FOOD VARIETY AND QUALITY	★★½ (breakfast) ★★★½ (dinner)
NOISE LEVEL	Very loud
CHARACTER-TO-GUEST RATIO	1:67 (breakfast) 1:89 (dinner)

5. 1900 PARK FARE

LOCATION	Grand Floridian
MEALS SERVED	Breakfast/dinner
CHARACTERS	*Breakfast:* Mary Poppins and friends
	Dinner: Cinderella and friends
SERVED	Daily
SETTING	★★★
TYPE OF SERVICE	Buffet
FOOD VARIETY AND QUALITY	★★★ (breakfast) ★★★ (dinner)
NOISE LEVEL	Moderate
CHARACTER-TO-GUEST RATIO	1:54 (breakfast) 1:44 (dinner)

6. GARDEN GRILL

LOCATION	Epcot
MEALS SERVED	Lunch/dinner
CHARACTERS	Chip 'n' Dale
SERVED	Daily
SETTING	★★★★½
TYPE OF SERVICE	Family-style
FOOD VARIETY AND QUALITY	★★½
NOISE LEVEL	Very quiet
CHARACTER-TO-GUEST RATIO	1:46

10. 'OHANA

LOCATION	Polynesian Resort
MEALS SERVED	Breakfast
CHARACTERS	Mickey, Pluto, Lilo, Stitch
SERVED	Daily
SETTING	★★
TYPE OF SERVICE	Family-style
FOOD VARIETY AND QUALITY	★★½
NOISE LEVEL	Moderate
CHARACTER-TO-GUEST RATIO	1:57

11. HOLLYWOOD & VINE

LOCATION	Disney-MGM Studios
MEALS SERVED	Breakfast/lunch
CHARACTERS	JoJo, Goliath, June, Leo
SERVED	Daily
SETTING	★★½
TYPE OF SERVICE	Buffet
FOOD VARIETY AND QUALITY	★★★
NOISE LEVEL	Moderate
CHARACTER-TO-GUEST RATIO	1:71

12. GULLIVER'S GRILL

LOCATION	Swan
MEALS SERVED	Dinner
CHARACTERS	Goofy and Pluto or Rafiki and Timon
SERVED	Daily
SETTING	★★★
TYPE OF SERVICE	Buffet
FOOD VARIETY AND QUALITY	★★★½
NOISE LEVEL	Moderate
CHARACTER-TO-GUEST RATIO	1:198

the Grand Floridian, most restaurants stick with the same characters. Even so, check the lineup when you call to make Advance Reservations.

A mom from Michigan offers this report:

Our character meal at 1900 Park Fare was a DISASTER!!! Please warn other readers with younger children that if they make Advance Reservations and the characters are villains, they may want to rethink their options. We went for my daughter's fifth birthday, and she was scared to death. The Queen of Hearts chased her sobbing and screaming down the hallway. Most young children we saw at the dinner were very frightened. Captain Hook and Prince John were laid-back, but Governor Ratcliff (from Pocahontas) and the Queen were amazingly rude and intimidating.

The villains have abdicated 1900 Park Fare in favor of more benign characters, but you never know where the baddies might show up next. Moral? Call before making Advance Reservations and ask with which characters you'll be dining.

2. **ATTENTION FROM THE CHARACTERS** At all character meals, characters circulate among guests, hugging children, posing for pictures, and signing autographs. How much time a character spends with you and your children depends primarily on the ratio of characters to guests. The more characters and fewer guests, the better. Because many character meals never fill to capacity, the character-to-guest ratios found in our Character-meal Hit Parade chart (pages 230–231) have been adjusted to reflect an average attendance. Even so, there's quite a range. The best ratio is at Cinderella's Royal Table, where there's approximately one character to every 26 guests.

Many kids take special delight in meeting the "face characters," such as Jasmine, Aladdin, and Cinderella, who can speak to them and engage them in a way that the mute animal characters can't.

Liliane

The worst ratio is at Gulliver's Grill–Garden Grove Cafe at the Swan Resort. Here, there's only one character for every 198 guests. In practical terms, this means your family will get eight times as much attention from characters at Cinderella's Royal Table as from those at Gulliver's Grill–Garden Grove Cafe.

3. **THE SETTING** Some character meals are in exotic settings. For others, moving the event to an elementary-school cafeteria would be an improvement. Our chart rates each meal's setting with the familiar scale of zero (worst) to five (best) stars. Two restaurants, Cinderella's Royal Table in the Magic Kingdom and the Garden Grill in the Land Pavilion at Epcot, deserve special mention. Cinderella's Royal Table is on the first and second floors of Cinderella Castle in Fantasyland, offering guests a look inside the castle. The Garden Grill is a revolving restaurant overlooking several

scenes from the Living with The Land boat ride. Also at Epcot, the popular Princesses Character Breakfast is held in the castlelike Akershus Royal Banquet Hall. Though Chef Mickey's at the Contemporary Resort is rather sterile in appearance, it affords a great view of the monorail running through the hotel. Themes and settings of the remaining character-meal venues, while apparent to adults, will be lost on most children.

4. **THE FOOD** Although some food served at character meals is quite good, most is average (palatable but nothing to get excited about). In variety, consistency, and quality, restaurants generally do a better job with breakfast than with lunch or dinner (if served). Some restaurants offer a buffet, while others opt for "one-skillet" family-style service, in which all hot items are served from the same pot or skillet. To help you sort it out, we rate the food at each character meal in our chart using the five-star scale.

5. **THE PROGRAM** Some larger restaurants stage modest performances where the characters dance, head-up a parade around the room, or lead songs and cheers. For some guests, these activities give the meal a celebratory air; for others, they turn what was already mayhem into absolute chaos. Either way, the antics consume time the characters could spend with families at their table.

6. **NOISE** If you want to eat in peace, character meals are a bad choice. That said, some are much noisier than others. Our chart gives you an idea of what to expect.

7. **WHICH MEAL** Although breakfasts seem to be most popular, character lunches and dinners are usually more practical because they don't interfere with early-morning touring. During hot weather, a character lunch can be heavenly.

8. **COST** Dinners cost more than lunches, and lunches are more than breakfasts. Prices for any meal vary about $14–$24 from the least expensive to the most expensive restaurant. Breakfasts run $17 to $32 for adults and $9 to $22 for ages 3 to 9. For character lunches, expect to pay $21 to $34 for adults and $12 to $23 for kids. Dinners are $25 to $49 for adults and $11 to $14 for children. Little ones 2 years and younger eat free. The meals at the high end of the price range are at Cinderella's Royal Table, located in the castle at the Magic Kingdom. The reasons for the sky-high prices are (1) Cinderella's Royal Table is small but in great demand, and (2) the price includes a set of photos of your group taken by a Disney photographer. Unlike other venues where photographers circulate and offer to take your picture for a price, at Cinderella's it's buy the photos or hit the road.

9. **ADVANCE RESERVATIONS** The Disney dining reservations system makes Advance Reservations for character meals up to 180 days before you wish to dine. Advance Reservations for most character meals are easy to obtain even if you call only a couple of weeks before you leave home. Breakfast and lunch at Cinderella's Royal Table are another story. To eat at Cinderella's, you'll need our strategy as well as help from Congress and the Pope.

Liliane

If you've secured Advance Reservations for a character meal, I say roll out the costume chest. Dress up your little tyke—from princess to pirate, everything goes. As a matter of fact. if your little princess wants to wear her princess dress when visiting the Magic Kingdom for the first time, indulge her. And don't worry about the unavoidable food landing on the precious dress; that is what stain removers are for. Besides, if not today, when?

10. **HOMELESS CHARACTERS**   Disney periodically pulls the plug on one or another of the character meals. Reconfirm all character-meal Advance Reservations three weeks or so before you leave home by calling ☎ 407-WDW-DINE.

11. **FRIENDS AND PALS**   For some venues, Disney has stopped specifying characters scheduled for a particular meal. Instead, they say it's a certain character "and friends (or pals)." For example, "Pooh and friends," meaning Eeyore, Piglet, and Tigger, or some combination thereof, or "Mickey's pals" with some assortment chosen among Minnie, Goofy, Pluto, Donald, and Daisy. Most are self-evident, but others such as "Mary Poppins and friends" are unclear. Who knows with whom Mary Poppins hangs out? (Don't expect Dick van Dyke.)

Boosting Sales of Mementos and Souvenirs

Usually when Disney sees a horse carrying moneybags, it rides it until it drops. Disney's latest scheme of bundling photos and souvenirs in the price of character meals at Cinderella's Royal Table is probably something we'll see again at other venues. Adding photos of your group taken by a Disney photographer is Disney's justification for raising the price of the character meals by about 60%. Disney insists that you're getting the photos at a bargain price. This is well and good if you're in the market, but if buying photos was not in your plans, well, they've gotcha. It's a matter of some conjecture how far Disney will run with this idea. Maybe next year the price will be $200 and include fanciful medieval costumes for your entire party (charges for the changing room and locker to store your street clothes not included).

CINDERELLA'S ROYAL TABLE

CINDERELLA'S ROYAL TABLE, IN CINDERELLA CASTLE in the Magic Kingdom, hosts the obsessively popular character breakfast starring Cinderella and a number of other Disney princesses. Admittedly, the toughest ticket at Disney World is an Advance Reservation for this character meal. Why? Cinderella's Royal Table is Disney's tiniest character-meal restaurant, accommodating only about 130 diners at a time. Demand so outdistances supply for this event that Walt Disney World visitors go to unbelievable lengths to secure an Advance Reservation. After decades of guests complaining and beating their chests over their inability to get a table, Disney finally is offering a noon-to-2 p.m. character lunch with the same cast of characters and a fixed-price evening meal presided over solo by the Fairy Godmother.

This frustrated reader from Golden, Colorado, complains:

I don't know what you have to do to get an Advance Reservation for Cinderella's [Royal] Table in the castle. I called Disney Dining every morning at 7 [a.m.], which was 5 [a.m.] where I live! It was like calling into one of those radio shows where the first person to call wins a prize. Every time I finally got through, all the tables were gone. I am soooo frustrated and mad I could spit. What do you have to do to get a table for Cinderella's breakfast?

The only way to get a table is to obtain an Advance Reservation through Disney reservations. You must call ☎ 407-WDW-DINE at 7 a.m. EST exactly 180 days before the day you want to eat at Cinderella's. If you live in California and have to get up at 4 a.m. Pacific time to call, Disney could care less. There's no limit to the number of hoops they can make their patrons jump through if demand exceeds supply.

Here's how it works. It's 6:50 a.m. EST and all the Disney dining reservationists are warming up their computers to begin filling available seats at 7 a.m. As the clock strikes seven, Disney dining is blasted with an avalanche of calls, all trying to make Advance Reservations for the character meals at Cinderella's Royal Table. There are more than 100 reservationists on duty, and most Advance Reservations can be assigned in two minutes or less. Thus, the coveted seats go quickly, selling out as early as 7:02 a.m. on many days.

To be among the fortunate few who score an Advance Reservation, try the following. First, call on the correct morning. Use a calendar and count backward exactly 180 days from (but not including) the day you wish to dine. (The computer doesn't understand months, so you can't, for example, call on January 1st to make an Advance Reservation for July 1st because that's more than 180 days.) If you want to eat on May 1st, for example, begin your 180-day backward count on April 30th. If you count correctly, you'll find that the correct morning to call is November 2nd. If you don't feel like counting days, call ☎ 407-WDW-DINE, and the Disney folks will calculate it for you. Call them during the afternoon, when they're less busy, about 195 days before your trip. Let them know when you'd like your Advance Reservation, and they'll tell you the correct date to call.

To get a table, you must dial at almost exactly 7 a.m. EST. Disney does not calibrate its clock with the correct time as determined by the U.S. Naval Observatory or the National Institute of Standards and Technology, but we conducted synchronizing tests and determined that Disney reservation-system clocks are accurate to within one to three seconds. Several Internet sites will give you the exact time. Our favorite is **www.atomictime.net,** which offers the exact time in displays that show hours, minutes, and seconds. Once the atomic time home page is up, click on "HTML multizone continuous" and look for the Eastern

Time Zone. Using this site or your local time-of-day number from the phone directory, synchronize your watch TO THE SECOND. About 18 to 20 seconds before 7 a.m., dial ☎ 407-WDW-DINE, waiting to dial the final E in DINE until seven seconds before the hour.

Hang up and redial until your call is answered. When it is, you will hear one of two recorded messages:

1. "Thank you for calling the Disney Reservation Center. Our office is closed. . . ." If you get this message, hang up the instant you hear the words "Our office," and hit redial.

Or

2. You'll get a recording with a number of prompts. The prompts change periodically. Call a few mornings before the day you actually make your reservation to learn what prompts are being used. Once you know the prompts, you can determine which numbers on your touch-tone phone to press in order to work through the prompts at warp speed. Some prompts begin with "If," others may request info such as your phone number or resort reservation number. Do not listen to the entire prompt. Immediately press the appropriate numbered key(s) as determined by your previous trial run.

Your call will be answered momentarily by a Disney Reservations Center (DRC) agent. Don't get nervous if you're on hold for a bit. The worst thing you can do now is hang up and try again.

As soon as a live DRC agent comes on the line, interrupt immediately and say, "I need Cindy's breakfast [lunch], for May 1st, for four people, any available time" (substituting your own breakfast or lunch dates, of course). Don't engage in "good mornings" or other pleasantries. Time is of the essence. You can apologize later to the DRC agent for your momentary rudeness if you feel the need to do so, but she already knows what's going on. Don't try to pick a specific time. Even two seconds to ask for a specific time will seriously diminish your chances of getting an Advance Reservation.

Make a test call a few days in advance to learn what the prompts are.

Bob

If the atomic-clock thing seems too complicated (not to mention anal), start dialing ☎ 407-WDW-DINE about 50 seconds before 7 a.m. If the reservation center isn't open yet, you'll get a recorded message saying so. When this happens, hang up and call back immediately. If you have a redial button on your phone, use it to speed the dialing process. Continue hanging up and redialing as fast as you can until you get the recording with the prompts. This recording verifies that your call has been placed in the service queue in the order in which it was received. What happens next depends on how many others got through ahead of you, but chances are good that you'll be able to get an Advance Reservation. Bear in mind that while you're talking, other agents are confirming Advance Reservations for other guests, so you want the transaction to go down as fast as possible. Flexibility on your part counts. It's much harder to get a seating for a large group; give some thought to breaking your group into numbers that can be accommodated at tables for four.

All Advance Reservations for Cinderella's Royal Table character meals require complete prepayment with a credit card at the time of the booking. The name on the booking can't be changed after the Advance Reservation is made. Advance Reservations may be canceled with the deposit refunded in full by calling ☎ 407-WDW-DINE at least 24 hours before the seating time.

While many readers have been successful using our strategies, some have not:

> [Regarding] reservations for breakfast at Cinderella's Castle, I did exactly what you suggested, five days in a row, and was unable to get through to an actual person until after 7:15 each day (although I was connected and put on hold at exactly 7 a.m. each time). Of course, by then, all reservations were gone (this was for the first week in May, not a peak time).

On most days, a couple of hundred calls slam Disney's automated call-queuing system within milliseconds of one another. With this call volume, a 20th of a second or less can make the difference between getting a table and not getting one. As it happens, there are variables beyond your control. When you hit the first digit of a long-distance number, your phone system leaps into action. As you continue entering digits, your phone system is already searching for the best path to the number you're calling. According to federal regulation, a phone system must connect the call to the target number within 20 seconds of your entering the last digit. In practice, most systems make the connection much faster, but your system could be pokey. How fast your call is connected, therefore, depends on your local phone system's connection speed, and even this varies according to traffic volume and available routing paths for individual calls. Distance counts too, though we're talking milliseconds. Thus, it takes just a bit longer for a call to reach Disney World from Chicago than from Atlanta, and longer yet if you're calling from San Francisco.

I'd ride The Mummy and The Hulk before I'd go through all this, and that means a lot coming from me! Liliane

So, if you're having trouble getting an Advance Reservation at Cinderella's Royal Table using the strategies outlined earlier, here are our suggestions. Make a test call to ☎ 407-WDW-DINE at 7 a.m. EST a couple of days before you call in earnest. Using a stopwatch or the stopwatch function on your watch, time the interval between entering the last digit of the number and when the phone starts to ring. This exercise will provide a rough approximation of the call connection speed at that time from your area, taking into account both speed of service and distance. For most of you, the connection interval will be very short. Some of you, however, might discover that your problem in getting through is because of slow service. Either way, factor in the connection interval in timing your call to Disney. Phone traffic is heavier on weekdays than weekends, so if you plan to call reservations on a weekday, conduct your test on a weekday. Finally, don't use a cell phone to make the call. The connection time will usually be slower and certainly less predictable.

This is one of the most widely used sections in this guidebook, but we're amazed that anyone would go to this much trouble to eat with Cinderella . . . atomic clocks, split-second timing, test calls . . . yikes!

As a postscript, we've found it's often easier to get through to reservations if you call on Saturday or Sunday. Presumably, folks don't mind calling at the break of dawn if they're up getting ready for work but object to interrupting their beauty rest on weekends.

If You Can't Get an Advance Reservation

If you insist on a meal at Cinderella's but can't get an Advance Reservation, go to the restaurant on the day you wish to dine and try for a table as a walk-in. This is a long shot, though it's possible during the least busy times of year. There's also a fair shot at success on cold or rainy days when there's an above-average probability of no-shows. If you try to walk in, your chances are best during the last hour of serving.

Landing an Advance Reservation for dinner is somewhat easier, but only the Fairy Godmother is present, and the price is a whopping $40 for adults and $25 for children ages 3 to 9. As at breakfast and lunch, five photos of your group are included in the price (like it or not), and a princess wand for girls, while boys receive a prince sword. If you're unable to lock up a table for breakfast or lunch, a dinner reservation will at least get your children inside the castle. Even without characters, a meal in the castle costs a bundle, as this Snellville, Georgia, mom points out:

> We ate [dinner] at Cinderella's Castle to fulfill my longtime dream. The menu was very limited and expensive. For three people, no appetizers or dessert, the bill was $100.

And no alcoholic beverages, either. Alcohol isn't served in the Magic Kingdom.

OTHER CHARACTER EVENTS

A CAMPFIRE AND SING-ALONG are held nightly (times vary with the season) near the Meadow Trading Post and Bike Barn at Fort Wilderness Resort & Campground. Chip 'n' Dale lead the songs, and two Disney films are shown. The program is free and open to resort guests (☎ 407-824-2900).

WONDERLAND TEA PARTY Although the name of this enchanting soirée is enough to give most boys hives, it's nevertheless available at the Grand Floridian's 1900 Park Fare restaurant, Monday through Friday, at 1:30 p.m. for about $29 per child (ages 3 to 10). The program consists of making cupcakes, arranging flower bouquets, and having lunch and tea with characters from Alice in Wonderland. Reserve up to 180 days in advance by calling ☎ 407-WDW-DINE.

STROLLERS

STROLLERS ARE AVAILABLE FOR RENT at all four theme parks and the Downtown Disney area (single stroller, $10 per day with no deposit, $8 per day for the entire stay; double stroller, $18 per day with no deposit, $16 per day for the entire stay; stroller rentals at Downtown Disney require a $250 credit-card deposit; double strollers are not available at Downtown Disney). Strollers are welcome at Blizzard Beach and Typhoon Lagoon, but no rentals are available. We recommend you pay in advance for your stroller rentals—this allows you to bypass the "paying" line and head straight for the "pickup" line. Make sure you keep the receipt in a safe place. If you rent a stroller at the Magic Kingdom and decide to go to Epcot, the Animal Kingdom, or Disney-MGM Studios, turn in your Magic Kingdom stroller and present your receipt at the next park. You will be issued another stroller without additional charge. Rental at all parks is fast and efficient, and returning the stroller is a breeze.

Readers inform us that there is a lively "gray market" for strollers at the parks. Families who arrive late look for families who are heading for the exit and "buy" their stroller at a bargain price.

I strongly recommend bringing your own stroller. In addition to the parks there is the walk from and to the parking lot or the bus/monorail/boat station to the park entrance, not to mention many other occasions at your hotel or during shopping when you will be happy to have a stroller handy.

Liliane

If you do not want to bring your own stroller you may consider buying one of the umbrella style collapsible strollers. Wal-Mart retails a very basic "Winnie the Pooh" collapsible stroller for $13.88. You may even consider ordering online at places such as **www.walmart.com, www.toysrus.com,** or **www.sears.com** and shipping it right to your hotel in Orlando. Make sure you leave enough time between your order and arrival dates. When you are ready to go home, keep it or chunk it.

Another important matter is protection against the sun. Liliane always used a stroller with an adjustable canopy and also had two to three lightweight pieces of

When you enter a show or board a ride, you must park your stroller, usually in an open area. Bring a cloth or towel to dry it if it rains before you return.

Bob

cloth handy to protect her child from the sun. You can use anything for that purpose; a receiving blanket works well. Liliane used clothespins and security pins to attach the pieces to the canopy.

Strollers are a must for infants and toddlers, but we have observed many sharp parents renting strollers for somewhat older children (up to age 5 or so). The stroller prevents parents from having to carry children when they sag and provides a convenient place to carry water and snacks.

A family from Tulsa, Oklahoma, recommends springing for a double stroller:

> We rent a double for baggage room or in case the older child gets tired of walking.

 Rental strollers are too large for all infants and many toddlers. If you plan to rent a stroller for your infant or toddler, bring pillows, cushions, or rolled towels to buttress him in.

Liliane

If you go to your hotel for a break and intend to return to the park, leave your rental stroller by an attraction near the park entrance, marking it with something personal, such as a bandanna. When you return, your stroller will be waiting.

Bringing your own stroller is permitted. However, only collapsible strollers are allowed on monorails, parking-lot trams, and buses. Your stroller is unlikely to be stolen, but mark it with your name.

Having her own stroller was indispensable to a Mechanicsville, Virginia, mother of two toddlers:

> How I was going to manage to get the kids from the parking lot to the park was a big worry for me before I made the trip. I didn't read anywhere that it was possible to walk to the entrance of the parks instead of taking the tram, so I wasn't sure I could do it.
>
> I found that for me personally, since I have two kids aged 1 and 2, it was easier to walk to the entrance of the park from the parking lot with the kids in [my own] stroller than to take the kids out of the stroller, fold the stroller (while trying to control the two kids and associated gear), load the stroller and the kids onto the tram, etc. . . No matter where I was parked I could always just walk to the entrance . . . it sometimes took awhile but it was easier for me.

An Oklahoma mom, however, reports a bad experience with bringing her own stroller:

> The first time we took our kids we had a large stroller (big mistake). It is so much easier to rent one in the park. The large [personally owned] strollers are nearly impossible to get on the buses and are a hassle at the airport. I remember feeling dread when a bus pulled up that was even semifull of people. People look at you like you have a cage full of live chickens when you drag heavy strollers onto the bus.

STROLLER WARS Sometimes strollers disappear while you're enjoying a ride or show. Disney staff will often rearrange strollers parked outside an attraction. This may be done to tidy up or to clear a walkway. Don't assume your stroller is stolen because it isn't where you left it. It may be neatly arranged a few feet away.

Sometimes, however, strollers are taken by mistake or ripped off by people not wanting to spend time replacing one that's missing. Don't be alarmed if yours disappears. You won't have to buy it, and you'll be issued a new one.

Keep in mind that it is very hard to navigate a stroller in a huge crowd, especially when in a hurry and when trying to exit after the fireworks and shows at closing time. Sometimes guests without strollers may try to get ahead of you, making you wish to use the stroller as a lethal weapon. Don't. Given the number of strollers, pedestrians, and tight spaces, mishaps are inevitable on both sides. A simple apology and a smile are usually the best remediation.

WHEN KIDS *get* LOST

IF ONE OF YOUR CHILDREN gets separated from you, don't panic. All things considered, Walt Disney World is about the safest place to get lost we can think of. Disney cast members are trained to watch for seemingly lost kids, and because children become detached from parents so frequently in the theme parks, cast members know exactly what to do.

If you lose a child in the Magic Kingdom, report it to a Disney employee, then check at the Baby Center and at City Hall, where lost-children logs are kept. At Epcot, report the loss, then check at Baby Services near the Odyssey Center. At Disney-MGM Studios, report the situation at the Guest Relations Building at the entrance end of Hollywood Boulevard. At Animal Kingdom, go to the Baby Center in Discovery Island. Paging isn't used, but in an emergency an "all points bulletin" can be issued throughout the park(s) via internal communications. If a Disney employee encounters a lost child, he or she will immediately take the child to the park's guest relations center or its baby-care center.

As comforting as this knowledge is, however, it's nevertheless scary when a child turns up missing. Fortunately, circumstances surrounding a child becoming lost are fairly predictable and, for the most part, preventable.

We suggest that children younger than age 8 be color-coded by dressing them in "vacation uniforms" with distinctively colored T-shirts or equally eye-catching apparel.

For starters, consider how much alike children dress, especially in warm climates where shorts and T-shirts are the norm. Throw your children in with 10,000 other kids the same size and suddenly that "cute little outfit" turns into theme-park camouflage. It's also smart to sew a label into each child's shirt that states your family name, your hometown, your cell phone number, and the name of your hotel. The same thing can be accomplished by writing the information on a strip of masking tape. Hotel security professionals suggest the information be printed in small letters and the tape be affixed to the outside of the child's shirt, five inches below the armpit or. alternatively, on the tongue of the child's shoe. Another way to skin the cat is to attach a luggage tag to a belt loop. Finally, special name tags can be obtained at the major theme parks.

Other than just blending in, children tend to become separated from their parents under remarkably similar circumstances:

1. PREOCCUPIED SOLO PARENT In this situation, the party's only adult is preoccupied with something like buying refreshments, loading the camera, or using the restroom. Junior is there one second and gone the next.

2. THE HIDDEN EXIT Sometimes parents wait on the sidelines while two or more young children experience a ride together. Parents expect the kids to exit in one place and, lo and behold, the youngsters pop out somewhere else. Exits from some attractions are distant from the entrances. Make sure you know exactly where your children will emerge before letting them ride by themselves. If in doubt, ask a cast member.

3. AFTER THE SHOW At the end of many shows and rides, a Disney staffer will announce, "Check for personal belongings and take small children by the hand." When dozens, if not hundreds, of people leave an attraction simultaneously, it's surprisingly easy for parents to lose contact with their children unless they have them directly in tow.

4. RESTROOM PROBLEMS Mom tells 6-year-old Tommy, "I'll be sitting on this bench when you come out of the restroom." Three possibilities: One, Tommy exits through a different door and becomes disoriented (Mom may not know there is another door). Two, Mom decides she also will use the restroom, and Tommy emerges to find her gone. Three, Mom pokes around in a shop while keeping an eye on the bench, but misses Tommy when he comes out.

If you can't be with your child in the restroom, make sure there's only one exit. The restroom on a passageway between Frontierland and Adventureland in the Magic Kingdom is the all-time worst for disorienting visitors. Children and adults alike have walked in from the Adventureland side and walked out on the Frontierland side (and vice versa). Adults realize quickly that something is wrong. Young children, however, sometimes fail to recognize the problem. Designate a meeting spot more distinctive than a bench, and be thorough in your instructions: "I'll meet you by this flagpole. If you get out first, stay right here." Have your child repeat the directions back to you.

5. PARADES There are many parades and shows at which the audience stands. Children tend to jockey for a better view. By moving a little this way and that, the child quickly puts distance between you before either of you notices.

6. MASS MOVEMENTS Be on guard when huge crowds disperse after fireworks or a parade, or at park closing. With 20,000 to 40,000 people at once in an area, it's very easy to get separated from a child or others in your party. Use extra caution after the evening parade and fireworks in the Magic Kingdom, *Fantasmic!* at the Disney-MGM Studios, or *IllumiNations* at Epcot. Families should have specific plans for where to meet if they get separated.

7. CHARACTER GREETINGS Activity and confusion are common when the Disney characters appear, and children can slip out of sight. See "Then Some Confusion Happened" (page 227).

8. GETTING LOST AT THE ANIMAL KINGDOM It's especially easy to lose a child at the Animal Kingdom, particularly in the Oasis entryway, on the Maharaja Jungle Trek, and on the Pangani Forest Exploration Trail. Mom and dad will stop to observe an animal. Junior stays close for a minute or so, and then, losing patience, wanders to the other side of the exhibit or to a different exhibit.

9. LOST . . . IN THE OZONE More often than you'd think, kids don't realize they're lost. They are so distracted that they sometimes wander around for quite a while before they notice that their whole family has mysteriously disappeared. Fortunately, Disney cast members are trained to look out for kids who have zoned out and will either help them find their family or deposit them at the Lost Child Center. There are times, however, when parents panic during the interval in which these scenarios play out. If you lose a child and he doesn't turn up at the Lost Child Center right away, take a deep breath. He's probably lost in the ozone.

10. TEACH YOUR KIDS WHO THE GOOD GUYS ARE On your very first day in the parks, teach your kids how to recognize a Disney cast member by pointing out the Disney name tags that they all wear. Instruct your children to find someone with such a name tag if they get separated from you.

LILIANE'S TIPS FOR KEEPING TRACK OF YOUR BROOD

ON A GOOD DAY, it's possible for Liliane to lose a cantaloupe in her purse. Being thus challenged she works overtime developing ways to hang on to her possessions, including her child. Here's what she has to say:

I've seen parents write their cell phone numbers on a child's leg with a felt-tip marker . . . effective but crude. Before you resort to a brand or tattoo, consider some of the tips I've busted my brain dreaming up. My friends (some much ditzier than I) have used them with great success.

- Same-colored T-shirts for the whole family will help you gather your troops in an easy and fun way. You can opt for just a uniform color or go the extra mile and have the T-shirts printed with a logo such as "The Brown Family's Assault on the Mouse." You might also include the date or the year of your visit. Your imagination is the limit. Light-colored T-shirts can even be autographed by the Disney characters.

- Clothing labels are great, of course. If you don't sew, buy labels that you can iron on the garment. If you own a cell phone, be sure to include the number on the label. If you do not own a cell phone, put in the phone number of the hotel where you'll be staying.

- In pet stores you can have name tags printed for a very reasonable price. These are great to add to necklaces and bracelets, or attach to your child's shoelace or beltloop.

- When you check into the hotel, take a business card of the hotel for each member in your party, especially those old enough to carry wallets and purses.

- Always agree on a meeting point before you see a parade, fireworks, and night-time spectacles such as *IllumiNations* and *Fantasmic!* Make sure the meeting place is in the park (as opposed to the car or someplace outside the front gate).

- If you have a digital camera you may elect to take a picture of your kids every morning. If they get lost the picture will show what they look like and what they are wearing.

- If all the members of your party have cell phones, it's easy to locate each other. Be aware, however, that the ambient noise in the parks is so loud that you probably won't hear your cell phone ring. Your best bet is to carry your phone in a front pants pocket and to program the phone to vibrate. If any of your younger kids carry cell phones, secure the phones with a strap.

- Save key tags and luggage tags for use on items you bring to the parks including your stroller, diaper bag, and backpack or hip pack.

- Don't underestimate the power of the permanent marker, such as a Sharpie. They are great for labeling pretty much anything. Mini-Sharpies are sold as clip-ons and are great for collecting character autographs. The Sharpie will also serve well for writing down (Bob suggests on my son's forehead) the location of your car in the parking lot.

A word about keeping track of your park-admission passes. One minute you have them, the next you don't. The passes (which for Disney hotel guests also serve as a credit card and room key) are precious. They are also your key to obtaining FASTPASSes and this, typically, is how they get lost. I have tried many ways of keeping track of my passes but my all-time favorite is a clear badge case that you wear around your neck. It is perfect for holding admission passes, room keys, and some cash; best of all it is completely waterproof, and you can wear the case in the pool or at the water parks.

PART SEVEN

The MAGIC KINGDOM

AT THE MAGIC KINGDOM, stroller and wheelchair rentals are to the right of the train station, and lockers are on the station's ground floor. On your left as you enter Main Street is City Hall, the center for information, lost and found, guided tours, and entertainment schedules. Automated tellers (ATMs) are underneath the Main Street railroad station. Down Main Street and left around the central hub (toward Adventureland) are the baby-changing/nursing center and a first-aid post.

If you don't already have a handout park map, get one at City Hall. The handout lists all attractions, shops, and eateries; provides helpful information about first aid, baby care, and assistance for the disabled; and gives tips for good photos. It also lists times for the day's special events, live entertainment, Disney character parades, concerts, and other activities. Additionally, it tells when and where to find Disney characters.

Often the guide map is supplemented by a daily entertainment schedule known as a *Times Guide,* which provides info on special Disney character appearances and what Disney calls Special Hours. This term refers to attractions that open late or close early and to the operating hours of park restaurants. If you are lodging at a Walt Disney World resort hotel and the park is operating on an Extra Magic Hour evening schedule, make sure you also pick up the Extra Magic Hours "Evenings" flyer. The flyer will list which attractions are open late and tells you where and when (usually two hours before regular closing time) to obtain the wristbands necessary for you to benefit from these special hours. All members of your party need to be present to obtain a wristband upon presenting your Disney lodging-room key.

Main Street ends at a central hub from which branch the entrances to five other sections of the Magic Kingdom: Adventureland, Frontierland, Liberty Square, Fantasyland, and Tomorrowland. Mickey's Toontown Fair doesn't connect to the central hub—it is wedged like a dimple between the cheeks of Fantasyland and Tomorrowland.

In this and the following three chapters we rate the individual attractions at each of the four major Disney theme parks. The authors' rating as well as ratings according to age group are given on a scale of zero to five stars—the more stars, the better the attraction. The authors' rating is from the perspective of an adult. The authors, for example, might rate a ride such as Dumbo much lower than the age group for which the ride is intended, in this case, children. This rating, therefore, will more closely approximate how another adult will experience the attraction than how your children will like it. The bottleneck rating ranges from one to ten; the higher the rating, the more congested the attraction. In general, try to experience attractions with a high bottleneck rating early in the morning (that is, between 8 and 10:30 a.m.) before the park gets crowded or late in the day when the crowd has diminished.

MAIN STREET, U.S.A.

BEGIN AND END YOUR VISIT ON MAIN STREET, which may open a half hour before and closes a half hour to an hour after the rest of the park. It is easy to get sidetracked when entering Main Street, as this Disneyfied turn-of-the-19th-century small town street is lovely, with exceptional attention to detail. But remember: Time is of the essence, and the rest of the park is waiting to be discovered. The same goes for the one and only Cinderella Castle. Stick with your touring plan and return to Cinderella Castle and Main Street after you've experienced the "Must-Do's" on your list.

 ### Walt Disney World Railroad ★★½

APPEAL BY AGE	PRESCHOOL ★★★★	GRADE SCHOOL ★★½	TEENS ★★★
YOUNG ADULTS ★★★		OVER 30 ★★	SENIORS ★★★

What it is Scenic railroad ride around perimeter of the Magic Kingdom, and transportation to Frontierland and Mickey's Toontown Fair. **Scope and scale** Minor attraction. **Fright potential** Not frightening in any respect. **Bottleneck rating** 6. **When to go** Anytime. **Special comments** Main Street is usually the least congested station. **Authors' rating** Plenty to see; ★★½. **Duration of ride** About 20 minutes for a complete circuit. **Average wait in line per 100 people ahead of you** 8 minutes. **Assumes** 2 or more trains operating. **Loading speed** Moderate.

Later in the day when you need a break, this full-circuit ride will give you and your feet 20 minutes of rest. You cannot take your rental stroller on  the train; but if you get off short of a complete circuit, you can get a free replacement. Be advised that the railroad shuts down immediately preceding and during parades.

Thumbs Up for the Whole Family

ADVENTURELAND

THE FIRST LAND TO THE LEFT OF MAIN STREET, Adventureland combines an African safari theme with an old New Orleans/Caribbean atmosphere.

Swiss Family Treehouse ★★★

APPEAL BY AGE	PRESCHOOL ★★★	GRADE SCHOOL ★★★½	TEENS ★★★
YOUNG ADULTS ★★★		OVER 30 ★★★	SENIORS ★★★

What it is Outdoor walk-through tree house. **Scope and scale** Minor attraction. **Fright potential** Not frightening in any respect. **Bottleneck rating** 6. **When to go** Before 11:30 a.m. or after 5 p.m. **Special comments** Requires climbing a lot of stairs. **Authors' rating** A visual delight; ★★★. **Duration of tour** 10–15 minutes. **Average wait in line per 100 people ahead of you** 7 minutes. **Loading speed** Doesn't apply.

This king of all tree houses is perfect for the 10-and-under crowd. Though a minor attraction, it's a great place expending pent-up energy. Parents might be inclined to sit across the walkway and watch their aspiring Tarzans, but in truth the tree house is fun for adults, too.

Thumbs Up for the Whole Family

 Swiss Family Robinson is a 1960 film adaptation of the Johann David Wyss novel and was the inspiration for the Swiss Family Treehouse.

Jungle Cruise (FASTPASS) ★★★

APPEAL BY AGE	PRESCHOOL ★★★½	GRADE SCHOOL ★★★½	TEENS ★★½
YOUNG ADULTS ★★★		OVER 30 ★★★	SENIORS ★★★

What it is Outdoor safari-themed boat ride adventure. **Scope and scale** Major attraction. **Fright potential** Moderately intense, some macabre sights; a good test attraction for little ones. **Bottleneck rating** 10. **When to go** Before 10 a.m. or 2 hours before closing. **Authors' rating** A long-enduring Disney masterpiece; ★★★. **Duration of ride** 8–9 minutes. **Average wait in line per 100 people ahead of you** 3½ minutes. **Assumes** 10 boats operating. **Loading speed** Moderate.

You have to put things into perspective to truly enjoy this ride and realize that it once was a super-headliner attraction at the Magic Kingdom. It still is a relaxing and enjoyable boat ride, but it won't capture the fascination of the high-tech savvy youngsters of the new millennium.

Thumbs Up for the Whole Family

Magic Carpets of Aladdin ★★★

APPEAL BY AGE	PRESCHOOL ★★★★½	GRADE SCHOOL ★★★★
TEENS ★½	YOUNG ADULTS ★½	OVER 30 ★½	SENIORS ★½

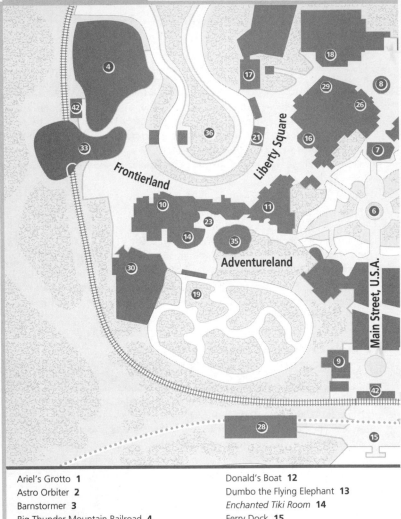

magic kingdom

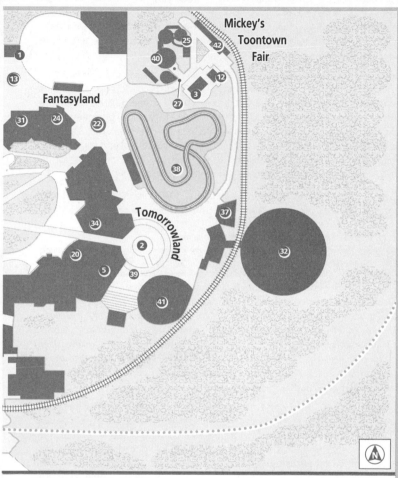

Magic Carpets of Aladdin **23**
Many Adventures of Winnie the Pooh **24**
Mickey's Country House and Judge's Tent **25**
Mickey's PhilharMagic **26**
Minnie's Country House **27**
Monorail Station **28**
Peter Pan's Flight **29**
Pirates of the Caribbean **30**
Snow White's Scary Adventures **31**
Space Mountain **32**
Splash Mountain **33**

Stitch's Great Escape **34**
Swiss Family Treehouse **35**
Tom Sawyer Island **36**
Tomorrowland Arcade **37**
Tomorrowland Speedway **38**
Tomorrowland Transit Authority **39**
Toontown Hall of Fame **40**
Walt Disney's Carousel of Progress **41**
WDW Railroad Station **42**

What it is Elaborate midway ride. **Scope and scale** Minor attraction. **Fright potential** Much like Dumbo; a favorite of most younger children. **Bottleneck rating** 10. **When to go** Before 10 a.m. or in the hour before park closing. **Authors' rating** An eye-appealing children's ride; ★★★★ **Duration of ride** 1½ minutes. **Average wait in line per 100 people ahead of you** 16 minutes. **Loading speed** Slow.

For parents with preschoolers there's no way out—like Dumbo, it is a must. Try to get your kids to ride in the first 30 minutes the park is open or just before park closing. Beware, the ride has a spitting camel positioned to spray jets of water on riders. The magic-carpet vehicles are rider-controlled, so you can fly your magic carpet up, down, or pitch forward or backward. The front-seat control is for up and down while the back-seat control pitches the carpet forward or backward. Sweet, but oh so slow loading. One more tip: Jasmine and Aladdin are often on hand for greeting and meeting.

 Of course the ride is inspired by the 1992 Disney movie *Aladdin*.
Movie Tip Did you know that Robin Williams is the voice of the Genie?

Pirates of the Caribbean ★★★★★

APPEAL BY AGE	PRESCHOOL ★★★	GRADE SCHOOL ★★★★★	TEENS ★★★★
YOUNG ADULTS ★★★★		OVER 30 ★★★★½	SENIORS ★★★★★

What it is Indoor pirate-themed adventure boat ride. **Scope and scale** Headliner. **Fright potential** Slightly intimidating queuing area; intense boat ride with gruesome (though humorously presented) sights and a short, unexpected slide down a flume. **Bottleneck rating** 7. **When to go** Before noon or after 5 p.m. **Special comments** Frightens some young children. **Authors' rating** Disney audio-animatronics at its best; not to be missed; ★★★★★. **Duration of ride** About 7½ minutes. **Average wait in line per 100 people ahead of you** 1½ minutes. **Assumes** Both waiting lines operating. **Loading speed** Fast.

   Yo ho, yo ho, a pirate's life for me! This indoor cruise through a series of sets depicting a pirate raid on an island settlement has been a favorite for decades, but with the

Scary   Dark   Loud

release of *Pirates of the Caribbean: The Curse of the Black Pearl* (2004) and *Pirates of the Caribbean: Dead Man's Chest* (2006), the popularity of the ride has soared to new heights. Oh yeah, the films' protagonist, Captain Jack Sparrow, has joined the attraction's animatronic cast.

 It's a fun ride because pirates aren't really living anymore. When you're entering the ride's line, you can look through the bars in the jail cells and see guns, barrels, and skeletons. The scariest part is when there's a cannon fight between the pirate's boat and the town. And Davy Jones looks kind of creepy.

Hannah

 For all fans of the *Pirates of the Caribbean* movies, rent the movies
Movie Tip before you go to Walt Disney World. They're a blast.

Enchanted Tiki Room—Under New Management ★★★½

APPEAL BY AGE	PRESCHOOL ★★★★	GRADE SCHOOL ★★★½	TEENS ★★★
YOUNG ADULTS ★★★		OVER 30 ★★★	SENIORS ★★★

What it is Audio-animatronic Pacific Island musical theater show. **Scope and scale** Minor attraction. **Fright potential** Young children might be frightened by the thunder and lightning storm, plus the theater is at times plunged into utter darkness. **Bottleneck rating** 4. **When to go** Before 11 a.m. or after 3:30 p.m. **Special comments** Frightens some preschoolers. **Authors' rating** Very, very unusual; ★★★½. **Duration of presentation** 15½ minutes. **Preshow entertainment** Talking birds. **Probable waiting time** 15 minutes.

The Tiki birds are a great favorite of the 8-and-under set. The sarcasm of Iago from *Aladdin* and Zazu from *The Lion King* save the show for older patrons. If you can look beyond the cheese, it is actually hilariously funny. The air-conditioned theater is a great place to cool off and rest your feet.

FRONTIERLAND

FRONTIERLAND ADJOINS ADVENTURELAND as you move clockwise around the Magic Kingdom. The focus is on the Old West, with stockade-type structures and pioneer trappings.

Splash Mountain (FASTPASS) ★★★★★

APPEAL BY AGE	PRESCHOOL †	GRADE SCHOOL ★★★★★	TEENS ★★★★★
YOUNG ADULTS ★★★★★		OVER 30 ★★★★★	SENIORS ★★★★★

† Many preschoolers are too short to meet the height requirement. Among preschoolers who actually ride, most give the attraction high marks.

What it is Indoor/outdoor water-flume adventure ride. **Scope and scale** Super headliner. **Fright potential** Visually intimidating from outside, with moderately intense visual effects. The ride, culminating in a 52-foot plunge down a steep chute, is somewhat hair-raising for all ages. **Bottleneck rating** 10. **When to go** As soon as the park opens, during afternoon or evening parades, just before closing, or use FASTPASS. **Special comments** Must be 40 inches tall to ride; children younger than 7 must ride with an adult. Switching-off option provided (page 220). **Authors' rating** A wet winner; not to be missed; ★★★★★. **Duration of ride** About 10 minutes. **Average wait in line per 100 people ahead of you** 3½ minutes. **Assumes** Operating at full capacity. **Loading speed** Moderate.

Zip-a-dee-doo-dah, are we having fun yet, my-o-my, did we get wet! The half-mile ride through swamps, caves, and backwood bayous is wonderful. Based on the 1946 Disney film *Song of the South,* you travel in a log through Uncle Remus's tales of Brer Rabbit. Three small drops lead up to the big one, a five-story drop at 40 mph.

A PEEK BEHIND THE SCENES WITH JIM HILL

NO RHYME OR REMUS

Fans of *Song of the South* (the 1946 Disney film on which Splash Mountain was based) may notice one very important character from that movie missing from this attraction: Uncle Remus himself. Supposedly out of concern that this character might offend African Americans, the Imagineers just cut Uncle Remus out of the show, replacing him with a new narrator for the ride, Brer Frog.

Splash Mountain. Way too cool! If you want to feel what it's like to go over a waterfall, sit in the front, but I prefer the back. I think you get wetter. Get as many big people sitting in front of you as you can. They weigh down the boat and make the biggest splash.

Ian

You get really wet on this ride, and there are a lot of surprises! When you get in, the seats are going to be really wet.

Hannah

Movie Tip

Unavailable in the United States, *Song of the South* will become public domain in 2039, and Disney might rerelease the movie before they lose the rights to it. If you are interested in the history of this controversial movie, check out **www.songofthesouth.net/home.html.**

Big Thunder Mountain Railroad ★★★★ (FASTPASS)

APPEAL BY AGE	PRESCHOOL ★★★	GRADE SCHOOL ★★★★	TEENS ★★★★
YOUNG ADULTS ★★★★		OVER 30 ★★★★	SENIORS ★★★

What it is Tame, Western-mining-themed roller coaster. **Scope and scale** Headliner. **Fright potential** Visually intimidating from outside, with moderately intense visual effects; the roller coaster is wild enough to frighten many adults, particularly seniors. **Bottleneck rating** 9. **When to go** Before 10 a.m., in the hour before closing, or use FASTPASS. **Special comments** Must be 40 inches tall to ride; children younger than age 7 must ride with an adult. Switching-off option provided (page 220). **Authors' rating** Great effects; relatively tame roller coaster; not to be missed; ★★★★. **Duration of ride** Almost 3½ minutes. **Average wait in line per 100 people ahead of you** 2½ minutes. **Assumes** 5 trains operating. **Loading speed** Moderate to fast.

Scary

Rough

Lose Things

Zooming on a runaway train around a mountain and through a deserted mining town is Disney at its best (if only one could concentrate on the scenery). The ride is rough, and if you do not like roller coasters, this one is going to remind you why. If you are a fan, however, the scenery deserves three rides in a row and an extra one for atmosphere after dark.

Ian

Big Thunder Mountain Railroad. Watch out on this one. Sitting in the back jerks me around too much. If you go in the front or the middle you'll have a smoother ride. It has a lot of dips but no flips because it is more like a wooden rollercoaster.

Hannah

I was not "feeling the love" the first time I went on this. You always feel like you're going to hit your head on one rock or another, and there are a lot of twists and turns. Eventually, I liked the bumps and how high the ride went, so I went on it again with my dad.

 ## Country Bear Jamboree ★★★

| APPEAL BY AGE | PRESCHOOL ★★★ | GRADE SCHOOL ★★★ | TEENS ★★½ |
| YOUNG ADULTS ★★½ | | OVER 30 ★★★ | SENIORS ★★★ |

What it is Audio-animatronic country hoedown theater show. **Scope and scale** Major attraction. **Fright potential** Not frightening in any respect. **Bottleneck rating** 8. **When to go** Before 11:30 a.m., before a parade, or during the 2 hours before closing. **Authors' rating** A Disney classic; ★★★. **Duration of presentation** 15 minutes. **Preshow entertainment** None. **Probable waiting time** This attraction is moderately popular but has a comparatively small capacity. Probable waiting time between noon and 5:30 p.m. on a busy day waits will average 15–45 minutes.

Kids up to age 10 especially will enjoy this funny country music show. The show is a little dusty but Teddi Bara, Big Al, Trixie, and the rest of the gang are Disney classics.

Thumbs Up for the Whole Family

Movie Tip

Kids will love watching *The Country Bears,* a live-action film produced by Walt Disney Pictures based loosely on the *Country Bear Jamboree* show. It was Disney's first movie based on a ride or attraction, released in 2002, almost a year before *Pirates of the Caribbean: The Curse of the Black Pearl.*

 ## Tom Sawyer Island and Fort Langhorn ★★★

| APPEAL BY AGE | PRESCHOOL ★★★★★ | GRADE SCHOOL ★★★★★ |
| TEENS ★★ | YOUNG ADULTS ★★ | OVER 30 ★★ | SENIORS ★★ |

What it is Outdoor walk-through exhibit/rustic playground. **Scope and scale** Minor attraction. **Fright potential** Not frightening in any respect. **Bottleneck rating** 4. **When to go** Midmorning through late afternoon. **Special comments** Closes at dusk. **Authors' rating** The place for rambunctious kids; ★★★.

This is a great place for kids ages 5 and up to unwind. The wildest and most uncooperative youngster will relax after exploring caves and climbing around in an old fort. While it is also a great place for a picnic, there is no

Hannah

I thought this was really cool because I like adventurous stuff like the rope bridges. There's also a playground. You take a boat across the lake to get there.

food, so bring your own. Access to the island is by raft with a (usually short) wait both coming and going. Plan to give your kids at least 20 minutes on the island. Left to their own devices they would likely stay all day.

Frontierland Shootin Arcade ★½

APPEAL BY AGE	PRESCHOOL ★★★	GRADE SCHOOL ★★★★	TEENS ★★★
YOUNG ADULTS ★★		OVER 30 ★★	SENIORS ★★

What it is Electronic shooting gallery. **Scope and scale** Diversion. **When to go** Whenever convenient. **Special comments** Costs 50 cents per play. **Authors' rating** Very nifty shooting gallery; ★½.

Bring quarters. It is big-time fun.

Idan

▌ LIBERTY SQUARE

LIBERTY SQUARE RE-CREATES COLONIAL AMERICA at the time of the American Revolution. The architecture is Federal or Colonial. A real, 130-year-old live oak (dubbed the "Liberty Tree") lends dignity and grace to the setting.

The Hall of Presidents ★★★

APPEAL BY AGE	PRESCHOOL ★	GRADE SCHOOL ★★½	TEENS ★★★
YOUNG ADULTS ★★★★		OVER 30 ★★★★	SENIORS ★★★★

What it is Audio-animatronic historical theater presentation. **Scope and scale** Major attraction. **Fright potential** Not frightening in any respect. **Bottleneck rating** 4. **When to go** Anytime. **Authors' rating** Impressive and moving; ★★★. **Duration of presentation** Almost 23 minutes. **Preshow entertainment** None. **Probable waiting time** Lines for this attraction look awesome but are usually swallowed up as the theater exchanges audiences. Your wait will probably be the remaining time of the show that's in progress when you arrive. Even during the busiest times, waits rarely exceed 40 minutes.

Thumbs Up for the Whole Family

Disney immortalizes the presidents of the United States with their own audio-animatronic counterparts. Did you know that President Bill Clinton was the very first presidential figure other than Lincoln to have a speaking role? Clinton recorded his speech at the White House specifically for the attraction, as did President George W. Bush when he was elected. Attention to detail is masterful. The show is definitively a must-see for adults. Kids will fidget or fall asleep.

★ *Liberty Belle* Riverboat ★★½

APPEAL BY AGE	PRESCHOOL ★★★½	GRADE SCHOOL ★★★	TEENS ★★½
YOUNG ADULTS ★★★		OVER 30 ★★★	SENIORS ★★★

What it is Outdoor scenic boat ride. **Scope and scale** Major attraction. **Fright potential** Not frightening in any respect. **Bottleneck rating** 4. **When to go** Anytime. **Authors' rating** Slow, relaxing, and scenic; ★★½. **Duration of ride** About 16 minutes. **Average wait to board** 10–14 minutes.

This fully narrated 16-minute trip is relaxing and offers great photo ops. It's a good choice also at night when the boat and the attractions along the waterfront are lighted. Did you know that the *Liberty Belle* Riverboat runs on a track hidden just below the water?

Thumbs Up for the Whole Family

The Haunted Mansion (FASTPASS) ★★★★

APPEAL BY AGE	PRESCHOOL [VARIES]	GRADE SCHOOL ★★★★★	TEENS ★★★★
YOUNG ADULTS ★★★★		OVER 30 ★★★★	SENIORS ★★★★

What it is Haunted-house dark ride. **Scope and scale** Major attraction. **Fright potential** The name raises anxiety, as do the sounds and sights of the waiting area. An intense attraction with humorously presented macabre sights, the ride itself is gentle. **Bottleneck rating** 8. **When to go** Before 11:30 a.m. use FASTPASS, or go after 8 p.m. **Special comments** Frightens some very young children. **Authors' rating** Some of Walt Disney World's best special effects; not to be missed; ★★★★. **Duration of ride** 7-minute ride plus a 1½-minute preshow. **Average wait in line per 100 people ahead of you** 2½ minutes. **Assumes** Both "stretch rooms" operating. **Loading speed** Fast.

Scary

Dark

Don't let the apparent spookiness of the old-fashioned Haunted Mansion put you off. This is one of the best attractions in the Magic Kingdom (and, in fact, one that seems to get a few new twists each year). It's not scary, except in the sweetest of ways, but it will remind you of the days before ghost stories gave way to slasher flicks. The Haunted Mansion takes less than 10 minutes to ride, preshow included, but you may have to do it more than once—it's jam-packed with visual puns, special effects, Hidden Mickeys, and really lovely Victorian-spooky sets.

Ian

It's freaky, man. One time I almost chickened out. Real people in costumes stare you down. There's lots of weird stuff going on, like eyes in paintings on the wall following you and a lady's face inside a crystal ball. At the end, a ghost rides in the car with you. Read the funny tombstones before you go in.

FANTASYLAND

FANTASYLAND IS THE HEART of the Magic Kingdom, a truly enchanting place spread gracefully like a miniature Alpine village beneath the lofty towers of the Cinderella Castle.

It's a Small World ★★★

APPEAL BY AGE	PRESCHOOL ★★★★	GRADE SCHOOL ★★★★	TEENS ★★★
YOUNG ADULTS ★★★		OVER 30 ★★★	SENIORS ★★★

What it is World brotherhood–themed indoor boat ride. **Scope and scale** Major attraction. **Fright potential** Not frightening in any respect. **Bottleneck rating** 6. **When to go** Anytime. **Authors' rating** Exponentially "cute"; ★★★. **Duration of ride** Approximately 11 minutes. **Average wait in line per 100 people ahead of you** 2 minutes. **Assumes** Busy conditions with 30 or more boats operating. **Loading speed** Fast.

Thumbs Up for the Whole Family

Small boats carry visitors on a tour around the world, with singing and dancing dolls showcasing the dress and culture of each nation. Totally re-habbed in 2005, Small World is one of Disney's oldest entertainments. Did you know that the ride originated at the 1964 New York World's Fair? If you listen closely you will realize that the theme song is actually sung in nu-merous languages as your boat is carried from one continent to the next. Of course, there's no escaping the brain-numbing little tune. You'll go home with it lodged in your brain like a bullet, and just when you think you've re-pressed it, the song will resurface without warning to torture you some more.

This ride is why MP3 players were invented. Just put on your headphones and listen to Velvet Revolver all the way through the ride. The Small World song won't bother you a bit. Promise.

Ian

I must be immune to the tune. I love the ride and would not miss riding It's a Small World anytime I visit.

Idan

Peter Pan's Flight (FASTPASS) ★★★★

APPEAL BY AGE	PRESCHOOL ★★★★	GRADE SCHOOL ★★★★	TEENS ★★★★
YOUNG ADULTS ★★★★		OVER 30 ★★★★	SENIORS ★★★★

What it is Indoor track ride. **Scope and scale** Minor attraction. **Fright potential** Not frightening in any respect. **Bottleneck rating** 8. **When to go** Before 10 a.m., or use FASTPASS after 6 p.m. **Authors' rating** Happy, mellow, and well done; ★★★★. **Duration of ride** A little more than 3 minutes. **Average wait in line per 100 people ahead of you** 5½ minutes. **Loading speed** Moderate to slow.

Take a snort of pixie dust and off you go soaring over London and on to Never-land. If your kids love Peter Pan, have them help Captain Hook find treasures at: **disney.go.com/characters/activities/toys/treasurequest/index.html.**

Thumbs Up for the Whole Family

Movie Tip

Disney's animated film version of *Peter Pan* is, of course, the inspiration for this wonderful ride. While the original is easy to find, the sequel, *Return to Neverland,* is not. Try to get a copy at a library or a used one at

www.amazon.com and reunite with Peter, Wendy, Tinker Bell, Mr. Smee, the Lost Boys, and Captain Hook. But most of all: don't grow up.

A PEEK BEHIND THE SCENES WITH JIM HILL

HOW DO THEY DO THAT?

What's the secret behind those tiny cars you see rolling through the streets of London as you fly off to Neverland? Those aren't really autos at all, just dots of glow-in-the-dark paint on bicycle chains. As these chains are pulled through the miniature version of the city, they give the impression that cars—with their headlights on—are rolling through London.

Mickey's PhilharMagic (FASTPASS) ★★★★

APPEAL BY AGE	PRESCHOOL ★★★★	GRADE SCHOOL ★★★★★	TEENS ★★★★
YOUNG ADULTS ★★★★		OVER 30 ★★★★	SENIORS ★★★★

What it is 3-D movie. **Scope and scale** Major attraction. **Special comments** Not to be missed. **When to go** Before 11 a.m., during parades, or use FASTPASS. **Authors' rating** ★★★★. A masterpiece. **Duration of presentation** About 20 minutes. **Probable waiting time** 12–30 minutes.

A real stunner, *Mickey's PhilharMagic* combines three fabulous ideas: Mickey and Donald mix and meet with latter-day Disney stars such as Aladdin, Jasmine, Ariel, the Beast's pantry servants (such as Lumière and Mrs. Potts), and Simba; it employs a form of computer-enhanced 3-D video technology that is truly impressive (it's the first time most of these characters have been digitally animated, which will make them more "flexible," so to speak, in the future); and the whole shebang is projected on a 150-foot-wide, 180-degree screen. *Mickey's PhilharMagic* even employs some of those famous Disney scent effects, and turns the old *Sorcerer's Apprentice* trick back on Mickey. Some preschoolers might be a little scared at first, but taking off the 3-D glasses tones down the effect.

Cinderella's Golden Carousel ★★★

APPEAL BY AGE	PRESCHOOL ★★★★	GRADE SCHOOL ★★½
TEENS —	YOUNG ADULTS —	OVER 30 —	SENIORS —

What it is Merry-go-round. **Scope and scale** Minor attraction. **Fright potential** Not frightening in any respect. **Bottleneck rating** 9. **When to go** Before 11 a.m. or after 8 p.m. **Special comments** Adults enjoy the beauty and nostalgia of this ride. **Authors' rating** A beautiful children's ride; ★★★. **Duration of ride** About 2 minutes. **Average wait in line per 100 people ahead of you** 5 minutes. **Loading speed** Slow.

It is a long wait, but the beauty of the carousel captures everyone. The carousel (built in 1917) was discovered in New Jersey, where it was once part of an amusement park. It is beautifully maintained and especially magical at night when all the lights are on. Check out your children's delighted expressions as the painted ponies go up and down.

The Many Adventures of Winnie the Pooh ★★★½
(FASTPASS)

APPEAL BY AGE	PRESCHOOL ★★★★½	GRADE SCHOOL ★★★★	TEENS ★★★
YOUNG ADULTS ★★★		OVER 30 ★★★	SENIORS ★★★

What it is Indoor track ride. **Scope and scale** Minor attraction. **Fright potential** Not frightening in any respect. **Bottleneck rating** 8. **When to go** Before 10 a.m., in the 2 hours before closing, or use FASTPASS. **Authors' rating** Cute as the Pooh-bear himself; ★★★½. **Duration of ride** About 4 minutes. **Average wait in line per 100 people ahead of you** 4 minutes. **Loading speed** Moderate.

Thumbs Up for the Whole Family

This ride is a romp through the Hundred-Acre Wood on a blustery day. The visuals are gentle and charming without being saccharine. The Many Adventures of Winnie the Pooh is a perfect test to assess how your very young children will react to the indoor, so-called dark rides.

Movie Tip

The ride is based on a 1977 Disney animated feature, *The Many Adventures of Winnie the Pooh.* The movie and Winnie the Pooh books are perfect for very young children. Did you know that Paul Winchell won a Grammy for his voicing of Tigger? Other Disney roles of Paul Winchell include parts in *The Aristocats* as a Chinese cat and *The Fox and the Hound* as Boomer the woodpecker. He also lends his voice to evil Gargamel in the Smurfs.

Snow White's Scary Adventures ★★½

APPEAL BY AGE	PRESCHOOL ★	GRADE SCHOOL ★★★	TEENS ★★
YOUNG ADULTS ★★½		OVER 30 ★★½	SENIORS ★★½

What it is Indoor track ride. **Scope and scale** Minor attraction. **Fright potential** Moderately intense spook-house-genre attraction with some grim characters. Terrifies many preschoolers. **Bottleneck rating** 8. **When to go** Before 11 a.m. or after 6 p.m. **Authors' rating** Worth seeing if the wait isn't long; ★★½. **Duration of ride** Almost 2½ minutes. **Average wait in line per 100 people ahead of you** 6¼ minutes. **Loading speed** Moderate to slow.

Dark   Scary

"I'm Wishing" is one of the most beloved songs from Disney's first animated feature, but experiencing Snow White's Scary Adventures gives this song a new twist. You end up wishing not for the Prince to come but for the wicked witch to GO AWAY. The ride is intimidating to many young children because Snow White's Scary Adventures is more about the witch, who's more persistent than a time-share salesman, than about Snow White.

Movie Tip

The movie, a classic of course, is scary for preschoolers but a timeless must-see for older childen. Walt Disney won an honorary Academy Award for significant screen innovation with this film and received a full-size Oscar statuette with seven miniature ones. The honorary award was presented in 1938 to Walt Disney by Shirley Temple; the seven miniatures represented Doc, Grumpy, Happy, Sneezy, Bashful, Sleepy, and Dopey.

WET!

?. Ariel's Grotto ★★★

APPEAL BY AGE	PRESCHOOL ★★★★★		GRADE SCHOOL ★★★★★
TEENS ★★	YOUNG ADULTS ★	OVER 30 ★	SENIORS ★

What it is Interactive fountain and character-greeting area. **Scope and scale** Minor attraction. **Fright potential** Not frightening in any respect. **Bottleneck rating** 9. **When to go** Before 10 a.m. or after 9 p.m. **Authors' rating** One of the most elaborate of the character-greeting venues; ★★★. **Average wait in line per 100 people ahead of you** 30 minutes.

If your children spot the Grotto before you do, you're hosed in more ways than one. First, there will be no bypassing Ariel, and you can count on a long, slow-moving queue. In addition to the long wait, your child will manage to get wetter than a trout in the interactive fountain at the entrance to the Grotto. The experience gives a whole new meaning to Sebastian's song "Under the Sea." By the time you finally make it to Ariel, that's exactly where it will appear your kids have been. Early in the mornings and on cool days keep your would-be mackerels on a short leash and out of the water.

 Disney released the movie _The Little Mermaid_ in 1989. A good night's entertainment for the whole family, the film is based on the Hans Christian Andersen fairy tale of the same name. In 1990, the animated feature won the Academy Award for original movie score, and "Under the Sea" won the Academy Award for best song.

✦ Dumbo the Flying Elephant ★★★

APPEAL BY AGE	PRESCHOOL ★★★★★	GRADE SCHOOL ★★★★	TEENS ★★
YOUNG ADULTS ★★		OVER 30 ★★	SENIORS ★★

What It Is Disneyfied midway ride. **Scope and scale** Minor attraction. **Fright potential** A tame midway ride; a great favorite of most young children. **Bottleneck rating** 10. **When to go** Before 10 a.m. or after 9 p.m. **Authors' rating** An attractive children's ride; ★★★. **Duration of ride** 1½ minutes. **Average wait in line per 100 people ahead of you** 20 minutes. **Loading speed** Slow.

Making sure your child gets his fill of this tame, happy children's ride is what mother love is all about. The 90-second ride is hardly worth the long lines, unless, of course, you're under 7 years old. If Dumbo's on your must-see list, try to get the kids on board during the first half hour the park is open.

 If you have not seen _Dumbo_ (first released in 1941 and winner of an Academy Award for original music score), you have an elephant-sized gap in your Disney education. Fun for all ages, rent the movie when you get home.

?. Mad Tea Party ★★

APPEAL BY AGE	PRESCHOOL ★★★★	GRADE SCHOOL ★★★★	TEENS ★★★★
YOUNG ADULTS ★★★★		OVER 30 ★★	SENIORS ★★

What it is Midway-type spinning ride. **Scope and scale** Minor attraction. **Fright potential** Low, but this type of ride can induce motion sickness in all ages. **Bottleneck rating** 9. **When to go** Before 11 a.m. or after 5 p.m. **Special**

comments You can make the teacups spin faster by turning the wheel in the center of the cup. **Authors' rating** Fun, but not worth the wait; ★★. **Duration of ride** 1½ minutes. **Average wait in line per 100 people ahead of you** 7½ minutes. **Loading speed** Slow.

It's a party, and a mad one at that. Prepare yourself for a whirling adventure inside a giant teacup (also known as the human centrifuge). Teenagers love to lure adults into the spinning teacups, then turn the wheel in the middle (making the cup spin faster) until the adults are plastered against the sides and on the verge of throwing up. The only sane way to experience this ride with teenagers is, paradoxically, to put them in straight jackets so they can't spin the wheel. We're dying to try this. Volunteers, anyone?

My son loves this ride, but then again he is a teenager. As for me, I love the ride, too. I'll take the Mad Tea Party over Big Thunder Mountain any day. Plus, it's good training for experiencing Mission: Space at Epcot.

Liliane

Researchers at NASA determined that you're less likely to experience motion sickness if you don't ride on an empty stomach.

Bob

The Mad Tea Party is inspired by the unusual tea party scene in the 1951 Disney adaptation of Lewis Carroll's *Alice in Wonderland*. Did you know that the voice of Alice, British voice actress and school teacher Kathryn Beaumont, is also the voice of Wendy in Disney's *Peter Pan*?

★ Pooh's Playfull Spot ★★★

APPEAL BY AGE	PRESCHOOL ★★★★	GRADE SCHOOL ★★★	TEENS —
YOUNG ADULTS —		OVER 30 —	SENIORS —

What it is Playground for young children. **Scope and scale** Minor attraction. **Fright potential** Not frightening in any respect. **Bottleneck rating** 4. **When to go** Anytime. **Special comments** Good resting place for adults. **Authors' rating** A favorite of the 7-and-under crowd; ★★★.

This playground is a great place for kids and parents alike. The best part of this mini-version of the Hundred-Acre Wood is that it's small enough and sufficiently enclosed for tired parents to turn the kids loose. When you're ready to collapse and your kids are still bouncing off the walls, Pooh's Playfull Spot is as good as Club Med.

MICKEY'S TOONTOWN FAIR

MICKEY'S TOONTOWN FAIR IS THE ONLY NEW "land" to be added to the Magic Kingdom since its opening and the only land that doesn't connect to the central hub. Attractions include an opportunity to meet

Mickey Mouse, tour Mickey's and Minnie's houses, and ride a child-sized roller coaster.

If you only have one day at the Magic Kingdom and the major attractions beckon, save Mickey's Toontown Fair for a return visit. For children ages 2 to 8, however, Mickey's Toontown Fair will be a highlight of their day.

Mickey's Country House and Judge's Tent ★★★

APPEAL BY AGE	PRESCHOOL ★★★½	GRADE SCHOOL ★★★	TEENS ★★½
YOUNG ADULTS ★★½	OVER 30 ★★½		SENIORS ★★½

What it is Walk-through tour of Mickey's house and meeting with Mickey. **Scope and scale** Minor attraction. **Fright potential** Not frightening in any respect. **Bottleneck rating** 9. **When to go** Before 11:30 a.m. or after 4:30 p.m. **Authors' rating** Well done; ★★★. **Duration of tour** 15–30 minutes (depending on the crowd). **Average wait in line per 100 people ahead of you** 20 minutes. **Touring speed** Slow.

Mickey's Country House is perfect for preschoolers who want to see how Mickey lives. If your child actually insists on seeing Mickey, you'll find him on duty in the Judge's Tent next door all day. His friends, including all the princesses you can count, can be found nearby at the Toontown Hall of Fame.

Minnie's Country House ★★

APPEAL BY AGE	PRESCHOOL ★★★	GRADE SCHOOL ★★★★
TEENS ★★½	YOUNG ADULTS ★★½	OVER 30 ★★½	SENIORS ★★½

What it is Walk-through exhibit. **Scope and scale** Minor attraction. **Fright potential** Not frightening in any respect. **Bottleneck rating** 9. **When to go** Before 11:30 a.m. or after 4:30 p.m. **Authors' rating** Great detail; ★★. **Duration of tour** About 10 minutes. **Average wait in line per 100 people ahead of you** 12 minutes. **Touring speed** Slow.

I see color! I see pink! Minnie's kitchen looks like a cartoon version of a set for *Martha Stewart Living*. The kitchen is filled with recipes, magazines, and awards Minnie has won for canning and baking. The attention to detail throughout gives the house a real lived-in feel. Occasionally Minnie appears in her backyard, but usually she's in Scrooge McDuck's vault reviewing stock options with Martha.

Toontown Hall of Fame ★★

APPEAL BY AGE	PRESCHOOL ★★★★	GRADE SCHOOL ★★★★★
TEENS ★★	YOUNG ADULTS ★★	OVER 30 ★★	SENIORS ★★

What it is Character-greeting venue. **Scope and scale** Minor attraction. **Fright potential** Not frightening in any respect. **Bottleneck rating** 10. **When to go** Before 10:30 a.m. or after 5:30 p.m. **Authors' rating** You want characters? We got 'em! ★★. **Duration of greeting** About 7–10 minutes. **Average wait in line per 100 people ahead of you** 35 minutes. **Touring speed** Slow.

If your child's heart is set on meeting as many characters as possible, you've come to the right place. Of course, the wait can be a long one. Make sure—especially when it comes to the Princess Room—to know which characters are present. Many adults would rather skip this time-consuming attraction, but a parent has to do what a parent has to do. Watching your children meet their favorite Disney characters one-on-one is, as the credit card commercial puts it, priceless.

The Barnstormer at Goofy's Wiseacres Farm ★★

| APPEAL BY AGE | PRESCHOOL ★★★★ | GRADE SCHOOL ★★★ | TEENS ★★½ |
| YOUNG ADULTS ★★½ | | OVER 30 ★★½ | SENIORS ★★ |

What it is Small roller coaster. **Scope and scale** Minor attraction. **Fright potential** A children's coaster; frightens some preschoolers. **Bottleneck rating** 9. **When to go** Before 10:30 a.m., during parades, or in the evening just before the park closes. **Special comments** Must be 35 inches or taller to ride. **Authors' rating** Great for little ones, but not worth the wait for adults; ★★. **Duration of ride** About 53 seconds. **Average wait in line per 100 people ahead of you** 7 minutes. **Loading speed** Slow.

Rough　　　Scary

Remember that the height requirement for this ride is 35 inches. If you want to see how your child handles riding coasters, Goofy's Barnstormer is the perfect testing ground.

Liliane

Yours truly screamed big-time from start to end (thankfully it only lasted a minute and a half), and no way would I let the apple of my eye ride alone unless he or she is 6 years or older.

Liliane is a gentle and sensitive soul. Most kids experience rides wilder than Goofy's Barnstormer on their tricycles. When I heard Liliane wailing like a banshee on this little coaster, my first thought was that her appendix must have ruptured.

Bob

WET!

Donald's Boat ★★½

| APPEAL BY AGE | PRESCHOOL ★★★★ | GRADE SCHOOL ★★½ | TEENS — |
| YOUNG ADULTS ★½ | | OVER 30 — | SENIORS — |

What it is Playground and (when the water is running) interactive fountain. **Scope and scale** Diversion. **Fright potential** Not frightening in any respect. **Bottleneck rating** 3. **When to go** Anytime. **Authors' rating** A favorite of the 5-and-under set; ★★½.

The S.S. *Miss Daisy,* Donald Duck's very leaky boat, is an interactive wet playground that offers yet another opportunity to succumb to hypothermia. What's insidious about the *Miss Daisy,* however, is that on first glance it doesn't look like your kids will get wet. But give them five minutes and they'll look like survivors of the *Titanic.*

TOMORROWLAND

TOMORROWLAND IS A MIX OF RIDES and experiences relating to the technological development of humankind and what life will be like in the future. When Disney overhauled Tomorrowland a few years back, it bailed on trying to predict how the future might appear, opting instead for a timeless, retro Buck Rogers look.

Keep an eye out for PUSH, the talking trash can of Tomorrowland. Kids love PUSH and delight in the opportunity to talk trash with the real thing.

Astro Orbiter ★★

APPEAL BY AGE	PRESCHOOL ★★★★		GRADE SCHOOL ★★★
TEENS ★★½	YOUNG ADULTS ★★½	OVER 30 ★★	SENIORS ★

What it is Buck Rogers–style rockets revolving around a central axis. **Scope and scale** Minor attraction. **Fright potential** Visually intimidating waiting area for a relatively tame ride. **Bottleneck rating** 10. **When to go** Before 11 a.m. or after 5 p.m. **Special comments** This attraction, formerly StarJets, is not as innocuous as it appears. **Authors' rating** Not worth the wait; ★★. **Duration of ride** 1½ minutes. **Average wait in line per 100 people ahead of you** 13½ minutes. **Loading speed** Slow.

Parents beware! If you are prone to motion sickness, this ride (a) spins round and round; (b) is faster than Dumbo; and (c) for added "fun," there's a joystick that lets you raise and lower the rocket throughout your 1½ minute journey. We like to ride the Astro Orbiter at night. The combination of lighting and the view are spectacular.

Buzz Lightyear's Space Ranger Spin (FASTPASS) ★★★★

APPEAL BY AGE	PRESCHOOL ★★★★	GRADE SCHOOL ★★★★★	TEENS ★★★★★
YOUNG ADULTS ★★★★	OVER 30 ★★★★		SENIORS ★★★★

What it is Combination space travel–themed indoor ride and shooting gallery. **Scope and scale** Minor attraction. **Fright potential** Dark ride with cartoonlike aliens may frighten some preschoolers. **Bottleneck rating** 8. **When to go** Before 10:30 a.m., after 6 p.m., or use FASTPASS. **Authors' rating** A real winner! ★★★★. **Duration of ride** About 4½ minutes. **Average wait in line per 100 people ahead of you** 3 minutes. **Loading speed** Fast.

Once you get the hang of it you will come back for more, to infinity and beyond.

Totally awesome! I earned my Space Ranger Wings on my first ride. Use the joystick to spin and set up your shots, but don't spin too much because that uses up time and energy. Always aim and never stop shooting, especially at the big alien targets. Those are the ones with lots of arms and legs, and four eyes. They get you the most points.

Ian

You'll see Zurg in jail at the end of the ride. Little kids can squeeze through the bars and pretend they're in jail, too.

Hannah

 Movie Tip

The ride is based on the space-commando character, Buzz Lightyear, from the 1995 Disney/Pixar feature, *Toy Story*. Did you know that Tom Hanks and Tim Allen are the voices of Woody and Buzz?

A PEEK BEHIND THE SCENES WITH JIM HILL

SIX MILLION AA BATTERIES REQUIRED Look for WDW's version of Buzz to incorporate a popular interactive feature from its Disneyland cousin. Through the magic of the Internet, people sitting at their home computers will be able to make some elements in the attraction move around, seriously increasing the point value of various targets. This is all part of an ongoing effort by the Mouse to make the GameBoy generation bond that much more strongly with the Disney theme parks.

Space Mountain (FASTPASS) ★★★★

APPEAL BY AGE	PRESCHOOL †	GRADE SCHOOL ★★★★★	TEENS ★★★★★
YOUNG ADULTS ★★★★★		OVER 30 ★★★★	SENIORS †

† *Some preschoolers loved Space Mountain; others were frightened. The sample size of senior citizens who experienced this ride was too small to develop an accurate rating.*

What it is Roller coaster in the dark. **Scope and scale** Super headliner. **Fright potential** Very intense roller coaster in the dark; the Magic Kingdom's wildest ride and a scary roller coaster by any standard. **Bottleneck rating** 10. **When to go** When the park opens, between 6 and 7 p.m., during the hour before closing, or use FASTPASS. **Special comments** Great fun and action; much wilder than Big Thunder Mountain Railroad. Must be 44 inches tall to ride; children younger than age 7 must be accompanied by an adult. Switching-off option provided (page 220). **Authors' rating** An unusual roller coaster with excellent special effects; not to be missed; ★★★★. **Duration of ride** Almost 3 minutes. **Average wait in line per 100 people ahead of you** 3 minutes. **Assumes** Two tracks, one dedicated to FASTPASS riders, dispatching at 21-second intervals. **Loading speed** Moderate to fast.

Dark   Scary   Rough   Motion Sickness

Space Mountain is one of the zipiest (and darkest) rides in Walt Disney World, lasting just under three minutes and including several abrupt turns and plummets. So, those with neck or back problems or vertigo should probably skip it. However, this ride achieves "only" about 28 mph, a leisurely pace by 21st-century standards.

Space Mountain also involves sudden blackouts, as do many thrill rides at Disney World. Those who suffer from claustrophobia (Liliane), tend to panic in the dark (Liliane), or have vision problems with extremes of light and darkness (Liliane) should avoid this attraction. Plunged into darkness and bouncing around like a marble in a spittoon, many warmly recall Space Mountain as the longest three minutes of their life. Your kids will love it, of course.

If you're not sure that you are brave enough to ride Space Mountain, you can always take the Tomorrowland Transit Authority and watch the actual ride in action before you get in line.

Ian

I dream of riding Space Mountain at the pace of Spaceship Earth in Epcot. At last, I would be able to enjoy the twinkling lights.

Liliane

All of the people screaming sort of scared me at first. I did like all the flashing lights and the astronaut stuff. Look for the giant chocolate-chip cookies flying by on the ceiling when you're in line.

Hannah

Tomorrowland Indy Speedway ★

APPEAL BY AGE	PRESCHOOL ★★★★		GRADE SCHOOL ★★★
TEENS ★	YOUNG ADULTS ½	OVER 30 ½	SENIORS ½

What it is Drive-'em-yourself miniature cars. **Scope and scale** Major attraction. **Fright potential** Not frightening in any respect. **Bottleneck rating** 9. **When to go** Before 11 a.m. or after 5 p.m. **Special comments** Must be 52 inches tall to drive unassisted. **Authors' rating** Boring for adults (★); great for preschoolers. **Duration of ride** About 4¼ minutes. **Average wait in line per 100 people ahead of you** 4½ minutes. **Assumes** 285-car turnover every 20 minutes. **Loading speed** Slow.

The sleek cars and racetrack noise will get your younger kids hopped up to ride this extremely prosaic attraction. The minimum height requirement of 52 inches means that the younger (or shorter) set will have to ride with an adult. We suggest you work the accelerator and brakes and let your future Kasey Kahne steer the car. Resist the urge to dispatch your little one with a taller sibling, unless the sibling is willing to hand over the steering wheel. The loading and unloading speed is excruciatingly slow, and the attraction offers hardly any protection from the sun.

What I like about this ride is you don't have to be 16 [years old] to drive! Dude, you've got total control, ... well, almost. Pretend you're an Indy car driver like Sam Hornish Jr. Turn the steering wheel, put your foot on the gas, and even hit the brakes ... just like a go-cart. Sweet!

Ian

Tomorrowland Transit Authority ★★★

APPEAL BY AGE	PRESCHOOL ★★★★	GRADE SCHOOL ★★★	TEENS ★★½
YOUNG ADULTS ★★★		OVER 30 ★★★	SENIORS ★★★

What it is Scenic tour of Tomorrowland. **Scope and scale** Minor attraction. **Fright potential** Not frightening in any respect. **Bottleneck rating** 3. **When to go** During hot, crowded times of day (11:30 a.m.–4:30 p.m.). **Special comments** A good way to check out the FASTPASS line at Space Mountain. **Authors'**

rating Scenic, relaxing, informative; ★★★. **Duration of ride** 10 minutes. **Average wait in line per 100 people ahead of you** 1½ minutes. **Assumes** 39 trains operating. **Loading speed** Fast.

Thumbs Up for the Whole Family

There is never a line, and the ride is ideal for taking a break. It's also a great way to see Tomorrowland all aglow at night. The route gives a sneak preview of Buzz Lightyear's Space Ranger Spin, and you can check on those screams emanating from Space Mountain. Most of the time cast members will let you ride several times in a row without having to get off. This last thing, according to many moms, makes the ride a great option for nursing.

It's good because you don't have to scream at anything, and there are no hills.

Hannah

Walt Disney's Carousel of Progress (open seasonally) ★★★

APPEAL BY AGE	PRESCHOOL ★★	GRADE SCHOOL ★★★	TEENS ★★★
YOUNG ADULTS ★★★		OVER 30 ★★★	SENIORS ★★★★

What it is Audio-animatronic theater production. **Scope and scale** Major attraction. **Fright potential** Not frightening in any respect. **Bottleneck rating** 4. **When to go** Anytime. **Authors' rating** Nostalgic, warm, and happy; ★★★. **Duration of presentation** 18 minutes. **Preshow entertainment** Documentary on the attraction's long history. **Probable waiting time** Less than 10 minutes.

A piece of Disney history not to be missed. The attraction offers a nostalgic look at how technology and electricity have changed the lives of an audio-animatronic family over several generations.

Laugh Floor Comedy Club ★★★

APPEAL BY AGE	PRESCHOOL ★★½	GRADE SCHOOL ★★★★	TEENS ★★★
YOUNG ADULTS ★★★½		OVER 30 ★★★½	SENIORS ★★★★

What it is Interactive comedy club starring Pixar characters from *Monsters, Inc.* **Scope and scale** Major attraction. **Fright potential** Not much is frightening, but they are monsters, after all. **Bottleneck rating** 8. **When to go** After 3 p.m. **Authors' rating** Good but doesn't live up to its potential; ★★★. **Duration of presentation** 20 minutes. **Preshow entertainment** Yes. **Probable waiting time** 25 minutes.

This attraction features the characters Mike and Sully from Disney/Pixar's animated film *Monsters, Inc.* If you've seen the movie, you'll recall that Mike and Sully are monsters living in Monstropolis, a city that derives its electricity from the screams of small children. In the film, the duo discovers that children's laughter makes much more electricity than screams.

The premise of the attraction is that Monstropolis still needs electricity and Mike and Sully have been recruited to do a stand-up comedy routine to harness the laughter of Walt Disney World guests.

Stitch's Great Escape (FASTPASS) ★★

APPEAL BY AGE	PRESCHOOL —	GRADE SCHOOL ★★★	TEENS ★★★
YOUNG ADULTS ★★½		OVER 30 ★★	SENIORS ★★

What it is Theater-in-the-round sci-fi adventure show. **Scope and scale** Major attraction. **When to go** Before 11 a.m. or after 6 p.m.; try during parades. **Special comments** Frightens children of all ages; 40-inch minimum height requirement. **Authors' rating** A cheap coat of paint on a broken car; ★★. **Duration of presentation** About 12 minutes. **Preshow entertainment** About 6 minutes. **Probable waiting time** 12–35 minutes.

Dark Scary Loud

Disney's press release touting *Stitch* as a child-friendly attraction was about as accurate as Enron's bookkeeping. You are held in your seat by overhead restraints and subjected to something weird clambering around you and whispering to you in a theater darker than a stack of black cats. Enough to scare the pants off many kids ages 10 and younger.

Liliane

Not fair! I love *Stitch* but agree with parents of young children who have complained about how scary the show is, especially because the overhead restraint prevents you from leaving your seat to comfort your child if need arises. Preteens and up, however, will enjoy the wicked fun of the show. All I could think of was the Pink Floyd song "Comfortably Numb": "Is there anybody in there?"

Movie Tip

Skip the show, but do not discount the movie. *Lilo & Stitch* (released in 2002) is a great family movie. The Hawaiian culture of Ohana, which in Hawaiian means extended family including friends, is the cornerstone philosophy of this wonderful flick. The movie reminds children about the importance of good behavior and points out to adults that there is good inside every child no matter how rotten he or she may behave at times.

LIVE ENTERTAINMENT
and PARADES *in the*
MAGIC KINGDOM

IT'S IMPOSSIBLE TO TAKE IN ALL THE MANY live entertainment offerings at the Magic Kingdom in a single day. To experience both the attractions and the live entertainment, we recommend you allocate at least two days to this park. In addition to parades, stage shows, and fireworks, check the daily entertainment schedule (*Times Guide*) or ask a cast member about concerts in Fantasyland, square dancing in front of the *Country Bear Jamboree,* the Flag Retreat at Town Square, and the appearances of the various bands, singers, and street performers that roam the park daily.

Following is a short list of daily events with special appeal for families with children:

CASTLE FORECOURT STAGE "DREAM ALONG WITH MICKEY" A daytime stage show in front of Cinderella Castle featuring a veritable pantheon of Disney characters and music.

STORYTIME WITH BELLE AT THE FAIRYTALE GARDEN Belle and several helpers select children from the small amphitheater audience and dress them up as characters from *Beauty and the Beast.* As Belle tells the story, the children act out the roles. There is a three- to five-minute meet-and-greet with photo and autograph opportunities afterward. Storytime takes place six to eight times a day; check the daily entertainment schedule (*Times Guide*) for show times. The Fairytale Garden is located next to the Enchanted Grove refreshment stand in Fantasyland, across from Cosmic Ray's in Tomorrowland.

Storytime with Belle reminds me of the movie *The Secret Garden.* It's possibly the only entertainment offering that can make you forget for a moment that you're in a bustling theme park with 50,000 other people. Don't forget to load your camera; the performance is a top photo op. Priceless!

Liliane

SWORD IN THE STONE CEREMONY Merlin the Magician selects youngsters from the audience to test their courage and strength by removing the sword, Excalibur, from the stone. The ceremony is performed about six times daily in front of Cinderella's Golden Carousel. Check your entertainment schedule (*Times Guide*) for show times.

The child who manages to pull Excalibur from the stone is crowned King for a day with a grown-up from the audience having to carry his robe so the "King" can take a majestic walk.

Liliane

The ceremony is based on the 1963 Walt Disney Production *The Sword in the Stone,* telling the legend of King Arthur and the famous wizard Merlin. The story is based on a book by T. H. White. Did you know that the voice of the narrator, Sebastian Cabot, is also the voice of Bagheera in the 1967 Disney Production *The Jungle Book?*

LET'S HAVE A BALL Consult your *Times Guide* for showings of this music-filled pageant, held daily in front of Cinderella Castle. Guests receive dancing and etiquette lessons in preparation for a royal ball. Once the ball gets started, your little prince and princess will dance and mingle with the royal court. Parents, get the cameras ready!

WOODY'S COWBOY CAMP Calling all cowboys and cowgirls for a fun time with Woody, Jesse, Sam, and Bullseye. Sam the Singin' Cowboy leads a western hoedown in Frontierland. Daily performances are listed in your *Times Guide.* Yee-haw!

MAIN STREET FAMILY FUN PARADE Don't miss this unique parade. Guests join Disney characters and a marching band for a fun-filled rally down Main Street. The grand finale is a flag-waving patriotic salute on Town Square. Check your *Times Guide* to join this small-town Fourth of July Parade.

CAPTAIN JACK SPARROW'S PIRATE TUTORIAL Sign up with Captain Jack Sparrow and his crewman Mack for a hilarious pirate one-on-one. Check your *Times Guide* for the scheduled daily encounters and meet the Johnny Depp look-alike right next to the Pirates of the Caribbean ride. The lucky chosen buccaneers are taught how to be pirates and receive an honorary pirate certificate at the end of the show.

The show is wonderful for little wannabe pirates and grown-ups alike and draws quite a crowd, especially ladies. I signed up for the pirate's life in a jiffy.

Liliane

PARADES Parades at the Magic Kingdom are full-fledged spectaculars with dozens of Disney characters and amazing special effects. An outstanding new afternoon parade is introduced every year or two; while some elements such as the Disney characters remain constant, the theme, music, and float design change. The evening parade is a high-tech affair and not to be missed. Always check your entertainment schedule (*Times Guide*) to make sure what parade is happening when as well as the guide map for the parade route.

Remember, parades disrupt traffic and it is nearly impossible to move around the park when one is going on. Parades also draw thousands of guests away from the attractions, making parade time the perfect moment to catch your favorite attraction with a shorter line. Finally, be advised that the Walt Disney World Railroad shuts down during parades.

The best place to view a parade is the upper platform of the Walt Disney Railroad station, but you will have to stake out your position 30 to 45 minutes before the event. Try also, especially on rainy days, the covered walkway between Liberty Tree Tavern and The Diamond Horseshoe Saloon on the border of Liberty Square and Frontierland.

FIREWORKS The nightly fireworks show starts just after Tinker Bell's flight in the sky above Cinderella Castle. The fireworks are synchronized to music from beloved Disney films.

View the fireworks from the upper platform of the railroad station. This vantage point also provides an easy path to the park exit when the fireworks are over. Our favorite spot, if we intend to remain in the park after the fireworks, is the roofless patio of the Plaza Pavilion located in Tomorrowland on the border with Main Street, U.S.A.

A very special spot to view the fireworks is atop the nearby Contemporary Resort at the California Grill. Once the fireworks begin, the restaurant dims its lights and broadcasts the music from the show.

BAY LAKE AND SEVEN SEAS LAGOON FLOATING ELECTRICAL PAGEANT Performed at nightfall at about 9 p.m. most of the year on Seven Seas Lagoon and Bay Lake, this pageant is the perfect culmination of a wonderful day. You have to leave the Magic Kingdom to see this floating electric light show. Take the monorail to the Polynesian Resort, get the kids a snack and yourself a drink, and walk to the end of the pier to watch the show. Pure magic, less the crowds.

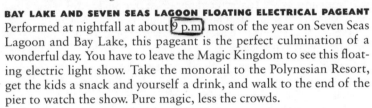

FAVORITE EATS IN MAGIC KINGDOM		
LAND	FOOD ITEM	WHERE THEY CAN BE FOUND
MAIN STREET	Homemade goodies and Krispie treats	Main Street Bakery
ADVENTURELAND	Churros and ice-cream bars	El Pirata y el Perico
FANTASYLAND	Sundaes, fudge brownies, and strawberry shortcake	Mrs. Pott's Cupboard
	Kids meals of mac and cheese and burgers	The Pinocchio Village Haus
	Frozen Cokes, soft pretzels, chips	Scuttle's Landing
	Fries	The Village Fry Shoppe
FRONTIERLAND	Burgers, use the great fixin's station	Pecos Bill's Tall Tale Inn & Cafe
LIBERTY SQUARE	Soup and sandwiches	Columbia Harbour House
	Funnel cake	Sleepy Hollow
TOMORROWLAND	Rotisserie chicken, ribs, kosher choices	Cosmic Ray's Starlight Cafe
	Turkey legs, pretzels, and frozen soda	The Lunching Pad
TOONTOWN	Fruits	Toontown Farmer's Market

EXIT STRATEGIES

LEAVING THE PARK AFTER EVENING PARADES and fireworks is no small matter. Huge throngs depart the Magic Kingdom after parades, fireworks, and at closing. Trust us, with small children, you don't want to be among them. The best strategy for avoiding the mass exodus is to view both fireworks and parades from the upper platform of the railroad station at the Town Square end of Main Street. As soon as the performance concludes, beat feet to the park exits. If you remain in the park after the fireworks and parades, don't wait until closing time to leave. On a busy day give yourself a 30- to 40-minute cushion.

Another strategy for beating the masses out of the park (if your car is in the TTC lot) is to watch the early parade and then leave before the fireworks begin. Line up for the ferry instead of the monorail. A ferry departs about every eight to ten minutes. Try to catch the ferry that will be crossing Seven Seas Lagoon while the fireworks are in progress. The best vantage point is on the top deck to the right of the pilothouse. Your chances are about 50/50 of catching it just right. If you are in front of the line for the ferry and you don't want to board the boat that's loading, stop at the gate and let people pass you. You'll be the first to board the next boat.

MAGIC KINGDOM TOURING PLANS

OUR STEP-BY-STEP TOURING PLANS are field-tested, independently verified itineraries that will keep you moving counter to the crowd flow and allow you to see as much as possible in a single day with a minimum of time wasted in line.

Don't worry that other people will be following the plans and render them useless. Fewer than 1 in every 350 people in the park will have been exposed to this information.

Bob

We developed many of these plans when preparing to visit the Magic Kingdom with our own children (ages 2 through 8). Some plans offer a midday break of at least three hours back at your hotel. It's debatable whether the kids will need the nap more than you, but you'll thank us later, we promise. Our kids are picky eaters, too: one went through a phase where she ate nothing but beige food (chicken fingers, pasta, macaroni and cheese, and the like). The restaurants we recommend in these plans are all kid friendly and should work for almost everyone.

If you've got just one day to spend in the Magic Kingdom, our single-day plans will allow you to see the best attractions for kids while avoiding crowds and long waits in line. If you're looking for a more relaxed, less structured tour of the park, try the one-and-a-half, two-day, or Sleepy Head plans. These alternatives have less backtracking, the same midday breaks, and a much more casual feel. The Sleepy Head plans assume you'll get to the park around 11 a.m., so they're great for mornings when you don't feel like getting out of bed early.

The different touring plans for each park are described below. The descriptions will tell you for whom (for example, tweens, parents with preschoolers, grandparents, and so on) or for what situation (such as sleeping late or enjoying the park at night) the plans are designed. The actual touring plans are located on pages 407–415 at the back of the book. Each plan includes a numbered map of the park in question to help you find your way around. Clip the plan of your choice out of the book by cutting along the line indicated, and take it with you to the park.

MAGIC KINGDOM HAPPY FAMILY ONE-DAY TOURING PLAN This is a one-day touring plan of the Magic Kingdom that includes something for everyone in the family: small children, tweens (children ages 8 to 12), teenagers, parents, and seniors. The plan keeps the entire family together for most of the day, plus lunch and dinner. A midday break is integrated into the day's touring.

The plan includes attractions very popular with small children, such as Dumbo and Ariel's Grotto in Fantasyland and the Magic Carpets of Aladdin in Adventureland. For older kids and teenagers, we recommend thrill rides such as Space Mountain and Big Thunder Mountain, with both groups getting back together when each is done.

MAGIC KINGDOM ONE-DAY TOURING PLAN FOR GRANDPARENTS WITH SMALL CHILDREN The attractions in this touring plan are generally those rated at least three stars (out of five) by both seniors and small children, plus a handful of senior-friendly attractions that kids just love. Specifically designed to minimize walking, this plan also includes a midday break of at least three hours and dining recommendations for lunch and dinner. We don't try to cover the entire park, either: most of Tomorrowland is left as an option if everyone's feeling up for it.

To convert this itinerary into a two-day plan, one option is to do steps 1 through 14 on Day One. If you're returning in the morning of Day Two, do steps 25 and 26 first, then steps 16 through 24. An alternate strategy for a morning and afternoon is to do steps 1 through 14 on the morning of Day One and steps 15 through 28 on the afternoon of Day Two.

MAGIC KINGDOM ONE-DAY TOURING PLAN FOR TWEENS AND THEIR PARENTS A one-day plan for parents with children ages 8 to 12. It includes every attraction rated three stars and higher by this age group and sets aside ample time for lunch and dinner.

MAGIC KINGDOM TWO-DAY TOURING PLAN FOR PARENTS WITH SMALL CHILDREN This is a two-day touring plan designed specifically to

eliminate extra walking and backtracking. It is a comprehensive touring plan of the Magic Kingdom and
includes every child-friendly attraction in the park. The plan features
long midday breaks for rest and naps
outside the park, as well as recommendations for good dining choices
inside the park.

Switching off allows
adults to enjoy the more
adventuresome attrac-
tions while keeping the
group together. Liliane

**MAGIC KINGDOM TWO-DAY SLEEPY HEAD TOURING PLAN FOR PARENTS
WITH SMALL CHILDREN** Another version of the two-day touring plan
described above, this plan allows families with young children to
sleep in, arrive at the park in the late morning, and still see the very
best attractions in the Magic Kingdom over two days. Each day also
contains a one-hour break inside the park, and we've made specific
recommendations on the best spots to rest and cool off. The plan
includes lunch and dinner suggestions for both days, with plenty of
time to explore the park on either day.

**PARENTS' MAGIC KINGDOM TOURING PLANS FOR AN AFTERNOON AND
ONE FULL DAY** This day-and-a-half plan works perfectly if you're
arriving in Orlando late in the morning of your first vacation day and
can't wait to start touring. It also works great for families who want
to sleep in one morning after spending a full day in the Magic Kingdom the day before.

The attractions in these plans are the same as those found in the
standard one-day plans for parents with small children, so these day-
and-a-half itineraries also work as relaxed versions of those plans.
Both plans employ FASTPASS and some version of a "wait 'em out"
crowd strategy, whereby you'll take advantage of lower evening
crowds to visit the more popular attractions. The plans should work
well during the more crowded times of the year, and we've provided
FASTPASS alternatives for the more popular attractions in case
they're out of passes by the time you arrive.

PRELIMINARY INSTRUCTIONS FOR
ALL MAGIC KINGDOM TOURING PLANS

ON DAYS OF MODERATE-TO-HEAVY ATTENDANCE, follow your
chosen touring plan exactly, deviating only:

1. When you aren't interested in an attraction it lists. For example, the
   plan may tell you to go to Tomorrowland and ride Space Mountain,
   a roller coaster. If you don't enjoy roller coasters, skip this step and
   proceed to the next.
2. When you encounter a very long line at an attraction the touring plan
   calls for. Crowds ebb and flow at the park, and an unusually long line
   may have gathered at an attraction to which you're directed. For example, you arrive at The Haunted Mansion and find extremely long lines.

It's possible that this is a temporary situation caused by several hundred people arriving en masse from a recently concluded performance of *The Hall of Presidents* nearby. If this is the case, skip The Haunted Mansion and go to the next step, returning later to retry.

WHAT TO DO IF YOU GET OFF TRACK

IF AN UNEXPECTED INTERRUPTION OR PROBLEM throws the touring plan off, consult the recommended attraction visitation times in the attraction profile for the preferred times of day to visit attractions.

BEFORE YOU GO

1. Call ☎ 407-824-4321 the day before you go to check the official opening time.
2. Purchase admission before you arrive.
3. Familiarize yourself with park-opening procedures (described on page 208) and reread the touring plan you've chosen so that you know what you're likely to encounter.

MAGIC KINGDOM TRIVIA QUIZ
By Lou Mongello

1. If you enter Adventureland from Main Street, which ride do you hit first?
   a. Pirates
   b. *Enchanted Tiki Room*
   c. Swiss Family Treehouse
   d. Magic Carpets of Aladdin

2. Which of these is not one of the lands in the Magic Kingdom?
   a. Adventureland
   b. Frontierland
   c. Discoveryland
   d. Mickey's Toontown Fair

3. On which ride can you hear singing dolls from around the world?
   a. *Mickey's PhilharMagic*
   b. It's a Small World
   c. The Jungle Cruise
   d. The Haunted Mansion

4. On what ride in the Magic Kingdom do you ride on elephants?
   a. Winnie the Pooh
   b. Dumbo
   c. Peter Pan's Flight
   d. The Many Adventures of Winnie the Pooh

5. What is the name of the log flume ride in the Magic Kindgom?
   a. Splash Mountain
   b. Big Thunder Mountain
   c. Space Mountain
   d. Expedition Everest

6. You can find rides in the Magic Kingdom based on all of these movies EXCEPT:
   a. *Tarzan*
   b. *Snow White and the Seven Dwarfs*
   c. *Peter Pan*
   d. *Aladdin*

7. What princess lives in the castle in the Magic Kingdom?
   a. Ariel
   b. Aurora
   c. Cinderella
   d. Snow White

8. What type of animal is Zazu?
   a. Dog
   b. Cat
   c. Bird
   d. Lion

9. How many "happy haunts" can be found in the Haunted Mansion?
   a. 1
   b. None
   c. 999
   d. 71

10. Where can you find "Big Al"?
   a. Splash Mountain
   b. Mickey's Toontown Fair
   c. *The Hall of Presidents*
   d. *Country Bear Jamboree*

11. In *Stitch's Great Escape,* what Experiment Number is Stitch?
   a. 1
   b. 626
   c. 1971
   d. S68

12. Who are the hosts of the *Enchanted Tiki Room?*
   a. Timon and Pumbaa
   b. Iago and Zazu
   c. Chip and Dale
   d. Zac and Cody

13. The spinning teacups at the Mad Tea Party are based on what Disney movie?
   a. *Chicken Little*
   b. *Aladdin*
   c. *Cinderella*
   d. *Alice in Wonderland*

14. Who gives a tutorial in Adventureland teaching kids how to be a pirate?
   a. Captain Barbossa
   b. Captain EO
   c. Captain Hook
   d. Captain Jack Sparrow

15. How many lanterns hang from the Liberty Tree in Liberty Square?
   a. 1
   b. 7
   c. 13
   d. 71

16. Where in the Magic Kingdom can you hear, "If you should decide to join us, final arrangements may be made at the end of the tour."
   a. *Monster's Inc. Laugh Floor Comedy Club*
   b. *Walt Disney's Carousel of Progress*
   c. The Haunted Mansion
   d. The Jungle Cruise

Answers can be found on page 386.

Trivia content courtesy of Lou Mongello, author of Disney Trivia; *www.disneyworldtrivia.com.*

PART EIGHT

EPCOT

EDUCATION, INSPIRATION, AND CORPORATE IMAGERY are the focus at Epcot, the most adult of the Walt Disney World theme parks. What it gains in taking a futuristic, visionary, and technological look at the world, it loses, just a bit, in warmth, happiness, and charm. Some people find the attempts at education to be superficial; others want more entertainment and less education. Most visitors, however, are in between, finding plenty of amusement *and* information alike.

Epcot's theme areas are distinctly different. Future World combines Disney creativity and major corporations' technological resources to examine where humankind has come from and where we're going. World Showcase features landmarks, cuisine, and culture from almost a dozen nations and is meant to be a sort of permanent World's Fair.

So you thought the Magic Kingdom was big? Epcot is more than twice as large as the Magic Kingdom; so unless one day is all you have, plan on spending two days at Epcot to savor all it has to offer. While Epcot, unlike the Magic Kingdom, does not stand out as a "natural" for kids, rest assured that families can have as much fun at Epcot as at any of the other theme parks.

Now for the practical stuff: Future World always opens first; that is where you start your day. The World Showcase opens later at 11 a.m. But first things first: call ☎ 407-824-4321 for exact park hours. If you are lodging at a Disney hotel, consider visiting when the park offers morning or evening Extra Magic Hours. Once you arrive, pick up a park map and the daily entertainment schedule (*Times Guide*). If you are a Disney hotel guest and the park offers Extra Magic (morning or evening) Hours, grab the extra flyer that lists all the attractions open during the additional hours. If you intend to stay for Extra Magic Hours in the evening, you'll need to obtain a special wristband. The wristband is available two hours prior to official closing time at several locations identified on the Extra Magic Evening

Hours flyer. You must show your room card, and all members of your party must be present to obtain the wristband.

EPCOT SERVICES

STROLLER AND WHEELCHAIR RENTAL are available inside the main entrance to the left toward the rear of the Entrance Plaza. For storage lockers, turn right at Spaceship Earth. The Baby-Care Needs Center is on the World Showcase side of the Odyssey restaurant complex to the rear of Test Track. At the same location are first-aid and lost-persons services. For a live entertainment schedule and dining reservations, stop at Guest Relations to the left of Spaceship Earth. Lost and Found is located at the main entrance. Banking services (ATMs) are available outside the main entrance, on the Future World Bridge, and in World Showcase at the Germany Pavilion. Air-conditioned Pet Care Kennels are located adjacent to the park entrance.

KIDCOT FUN STOPS

THIS PROGRAM, DESIGNED TO MAKE EPCOT more interesting for younger visitors, is basically a movable feast of simple arts and crafts projects. Tables are set up at some locations in Future World and at each pavilion in World Showcase. The tables are staffed by cast members who discuss their native country with the children and engage them in a craft project. Look for the brightly colored Kidcot signs. Participation is free. For a memento and to augment the experience, you can purchase a World Showcase Passport for your children. The passports are sold for $10 at most stores throughout Epcot. As you visit the different lands, cast members at the Kidcot stations will stamp the passport. If your child is really interested in different lands, Guest Relations offers free fact sheets for each country.

Children as young as age 3 will enjoy the Kidcot Fun Stops. If you do not want to spring for the Passport, the Disney folks will be happy to stamp an autograph book or just about anything else, including you child's forehead.

FUTURE WORLD

Spaceship Earth ★★★★

APPEAL BY AGE	PRESCHOOL ★★★	GRADE SCHOOL ★★★★	TEENS ★★★½
YOUNG ADULTS ★★★½		OVER 30 ★★★★	SENIORS ★★★★

What it is Educational dark ride through past, present, and future. **Scope and scale** Headliner. **Fright potential** Dark and imposing presentation intimidates a few preschoolers. **Bottleneck rating** 7. **When to go** Before 10 a.m. or after 4 p.m.

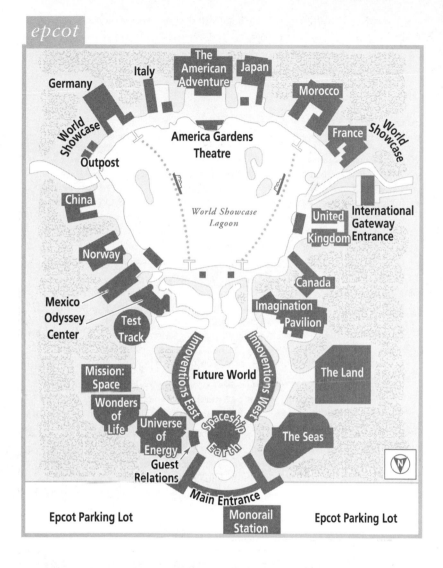

epcot

Germany

Italy

The American Adventure

Japan

Morocco

World Showcase

Outpost

America Gardens Theatre

France

World Showcase

China

World Showcase Lagoon

United Kingdom

International Gateway Entrance

Norway

Mexico

Odyssey Center

Test Track

Canada

Imagination Pavilion

Mission: Space

Wonders of Life

Universe of Energy

Innoventions East

Future World

Innoventions West

Spaceship Earth

The Land

The Seas

Guest Relations

Main Entrance

Epcot Parking Lot

Monorail Station

Epcot Parking Lot

Special comments If lines are long when you arrive, try again after 4 p.m. **Authors' rating** One of Epcot's best; not to be missed; ★★★★. **Duration of ride** About 16 minutes. **Average wait in line per 100 people ahead of you** 3 minutes. **Loading speed** Fast.

This ride spirals through the 18-story interior of Epcot's premier landmark, taking guests through audio-animatronic scenes depicting mankind's development in communications from cave

Thumbs Up for the Whole Family

> I hate this ride because it's boring. Most of these people didn't
> have cars or TV or anything we have today.
>
> Hannah

painting to the Internet. It's actually more fun than it sounds and
is carried off with a lot of humor. Spaceship Earth draws crowds
like a magnet first thing in the morning because it is so close to
the park entrance.

Innoventions ★★★½

APPEAL BY AGE	PRESCHOOL ★½	GRADE SCHOOL ★★★½	TEENS ★★★
YOUNG ADULTS ★★★½		OVER 30 ★★★	SENIORS ★★★

What it is Static and hands-on exhibits relating to products and technologies of
the near future. **Scope and scale** Major diversion. **Fright potential** Not
frightening in any respect. **Bottleneck rating** 8. **When to go** On your second
day at Epcot or after seeing all major attractions. **Special comments** Most
exhibits demand time and participation to be rewarding; not much gained here
by a quick walk-through. **Authors' rating** Vastly improved; ★★★½.

Innoventions consists of two huge, crescent-shaped structures separated by
a central plaza. Innoventions East and West provide visitors with an opportunity to preview products of tomorrow in a fun, hands-on manner.
Nothing is gained from a quick walk through and if you are short on time,
save this vast display of forward-looking technology for another day. If you
can dedicate two days to Epcot, by all means go on the second day and discover the latest virtual-reality games, high-definition TV, and voice-
activated appliances. Get a floor plan; you'll need it!

> This is a great place for parents to abandon their teenagers—at
> least for a while—to enjoy a meal of pan-seared foie gras and
> roasted quail at Le Bistro de Paris (France).
>
> Liliane

> Whoa! You gotta check out the e-mail postcards. Star in your
> own cartoon and e-mail it to all your friends. The best is in
> Innoventions. I put myself in an alien movie and landed on
> Mars! On the way home we couldn't wait to get there to see it
> on our computer. A very cool souvenir—and it's free.
>
> Ian

ICE STATION COOL

ATTACHED TO THE FOUNTAIN SIDE OF INNOVENTIONS WEST is a
sort of international soda fountain called Club Cool. The exhibit provides free unlimited samples of soft drinks from around the world.
Kids will love to fill their own tasting cups and move from one sampling
station to the next. Mix lemon, water, and honey and you get Kinley,
popular in Israel. In Mozambique Krest Ginger Ale is in, and in China
a drink based on watermelon is highly popular. The Japanese recommend the nutrition and health benefits of a vitamin drink, and the Ital-
ians are in love with a beverage that could chalk up great sales as an
emetic in the U.S. Vegetabeta, anyone?

Ice Station Cool also lives up to its name; it is cool inside and makes for a good meeting place.

[Ice Station Cool is] my favorite place to go when I'm thirsty, and the drinks are FREE. You can have as much as you want, soft drinks that is, from all over the world. Some are pretty yucky but some are pretty good. Give it a try and see what you think. Coke from China is not bad.

Ian

THE SEAS PAVILION

THE SEAS IS HOME TO ONE OF AMERICA'S top marine aquariums, a ride, an interactive animated film, and a number of first-class educational exhibits. A comprehensive makeover featuring characters from the animated feature *Finding Nemo* brings some whimsy and much-needed levity to what was heretofore educationally brilliant but somewhat staid. Before the makeover, The Seas (or The Living Seas, as it was previously known) was a snoozer for children. In its new incarnation, it ranks near the top of the kids' hit parade.

✻ The Seas Main Tank and Exhibits ★★★½

APPEAL BY AGE	PRESCHOOL ★★★	GRADE SCHOOL ★★★	TEENS ★★★
YOUNG ADULTS ★★★		OVER 30 ★★★	SENIORS ★★★★

What it is A huge saltwater aquarium, plus exhibits on oceanography, ocean ecology, and sea life. **Scope and scale** Major attraction. **Fright potential** Not frightening in any respect. **Bottleneck rating** 7. **When to go** Before 11:30 a.m. or after 5 p.m. **Authors' rating** An excellent marine exhibit; ★★★½. **Average wait in line per 100 people ahead of you** 3½ minutes. **Loading speed** Fast.

Take a *Finding Nemo*–themed ride to Sea Base to start your discovery of The Seas' main tank and exhibits. Watch scientists and divers conduct actual marine experiments in the main tank containing fish, mammals, and crustaceans in a simulation of an ocean ecosystem. Visitors can observe the

Thumbs Up for the Whole Family

activity through windows below the surface (including inside the Coral Reef restaurant). Children will be enchanted to discover the substantial fish population and the many exhibits offered.

✻ The Seas with Nemo and Friends ★★★½

APPEAL BY AGE	PRESCHOOL ★★★★	GRADE SCHOOL ★★★★½	TEENS ★★★★
YOUNG ADULTS ★★★★		OVER 30 ★★★★	SENIORS ★★★★

What it is Ride through a tunnel in The Seas' main tank. **Scope and scale** Major attraction. **Fright potential** Not frightening in any respect. **Bottleneck rating** 7. **When to go** Before 11 a.m. or after 5 p.m. **Special comments** Ride features characters from the animated hit *Finding Nemo*. **Authors' rating** Educational *and* fun; ★★★½. **Duration of ride** 4 minutes. **Probable average wait in line per 100 people ahead of you** 3½ minutes. **Probable loading speed** Fast.

Upon entering The Seas, you proceed to the loading area where you'll be made comfortable in a "clam-mobile" for your journey through the aquarium. The technology used makes it seem as if the animated characters are swimming with the live fish. Meet Mr. Ray and help Dory, Bruce, Marlin, Squirt, and Crush find Nemo. This new cool ride attracts lots of the lovable clownfish's fans, so ride early.

Clam-mobiles! This ride is fun because it shows real fish and real dolphins, and sometimes real scuba divers! I still get really cautious when I see real sharks, but they can't break the glass and attack you.

Hannah

 If you have not seen *Finding Nemo,* rent it prior to your visit. You will not soon forget this superb family movie that won the 2004 Oscar for best animated feature. Did you know that Alexander Gould, who gives his voice to little Nemo, is also the voice behind Bambi in the Disney animated sequel *Bambi II*?

 ### *Turtle Talk with Crush* ★★★★

APPEAL BY AGE	**PRESCHOOL** ★★★★½	**GRADE SCHOOL** ★★★★½	**TEENS** ★★★★
YOUNG ADULTS ★★★★		**OVER 30** ★★★★	**SENIORS** ★★★½

What it is An interactive animated film. **Scope and scale** Minor attraction. **Fright potential** Not frightening in any respect. **Bottleneck rating** 9. **When to go** Before 11 a.m. or after 5 p.m. **Special comments** Get there early to avoid long lines; a real spirit lifter. **Authors' rating** Amazing technology; ★★★★. **Duration of the presentation** 17 minutes. **Probable waiting time** 10–20 minutes before 11 a.m. and after 5 p.m.; as much as 40–60 minutes during the more crowded part of the day.

Thumbs Up for the Whole Family

This interactive theater show starring the 153-year-old surfer-turtle from the film *Finding Nemo* starts like a typical Disney theme-park movie but quickly turns into an interactive encounter as Crush begins conversations with guests in the audience. Not to be missed!

Turtle Talk with Crush? I like this show a lot. Don't miss it. You actually feel like you're in the movie *Finding Nemo.* Turtle talk comes alive when Crush swims up on the movie screen and talks to people. I mean really talks to people. He saw me raise my hand and—Dude!—he said my name and we had a conversation. I don't know how they do it, but it was great.

Ian

THE LAND PAVILION

THE LAND IS A HUGE PAVILION containing three attractions and several restaurants. When the pavilion was originally built, its emphasis was on farming, but now it focuses on environmental concerns. Dry as that sounds, kids really enjoy The Land's attractions, especially Soarin', a thrill ride where the operative word is "thrill," not terror.

Living with the Land (FASTPASS) ★★★★

APPEAL BY AGE	PRESCHOOL ★★½	GRADE SCHOOL ★★★	TEENS ★★★½
YOUNG ADULTS ★★★★		OVER 30 ★★★★	SENIORS ★★★★

What it is Indoor boat-ride adventure through the past, present, and future of U.S. farming and agriculture. **Scope and scale** Major attraction. **Fright potential** Not frightening in any respect, but loud. **Bottleneck rating** 9. **When to go** Before 11 a.m., or use FASTPASS. **Authors' rating** Interesting and fun; not to be missed; ★★★★. **Duration of ride** About 12 minutes. **Average wait in line per 100 people ahead of you** 3 minutes. **Assumes** 15 boats operating. **Loading speed** Moderate.

This boat ride through four experimental growing areas is inspiring and educational. Kids like seeing the giant pumpkins and hearing about the tomato tree that has produced 20,000 tomatoes. Teens will be fascinated by the imaginative ways to grow crops—without soil, hanging in the air, even on a space station. A lot of the fruits and vegetables grown here are served to guests in the restaurants at Epcot, such as the Garden Grill and the Coral Reef.

Thumbs Up for the Whole Family

I like the gardening part and looking at the fruits and vegetables. They need to make Living with the Land into a rock song.

Hannah

Soarin' (FASTPASS) ★★★★½

APPEAL BY AGE	PRESCHOOL —	GRADE SCHOOL ★★★★★	TEENS ★★★★½
YOUNG ADULTS ★★★★★		OVER 30 ★★★★★	SENIORS ★★★★

What it is Flight simulation ride. **Scope and scale** Super headliner. **Fright potential** Frightens almost no one who meets the minimum height requirements. **When to go** First 30 minutes the park is open or use FASTPASS. **Special comments** Entrance on the lower level of The Land pavilion. May induce motion sickness; 40-inch minimum-height requirement; switching off available (see page 220). **Authors' rating** Exciting and mellow at the same time; ★★★★½. Not to be missed. **Duration of ride** 5½ minutes. **Average wait in line per 100 people ahead of you** 4 minutes. **Assumes** 2 concourses operating. **Loading speed** Moderate.

This is the closest to hang gliding you will come without trying the real thing. Once airborne, you are flying over California with IMAX-quality images projected all around you while a flight simulator moves your hang glider in sync with the movie. The experience is extremely mellow and nonthreatening. Any child (or adult) who meets the 40-inch minimum height requirement will love Soarin'.

Ian

Now I know what it feels like to be a kite. Fly high into the clouds and soar like a bird! It's like you have a front row seat to see the world. You feel the wind in your face and smell the oranges as you fly over the trees. I'll never forget flying through the golf course when all of a sudden—oh, dude!— a golf ball whooshed by my head.

It's a ride, but you don't really move that much. There's a huge movie screen in front of you. You go past an orange farm in the ride, and it starts to smell like oranges. It's a good thing you don't go near any wet dogs!
Hannah

The Circle of Life ★★★½

| APPEAL BY AGE | PRESCHOOL ★★½ | GRADE SCHOOL ★★★ | TEENS ★★½ |
| YOUNG ADULTS ★★★ | | OVER 30 ★★★ | SENIORS ★★★ |

What it is Film exploring man's relationship with his environment. **Scope and scale** Minor attraction. **Fright potential** Not frightening in any respect. **Bottleneck rating** 5. **When to go** Before 11 a.m. or after 2 p.m. **Authors' rating** Highly interesting and enlightening; ★★★½. **Duration of presentation** About 12½ minutes. **Preshow entertainment** None. **Probable waiting time** 10–15 minutes.

The Swahili saying *hakuna matata* (don't worry) does not apply to this movie. On the contrary, Simba, Pumbaa, and Timon from Disney's animated feature *The Lion King* offer a sugar-coated lesson on how to protect and care for the environment.

Movie Tip

Did you know that Elton John wrote the music to the song "Hakuna Matata"?

IMAGINATION PAVILION

THIS MULTIATTRACTION PAVILION is situated on the west side of Innoventions West and down the walk from The Land. Outside is an "upside-down waterfall" and one of our favorite Future World landmarks, the "jumping water," a fountain that hops over the heads of unsuspecting passersby.

Ian

When it's hot, all I want to do is wear my swim trunks and get wet. One of the best places is outside of [the] Imagination [Pavilion]. They have dancing waters skipping through the air. I like to follow where the water is flying and let it splash my face. Another place to get wet is near Test Track. Water shoots up from the ground. It's fun!

Journey into Imagination with Figment ★★½

| APPEAL BY AGE | PRESCHOOL ★★ | GRADE SCHOOL ★★ | TEENS ★★ |
| YOUNG ADULTS ★★★ | | OVER 30 ★★★ | SENIORS ★★★ |

What it is Dark fantasy-adventure ride. **Scope and scale** Major attraction wannabe. **Fright potential** Frightens a small percentage of preschoolers. **Bottleneck rating** 6. **When to go** Anytime. **Authors' rating** Vacuous; ★★½. **Duration of ride** About 6 minutes. **Average wait in line per 100 people ahead of you** 2 minutes. **Loading speed** Fast.

"One little spark of inspiration is at the heart of all creation" croons the ever-popular Figment as he takes you on a tour of the zany Imagination Institute with the help of your five senses. Young children will love the little purple dragon, but grown-ups and teens will be mildly amused at best. An adjacent interactive exhibit area has unique offerings, however, including a photo-morphing computer. First the machine takes your picture, then you select an image from several categories into which your photo is integrated. The final result can be e-mailed free of charge and on the spot to family and friends.

Honey, I Shrunk the Audience (FASTPASS) ★★★★½

APPEAL BY AGE PRESCHOOL ★★★★ GRADE SCHOOL ★★★★★ TEENS ★★★★★
YOUNG ADULTS ★★★★★ OVER 30 ★★★★★ SENIORS ★★★★

What it is 3-D film with special effects. **Scope and scale** Headliner. **Fright potential** Extremely intense visual effects and loudness frighten many young children. **Bottleneck rating** 8. **When to go** Before 11:30 a.m., after 6 p.m., or use FASTPASS. **Special comments** Adults should not be put off by the sci-fi theme. The loud, intense show with tactile effects frightens some young children. **Authors' rating** An absolute hoot! Not to be missed; ★★★★½. **Duration of presentation** About 17 minutes. **Preshow entertainment** 8 minutes. **Probable waiting time** 12 minutes (at suggested times).

   This show is hilariously funny. The audience is attacked by a multitude of special effects, including simulated explosions,

Dark Loud Scary smoke, fiber optics, lights, simulated mice, water spray, moving seats, and unfortunately by an earsplitting soundtrack. If you're perplexed concerning how exactly mice are simulated, one performance of *Honey, I Shrunk the Audience* will make it abundantly clear.

It is fitting that the role of the Chairman of the Imagination Institute, Dr. Nigel Channing, is played by Eric Idle, who wrote the song "Always Look on the Bright Side of Life," which was originally featured in the 1979 film *Monty Python's Life of Brian.*

 Young children will be frightened at times. If, however, they want to see the show, I recommend letting them watch first without the 3-D glasses and with earplugs.

Liliane

Yikes Liliane, you could cover them up with a blanket, too! About those mice: if the thought of several thousand (simulated) mice loose in the theater gives you the willies, sit with your feet crossed in yoga position. You'll never know the mice are there (except for the screamimg of everyone around you, of course).

Bob

Test Track Ride (FASTPASS) ★★★½

APPEAL BY AGE	PRESCHOOL ★★★★	GRADE SCHOOL ★★★★	TEENS ★★★★
YOUNG ADULTS ★★★★		OVER 30 ★★★★	SENIORS ★★★★

What it is Automobile test-track simulator ride. **Scope and scale** Super headliner. **Fright potential** Intense thrill ride may frighten guests of any age. Switching-off option provided (see page 220). **Bottleneck rating 10. When to go** First 30 minutes the park is open, just before closing, or use FASTPASS. **Special comments** 40-inch height minimum. **Authors' rating** Good but not worth a 40-minute or longer wait; ★★★½. **Duration of ride** About 4 minutes. **Average wait in line per 100 people ahead of you** 4½ minutes. **Loading speed** Moderate to fast.

Scary   Rough

Visitors test a future model car at high speeds through hairpin turns, up and down steep hills, and over rough terrain. The six-guest vehicle is a motion simulator that rocks and pitches. The grand finale is a spin around a steep-banked loop at 65 mph! It is much fun if you meet the height requirements. Test Track is a favorite attraction of teens.

Idan

If nobody in your family wants to join you on the ride and you don't have a FASTPASS, join the singles line. It moves much faster.

Man, this is about as scary as driving with my 17-year-old sister! The ride is pretty cool, especially driving in a car that nearly wipes out and hits a truck. If you like those test dummies, you'll know what it's like to be one. The best time is when you hit the speed track outside and rip around an oval like you're a NASCAR driver.

Ian

I love fast things, and this was more than fast! You ride in a really cool car on what looks like a real road. There's no radio, but it's a convertible, and I like convertibles!

Hannah

There is a Kidcot Fun Stop at Test Track where those too short to ride can occupy themselves with arts and crafts. When the temperature's boiling, try the neighboring Cool Wash misting station.

Liliane

WONDERS OF LIFE PAVILION
(open seasonally)

THIS MULTIFACETED PAVILION deals with the human body, health, and medicine. Housed in a 100,000-square-foot, gold-domed structure, Wonders of Life focuses on the capabilities of the human body and the importance of keeping fit.

Body Wars ★★★½

APPEAL BY AGE	PRESCHOOL ★★★	GRADE SCHOOL ★★★★	TEENS ★★★★
YOUNG ADULTS ★★★★		OVER 30 ★★★½	SENIORS ★★½

What it is Flight-simulator ride through the human body. **Scope and scale** Headliner. **Fright potential** Very intense, with frightening visual effects. Ride may cause motion sickness in riders of all ages. Switching-off option provided (see page 220). **Bottleneck rating** 9. **When to go** Anytime. **Special comments** Not recommended for pregnant women or people prone to motion sickness; 40-inch height minimum. **Authors' rating** Anatomy made fun; not to be missed; ★★★½. **Duration of ride** 5 minutes. **Average wait in line per 100 people ahead of you** 4 minutes. **Assumes** All simulators operating. **Loading speed** Moderate to fast.

Motion Sickness

If you enjoyed Star Tours at Disney-MGM Studios you will love this simulated microscopic ride through the human organs. The ride has a minimum height requirement of 40 inches and has the bad, albeit deserved, reputation of inducing motion sickness (heightened we're sure by the visuals—imagine a warp-speed romp through the small intestines on a microscopic roller coaster). Body Wars, maybe for the better, is only open seasonally.

Cranium Command ★★★★½

APPEAL BY AGE	PRESCHOOL ★★	GRADE SCHOOL ★★★★	TEENS ★★★★
YOUNG ADULTS ★★★★★		OVER 30 ★★★★★	SENIORS ★★★★★

What it is Audio-animatronic theater show about the brain. **Scope and scale** Major attraction. **Fright potential** Not frightening in any respect. **Bottleneck rating** 5. **When to go** Before 11 a.m. or after 3 p.m. **Authors' rating** Funny, outrageous, and educational; not to be missed; ★★★★½. **Duration of presentation** About 20 minutes. **Preshow entertainment** Explanatory lead-in to feature presentation. **Probable waiting time** Less than 10 minutes at times suggested.

You may not want to ride Body Wars, but don't miss this clever show in the same pavilion. Characters called "Brain Pilots" are trained to operate human brains. The show consists of a day in the life of one of these Cranium Commanders as he tries to pilot the brain of an adolescent boy. A real sleeper attraction, *Cranium Command* is regarded by veteran guests as one of the funniest attractions at Walt Disney World. Unfortunately, it's open only seasonally (which basically means when Disney feels like offering it).

Thumbs Up for the Whole Family

The Making of Me ★★★

APPEAL BY AGE	PRESCHOOL ★½	GRADE SCHOOL ★★★½	TEENS ★★½
YOUNG ADULTS ★★★		OVER 30 ★★★	SENIORS ★★★

What it is Humorous movie about human conception and birth. **Scope and scale** Minor attraction. **Fright potential** Not frightening in any respect.

Bottleneck rating 10. **When to go** Early in the morning or after 4:30 p.m. **Authors' rating** Sanitized sex education; ★★★. **Duration of presentation** 14 minutes. **Preshow entertainment** None. **Probable waiting time** 25 minutes or more, unless you go at suggested times.

The Making of Me is an excellent movie about human conception, gestation, and birth. Parents of children younger than age 7 tell us the sexual information went over their children's heads, for the most part. With older children, however, the film can precipitate questions, so be prepared.

Mission: Space (FASTPASS) ★★★★

APPEAL BY AGE	PRESCHOOL —	GRADE SCHOOL ★★★★★	TEENS ★★★★½
YOUNG ADULTS ★★★★★		OVER 30 ★★★★	SENIORS ★★★★

What it is Space flight simulation ride. **Scope and scale** Super headliner. **Scope and scale** Intense thrill ride may frighten guests of any age. Switching-off option provided (see page 220). **Bottleneck rating** 9. **When to go** First 30 minutes the park is open, or use FASTPASS. **Special comments** Not recommended for pregnant women or people prone to motion sickness; 44-inch minimum-height requirement; a gentler, nonspinning version is also available. **Authors' rating** Impressive; ★★★★. **Duration of ride** About 5 minutes plus preshow. **Average wait in line per 100 people ahead of you** 4 minutes.

Motion Sickness   Rough

In this attraction, you join three other guests in a four-man crew to fly a space mission. Each guest plays a role (commander, pilot, navigator, or engineer) and is required to perform certain functions during the flight. A cleverly conceived, technological marvel, Mission: Space made national news when, in separate incidents, two guests died after riding it. While neither of the deaths were linked to the attraction (the victims had unknown preexisting conditions), the negative publicity caused many guests to skip it entirely. In response, Disney has added a less stressful nonspinning version of Mission: Space. If you want to experience the spinning version of the ride, join the "orange" team, and if you prefer to check it out without those pesky g-forces, join the "green" team.

Follow the orange brick road because it's much more fun. The ride is too intense for little ones and anybody prone to motion sickness, but grade-schoolers, teens, and brave moms and dadstronauts will love it! And don't worry about the job assignments—do you really think Disney is going to let you

Liliane

meddle around with their multimillion-dollar high-tech toys?

Movie Tip

The host during your expedition is Gary Sinise, known for his roles in the space flicks *Apollo 13* and *Mission to Mars.*

Universe of Energy: Ellen's Energy Adventure ★★★★

APPEAL BY AGE	PRESCHOOL ★★★	GRADE SCHOOL ★★★★	TEENS ★★★½
YOUNG ADULTS ★★★★		OVER 30 ★★★★	SENIORS ★★★★

What it is Combination ride/theater presentation about energy. **Scope and scale** Major attraction. **Fright potential** Dinosaur segment frightens some preschoolers; visually intense, with some intimidating effects. **Bottleneck rating** 7. **When to go** Before 11:15 a.m. or after 4:30 p.m. **Special comments** Don't be dismayed by long lines; 582 people enter the pavilion each time the theater changes audiences. **Authors' rating** The most unique theater in Walt Disney World; ★★★★. **Duration of presentation** About 26½ minutes. **Preshow entertainment** 8 minutes. **Probable waiting time** 20–40 minutes.

Scary

Join Ellen DeGeneres and Bill Nye, the science guy, who star in this 26-minute presentation about energy. Visitors are seated in what appears to be an ordinary theater. After a short film, the theater seats divide into six 97-passenger traveling cars that glide among swamps and through a prehistoric forest full of animatronic dinosaurs. The ride itself is smooth and not scary at all, though some children are frightened by the dinosaurs.

Movie Tip

Ellen DeGeneres lent her voice to the role of Dory, a fish with short-term memory loss, in the animated Disney/Pixar film *Finding Nemo*.

The "Mom, I Can't Believe It's Disney!" Fountain ★★★★★

APPEAL BY AGE	PRESCHOOL ★★★★★	GRADE SCHOOL ★★★★★
TEENS ★★★★	YOUNG ADULTS ★★★★ OVER 30 ★★★★	SENIORS ★★★★★

What it is Combination fountain and shower. **Scope and scale** Diversion. **Fright potential** Not frightening in any respect. **When to go** When it's hot. **Special comments** Secretly installed by Martians during *IllumiNations*. **Authors' rating** Yes!! ★★★★★. **Duration of experience** Indefinite. **Probable waiting time** None.

On a broiling Florida day, when you think you might suddenly combust, fling yourself into the fountain and do decidedly un-Disney things. Dance, skip, sing, jump, splash, stick your toes down the spouts, or catch the water in your mouth! Toddlers and preschoolers, along with

Thumbs Up for the Whole Family

hippies, especially love the fountain. Let your little ones cavort in their underwear (to be exchanged afterward for a pair of dry ones you brought along just for this occasion). Needless to say, this is photo-op territory.

▌ WORLD SHOWCASE

WORLD SHOWCASE, EPCOT'S SECOND THEME AREA, is an ongoing World's Fair encircling a picturesque, 40-acre lagoon. The cuisine, culture, history, and architecture of almost a dozen countries are permanently displayed in individual national pavilions spaced along a 1.2-mile promenade. Pavilions replicate familiar landmarks and street scenes from the host countries.

MEXICO PAVILION

SPANISH ONE-ON-ONE

Hello: *Hola*	Pronunciation: *Oh-la*
Goodbye: *Adios*	Pronunciation: *Ah-dee-ohs*
Thank you: *Gracias*	Pronunciation: *Grah-see-ahs*
Mickey Mouse: *El Ratón Miguelito*	Pronunciation: *El Rah-tone Mee-gell-lee-toe*

PRE-COLUMBIAN PYRAMIDS dominate the architecture of this exhibit. Inside you will find authentic and valuable artifacts, a village scene complete with restaurant, and the boat ride.

Gran Fiesta Tour Starring the Three Caballeros ★★★

APPEAL BY AGE	PRESCHOOL ★★★½	GRADE SCHOOL ★★★	TEENS ★★½
YOUNG ADULTS ★★★		OVER 30 ★★★	SENIORS ★★★

What it is Indoor scenic boat ride. **Scope and scale** Minor attraction. **Fright potential** Not frightening in any respect. **Bottleneck rating** 5. **When to go** Before noon or after 3 p.m. **Authors' rating** New role for classic Disney characters; ★★★. **Duration of ride** About 7 minutes (plus 1½-minute wait to disembark). **Average wait in line per 100 people ahead of you** 4½ minutes. **Assumes** 16 boats in operation. **Loading speed** Moderate.

Thumbs Up for the Whole Family

Gran Fiesta Tour replaces El Río del Tiempo which had run since Epcot's opening in 1982. A new storyline featuring Donald Duck, José Carioca (a parrot), and Panchito (a Mexican charro rooster) from the 1944 Disney film, *The Three Caballeros,* has our heroes racing to Mexico City for a gala reunion performance. The sets were refurbished to enhance the new film.

NORWAY PAVILION

NORWEGIAN ONE-ON-ONE

Hello: *God dag*	Pronunciation: *Good dagh*
Goodbye: *Ha det*	Pronunciation: *Hah deh*
Thank you: *Takk*	Pronunciation: *Tahk*
Mickey Mouse: Mikke Mus	Pronunciation: *Mikeh Moose*

SURROUNDING A COURTYARD is an assortment of traditional Scandinavian buildings, including a replica of the 14th-century Akershus Castle, now home to Princesses-hosted character meals. Other attractions include Maelstrom, a ride, and a Viking ship playground (the only dedicated playground at Epcot).

It is hard to say no to one of the mouthwatering pastries at Kringla Bakeri og Kafé.

Liliane

🏃 Maelstrom (FASTPASS) ★★★

APPEAL BY AGE	PRESCHOOL ★★★½	GRADE SCHOOL ★★★½	TEENS ★★★
YOUNG ADULTS ★★★		OVER 30 ★★★	SENIORS ★★★

What it is Indoor adventure boat ride. **Scope and scale** Major attraction. **Fright potential** Dark, visually intense in parts. Ride ends with a plunge down a 20-foot flume. **Bottleneck rating** 9. **When to go** Before noon, after 4:30 p.m., or use FAST-PASS. **Authors' rating** Too short, but has its moments; ★★★. **Duration of ride** 4½ minutes, followed by a 5-minute film with a short wait in between; about 14 minutes for the ride and show combo. **Average wait in line per 100 people ahead of you** 4 minutes. **Assumes** 12 or 13 boats operating. **Loading speed** Fast.

Dark

Scary

Board a dragon-headed ship for a voyage through the fabled seas of Viking history and legends, brave trolls, rocky gorges, and a storm at sea. Sounds dangerous? The ride can be intense at times, but the only hold-your-breath moment is when your boat descends a 20-foot slide.

CHINA PAVILION

CHINESE (MANDARIN) ONE-ON-ONE

Hello: *Ni hao*	Pronunciation: *Knee how*
Goodbye: *Zai jian*	Pronunciation: *Zy jehn*
Thank you: *Xiè xie*	Pronunciation: *Chi-eh chi-eh*
Mickey Mouse: *Mi Lao Shu*	Pronunciation: *Me Lah-oh Su*

THERE IS NO RIDE AT THE CHINA PAVILION, but the majestic half-sized replica of the Temple of Heaven in Beijing will surely make it into your photo album. Inside the pavilion see *Reflections of China,* an impressive film about the people and natural beauty of China. Children will enjoy the regularly scheduled performances of Chinese acrobats. Check your entertainment schedule (*Times Guide*) for show times.

Reflections of China ★★★½

APPEAL BY AGE	PRESCHOOL ★★	GRADE SCHOOL ★★½	TEENS ★★★
YOUNG ADULTS ★★★½		OVER 30 ★★★★	SENIORS ★★★★

What it is Film about the Chinese people and country. **Scope and scale** Major attraction. **Fright potential** Not frightening in any respect. **Bottleneck rating** 4. **When to go** Anytime. **Special comments** Audience stands throughout performance. **Authors' rating** This beautifully produced film was introduced in 2003; ★★★½. **Duration of presentation** About 14 minutes. **Preshow entertainment** None. **Probable waiting time** 10 minutes.

GERMANY PAVILION

THE GERMANY PAVILION DOES NOT HAVE ATTRACTIONS. The main focus is the Biergarten, a full-service (priority seating required)

GERMAN ONE-ON-ONE

Hello: *Guten Tag*	Pronunciation: *Gooh-ten tak*
Goodbye: *Auf wiedersehen*	Pronunciation: *Ow-f veeh-der-zain*
Thank you: *Danke*	Pronunciation: *Dan-keh*
Mickey Mouse: *Micky Maus*	Pronunciation: *Me-key Mouse*

restaurant serving German food and beer. Yodeling, folk dancing, and oompah-band music are regularly performed during mealtimes. Be sure to check out the large, elaborate model railroad located just beyond the restrooms as you walk from Germany toward Italy.

Biergarten German restaurant: The best party I ever went to. Good chicken fingers, lots of salads, yummy desserts. My dad liked the beer band, and so did I. They shouted "Ticky tocky, ticky tocky!" and we yelled back "Oy, oy, oy!" (whatever that means). Everybody raised their beer glasses, sang songs, and did goofy dances. I think I had one too many root beers.

Ian

This is the perfect place to introduce your kids to a great snack: *Gummibaerchen*, (gummy bears), my favorite childhood candy.

Liliane

ITALY PAVILION

ITALIAN ONE-ON-ONE

Hello: *Buon giorno*	Pronunciation: *Bon jor-no*
Goodbye: *Ciao* (informal)	Pronunciation: *Chow*
Thank you: *Grazie*	Pronunciation: *Grah-zee-eh*
Mickey Mouse: *Topolino*	Pronunciation: *To-po-lee-no*

THE ENTRANCE TO ITALY IS MARKED by a 105-foot-tall campanile (bell tower) intended to mirror the tower in St. Mark's Square in Venice. Left of the campanile is a replica of the 14th-century Doge's Palace.

Streets and courtyards in the Italy Pavilion are among the most realistic in the World Showcase. You really feel as if you're in Italy. Because there's no film or ride, tour any time.

I don't know how they do this, but I couldn't stop watching. A lady statue comes alive and messes with people. She stands perfectly still in front of Italy. When people have their pictures taken next to her, she moves and does crazy things to them. My family laughed a lot, but I was too chicken to go up to her.

Ian

UNITED STATES PAVILION

THE UNITED STATES PAVILION is an imposing brick structure reminiscent of colonial Philadelphia, and is home to a very moving and patriotic, albeit sanitized, retrospective of U.S. history. Street entertainment outside includes the Voices of Liberty choral ensemble and the Spirit of America Fife and Drum Corps, among others. Across the plaza is the American Gardens Theatre, Epcot's premier venue for concerts and stage shows.

The American Adventure ★★★★

APPEAL BY AGE	PRESCHOOL ★★	GRADE SCHOOL ★★★	TEENS ★★★
YOUNG ADULTS ★★★★	OVER 30 ★★★★½		SENIORS ★★★★★

What it is Patriotic mixed-media and audio-animatronic theater presentation on U.S. history. **Scope and scale** Headliner. **Fright potential** Not frightening in any respect. **Bottleneck rating** 6. **When to go** Anytime. **Authors' rating** Disney's best historic/patriotic attraction; not to be missed; ★★★★. **Duration of presentation** About 29 minutes. **Preshow entertainment** Voices of Liberty chorale singing. **Probable waiting time** 16 minutes.

The 29-minute multimedia show is narrated by animatronic Mark Twain and Ben Franklin. *The American Adventure* reminds you of a contest: tell us everything you love about America in 30 minutes or less. There are only four female figures among the 12 personified ideals around the theater, one of them representing the rather ambiguous "tomorrow" by virtue of holding a baby. The North American continent seemingly does not exist prior to the landing of the *Mayflower*.

Thumbs Up for the Whole Family

JAPAN PAVILION

JAPANESE ONE-ON-ONE

Hello: *Konnichi wa*	Pronunciation: *Ko-nee-chee wah*
Goodbye: *Sayounara*	Pronunciation: *Sigh-yo-nah-ra*
Thank you: *Arigatou*	Pronunciation: *Ah-ree-gah-to*
Mickey Mouse: *Mikki Mausu*	Pronunciation: *Mikkee Mou-su*

THE FIVE-STORY, BLUE-ROOFED PAGODA, inspired by a 17th-century shrine in Nara, sets this pavilion apart. A hill garden behind it encompasses waterfalls, rocks, flowers, lanterns, paths, and rustic bridges. There are no attractions unless you count the huge Japanese retail venue.

MOROCCO PAVILION

ARABIC ONE-ON-ONE

Hello: *Salaam alekoum*	Pronunciation: *Sah-lahm ah-leh-koom*
Goodbye: *Ma'salama*	Pronunciation: *Mah sah-lah-mah*
Thank you: *Chokrane*	Pronunciation: *Shoe-krah-n*
Mickey Mouse: *Mujallad Miki*	Pronunciation: *Muh-jahl-lahd Me-key*

THE BUSTLING MARKET, WINDING STREETS, lofty minarets, and stuccoed archways re-create the romance and intrigue of Marrakesh and Casablanca. Attention to detail makes Morocco one of the most exciting World Showcase pavilions, but there are no attractions.

Idan

I love Middle Eastern food and enjoy the music and belly dancing at Restaurant Marrakech. Try the falafel; it's delicious. In the courtyard Aladdin and Jasmine come to greet kids several times a day. I wish Disney would bring out Jaffar, my favorite character from *Aladdin,* more often.

FRANCE PAVILION

FRENCH ONE-ON-ONE	
Hello: *Bonjour*	Pronunciation: *Bon-jure*
Goodbye: *Au revoir*	Pronunciation: *Oh reh-vwa*
Thank you: *Merci*	Pronunciation: *Maer-si*
Mickey Mouse: *Mickey*	Pronunciation: *Mee-keh*

WELCOME AND BIENVENUE to Paris, Eiffel Tower, and all. There is not much to do for the kids here, but you won't have any trouble luring them into Boulangerie Patisserie for a scrumptious French pastry.

Impressions de France ★★★½

APPEAL BY AGE	PRESCHOOL ★½	GRADE SCHOOL ★★½	TEENS ★★★
YOUNG ADULTS ★★★★		OVER 30 ★★★★	SENIORS ★★★★

What it is Film essay on the French people and country. **Scope and scale** Major attraction. **Fright potential** Not frightening in any respect. **Bottleneck rating** 7. **When to go** Anytime. **Authors' rating** Exceedingly beautiful film; not to be missed; ★★★½. **Duration of presentation** About 18 minutes. **Preshow entertainment** None. **Probable waiting time** 15 minutes (at suggested times).

France, here I come! This truly lovely 18-minute movie will make you want to pack your suitcase. An added bonus is that the showing is "très civilizé" as you get to sit down and rest your weary feet.

UNITED KINGDOM PAVILION

A BLEND OF ARCHITECTURE ATTEMPTS to capture Britain's city, town, and rural atmospheres. One street alone has a thatched-roof cottage, four-story timber-and-plaster building, pre-Georgian plaster building, formal Palladian dressed stone exterior, and a city square with a Hyde Park bandstand (whew!). There are no attractions.

Liliane

If your child loves Mary Poppins, your best chance to meet her is here. Teens and yours truly have a good time with the Beatles impersonation band. Check your entertainment schedule (*Times Guide*) for a trip down Abbey Road.

CANADA PAVILION

CANADA'S CULTURAL, NATURAL, AND architectural diversity is reflected in this large and impressive pavilion. Older kids will be interested in the 30-foot-tall totem poles that embellish a Native American village. Canada is also home to a sort of punk-Celtic-country band called Off Kilter—yes, the lead singer wears a kilt—that performs in front of the showcase entrance. Check your entertainment schedule (*Times Guide*) for performance times.

O Canada! ★★★½

APPEAL BY AGE	PRESCHOOL ★★	GRADE SCHOOL ★★½	TEENS ★★★
YOUNG ADULTS ★★★½		OVER 30 ★★★★	SENIORS ★★★★

What it is Film essay on the Canadian people and their country. **Scope and scale** Major attraction. **Fright potential** Not frightening in any respect. **Bottleneck rating** 5. **When to go** Anytime. **Special comments** Audience stands during performance. **Authors' rating** Makes you want to catch the first plane to Canada! ★★★½. **Duration of presentation** About 18 minutes. **Preshow entertainment** None. **Probable waiting time** 10 minutes.

Canadians who see this 360-degree Circle Vision flick (running since 1982) claim it's out-of-date and doesn't accurately characterize their country. Be that as it may, the film effectively showcases the beauty and diversity of Canada, and like any good travelogue, makes you want to go there.

LIVE ENTERTAINMENT *at* EPCOT

IN FUTURE WORLD

KIDS WILL LOVE THE CREW OF DRUMMING JANITORS (The JAM-Mitors), as well as the Krystos gymnasts in alien attire and the dancing fountains show in the plaza between the Innoventions East and West buildings.

 Combine a rest break with a little fun. Let your kids experience one of the special talking water fountains at Epcot (located outside the Mouse Works shop, behind Innoventions West; between Innoventions and *Honey, I Shrunk the Audience* in the Imagination Pavilion; and next to the play fountain between Future World and World Showcase). For a hilarious chat seek out PUSH the talking trash can at the Electric Umbrella Restaurant in Innoventions East.

Liliane

AROUND THE WORLD SHOWCASE

STREET PERFORMANCES IN AND AROUND the World Showcase are what set live entertainment at Epcot apart from the other Disney parks. A strolling mariachi group can be found in Mexico, street actors in Italy; a fife-and-drum corps or The Voices of Liberty at The

American Adventure; traditional songs, drums, and dances in Japan; street comedy and a Beatles impersonation band in the United Kingdom; white-faced mimes in France; bagpipes in Canada, among other performances. Check your entertainment schedule (*Times Guide*) for performance times. Some restaurants get in on the act, too. You can dine among singing waiters in Italy, enjoy Oktoberfest entertainment in Germany, and belly dancing in Morocco.

AMERICA GARDENS THEATRE

THE AMERICA GARDENS THEATRE, a pleasant amphitheater on the lagoon across from the U.S. Pavilion, showcases stage shows featuring Disney characters, international dance troupes, acrobatic companies, choruses, musical groups, dinosaur rock bands (particularly appropriate), comedians who book engagements of several weeks, and even cheerleading competitions. Some of these are very good indeed, although whether you're interested in a particular show may depend on how tired you are and what else you have scheduled. Show times (all free, of course) are listed on a board outside the exits and in the daily *Times Guide*.

ILLUMINATIONS

A nightly capstone event at Epcot called *IllumiNations* features a program of music, fireworks, erupting fountains, special lightning, and laser technology performed on World Showcase Lagoon. This enchanting and ambitious show (it tells the history of the universe starting with the Big Bang) is well worth keeping the kids up late. The best place to view the show is from the lakeside veranda of the Cantina de San Angel Inn at the Mexico Pavilion. Come early and relax with a drink or snack. The drawback is, you guessed it, that you will have to claim this spot at least 90 minutes before *IllumiNations*. Also consider dinner on the patio of the Rose & Crown Pub in the U.K. Pavilion (Advance Reservations recommended).

For other great viewing spots, check out our "Where to View *IllumiNations*" map.

IllumiNations is the climax of every day at Epcot, so keep in mind that once the show is over you will be leaving the park, and so will almost everybody else. For suggested exit strategies, see below.

For a really good view of the show, you can charter a pontoon boat for $251. Captained by a Disney cast member, the boat holds up to ten guests. Your captain will take you for a little cruise and then position the boat in a perfect place to watch *IllumiNations*. For more information, call ☎ 407-934-3160.

IllumiNations ★★★★½

| APPEAL BY AGE | PRESCHOOL ★★★ | GRADE SCHOOL ★★★★ | TEENS ★★★★ |
| YOUNG ADULTS ★★★★ | | OVER 30 ★★★★ | SENIORS ★★★★ |

where to view illuminations

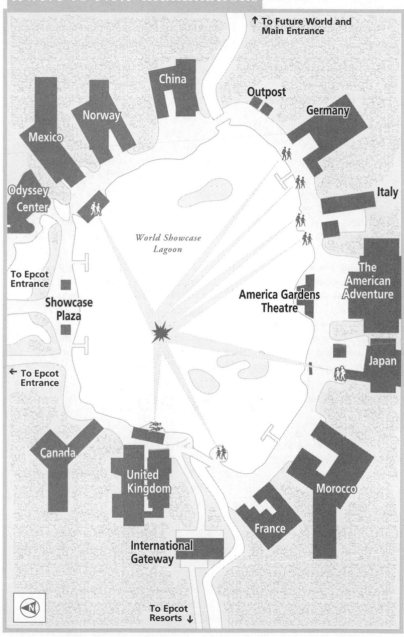

↑ To Future World and Main Entrance

China

Outpost

Germany

Norway

Mexico

Italy

Odyssey Center

World Showcase Lagoon

The American Adventure

To Epcot Entrance

Showcase Plaza

America Gardens Theatre

Japan

← To Epcot Entrance

Canada

United Kingdom

Morocco

International Gateway

France

To Epcot Resorts ↓

What it is Nighttime fireworks and laser show at World Showcase Lagoon. **Scope and scale** Super headliner. **Fright potential** Not frightening in any respect. **When to go** Stake out viewing position 20–40 minutes before showtime. **Special comments** Showtime is listed in the daily entertainment schedule on the handout park map. Audience stands during performance. **Authors' rating** Epcot's most impressive entertainment event; ★★★★½. **Duration of presentation** About 18 minutes.

EXIT STRATEGIES

MORE GROUPS GET SEPARATED AND MORE CHILDREN lost after *IllumiNations* than at any other time. Make sure that you have preselected a meeting point in the Epcot entrance area. Warn your group not to leave through the exit turnstiles until everyone is reunited.

Suggested meeting point: the fountain just inside the main entrance.

- If you are staying at the Swan, Dolphin, Yacht and Beach Club Resorts, or BoardWalk Inn and Villas, watch *IllumiNations* from somewhere between Italy and the United Kingdom and exit the park through the International Gateway between France and the United Kingdom. You can walk or take a boat back to your hotel.

- If you have a car in the Epcot lot, find a viewing spot at the Future World end of World Showcase Lagoon (Showcase Plaza) and leave immediately as soon as *IllumiNations* ends. The problem is not the traffic in the parking lot—it actually moves pretty well—it's making your way to, and finding, your car. Make sure you write down where you are parked—this is not the time to rely on your memory. If you are parked near the entrance, skip the tram and walk. If you walk, watch your children closely and hang on to them for all you're worth. The parking lot is pretty wild at this time of night.

EPCOT TOURING PLANS

OUR STEP-BY-STEP TOURING PLANS ARE FIELD-TESTED, independently verified itineraries that will keep you moving counter to the crowd flow and allow you to see as much as possible in a single day with a minimum of time wasted in line. We present three Epcot one-day touring plans specifically geared toward visiting with children. We also offer, and recommend, a two-day touring plan that is much more relaxing and far less tiring.

Touring Epcot is much more strenuous and demanding than touring the other theme parks. Epcot requires about twice as much walking. And, unlike the Magic Kingdom, Epcot has no effective in-park transportation—wherever you want to go, it's always quicker to walk. Our plans will help you avoid crowds and bottlenecks on days of moderate to heavy attendance, but they can't shorten the distance you have to walk. (Wear comfortable shoes.) On days of lighter attendance, when crowd conditions aren't a critical factor, the plans will help you organize your tour.

FAVORITE EATS AT EPCOT

LAND	FOOD ITEM	WHERE THEY CAN BE FOUND
JAPAN	Beef & chicken teriyaki (adult & child versions)	Yakitori House
	Shaved ice in unique flavors (honeydew melon & tangerine)	Kaki Gori
FRANCE	Croissants, chocolate mousse, yummy sandwiches on baguettes	Boulangerie Patisserie
	Crêpes (pancakes) & espresso	Crepes des Chefs de France
MEXICO	Children's plate with burrito, chips, and beverage	Cantina de San Angel
NORWAY	Smoked salmon sandwiches and pastries	Kringla Bakeri og Kafé
GERMANY	Bratwurst and frankfurter with kraut and apple strudel	Sommerfest
MOROCCO	Shawarma, hummus, couscous, and kids' meals—outdoor seating	Tangierine Cafe
UNITED KINGDOM	You must have an English Cadbury bar once in your life	UK Shop
CHINA	Beef and chicken rice bowls, vegetable lo mein, and egg rolls	Lotus Blossom Cafe
ITALY	Reasonable pasta, kids' menu*	L'Originale Alfredo di Roma
	Kids can watch pasta being made	
UNITED STATES	If you are craving all-American food	Liberty Inn
CANADA	The Northern Lights dessert for kids* Great steaks for mom and dad	Le Cellier
INNOVENTIONS EAST	French toast, bagels, and talking trash can	Electric Umbrella Restaurant
THE LAND PAVILION	Healthy choices—our all-time favorite	Sunshine Season Food Fair
THE SEAS PAVILION	Food with a view—fish menu* The aquarium will keep the kids happy for quite some time	The Coral Reef Restaurant

*table service only—Advance Reservations highly recommended

As a group, the *Unofficial Guide* research staff loves Epcot. Because we spend so much time there, we really wanted our small children to enjoy it, too. The challenge was figuring out how to get the kids connected to the theme or presentation at each pavilion, especially in Future World. Let's face it—a 7-year-old is only going to take so much talk about hydroponic vegetables, nuclear fission, or communication systems before tuning out.

The key for us was to brief our children on what they were likely to see in each attraction and then tie it back to something they could relate to in their everyday lives. During the tour of the greenhouse in Living with the Land, for example, we made a game of finding foods they like. (They've got cocoa beans—chocolate—so we think that covers almost everyone.) While riding Test Track, we asked our daughter to figure out which parent's driving was most like the ride's. (To avoid further sleeping in the garage, we'll not disclose who "won" that contest.) Our point here is that Epcot's Future World attractions can be a lot more palatable to young children if they're engaged and prepared going in. It's all about presentation.

The different touring plans are described below. The descriptions will tell you for whom (for example, tweens, parents with preschoolers, grandparents, and so on) or for what situation (such as sleeping late or enjoying the park at night) the plans are designed. The actual touring plans are located on pages 416–420 at the back of the book. Each plan includes a numbered map of the park in question to help you find your way around. Clip the plan of your choice out of the book by cutting along the line indicated, and take it with you to the park.

EPCOT ONE-DAY TOURING PLAN FOR PARENTS WITH SMALL CHILDREN
This plan is designed for parents of children ages 3 to 8 who wish to see the very best age-appropriate attractions in Epcot. Every attraction has a rating of at least three stars (out of five) from preschool and grade-school children surveyed by the *Unofficial Guide*. Special advice is provided for touring the park with small children, including restaurant recommendations. The plan keeps walking and backtracking to a minimum.

EPCOT ONE-DAY SLEEPY HEAD TOURING PLAN FOR PARENTS WITH SMALL CHILDREN A relaxed plan that allows families with small children to sleep late and still see the highlights of Epcot. The plan begins around 11 a.m., sets aside ample time for lunch, and includes the very best child-friendly attractions in the park. The plan also points out where FASTPASS can best be used.

EPCOT ONE-DAY TOURING PLAN FOR TWEENS AND THEIR PARENTS A one-day touring plan for parents with children ages 8 to 12. It includes every attraction rated three stars and higher by this age group, and sets aside ample time for lunch and dinner.

PARENTS' EPCOT TOURING PLANS FOR AN AFTERNOON AND ONE FULL DAY This touring plan is for families who want to tour Epcot comprehensively over two days. Day One takes advantage of early-morning touring opportunities. Day Two begins in the afternoon and continues until closing.

BE PREPARED

ALWAYS DETERMINE THE OFFICIAL PARK OPENING TIME. Call ☎ 407-824-4321 the day before you plan to visit. Purchase your admission tickets before you arrive and familiarize yourself with the touring plan you have chosen.

PRELIMINARY INSTRUCTIONS FOR ALL EPCOT TOURING PLANS

1. Call ☎ 407-824-4321 in advance for the hours of operation on the day of your visit.
2. Make reservations at the Epcot full-service restaurant(s) of your choice in advance of your visit.

EPCOT TRIVIA QUIZ
By Lou Mongello

1. What is the name of the purple dragon in Journey Into Imagination?
   a. Waldo
   b. Figment
   c. Pumbaa
   d. Meeko

2. What is the name of the 3-D movie in Epcot?
   a. *Honey, the Audience is Ugly*
   b. *Honey, I Shrunk the Audience*
   c. *Dude, Where's My Car?*
   d. *Muppet-Vision 3-D*

3. The area of Epcot that features pavilions of various countries from around the world is called:
   a. Epcot's World's Fair
   b. Future World
   c. World Showcase
   d. It's a Small World After All

4. The attraction inside the "giant golf ball" at the entrance to Epcot is called:
   a. Innoventions
   b. Journey Into Imagination
   c. Mission: Space
   d. Spaceship Earth

5. If you wanted to take pictures with Aladdin, Jasmine, and the Genie, what country's pavilion would you visit?
   a. China
   b. Morocco
   c. Japan
   d. Germany

6. Where in Epcot can you find a three-headed troll?

a. Germany

b. Norway

c. Ellen's Energy Adventure

d. Wonders of Life

7. "The Seas with Nemo and Friends" pavilion has an attraction called *Turtle Talk with* _____:

a. Crush

b. Squirt

c. Nemo

d. Bruce

8. Where can kids learn to make masks and find out more about the people from the different countries in Epcot?

a. Epcot Fun Stations

b. Discovery Outposts

c. Kidcot Fun Stops

d. Epcot Kids World

9. *The Circle of Life* film in the Land pavilion features Timon and Pumbaa from *The Lion King* movie. What type of animal is Timon?

a. Warthog

b. Lion

c. Giraffe

d. Meercat

10. What pavilion in Epcot has solar panels on top of it to help provide power to the building and attraction?

a. Test Track

b. Spaceship Earth

c. Universe of Energy

d. Imagination!

11. If you wanted to get some "astronaut training," which attraction would you go to?

a. Spaceship Earth

b. Journey Into Imagination with Figment

c. Mission: Space

d. Wonders of Life

12. You can ride through the Seas with Nemo and Friends to see characters from the movie swimming with real fish. In what part of the world did the movie take place?

a. Australia

b. Florida

c. California

d. Austria

Answers can be found on page 386.

Trivia content courtesy of Lou Mongello, author of Disney Trivia; *www.disneyworldtrivia.com.*

PART NINE

ANIMAL KINGDOM

WITH ITS LUSH FLORA, WINDING STREAMS, meandering paths, and exotic setting, the Animal Kingdom is a stunningly beautiful theme park. The landscaping alone conjures images of rain forest, veldt, and even formal gardens. Add to this loveliness a population of more than 1,000 animals, replicas of Africa's and Asia's most intriguing architecture, and a diverse array of singularly original attractions, and you have the most unique of all Walt Disney World theme parks. The Animal Kingdom's six sections, or "lands," are the Oasis, Discovery Island, DinoLand U.S.A., Camp Minnie-Mickey, Africa, and Asia.

On Discovery Island, next to Creature Comforts Shop, is the baby-care center with supplies, changing tables, and a quiet place to nurse. Garden Gate Gifts at the main entrance and Duka La Filimu in Africa will save the day if you run out of film.

At the entrance plaza, ticket kiosks front the main entrance. To your right before the turnstiles, you'll find the kennel and an ATM. Passing through the turnstiles, wheelchair and stroller rentals are to your right. Guest Relations, the park headquarters for information, handout park maps, entertainment schedules, missing persons, and lost and found, is to the left.

The park is arranged somewhat like the Magic Kingdom. The lush, tropical Oasis serves as Main Street, funneling visitors to Discovery Island at the center of the park. Discovery Island is the park's retail and dining center. From Discovery Island, guests can access the respective theme areas: Africa, Camp Minnie-Mickey, Asia, and DinoLand U.S.A.

Extra Magic Hours are offered to guests lodging at the Disney hotels. Should you take advantage of these hours, keep in mind that you will see very little of the animals after 5 p.m. Evenings, however, are a cooler, more relaxed time to take in the shows and live entertainment offerings.

disney's animal kingdom

The Boneyard **1**
Character Greeting Area **2**
Conservation Station **3**
Dinosaur **4**
Expedition Everest **5**
Festival of the Lion King **6**
Flights of Wonder **7**
Gibbon Pool **8**
Guest Relations **9**
Harambe Village **10**
Kali River Rapids **11**
Kilimanjaro Safaris **12**
Maharaja Jungle Trek **13**
Main Entrance **14**
Pangani Forest
   Exploration Trail **15**
Pizzafari **16**
*Pocahontas and Her
   Forest Friends* **17**
Primeval Whirl **18**
Rafiki's Planet Watch **19**
Rainforest Cafe **20**
Restaurantosaurus **21**
Theater in the Wild/
   *Finding Nemo—
   The Musical* **22**
Ticket Booths **23**
The Tree of Life/*It's Tough
   to Be a Bug!* **24**
TriceraTop Spin **25**
Wildlife Express (Train) **26**

Africa

Camp Minnie-Mickey

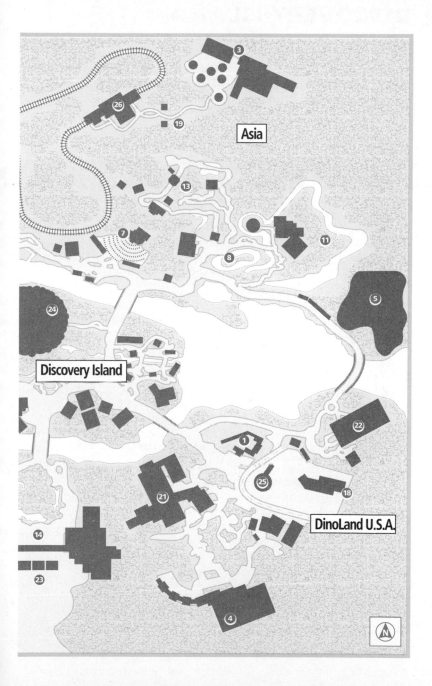

Asia

Discovery Island

DinoLand U.S.A.

DISCOVERY ISLAND

DISCOVERY ISLAND IS AN ISLAND OF TROPICAL GREENERY and whimsical equatorial African architecture, executed in vibrant hues of teal, yellow, red, and blue. Connected to the other lands by bridges, the island is the hub from which guests can access the park's various theme areas. In addition to several wildlife exhibits, Discovery Island's Tree of Life hosts the film *It's Tough to Be a Bug!*

The Tree of Life/It's Tough to Be a Bug! ★★★★ (FASTPASS)

| APPEAL BY AGE | PRESCHOOL ★★★½ | GRADE SCHOOL ★★★½ | TEENS ★★½ |
| YOUNG ADULTS ★★★ | | OVER 30 ★★★ | SENIORS ★★★ |

What it is 3-D theater show. **Scope and scale** Major attraction. **Fright potential** Very intense and loud, with special effects that startle viewers of all ages and potentially terrify young children. **Bottleneck rating** 9. **When to go** Before 10:30 a.m., after 4 p.m., or use FASTPASS. **Special comments** The theater is inside the tree. **Authors' rating** Zany and frenetic; ★★★★. **Duration of presentation** Approximately 7½ minutes. **Probable waiting time** 12–30 minutes.

Before entering the show take a close look at the Tree of Life, the remarkable home of this 3-D movie. The primary icon and focal point of the Animal Kingdom, the tree features a trunk with high-relief carving depicting 325 animals.

Dark   Loud   Scary

It's Tough to Be a Bug! is a zany, cleverly conceived, but very intense 3-D show housed below the Tree of Life. For starters, the show is about bugs and bugs always rank high on the ick-factor scale. That coupled with some startling special effects and a very loud soundtrack make *It's Tough to Be a Bug!* a potential horror show for the 7-and-under crowd. Tread cautiously, but don't write off the attraction. You can prepare by watching the animated feature *A Bug's Life* before you leave home—many of the characters are the same.

The closing lines of the show tipped me off when it was announced that "honorary bugs [read: audience members] remain seated while all the lice, bed bugs, maggots, and cockroaches exit first." In plain English, this means if

Liliane

you don't like bugs crawling on you, even simulated ones, keep your feet off the floor. And thanks to Disney ingenuity, the bugs sting, too—they do, they do.

CAMP MINNIE-MICKEY

THIS LAND IS DESIGNED TO BE THE DISNEY characters' Animal Kingdom headquarters. A small land, Camp Minnie-Mickey is about the size of Mickey's Toontown Fair but has a rustic and woodsy theme like a summer camp. In addition to a character meeting and greeting area, Camp Minnie-Mickey is home to two live stage productions featuring Disney characters.

Character Trails

Characters can be found at the end of each of several "character trails." Each trail has its own private reception area and, of course, its own queue. Unless your child is really into character autograph and photo-op sessions, skip this part of Camp Minnie-Mickey and experience the real gem, the *Festival of the Lion King* stage show.

Festival of the Lion King ★★★★

APPEAL BY AGE	PRESCHOOL ★★★★		GRADE SCHOOL ★★★★½
TEENS ★★★★	YOUNG ADULTS ★★★★	OVER 30 ★★★★	SENIORS ★★★★

What it is Theater-in-the-round stage show. **Scope and scale** Major attraction. **Fright potential** A bit loud, but otherwise not frightening in any respect. **Bottleneck rating** 9. **When to go** Before 11 a.m. or after 4 p.m. **Special comments** Performance times are listed in the handout park map or *Times Guide*. **Authors' rating** Upbeat and spectacular, not to be missed; ★★★★. **Duration of presentation** 25 minutes. **Preshow entertainment** None. **Probable waiting time** 20–35 minutes.

Great pageantry, dazzling costumes, a mini–Broadway show, and air-conditioning, too. *Festival of the Lion King* at the Animal Kingdom was the precursor of the Broadway production of *The Lion King*.

Thumbs Up for the Whole Family

Liliane

Try to score front row seats. Kids are invited to play musical instruments and join the performance.

The show is based on the animated feature *The Lion King,* a must-see movie. Did you know that James Earl Jones, the voice behind Mufasa (father of Simba), is also the voice behind Darth Vader in *Star Wars*?

Movie Tip

Pocahontas and Her Forest Friends ★★½

APPEAL BY AGE	PRESCHOOL ★★★½	GRADE SCHOOL ★★★½	TEENS ★★★
YOUNG ADULTS ★★★½		OVER 30 ★★★	SENIORS ★★★

What it is Conservation-themed stage show. **Scope and scale** Major attraction. **Fright potential** Not frightening in any respect. **Bottleneck rating** 7. **When to go** Before 11 a.m. or after 4 p.m. **Special comments** Performance times are listed in the daily entertainment schedule *Times Guide*. **Authors' rating** A little sappy; ★★½. **Duration of presentation** 15 minutes. **Preshow entertainment** None. **Probable waiting time** 20–30 minutes.

This is a great show for small children. If your kids are comfortable sitting a few rows away

Thumbs Up for the Whole Family

from you, encourage them to sit in the front. The story line is not very compelling but the message is wholesome, and the live animals, especially when they don't stick to the script, are a hoot!

A PEEK BEHIND THE SCENES WITH JIM HILL

COULD MEEKO SOON BE REPLACED BY LUCKY?

As the Imagineers continue to puzzle about what they should do with Lucky the Dinosaur, that walk-around audio-animatronic reptile that WDI created a few years back. One of the ideas being considered is shutting down the *Pocahontas and Her Forest Friends* show and creating a new theater space that would allow Merlin the Magician to show off his newest pet, Lucky the baby dragon (picture a dinosaur with a few more rubber spikes on its back). The cool thing about this idea is that it would give WDI a logical starting point for Animal Kingdom's long-delayed Beastly Kingdom expansion area, a whole new "land" that would celebrate mythological animals like unicorns and dragons.

AFRICA

AFRICA IS THE LARGEST OF THE ANIMAL KINGDOM'S lands, and guests enter through Harambe, Disney's idealized and immensely sanitized version of a modern, rural African town. There is a market (with modern cash registers), and counter-service food is available.

Kilimanjaro Safaris (FASTPASS) ★★★★★

APPEAL BY AGE	PRESCHOOL ★★★★	GRADE SCHOOL ★★★★★	TEENS ★★★★½
YOUNG ADULTS ★★★★½		OVER 30 ★★★★½	SENIORS ★★★★★

What it is Truck ride through an African wildlife reservation. **Scope and scale** Super headliner. **Fright potential** A "collapsing" bridge and the proximity of real animals make a few young children anxious. **Bottleneck rating** 10. **When to go** As soon as the park opens, in the 2 hours before closing, or use FASTPASS. **Authors' rating** Truly exceptional; ★★★★★. **Duration of ride** About 20 minutes. **Average wait in line per 100 people ahead of you** 4 minutes. **Assumes** Full-capacity operation with 18-second dispatch interval. **Loading speed** Fast.

Thumbs Up for the Whole Family

Off you go in an open safari vehicle through a simulated African savanna. Preschoolers will enjoy looking for hippos, zebras, giraffes, lions, and rhinos while the older kids will get a kick out of the story line about poachers.

Feast your eyes on the habitat and the animals and forget the story (which can really get to you if you ride more than once). The experience would be infinitely more educational if Disney ditched the hokey poacher plot and replaced it with interesting facts about the animals.

Liliane

There are animals here that I've never heard of. It was cool to discover new animals, learn about them, and see what they look like. I didn't know how big a baby giraffe really is!

Hannah

A PEEK BEHIND THE SCENES WITH JIM HILL

REMEMBER WHEN A SHINY PLASTIC BINDER WAS COOL?

In an effort to make Kilimanjaro Safaris even more appealing to younger folks, the Imagineers have been experimenting with the use of handheld devices, so that in theory children could note on a PDA all of the animals that they saw on that safari. This information would be stored under a given kid's name, enabling him or her to download photos once back at home. It'd make it that much easier to prepare that "What I Did on My Summer Vacation" presentation for class.

Pangani Forest Exploration Trail ★★★

APPEAL BY AGE	PRESCHOOL ★★★	GRADE SCHOOL ★★★	TEENS ★★½
YOUNG ADULTS ★★★		OVER 30 ★★★	SENIORS ★★★

What it is Walk-through zoological exhibit. **Scope and scale** Major attraction. **Fright potential** Not frightening in any respect. **Bottleneck rating** 9. **When to go** Before 11 a.m. and after 2:30 p.m. **Authors' rating** ★★★. **Duration of tour** About 20–25 minutes.

The Pangani Forest Exploration Trail is lush, beautiful, and jammed to the gills with people much of the time. This is particularly unpleasant if you have to wiggle your way through with a stroller. Walk the trail before 11 a.m. or after 2:30 p.m.

A PEEK BEHIND THE SCENES WITH JIM HILL

ELEPHANT RIDES WOULDN'T BE AN OPTION, WOULD THEY?

Long considered one of the least successful attractions at Disney's Animal Kingdom both for its remote location as well as its somewhat uninspiring theme, Rafiki's *Planet Watch* is slated to get a makeover in the coming months. The Imagineers will first try to figure out how to solve this attraction's traffic issues (including getting folks there some way other than riding on the train), then retool *Planet Watch*'s theme. Among some of the ideas currently being floated is making this part of the park the only area where you can interact with the characters from Pixar's newest film, *Ratatouille*, due in theaters in June 2007.

Rafiki's *Planet Watch*

Rafiki's *Planet Watch* showed up on park maps a couple years back. It's not a "land" and not really an attraction either. Our best guess is that Disney is using the name as an umbrella for Conservation Station, the petting zoo, and the environmental exhibits accessible from Harambe via the Wildlife Express train. Presumably, Disney hopes that invoking Rafiki (a beloved character from *The Lion King*) will stimulate guests to make the effort to check out things in this far-flung corner of the park. As for your kids seeing Rafiki, don't bet on it. The closest likeness we've seen here is a two-dimensional wooden cutout.

Wildlife Express Train ★★

APPEAL BY AGE	PRESCHOOL ★★★	GRADE SCHOOL ★★★	TEENS ★½
YOUNG ADULTS ★★½		OVER 30 ★★½	SENIORS ★★½

What it is Scenic railroad ride to Rafiki's *Planet Watch* and Conservation Station. **Scope and scale** Minor attraction. **Fright potential** Not frightening in any respect. **Bottleneck rating** 7. **When to go** Anytime. **Special comments** Opens 30 minutes after the rest of the park. **Authors' rating** Ho hum; ★★. **Duration of ride** About 5–7 minutes one way. **Average wait in line per 100 people ahead of you** 9 minutes. **Loading speed** Moderate.

Take the train only if you have small kids who would really enjoy the Affection Section <u>petting zoo</u> at Rafiki's *Planet Watch*. If you have a future veterinarian in your family it is also well worth checking out the behind-the-scenes exhibits at Conservation Station.

Conservation Station and Affection Section ★★★

APPEAL BY AGE	PRESCHOOL ★★★	GRADE SCHOOL ★★	TEENS ★★
YOUNG ADULTS ★★★		OVER 30 ★★★	SENIORS ★★★

What it is Behind-the-scenes walk-through educational exhibit and petting zoo. **Scope and scale** Minor attraction. **Fright potential** Not frightening in any respect. **Bottleneck rating** 6. **When to go** Anytime. **Special comments** Opens 30 minutes after the rest of the park. **Authors' rating** Evolving; ★★★. **Probable waiting time** None.

This is the Animal Kingdom's veterinary and conservation headquarters. Guests can meet wildlife experts, observe some of the station's ongoing projects, and learn about the operations of the park. The station includes a rehabilitation area for injured animals and a nursery for recently born or hatched critters.

ASIA

CROSSING THE ASIA BRIDGE FROM DISCOVERY ISLAND, you enter Asia through the village of Anandapur, a veritable collage of Asian themes inspired by the architecture and ruins of India, Thailand, Indonesia, and Nepal.

Expedition Everest (FASTPASS) ★★★★½

APPEAL BY AGE	PRESCHOOL —	GRADE SCHOOL ★★★★	TEENS ★★★★★
YOUNG ADULTS ★★★★		OVER 30 ★★★★½	SENIORS ★★★

What it is High-speed roller coaster through Mount Everest. **Scope and scale** Super headliner. **Fright potential** Frightens guests of all ages. **When to go** Before 9:30 a.m., after 4 p.m., or use FASTPASS. **Special comments** Contains some of the park's most stunning visual elements. **Authors' rating** ★★★★½. **Duration of ride** 4 minutes. **Average wait in line per 100 people ahead of you** Just under 4 minutes. **Assumes** 2 tracks operating. **Loading speed** Moderate to fast.

Scary   Lose Things

As you enjoy one of the most spectacular panoramas in Walt Disney World, you wish this expedition would never end. But you get over that in a hurry as the train starts whirring through the guts of Disney's largest man-made mountain (not only the largest in Florida, but it also beats out Mount Petty Poot Poot in Kansas by two feet). After a high-speed encounter with a large, smelly Yeti and a dead stop at the top of the mountain, the 50-miles-per-hour chase continues backward. The ride is very smooth and rich both in visuals and special effects. The backward segment is one of the most creative and exciting 20 seconds in roller coaster annals.<UTx2>

Having escaped the anger of the Abominable Snowman once, I am not ready to try my luck again anytime soon. I'll leave this one for roller coaster aficionados.

Liliane

I think it's cool because there are a lot of big hills. There's a Yeti, and he tries to eat you. If you're a big screamer like me, you'll probably just close your eyes and open your mouth.

Hannah

Flights of Wonder ★★★★

APPEAL BY AGE	PRESCHOOL ★★★★	GRADE SCHOOL ★★★★	TEENS ★★★½
YOUNG ADULTS ★★★★		OVER 30 ★★★★	SENIORS ★★★★

What it is Stadium show about birds. **Scope and scale** Major attraction. **Fright potential** Swooping birds startle some younger children. **Bottleneck rating** 6. **When to go** Anytime. **Special comments** Performance times are listed in the handout park map or *Times Guide*. **Authors' rating** Unique; ★★★★. **Duration of presentation** 30 minutes. **Preshow entertainment** None. **Probable waiting time** 20 minutes.

Humorously presented, the show is ideal for kids. Don't expect parrots riding unicycles though. *Flights of Wonder* is about the natural talents and characteristics of various bird species. If your child is comfortable with you sitting a few rows behind, encourage him or her to take a seat in the up-front "for kids only" section. When the show is over, stick around

Thumbs Up for the Whole Family

and talk to the bird trainers and meet the feathery cast of the show up close and personal. It is a great opportunity to ask questions and take pictures.

Kali River Rapids (FASTPASS) ★★★½

APPEAL BY AGE	PRESCHOOL ★★★★	GRADE SCHOOL ★★★★	TEENS ★★★★
YOUNG ADULTS ★★★½		OVER 30 ★★★½	SENIORS ★★★

What it is Whitewater raft ride. **Scope and scale** Headliner. **Fright potential** Potentially frightening and certainly wet for guests of all ages; height requirement is 38 inches. **Bottleneck rating 9. When to go** Before 11 a.m., after 4:30 p.m., or use FASTPASS. **Special comments** You are guaranteed to get wet. Opens 30 minutes after the rest of the park. Switching-off option provided (see page 220). **Authors' rating** Short but scenic; ★★★½. **Duration of ride** About 5 minutes. **Average wait in line per 100 people ahead of you** 5 minutes. **Loading speed** Moderate.

Scary   Wet

The ride itself is tame and allows you to take in the outstanding scenery as you drift through a dense rain forest, past waterfalls and temple ruins. There are neither big drops nor terrifying rapids waiting to swallow the raft and all inside. The forgoing information notwithstanding, Disney still manages to drench you. Nonriding park guests will take great pleasure squirting water at the rafters from above. The water-squirting elephant stations are a great consolation prize for young ones who do not meet the 38-inch height requirement.

On a hot summer day, the Kali River Rapids are just what the doctor ordered. However, if you ride early in the morning or on a cool day, use rain gear to protect yourselves and make sure your shoes stay dry. Touring in wet clothes is unpleasant, and walking all day in soaked sneakers is a recipe for blisters.

Liliane

Don't wear anything fancy because you're going to get soaked.

Hannah

Maharaja Jungle Trek ★★★★

APPEAL BY AGE	PRESCHOOL ★★★	GRADE SCHOOL ★★★½	TEENS ★★★
YOUNG ADULTS ★★★½		OVER 30 ★★★½	SENIORS ★★★★

What it is Walk-through zoological exhibit. **Scope and scale** Headliner. **Fright potential** Some children may balk at the bat exhibit. **Bottleneck rating 5. When to go** Anytime. **Special comments** Opens 30 minutes after the rest of the park. **Authors' rating** A standard-setter for natural habitat design; ★★★★. **Duration of tour** About 20–30 minutes.

The Jungle Trek is less congested than the Pangani Forest Exploration Trail and is a good choice for midday touring. Tigers, gibbons, bats, and birds are waiting to be discovered along a path winding through the fabulous ruins of the maharaja's palace.

The bat enclosure is outstanding and my favorite section of the trek. From Batman to Dracula, this is the opportunity to increase your knowledge of these mysterious mammals.

Liliane

DINOLAND U.S.A.

THIS MOST TYPICALLY DISNEY OF THE Animal Kingdom's lands is a cross between an anthropological dig and a quirky roadside attraction. Accessible via the bridge from Discovery Island, DinoLand U.S.A. is home to a children's play area, a nature trail, a 1,500-seat amphitheater, and Dinosaur, one of the Animal Kingdom's three thrill rides.

Children ages 4 to 12 will feel right at home at DinoLand U.S.A. Speaking of home, DinoLand U.S.A. is the residence of *Finding Nemo— The Musical*, replacing *Tarzan Rocks!* at the Theater in the Wild.

Dinosaur (FASTPASS) ★★★★½

APPEAL BY AGE	PRESCHOOL †	GRADE SCHOOL ★★★★½	TEENS ★★★★½
YOUNG ADULTS ★★★★½		OVER 30 ★★★★½	SENIORS ★★★½

† Sample size too small for an accurate rating.

What it is Motion-simulator dark ride. **Scope and scale** Super headliner. **Fright potential** High-tech thrill ride rattles riders of all ages. **Bottleneck rating** 8. **When to go** Before 10:30 a.m., in the hour before closing, or use FASTPASS. **Special comments** Must be 40 inches tall to ride. Switching-off option provided (see page 220). **Authors' rating** Really improved; ★★★★½. **Duration of ride** 3⅓ minutes. **Average wait in line per 100 people ahead of you** 3 minutes. **Assumes** Full-capacity operation with 18-second dispatch interval. **Loading speed** Fast.

Dark

Scary

Rough

Here you board a time capsule to return to the Jurassic age in an effort to bring back a live dinosaur before a meteor hits the Earth and wipes them out. The bad guy in this epic is the little known carnotaurus, an evil-eyed, long in the tooth, Tyrannosaurus rex–type fellow. A combination track ride and motion simulator, Dinosaur is not for the faint-hearted. You get tossed and pitched around in the dark with pesky dinosaurs jumping out at you. Dinosaur has left many an adult weak-kneed. Most kids under 9 find it terrifying.

Liliane

Dinosaur is an absolute no-no for preschoolers and any child easily frightened. The carnotaurus, unlike Barney and Figment, did not make my favorite dino list.

It doesn't really go up any hills, and it didn't make me scream, but it scared my cousin half to death when she was 4. Even if you're 5 or 6, the dinosaurs might scare you.
Hannah

TriceraTop Spin ★★

APPEAL BY AGE	PRESCHOOL ★★★★	GRADE SCHOOL ★★★	TEENS ★★
YOUNG ADULTS ★★		OVER 30 ★★	SENIORS ★★

What it is Hub-and-spoke midway ride. **Scope and scale** Minor attraction. **Fright potential** May frighten preschoolers. **Bottleneck rating 9. When to go** First 90 minutes the park is open and in the hour before park closing. **Authors' rating** Dumbo's prehistoric forebear; ★★. **Duration of ride** 1½ minutes. **Average wait in line per 100 people ahead of you** 10 minutes. **Loading speed** Slow.

Motion Sickness

Instead of Dumbo you got Dino spinning around a central axis. The ride is fun for young children, but the slow-loading ride is infamous for inefficiency and long waits.

Primeval Whirl (FASTPASS) ★★★

APPEAL BY AGE	PRESCHOOL ★★★	GRADE SCHOOL ★★★★½	TEENS ★★★½
YOUNG ADULTS ★★★		OVER 30 ★★★	SENIORS ★★

What it is Small coaster. **Scope and scale** Minor attraction. **Fright potential** Scarier than it looks. **Bottleneck rating 9. When to go** During the first 2 hours the park is open, in the hour before park closing, or use FASTPASS. **Special comments** 48-inch minimum height. Switching-off option provided (see page 220). **Authors' rating** "Wild Mouse" on steroids; ★★★. **Duration of ride** Almost 2½ minutes. **Average wait in line per 100 people ahead of you** 4½ minutes. **Loading speed** Slow.

Scary

Motion Sickness

Rough

This is a tricky little coaster with short drops, curves, and tight loops. As if that's not enough, the coaster cars also spin. The problem is, unlike with the evil teacups, guests cannot control the spinning. Complete spins are fun, but watch out for the screeching-stop half-spins.

Theater in the Wild
Finding Nemo–The Musical ★★★★

APPEAL BY AGE	PRESCHOOL ★★★	GRADE SCHOOL ★★★	TEENS ★★★
YOUNG ADULTS ★★★		OVER 30 ★★½	SENIORS ★★½

What it is Open-air venue for live stage shows. **Scope and scale** Major attraction. **Fright potential** Not frightening in any respect. **Bottleneck rating 6. When to go** Anytime. **Special comments** Performance times are listed in the handout park map or *Times Guide*. **Authors' rating** ★★★★. **Duration of presentation** 25–35 minutes. **Preshow entertainment** None. **Probable waiting time** About 30 minutes.

Thumbs Up for the Whole Family

Based on the Disney/Pixar animated feature, *Finding Nemo–The Musical* is an elaborate stage show headlining puppets, dancing, acrobats, and special effects. Replacing the long-running *Tarzan Rocks!*, Nemo is sweet and funny and a must-see. To get a seat, arrive half an hour before the show.

The Boneyard ★★★½

APPEAL BY AGE			
PRESCHOOL ★★★★★		GRADE SCHOOL ★★★★★	
TEENS —	YOUNG ADULTS —	OVER 30 —	SENIORS —

What it is Elaborate playground. **Scope and scale** Diversion. **Fright potential** Not frightening in any respect. **Bottleneck rating** 5. **When to go** Anytime. **Special comments** Opens 30 minutes after the rest of the park. **Authors' rating** Stimulating fun for children; ★★★½. **Duration of visit** Varies. **Probable waiting time** None.

It's playtime! The Boneyard is an elaborate playground for the 12-and-younger crowd and a great place for kids to let off steam and get dirty (or at least sandy). The playground equipment consists of skeletons of triceratops, Tyrannosaurus rex, brachiosaurus, and the like. In addition, there are climbing mazes as well as sand pits where little ones can scrounge around for bones and fossils.

The Boneyard can get very hot in the scorching Florida sun, so make sure your kids are properly hydrated and protected against sunburn. The playground is huge and parents might lose sight of a small child. Fortunately, however, there's only one entrance and exit. Your little ones are going to love the Boneyard, so resign yourself to staying awhile.

Hannah

Tusker House is my favorite. It has a lot of choices, and there are always a lot of people there because the food is good. You can get cinnamon rolls here as big as a stuffed animal!

FAVORITE EATS AT ANIMAL KINGDOM

LAND	FOOD ITEM	WHERE THEY CAN BE FOUND
DISCOVERY ISLAND	Ribs, chicken with beans and corn on the cob	Flame Tree Barbecue
	Pizza and chicken Caesar salad, breadsticks	Pizzafari
DINOLAND U.S.A.	McDonald's Happy Meals (character breakfast daily)	Restaurantosaurus
ASIA	Pastries, fruits, and a variety of teas	Royal Anandapur Tea Company
AFRICA	Ice cream and smoothies	Tamu Tamu
	Macaroni and cheese served with applesauce and Mickey cheddar crackers	Tusker House Restaurant
OUTSIDE ENTRANCE	Breakfast, lunch, and dinner in a tropical rain forest setting with huge saltwater aquarium, gorillas going wild once in a while, and simulated thunderstorms. The place to take the kids if you want to sit down! They'll love you for it, cross my heart, hope to die. (*table service only*)	Rainforest Cafe

LIVE ENTERTAINMENT *at* ANIMAL KINGDOM

STAGE SHOWS ARE PERFORMED DAILY at the Animal Kingdom; check your entertainment schedule (*Times Guide*) for show times. Street performers can be found most of the time at Discovery Island; in Harambe, Africa; Anandapur, Asia; and in DinoLand U.S.A.

LOOK WHO'S TALKING At the Oasis, don't miss introducing your kids to **Wes Palm,** the talking palm tree who loves to poke fun at unsuspecting guests. At Conservation Station have a silly-dilly (Liliane's term) chat with **Pipa,** the recycling trash can.

Though Wes Palm and Pipa will have you roaring with laughter, **DiVine** will leave you speechless. A perfect fusion between fantasy and reality, DiVine is an artist in a garb half-vine and half-creeping plant. She blends perfectly with the foliage at the Animal Kingdom and is only noticeable when she moves (which can be quite startling if you're not aware of her presence). DiVine travels around the park but seems to love the vicinity of the Rainforest Cafe entrance. The silent gracefulness of her movements and the serenity of her demeanor are totally captivating.

 AFTERNOON PARADE Mickey's Jammin' Jungle Parade features characters from *The Lion King, The Jungle Book, Tarzan,* and *Pocahontas.* The parade starts in Africa, crosses the bridge to Discovery Island, proceeds counterclockwise around the island, and then crosses the bridge to Asia. In Asia, the parade turns left and follows the walkway paralleling the river back to Africa.

The walking path between Africa and Asia has small cutouts that offer good views of the parade and excellent sun protection. Most guests scramble to Harambe, the starting point of the parade, and leave this area as soon as the parade crosses over the bridge to Discovery Island. Because guests don't realize that the parade cycles back

---

A PEEK BEHIND THE SCENES WITH JIM HILL

STAY AFTER DARK SO YOU CAN SEE THE LIGHT

Now that Expedition Everest and the new *Finding Nemo* musical show have allowed Disney's Animal Kingdom to extend its operating hours, this theme park is finally getting serious about providing WDW visitors with some after-dark entertainment. But since Animal Kingdom obviously can't do a fireworks display (out of concern for the animals' safety), one of the ideas currently being considered is a nighttime lantern-light parade. This project is currently being developed by Steve Davison, the same very creative gentleman who created the *Wishes* fireworks show for the Magic Kingdom. Look for Animal Kingdom's new lantern-light show to debut in late 2007 or early 2008.

through Harambe, there is never much of a crowd when the parade rumbles through the second time en route to going offstage. Therefore, if you make your way to Harambe about 20 minutes after the parade time listed in the *Times Guide* you'll be able to score a super vantage point at the last minute.

ANIMAL KINGDOM TOURING PLANS

OUR STEP-BY-STEP TOURING PLANS ARE FIELD-TESTED, independently verified itineraries that will keep you moving counter to the crowd flow and allow you to see as much as possible in a single day with a minimum of time wasted in line.

You can take in all the attractions at the Animal Kingdom in a single day even when traveling with young children.

If you are not interested in an attraction listed on the touring plan, just skip that step and proceed to the next one. Should you encounter a very long line at an attraction the touring plan calls for, skip the attraction and go to the next step, returning later to retry. The use of FASTPASS is factored into the touring plans.

The different touring plans are described below. The descriptions will tell you for whom (for example, tweens, parents with preschoolers, grandparents, and so on) or for what situation (such as sleeping late or enjoying the park at night) the plans are designed. The actual touring plans are located on pages 421–424 at the back of the book. Each plan includes a numbered map of the park in question to help you find your way around. Clip the plan of your choice out of the book by cutting along the line indicated, and take it with you to the park.

ANIMAL KINGDOM ONE-DAY TOURING PLAN FOR PARENTS WITH SMALL CHILDREN This plan is designed for parents of children ages 3 to 8 who wish to see the very best age-appropriate attractions in the Animal Kingdom. Every attraction has a rating of at least three stars (out of five) from preschool and grade-school children surveyed by the *Unofficial Guide*. Special advice is provided for touring the park with small children, including restaurant recommendations. The plan keeps walking and backtracking to a minimum, with no crisscrossing of the park.

ANIMAL KINGDOM ONE-DAY SLEEPY HEAD TOURING PLAN FOR PARENTS WITH SMALL CHILDREN A relaxed plan that allows families with small children to sleep late and still see the highlights of the Animal Kingdom. The plan begins around 11 a.m., sets aside ample time for lunch, and includes the very best child-friendly attractions in the park.

ANIMAL KINGDOM ONE-DAY TOURING PLAN FOR TWEENS AND THEIR PARENTS A one-day plan for parents with children ages 8 to 12. It includes every attraction rated three stars and higher by this age group and sets aside ample time for lunch and dinner.

ANIMAL KINGDOM ONE-DAY HAPPY FAMILY TOURING PLAN A plan for families of all ages. Includes time-saving tips for teens and adults visiting the Animal Kingdom's thrill rides, and age-appropriate attractions for parents with small children. The entire family stays together as much as possible (including lunch), but this plan allows groups with different interests to explore their favorite attractions without having everyone wait around.

BE PREPARED

ALWAYS CALL ☎ 407-824-4321 the day before you plan to visit to confirm the official park opening time. Purchase your admission tickets before you arrive and familiarize yourself with the touring plan you have chosen.

BEFORE YOU GO

1. Call ☎ 407-824-4321 before you go for the park's operating hours.
2. Purchase your admission prior to arrival.

DISNEY'S ANIMAL KINGDOM TRIVIA QUIZ
By Lou Mongello

1. What can you find in the middle of Animal Kingdom?
   a. A giant tree
   b. A giant castle
   c. A merry-go-round
   d. The Rainforest Cafe

2. What land in the Animal Kingdom is Expedition Everest located in?
   a. Africa
   b. Asia
   c. DinoLand U.S.A.
   d. Discovery Island

3. How tall is the highest mountain peak on Expedition Everest?
   a. 65 feet
   b. 117 feet
   c. 199 feet
   d. 279 feet

4. On what memorable day did Disney's Animal Kingdom open?
   a. Earth Day
   b. Groundhog Day
   c. Arbor Day
   d. Christmas Day

5. Which of these structures in Disney's Animal Kingdom is the tallest?
   a. The Tree of Life
   b. Expedition Everest
   c. *The Festival of the Lion King* Theater
   d. Dino-Sue

6. In the *Festival of the Lion King* show, which of these is NOT one of the animal sections you can sit in?
   a. Giraffe
   b. Warthog
   c. Meercat
   d. Lion

7. What attraction in the Animal Kingdom is similar to Dumbo in the Magic Kingdom?
   a. TriceraTop Spin
   b. Primeval Whirl
   c. Dinosaur
   d. Flights of Wonder

8. About how many different animals are carved into the Tree of Life?
   a. 55
   b. 175
   c. 325
   d. 500

9. What is the name of the animal you are trying to help save on the Kilimanjaro Safaris?
  a. Simba
  b. Little Red
  c. King Louie
  d. Hanna Montana

10. Where in Disney's Animal Kingdom can you find the "Tumble Monkeys"?
  a. Maharajah Jungle Trek
  b. *It's Tough to Be a Bug!*
  c. Kilimanjaro Safaris
  d. *Festival of the Lion King*

11. Who is the guardian of the mountain on Expedition Everest?
  a. Chernabog
  b. The Yeti
  c. Scar
  d. The Loch Ness Monster

Answers can be found on page 386.

Trivia content courtesy of Lou Mongello, author of Disney Trivia; *www.disneyworldtrivia.com.*

"OK, now let's try the Animal Kingdom to Epcot."

PART TEN

DISNEY-MGM STUDIOS

ABOUT HALF OF DISNEY-MGM STUDIOS is set up as a theme park. The other half, off limits except by guided tour, is a working motion picture and television studio. Though modest in size, the Studios' open-access areas are confusingly arranged (a product of the park's hurried expansion in the early 1990s). As at the Magic Kingdom, you enter the park and pass down a main street, only this time it's Hollywood Boulevard of the 1920s and 1930s. Because there are no "lands" as in the other parks, the easiest way to navigate is by landmarks and attractions using the park map.

Guest Relations, on your left as you enter, serves as the park headquarters and information center, similar to City Hall in the Magic Kingdom. Go there for a schedule of live performances, lost persons, package pick-up, lost and found (on the right side of the entrance), general information, or in an emergency. If you haven't received a map of the Studios, get one here. To the right of the entrance are locker, stroller, and wheelchair rentals.

A baby-care center is located at Guest Relations while Oscar's sells baby food and other necessities. More film for those precious moments can be purchased at The Darkroom on the right side of Hollywood Boulevard, just past Oscar's. Oddly enough the closest ATM is located outside the park to the right of the turnstiles.

Guests enter the park on Hollywood Boulevard, a palm-lined street reminiscent of the famous Hollywood main avenue of the 1930s. The best way to navigate is to decide what you really want to see and go for it! If you want the whole enchilada, it can be done in one day. But, as with the other parks, this is best accomplished by using one of our touring plans.

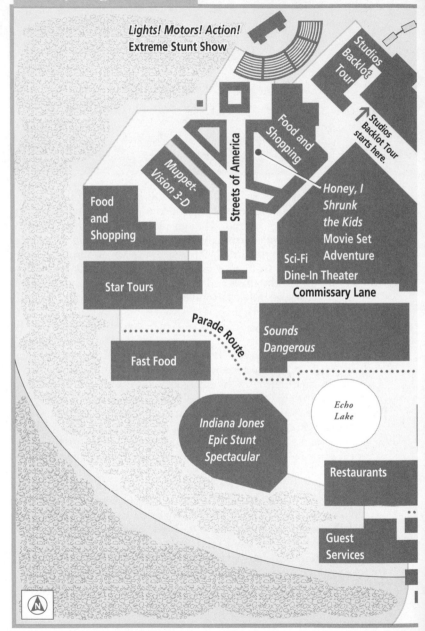

disney-mgm studios

Lights! Motors! Action!
Extreme Stunt Show

Studios
Backlot
Tour

Studios
Backlot Tour
starts here.

Food and
Shopping

Muppet-
Vision 3-D

Streets of America

Honey, I
Shrunk
the Kids
Movie Set
Adventure

Sci-Fi
Dine-In Theater

Commissary Lane

Food
and
Shopping

Star Tours

Parade Route

Sounds
Dangerous

Fast Food

Echo
Lake

Indiana Jones
Epic Stunt
Spectacular

Restaurants

Guest
Services

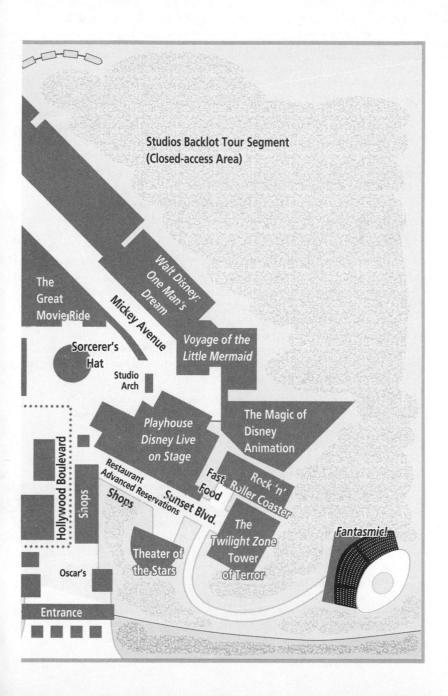

Studios Backlot Tour Segment
(Closed-access Area)

The Great Movie Ride

Walt Disney: One Man's Dream

Mickey Avenue

Sorcerer's Hat

Studio Arch

Voyage of the Little Mermaid

The Magic of Disney Animation

Playhouse Disney Live on Stage

Hollywood Boulevard

Shops

Restaurant Advanced Reservations

Shops

Sunset Blvd.

Fast Food

Rock 'n' Roller Coaster

Fantasmic!

Theater of the Stars

The Twilight Zone Tower of Terror

Oscar's

Entrance

The Twilight Zone **Tower of Terror (FASTPASS)** ★★★★★

APPEAL· BY AGE   PRESCHOOL ★★★   GRADE SCHOOL ★★★★★   TEENS ★★★★★
YOUNG ADULTS ★★★★★   OVER 30 ★★★★★   SENIORS ★★★★★

What it is Sci-fi-theme indoor thrill ride. **Scope and scale** Super headliner.
Fright potential Visually intimidating to young children; contains intense and
realistic special effects. The plummeting elevator at the ride's end frightens many
adults. Switching-off option provided (see page 220). **Bottleneck rating** 10.
When to go Before 9:30 a.m., after 6 p.m., or use FASTPASS. **Special comments**
Must be 40 inches tall to ride. **Authors' rating** Walt Disney World's best attraction; not to be missed; ★★★★★. **Duration of ride** About 4 minutes plus
preshow. **Average wait in line per 100 people ahead of you** 4 minutes. **Assumes**
All elevators operating. **Loading speed** Moderate.

Dark   Scary   Rough

And suddenly the cable went snap. If riding a
capricious elevator in a haunted hotel sounds
like fun to you, this is your ride. Erratic yet
thrilling, the Tower of Terror is an experience
to savor. The Tower has great potential for
terrifying young children and rattling more mature visitors. Recently, random ride-and-drop sequences were introduced to make the attraction
wilder and to keep you guessing about when, how far, and how many times
the elevator drops. We suggest you use teenagers in your party as experimental probes. If they report back that they really, really liked the Tower of
Terror, run as fast as you can in the opposite direction. Tower of Terror is
one of the hottest tickets in the park. If you're up to it, experience the ride
first thing in the morning or use FASTPASS.

Another ride that gives you surprises. I like it when you go up
and think you're going to stay up but end up zooming down.
There's a part of the ride where it looks like you're in outer
Hannah   space, then it turns back into the hotel.

Rock 'n' Roller Coaster (FASTPASS) ★★★★

APPEAL BY AGE   PRESCHOOL ★★★   GRADE SCHOOL ★★★★   TEENS ★★★★
YOUNG ADULTS ★★★★   OVER 30 ★★★★   SENIORS ★★★

What it is Rock music–themed roller coaster. **Scope and scale** Headliner. **Fright
potential** Extremely intense for all ages; the ride is one of Disney's wildest. 40-
inch minimum height requirement. **Bottleneck rating** 10. **When to go** Before 10
a.m. or in the hour before closing. **Special comments** Must be 48 inches tall to
ride; children younger than age 7 must ride with an adult. Switching-off option
provided (page 220). **Authors' rating** Disney's wildest American coaster; not to
be missed; ★★★★. **Duration of ride** Almost 1½ minutes. **Average wait in line
per 100 people ahead of you** 2½ minutes. **Assumes** All trains operating. **Loading speed** Moderate to fast.

Dark   Scary   Rough   Motion Sickness   Lose Things

Aerosmith's recent tour was called "Route of All Evil," and the notorious ride at Disney-MGM Studios will make good on fans' expectations. Loops, corkscrews, and drops that make Space Mountain seem like the Jungle Cruise is what to expect and what is delivered—pronto. You will be launched from 0 to 57 miles per hour in less than three seconds, and by the time you enter the first loop you'll be pulling five Gs. By comparison, that is two more Gs than astronauts experience at lift-off on a space shuttle.

Aerosmith describes this ride best in one of their songs: "Living on the Edge."

Liliane

The Great Movie Ride ★★★½

| APPEAL BY AGE | PRESCHOOL ★★½ | GRADE SCHOOL ★★★½ | TEENS ★★★½ |
| YOUNG ADULTS ★★★★ | | OVER 30 ★★★★ | SENIORS ★★★ |

What it is Movie-history indoor adventure ride. **Scope and scale** Headliner. **Fright potential** Intense in parts, with very realistic special effects and some visually intimidating sights. **Bottleneck rating** 8. **When to go** Before 11 a.m. or after 4:30 p.m. **Special comments** Elaborate, with several surprises. **Authors' rating** Unique; ★★★½. **Duration of ride** About 19 minutes. **Average wait in line per 100 people ahead of you** 2 minutes. **Assumes** All trains operating. **Loading speed** Fast.

Dark   Scary

Inside the re-creation of Hollywood's Chinese Theater awaits a trip down memory lane. From *Casablanca* to *Raiders of the Lost Ark,* classic movies are showcased in this ride through some of the movies' most memorable sets. Young movie buffs might be flipped out along the way (*Alien* is one of the movies represented), but the wonderful Munchkins from *The Wizard of Oz* scene will make up for it—Wicked Witch of the North notwithstanding.

I've only seen some of these movies, so I like how it's not just a ride, but there's a hostess that tells you about the movies, like if it's a western or something. There's the yellow-brick road from *The Wizard of Oz,* and the Munchkins sing "Follow the Yellow Brick Road."

Hannah

Star Tours (FASTPASS) ★★★★

| APPEAL BY AGE | PRESCHOOL ★★★★ | GRADE SCHOOL ★★★★ | TEENS ★★★★ |
| YOUNG ADULTS ★★★★ | | OVER 30 ★★★★ | SENIORS ★★★★ |

What it is Indoor space flight–simulation ride. **Scope and scale** Headliner. **Fright potential** Extremely intense visually for all ages; the ride is one of Disney's wildest. Likely to cause motion sickness. Switching-off option provided (see page 220); 40-inch minimum height requirement. **Bottleneck rating** 8. **When to go** Before 11 a.m. or after 4:30 p.m. **Special comments** Expectant mothers and anyone prone to motion sickness are advised against riding. Too intense for many children younger than age 8. Must be 40 inches tall to ride. **Authors' rating** Not to be missed; ★★★★. **Duration of ride** About 7 minutes. **Average wait in line per 100 people ahead of you** 5 minutes. **Assumes** All simulators operating. **Loading speed** Moderate to fast.

Scary

Rough

Motion Sickness

Based on the *Star Wars* movie series, this attraction takes guests on a flight-simulator ride to Endor. You could swear you are moving at light speed and somehow when all hell breaks loose you are confident that, total mayhem aside, the force will be with you. This ride is wonderful for all *Star Wars* fans and a living nightmare for guests prone to motion sickness.

Movie Tip

Every year (usually mid-May to mid-June) Walt Disney World hosts four *Star Wars* weekends. Celebrities from the saga and fans converge at the park in celebration of George Lucas's epic series. Even Mickey turns into a Jedi and joins Ewoks, Jawas, and Wookies for a ride to a galaxy far, far away.

Oh, no! We're caught in a tractor beam!

Liliane

Idan

Star Wars weekends are a must for any and all *Star Wars* fans. Shame on Disney for keeping Darth Vader away from his fans. Why does he only appear in the parade? He deserves better than one outing a day. And what about that lovable Wookie? I say *Star Wars* characters on Hollywood Boulevard—now.

Sounds Dangerous ★★★

APPEAL BY AGE	PRESCHOOL ★★½	GRADE SCHOOL ★★★½	TEENS ★★★
YOUNG ADULTS ★★★		OVER 30 ★★★	SENIORS ★★★★

What it is Show demonstrating sound effects. **Scope and scale** Minor attraction. **Fright potential** Sounds in darkened theater frighten some preschoolers. **Bottleneck rating** 6. **When to go** Before noon or after 4 p.m. **Authors' rating** Funny and informative; ★★★. **Duration of presentation** 12 minutes. **Preshow entertainment** Video introduction to sound effects. **Probable waiting time** 15–30 minutes.

Dark

Put on your headphones, turn off the lights, and join Drew Carey in a hilarious presentation about sound effects. The show is not geared toward preschoolers. The theater is completely dark during much of the presentation, and the sound effects are very realistic and not a little disconcerting.

Indiana Jones Epic Stunt Spectacular (FASTPASS) ★★★★

APPEAL BY AGE	PRESCHOOL ★★★	GRADE SCHOOL ★★★★	TEENS ★★★★
YOUNG ADULTS ★★★★		OVER 30 ★★★★	SENIORS ★★★★

What it is Movie-stunt demonstration and action show. **Scope and scale** Headliner. **Fright potential** An intense show with powerful special effects, including explosions. Presented in an educational context that young children generally handle well. **Bottleneck rating** 8. **When to go** First 3 morning shows or last evening show. **Special comments** Performance times posted on a sign at the entrance to the theater. **Authors' rating** Done on a grand scale; ★★★. **Duration of presentation** 30 minutes. **Preshow entertainment** Selection of "extras" from audience. **Probable waiting time** None.

Professional stunt men and women demonstrate dangerous stunts with a behind-the-scenes look at how it is done. Most kids handle the show well. The show always needs a few "extras." To be chosen from the audience, arrive early, sit down front, and display unmitigated enthusiasm. Unfortunately "victims" must be 18 years old and up.

An amazing show with fiery explosions and nonstop action. Did you know that the folks at Disney have a vault filled with sound-effects CDs ranging from gunshots to magical twinkles? When a show is created, they pick and choose from this treasure chest and upload the sounds into their state-of-the-art computerized mixing table.

Idan

Huh? What's a "magical twinkle" sound like? But now that I think about it, I sure remember the noise my innards made after eating about a dozen magical twinkles.

Bob

Those were Twinkies, Mr. Tiki-Birdbrain!

Liliane

Beauty and the Beast—Live on Stage ★★★★

APPEAL BY AGE	PRESCHOOL ★★★★	GRADE SCHOOL ★★★★	TEENS ★★★
YOUNG ADULTS ★★★		OVER 30 ★★★★	SENIORS ★★★★

What it is Live musical, featuring Disney characters; performed in an open-air theater. **Scope and scale** Major attraction. **Fright potential** Not frightening in any respect. **Bottleneck rating** 5. **When to go** Anytime; evenings are cooler. **Special comments** Performances are listed in the daily *Times Guide*. **Authors' rating** Excellent; ★★★★. **Duration of presentation** 25 minutes. **Preshow entertainment** Sometimes. **Probable waiting time** 20–30 minutes.

Join Cogsworth, Lumiere, Chip, and Mrs. Potts as they help Belle to break the spell. This 25-minute musical stage show of Disney's *Beauty and the Beast* feature will charm everybody. The show is popular, so show up half an hour early to get a seat.

The décor and the costumes, the actors and the music: everything is in perfect harmony. Little girls fond of Belle will want to have that ball gown and young boys will be eager to teach that mean Gaston a lesson!

Liliane

Voyage of the Little Mermaid (FASTPASS) ★★★★

APPEAL BY AGE   PRESCHOOL ★★★★   GRADE SCHOOL ★★★★   TEENS ★★★½
YOUNG ADULTS ★★★★   OVER 30 ★★★★   ·SENIORS ★★★★

What it is Musical stage show featuring characters from the Disney movie *The Little Mermaid.* **Scope and scale** Major attraction. **Fright potential** Ursula the sea witch may frighten preschoolers. **Bottleneck rating** 10. **When to go** Before 9:45 a.m., just before closing, or use FASTPASS. **Authors' rating** Romantic, lovable, and humorous in the best Disney tradition; not to be missed; ★★★★. **Duration of presentation** 15 minutes. **Preshow entertainment** Taped ramblings about the decor in the preshow holding area. **Probable waiting time** Before 9:30 a.m., 10–30 minutes; after 9:30 a.m., 35–70 minutes.

Thumbs Up for the Whole Family

See this most tender and romantic stage show before Disney pulls the plug. Once inside the theater, the audience is transported into the wonderful underwater world of Ariel and her friends. Very young children might be frightened by Ursula the sea witch (she is actually a puppet standing 12 feet tall).

The scary characters like the eels just show up on the side—they don't come out at you. Ariel's hair is really, really bright red.

Hannah

A PEEK BEHIND THE SCENES WITH JIM HILL

HAVE I EVER BEEN WRONG? I MEAN, WHEN IT'S IMPORTANT

Though *Voyage of the Little Mermaid* is still one of Disney-MGM's most popular attractions, this live stage show will be closing for good sometime in 2007. And why would the Mouse do something stupid like that, you ask? Back in January 2006, Disney Theatrical Productions was readying the stage-musical version of *Tarzan* for its Broadway debut. Theatrical saw Animal Kingdom's *Tarzan Rocks!* show as competition for its Broadway show, so *Tarzan Rocks!* had to close before the New York show could open. And since the Broadway musical version of *The Little Mermaid* is supposed to open in the 2007–08 season . . . well, I guess you can see why Ariel's days of performing at Disney-MGM are now numbered.

Jim Henson's Muppet-Vision 3-D ★★★★½

APPEAL BY AGE   PRESCHOOL ★★★★½   GRADE SCHOOL ★★★★★   TEENS ★★★★½
YOUNG ADULTS ★★★★½   OVER 30 ★★★★½   SENIORS ★★★★½

What it is 3-D movie starring the Muppets. **Scope and scale** Major attraction. **Fright potential** Intense and loud, but not frightening. **Bottleneck rating** 8. **When to go** Before 11 a.m. or after 3 p.m. **Authors' rating** Uproarious; not to be missed; ★★★★½. **Duration of presentation** 17 minutes. **Preshow entertainment** Muppets on television. **Probable waiting time** 12 minutes.

Kermit, Miss Piggy, and the rest of the gang will lift your spirits as they unleash their hilarious mayhem. Because adults tend to associate Muppet characters with the children's show *Sesame Street*, many bypass this attraction. Big mistake. *Muppet-Vision 3-D* operates on several planes, and there's as much here for oldsters as for youngsters. The presentation is intense and sometimes loud, but most preschoolers handle it well. If your child is a little scared, encourage him to watch without the 3-D glasses at first.

Thumbs Up for the Whole Family

Honey, I Shrunk the Kids Movie Set Adventure ★★½

APPEAL BY AGE	PRESCHOOL ★★★★½	GRADE SCHOOL ★★★½	TEENS ★★
YOUNG ADULTS ★★½	OVER 30 ★★★		SENIORS ★★½

What it is Small but elaborate playground. **Scope and scale** Diversion. **Fright potential** Everything is oversized, but nothing is scary. **Bottleneck rating** 8. **When to go** Before 11 a.m. or after dark. **Special comments** Opens an hour later than the rest of the park. **Authors' rating** Great for young children, more of a curiosity for adults; ★★½. **Average wait in line per 100 people ahead of you** 20 minutes.

This elaborate playground appeals particularly to kids age 11 and younger. Tunnels, slides, rope ladders, and a variety of oversized props offer lots of playtime fun. There are a few problems with the attraction, though. The place is too small to accommodate all the children who would like to play and supervision inside the jam-packed and poorly ventilated playground can be trying. Last but not least, kids play as long as parents allow, so be prepared for this stop to take a big chunk of time out of your touring day. If you visit during the warmer months and want your children to experience the playground, get them in and out before 11 a.m. By late morning, this attraction is way too hot and crowded for anyone to enjoy.

Lights! Motors! Action! Extreme Stunt Show ★★★½

APPEAL BY AGE	PRESCHOOL ★★	GRADE SCHOOL ★★★★	TEENS ★★★★
YOUNG ADULTS ★★★½	OVER 30 ★★★½		SENIORS ★★★½

What it is Auto stunt show. **Scope and scale** Headliner. **Fright potential** Loud with explosions but not scary. **When to go** First show of the day or after 4 p.m. **Authors'**

rating Good stunt work, slow pace; ★★★½. **Duration of presentation** 25–30 minutes. **Preshow entertainment** Selection of audience "volunteers."

This show features cars and motorcycles in a blur of chases, crashes, jumps, and explosions. The secrets behind the special effects are explained after each stunt sequence. The show runs 25 to 30 minutes, and small children may become restless. Teens, however, will be gobsmacked. Note that FASTPASS for this attraction is not linked to the rest of the Studios' FASTPASS rides, so you can obtain FASTPASSes for this show immediately after obtaining them for any other FASTPASS attraction.

> The show left me speechless. This is one of the most amazing, unbelievable shows of all. You won't believe your eyes.

Idan

> Maybe it's an age thing, but I'm less impressed than Idan. The stunts are super, but there's too much dead time and redundancy in this show.

Bob

Streets of America ★★★

APPEAL BY AGE	PRESCHOOL ★½	GRADE SCHOOL ★★★	TEENS ★★★
YOUNG ADULTS ★★★		OVER 30 ★★★	SENIORS ★★★

What it is Walk-through backlot movie set. **Scope and scale** Diversion. **Fright potential** Not frightening in any respect. **Bottleneck rating** 1. **When to go** Anytime. **Authors' rating** Interesting, with great detail; ★★★. **Duration of presentation** Varies. **Average wait in line per 100 people ahead of you** No waiting.

There is never a wait to enjoy the Streets of America; save your visit here until you have seen those attractions that develop long lines. During the Christmas season, Streets of America are decorated with millions of Christmas lights and serve as a backdrop for the Osborne Family Spectacle of Lights.

One Man's Dream ★★★★

APPEAL BY AGE	PRESCHOOL ★	GRADE SCHOOL ★★½	TEENS ★★★
YOUNG ADULTS ★★★½		OVER 30 ★★★★	SENIORS ★★★★

What it is Tribute to Walt Disney. **Scope and scale** Minor attraction. **Fright potential** Not frightening in any respect. **Bottleneck rating** 2. **When to go** Anytime. **Authors' rating** Excellent! . . . and about time; ★★★★. **Duration of presentation** 25 minutes. **Preshow entertainment** Disney memorabilia. **Probable waiting time** For film, 10 minutes.

One Man's Dream is a long-overdue tribute to Walt Disney. The attraction consists of an exhibit area showcasing Disney memorabilia followed by a film documenting Disney's life. Teens and adults, especially those old enough to remember Walt Disney, will enjoy this homage to the man behind the mouse.

Playhouse Disney Live on Stage ★★★★

APPEAL BY AGE	PRESCHOOL ★★★★★	GRADE SCHOOL ★★★½	TEENS ★★
YOUNG ADULTS ★★★		OVER 30 ★★	SENIORS ★★★

What it is Live show for children. **Scope and scale** Minor attraction. **Fright potential** Not frightening in any respect. **Bottleneck rating 8. When to go** Per the daily entertainment schedule. **Authors' rating** A must for families with preschoolers; ★★★★. **Duration of presentation** 20 minutes. **Special comments** Audience sits on the floor. **Probable waiting time** 10 minutes.

This show features characters from the Disney Channel's *Rolie Polie Olie, The Book of Pooh, Bear in the Big Blue House,* and *Stanley.* A simple plot serves as the platform for singing, dancing, some dynamite puppetry, and a great deal of audience participation. The characters rally throngs of tots and preschoolers to sing and dance along with them. All the jumping, squirming, and high-stepping is facilitated by having the audience sit on the floor so that kids can spontaneously erupt into motion when the mood strikes. For preschoolers, *Playhouse Disney* will be the highlight of their day. For parents, this is the time for pictures and a video featuring your very own star.

The Magic of Disney Animation ★★½

APPEAL BY AGE	PRESCHOOL ★★★	GRADE SCHOOL ★★★	TEENS ★★★
YOUNG ADULTS ★★★★		OVER 30 ★★★★	SENIORS ★★★★

What it is Overview of Disney Animation process with limited hands-on demonstrations. **Scope and scale** Minor attraction. **Fright potential** Not frightening in any respect. **Bottleneck rating 7. When to go** Before 11 a.m. or after 5 p.m. **Special comment** Opens an hour later than the rest of the park. **Authors' rating** Not as good as previous renditions; ★★½. **Duration of presentation** 30 minutes. **Preshow entertainment** Gallery of animation art in waiting area. **Average wait in line per 100 people ahead of you** 7 minutes.

The consolidation of Disney Animation at the Burbank, California, studio has left this attraction without a story to tell. A mere shadow of its former self, the attraction does not warrant waiting in line. Guests learn very little about animation and the only interesting part, especially for children, is Animation Academy, an optional stop after the presentation is over. Here, kids and grown-ups alike have a chance to draw their own cartoon under the guidance of an animator. (Space is limited and is on a first-come, first-serve basis.) The presentation is compelling and provides a good idea of how difficult hand-drawn animation really is. Young children who need more time or assistance with their drawing will quickly become frustrated.

Mickey Avenue Movie Promo Soundstage

Disney uses this soundstage to promote its latest films. Disney's biggest effort went into building the set's doors in the shape of the wardrobe described in *The Chronicles of Narnia.*

Disney-MGM Studios Backlot Tour ★★★★

What it is Combination tram and walking tour of modern film and video production. **Scope and scale** Headliner. **Fright potential** Sedate and nonintimidating except for Catastrophe Canyon, where an earthquake and flash flood are simulated. Prepare younger children for this part of the tour. **Bottleneck rating** 6. **When to go** Anytime. **Special comments** Use the restroom before getting in line. **Authors' rating** Educational and fun; not to be missed; ★★★★. **Duration of presentation** About 30 minutes. **Preshow entertainment** A video before the special effects segment and another video in the tram boarding area.

Loud

About two-thirds of the Disney-MGM Studios is a working film and television facility, where actors, artists, and technicians work on productions year-round. The tour is an absolute must. Special effects are explained with demonstrations of rain and a naval battle. Next, visitors board a tram that takes them through wardrobe and craft shops where costumes, sets, and props are designed. The tour continues through the backlot, where western canyons exist side-by-side with New York City brownstones. The tour's highlight is Catastrophe Canyon, an elaborate special-effects movie set where a thunderstorm, earthquake, oil-field fire, and a flash flood are simulated. Prepare young children for Catastrophe Canyon as the rattling earthquake and the sudden flood shakes the tram and yes, if you are sitting on the left side facing the canyon, you will get wet.

Idan

I took the tour first at age 3 and was very scared. Now, of course, Catastrophe Canyon is my most favorite part of the ride. I also love to see the costumes and props and wish I could pack all of it up to take home with me.

LIVE ENTERTAINMENT *at* DISNEY-MGM STUDIOS

HIGH SCHOOL MUSICAL PEP RALLY

JOIN THE WILDCATS as they lead guests in cheers, dances, and pom-pom waving. Formerly held in Tomorrowland at the Magic Kingdom, the Pep Rally begins near Star Tours and proceeds clockwise around the border of Echo Lake, ending at the Sorcerer Mickey hat in front of the Great Movie Ride. Check your *Times Guide* for performance times. Go Wildcats!

STARS AND MOTORCARS PARADE

STAGED ONCE A DAY, THE PARADE BEGINS near the park's entrance, continues down Hollywood Boulevard, and circles in front

of the giant sorcerer's hat. From there, it passes in front of *Sounds Dangerous* and ends by Star Tours. Claim a spot along the route 30 minutes prior to the beginning of the parade. Good viewing spots are the stairs to the right of *Sounds Dangerous,* the outdoor seating area of Backlot Express restaurant, or right in front of Star Tours.

This is a great parade for children because Disney characters frequently interact with kids along the parade route. Characters from the early Disney films are joined by such new generation stars as Lilo and Stitch and *Disney Playhouse* characters Bear and Stanley. *Star Wars* aficionados get to see Luke Skywalker, Princess Leia, R2D2, and Darth Vader.

STREETMOSPHERE

PRACTICALLY AN ATTRACTION UNTO THEMSELVES are the cast members performing randomly along Hollywood Boulevard and elsewhere around the park. Specializing in skits and audience-participation routines, most of the street entertainment has a Hollywood theme. At any given time you might encounter Otto, a famous movie director; Cecily DeMille; or the Great Garbage, laundress to the stars. Streetmosphere is a hoot for the whole family, but smaller kids really need to be up front to appreciate what's going on.

FANTASMIC! ★★★★★

APPEAL BY AGE	PRESCHOOL ★★★★	GRADE SCHOOL ★★★★★	TEENS ★★★★½
YOUNG ADULTS ★★★★½		OVER 30 ★★★★½	SENIORS ★★★★½

What it is Mixed-media nighttime spectacular. **Scope and scale** Super headliner. **Fright potential** Loud and intense with fireworks and some scary villains, but most young children like it. **Bottleneck rating** 9. **When to go** Only staged in the evening. **Special comments** Disney's best nighttime event. **Authors' rating** Not to be missed; ★★★★★. **Duration of presentation** 25 minutes. **Probable waiting time** 50–90 minutes for a seat; 35–40 minutes for standing room.

Scary

Loud

Fantasmic! is far and away the most unique outdoor spectacle ever attempted in any theme park and a must-see for the whole family. Starring Mickey Mouse in his role as the Sorcerer's apprentice from *Fantasia,* the production uses lasers, images projected on a shroud of mist, dazzling fireworks, lightning effects, and powerful music. *Fantasmic!* has the potential to frighten young children. Prepare your child for the show and make sure they know that in addition to all the favorite Disney characters, the maleficent dragon and the evil Jafar will make appearances. To give you an idea, just picture this: The evil Jafar turns into a cobra 100 feet long and 16 feet high. Rest assured, however, that during the final parade your kids will cheer on Cinderella and Prince Charming, Belle, Snow White, Ariel and Prince Eric, Jasmine and Aladdin, Donald Duck, Minnie, and Mickey.

You can alleviate the fright factor somewhat by sitting back a bit. Also, if you are seated in the first twelve rows you will get sprayed with water at times.

The theater is huge but so is the popularity of the show. If there are two performances, the second show will almost always be less crowded. If you attend the first (or only) scheduled performance, show up at least an hour in advance. Plan to use that time for a picnic. Bring food and drinks and something to entertain the younger kids. If you forget to bring munchies, not to worry, there are food concessions in the theater.

Unless you buy a *Fantasmic!* dinner package, you will not have assigned seats, so arrive early for best choice. Try to sit in the middle three or four sections, a bit off center. Finally, understand that you are out of luck if *Fantasmic!* is cancelled due to weather or other circumstances.

Fantasmic! Dinner Packages

Three restaurants offer a ticket-voucher for the members of your dining party to enter *Fantasmic!* via a special entrance and sit in a reserved section of seats. The package consists of a buffet at Hollywood & Vine (buffet), or a fixed-price dinner at Mama Melrose's Ristorante Italiano or Brown Derby Restaurant (full-service restaurants). You can call ☎ 407-WDW-DINE up to 90 days in advance and request the *Fantasmic!* Dinner Package. This is a real reservation and must be guaranteed by a credit card at the time of booking. There's a 48-hour cancellation policy.

	HOLLYWOOD BROWN DERBY	MAMA MELROSE'S RISTORANTE ITALIANO	HOLLYWOOD & VINE BUFFET
Adult	$37	$29	$22
Child (3-9)	$10	$10	$10

Nonalcoholic drinks are included; park admission, tax, and gratuity are not.

Allow yourselves a minimum of two hours to eat. You will receive the vouchers (tickets for the show) at the restaurants. After dinner, report to the *Fantasmic!* sign on Hollywood Boulevard next to Oscar's Super Service filling station (just inside the front entrance to the park) no later than 35 minutes prior to show time. A cast member will collect the vouchers and escort you to the reserved section. If *Fantasmic!* is cancelled for any reason such as weather, technical problems, and the like, you'll not receive a refund or even a voucher for another performance.

EXIT STRATEGIES

EXITING THE STUDIOS at the end of the day following *Fantasmic!* is not nearly as difficult as leaving Epcot after *IllumiNations*. We recommend you take it easy and make your way out of the park after the first wave of guests has departed. Pick a spot inside the park and give instructions that nobody is to go through the turnstiles before the group is reunited. Most importantly, latch on to your kids.

Hannah

Toy Story Pizza Planet—I love their pizza, and their salads are really good, too. Plus, you can see the aliens in the spaceship right above you.

FAVORITE EATS AT DISNEY-MGM STUDIOS		
LAND	FOOD ITEM	WHERE THEY CAN BE FOUND
BACKLOT	Great traditional breakfast Chicken nuggets and strips with veggies	ABC Commissary
	Great burgers and fixin's Gyro-style steak and lamb kefta on flatbread	Backlot Express
	Good place for a break while your kids check out *Honey, I Shrunk the Kids* playground	Studios Catering Co.
	THE place for pizza	Toy Story Pizza Planet
SUNSET BOULEVARD	Your salad headquarters	Catalina Eddie's
COMMISSARY LANE	It's not about the food (dismal) but about eating in a vintage convertible car watching old sci-fi movie previews. Teens love it! Great place to cool off. (*table service only*)	Sci-Fi Dine-In Theater

DISNEY-MGM STUDIOS TOURING PLANS

OUR STEP-BY-STEP TOURING PLANS ARE FIELD-TESTED, independently verified itineraries that will keep you moving counter to the crowd flow and allow you to see as much as possible in a single day with a minimum of time wasted in line.

The different touring plans are described below. The descriptions will tell you for whom (for example, tweens, parents with preschoolers, grandparents, and so on) or for what situation (such as sleeping late or enjoying the park at night) the plans are designed. The actual touring plans are located on pages 425–428 at the back of the book. Each plan includes a numbered map of the park in question to help you find your way around. Clip the plan of your choice out of the book by cutting along the line indicated, and take it with you to the park.

You can take in all the attractions at the Disney-MGM Studios in one day, even when traveling with young children. If you are not interested in an attraction listed on the touring plan, just skip that attraction and proceed to the next step. Likewise, should you encounter a very long line at an attraction, skip it. Use of FASTPASS is factored into the touring plans.

DISNEY-MGM STUDIOS ONE-DAY TOURING PLAN FOR PARENTS WITH SMALL CHILDREN This plan is designed for parents of children ages 3 to 8 who wish to see the very best age-appropriate attractions and shows in the Disney-MGM Studios. Every attraction has a rating of at least three stars (out of five) from preschool and grade-school children surveyed by the *Unofficial Guide*. The plan includes a midday break inside the park so families can rest, relax, and regroup. The plan keeps walking and backtracking to a minimum, with no crisscrossing of the park.

DISNEY-MGM STUDIOS ONE-DAY SLEEPY HEAD TOURING PLAN FOR PARENTS WITH SMALL CHILDREN A relaxed plan that allows families with small children to sleep late and still see the highlights of the Disney-MGM Studios. The plan begins around 11 a.m., sets aside ample time for lunch, and includes the very best child-friendly attractions and shows in the park. Special advice is provided for touring the park with small children. The plan points out where FASTPASS can best be used.

DISNEY-MGM STUDIOS ONE-DAY TOURING PLAN FOR TWEENS AND THEIR PARENTS A one-day plan for parents with children ages 8 to 12. It includes every attraction rated three stars and higher by this age group and sets aside ample time for lunch and dinner.

DISNEY-MGM STUDIOS ONE-DAY HAPPY FAMILY TOURING PLAN A one-day itinerary for multigenerational families, this plan allows teens and older children to experience the Studios' thrill rides while parents and small children visit more age-appropriate attractions. The family stays together most of the day, including lunch and dinner, and each attraction in the plan is rated three stars or higher.

BE PREPARED

ALWAYS CALL ☎ 407-824-4321 the day before you plan to visit to confirm the official park opening time. Purchase your admission tickets before you arrive and familiarize yourself with the touring plan you have chosen.

BEFORE YOU GO

1. Call ☎ 407-824-4321 to verify the park's hours.
2. Buy your admission before arriving.
3. Make lunch and dinner advance reservations or reserve the *Fantasmic!* dinner package (if desired) before you arrive by calling ☎ 407-WDW-DINE.
4. The schedule of live entertainment changes from month to month and even from day to day. Review the handout daily *Times Guide* to get a fairly clear picture of your options.

DISNEY-MGM STUDIOS TRIVIA QUIZ

By Lou Mongello

1. Which of these characters can you find in *Playhouse Disney Live on Stage?*
   a. Stanley
   b. Mickey Mouse
   c. Buzz Lightyear
   d. Handy Manny

2. In *Muppet-Vision 3-D,* one live character walks out in front of the stage. Who is it?
   a. Dr. Bunsen Honeydew
   b. Beaker
   c. Fozzie
   d. Sweetums

3. What old TV show was made into a ride at the Disney-MGM Studios?
   a. *Star Trek*
   b. *The Twilight Zone*
   c. *The Honeymooners*
   d. *Fraggle Rock*

4. Which of these action movie stars has his own stage show at the Disney-MGM Studios?
   a. Indiana Jones
   b. James Bond
   c. Harry Potter
   d. Happy Gilmore

5. In what restaurant must you eat all of your meal or get no dessert?
   a. Hollywood & Vine
   b. Sci-Fi Dine-In Theater Restaurant
   c. '50s Prime Time Café
   d. The Hollywood Brown Derby

6. How tall is the mountain in *Fantasmic!*?
   a. 29 feet
   b. 59 feet
   c. 99 feet
   d. 129 feet

7. The voice of your pilot in Star Tours is the same person who played:
   a. Darth Vader
   b. Woody from *Toy Story*
   c. Pee Wee Herman
   d. Chicken Little

8. What TV game show could once be played by guests who visited at the Disney-MGM Studios?
   a. *Who Want to Be a Millionaire?*
   b. *Jeopardy!*
   c. *Deal or No Deal*
   d. *Dancing with the Stars*

9. What movie set has been turned into a giant-sized playground at the Disney-MGM Studios?
   a. *The Chronicles of Narnia: The Lion, The Witch and the Wardrobe*
   b. *Lilo and Stitch*
   c. *The Lion King*
   d. *Honey, I Shrunk the Kids*

10. What did Disney add to the Disney-MGM Studios to celebrate Walt Disney's 100th birthday?
    a. The giant Sorcerer Mickey hat
    b. *The Twilight Zone* Tower of Terror
    c. Free parking
    d. The Walt Disney Restaurant

11. In the *Wizard of Oz* scene from the Great Movie Ride, Dorothy and her friends are told to follow:
    a. The Munchkins to Neverland
    b. The signs for the nearest McDonald's
    c. The directions their parents gave them
    d. The yellow brick road

Answers can be found on page 386.

Trivia content courtesy of Lou Mongello, author of Disney Trivia; *www.disneyworldtrivia.com.*

PART ELEVEN

UNIVERSAL ORLANDO *and* SEAWORLD

DISNEY-MGM STUDIOS *versus* UNIVERSAL STUDIOS FLORIDA

DISNEY-MGM STUDIOS AND UNIVERSAL STUDIOS FLORIDA are direct competitors. Because both are large and expensive and they take at least one day to see, some guests must choose one park over the other. To help you decide, we present a head-to-head comparison of the two parks, followed by a description of Universal Studios in detail. In the summer of 1999, Universal launched its second major theme park, Universal's Islands of Adventure, which competes directly with Disney's Magic Kingdom. (Universal Studios Florida theme park, Islands of Adventure theme park, the three Universal hotels, and the CityWalk complex are collectively known as Universal Orlando.) Lastly, a summary profile of SeaWorld concludes this chapter.

Half of Disney-MGM Studios is off limits to guests—except by guided tour—while most all of Universal Studios Florida is open to exploration.

Bob

Both Disney-MGM Studios and Universal Studios Florida draw their themes and inspiration from film and television. Both offer movie- and TV-themed rides and shows, some of which are just for fun, while others provide an educational, behind-the-scenes introduction to the cinematic arts.

Unlike Disney-MGM, Universal Studios Florida's open area includes the entire back lot, where guests can walk at leisure among movie sets. Universal Studios Florida is about twice as large as Disney-MGM, and because almost all of it is open to the public, the crowding and congestion so familiar at Disney-MGM are largely mitigated. Universal Studios has plenty of elbow room.

Both parks include working film and television-production studios. Guests are more likely, however, to see a movie, commercial, or television production in progress at Universal Studios than at Disney-MGM. On most days, production crews will be shooting on the Universal back lot in full view of guests who care to watch.

Attractions are excellent at both parks, though Disney-MGM attractions are on average engineered to move people more efficiently. Each park offers stellar attractions that break new ground, transcending in power, originality, and technology any prior standard for theme-park entertainment. Universal offers Revenge of the Mummy, an indoor roller coaster that combines space-age robotics with live effects and pyrotechnics; *Terminator 2: 3-D*, which we consider the most extraordinary theater attraction in any American theme park; and *Men in Black* Alien Attack, an interactive high-tech ride where guests' actions determine the ending of the story. Disney-MGM Studios features *The Twilight Zone* Tower of Terror, Disney's best attraction to date in our book; Rock 'n' Roller Coaster, an indoor coaster that's launched like a jet off an aircraft carrier; and Jim Henson's *Muppet-Vision 3-D*, a zany theater attraction.

Amazingly, and to the visitor's advantage, each park offers a completely different product mix, so there is little or no redundancy for a person who visits both. Disney-MGM and Universal Studios Florida each provide good exposure to the cinematic arts. Disney-MGM over the years has turned several of its better tours into infomercials for Disney films. At Universal, you can still learn about postproduction, soundstages, set creation, and special effects without being bludgeoned by promotional hype.

We recommend you try one of the studios. If you enjoy one, you probably will enjoy the other. If you have to choose, consider these things:

1. TOURING TIME If you tour efficiently, it takes about 7 to 9 hours to see Disney-MGM Studios (including a lunch break). Because Universal Studios Florida is larger and contains more rides and shows, touring, including one meal, takes about 8 to 10 hours.

2. CONVENIENCE If you're lodging along International Drive, Interstate 4's northeast corridor, the Orange Blossom Trail (US 441), or in Orlando, Universal Studios Florida is closer. If you're lodging along US 27 or FL 192 or in Kissimmee or Walt Disney World, Disney-MGM Studios is more convenient.

3. ENDURANCE Universal Studios Florida is larger and requires more walking than Disney-MGM, but it is also much less congested, so the walking is easier. Both parks offer wheelchairs and disabled access.

4. COST Both parks cost about the same for one-day admission, food, and incidentals, though Universal admission can be purchased in combo packages that include discounted passes to SeaWorld, Busch Gardens, and/or Wet 'n Wild. When Disney instituted the multiday Magic Your

Way admission system in which you pay extra for park-hopping privileges, admissions to the minor parks, and the nonexpiring-pass option, Universal was quick to move in the opposite direction. With Universal multiday passports, all these extras are included at no extra charge. Also consider that Universal discounts its admission tickets more deeply on its Web site than does Disney.

5. BEST DAYS TO GO In order, Tuesdays, Mondays, Thursdays, and Wednesdays are best to visit Universal Studios Florida. For Disney-MGM Studios, see the crowd-level calendar at **www.touringplans.com.**

6. WHEN TO ARRIVE For Disney-MGM, arrive with your ticket in hand 30 to 40 minutes before official opening time. For Universal Studios, arrive with your admission already purchased about 25 minutes before official opening time.

7. YOUNG CHILDREN Both Disney-MGM Studios and Universal Studios Florida are relatively adult entertainment offerings. By our reckoning, half the rides and shows at Disney-MGM and about two-thirds at Universal Studios have a significant potential for frightening young children.

8. FOOD For counter-service food, Universal Studios has a decided edge. Disney-MGM full-service restaurants are marginally better.

9. FASTPASS VERSUS UNIVERSAL EXPRESS Until recently, Disney's FASTPASS and Universal Express were roughly comparable. They both offered a system whereby any guest could schedule an appointment to experience an attraction later in the day with little or no waiting. Universal was the first to monkey with the status quo by making unlimited Universal Express passes available to guests of Universal-owned resorts. This meant that resort guests could go right to the front of the line any time they wished. Next, Universal cooked up an enhanced Express pass, called Universal Express Plus, available to anyone but for an extra charge. Then they got really greedy. In the last installment, Universal terminated Universal Express privileges for all day guests unless they were willing to cough up the extra bucks for Universal Express Plus.

For the moment at least, here is how the current Universal Express program works. Guests at Universal hotels can access the Universal Express lines all day long simply by flashing their hotel keys. This can be especially valuable during peak season. With Universal Express Plus, for an extra $15 or $25 (depending on the season) you can buy a pass that provides line-cutting privileges at each Universal Express attraction at a given park. The Plus feature is good for only one day at one park (in other words, no park hopping), and for one ride only on each participating attraction. Speaking of participating attractions, more than 90% of rides and shows are included in the Universal Express program, a much higher percentage than are included in the FASTPASS program at the Disney parks.

UNIVERSAL ORLANDO

UNIVERSAL ORLANDO HAS TRANSFORMED into a complete destination resort, with two theme parks, three hotels, and a shopping, dining, and entertainment complex. The second theme park, Islands of Adventure, opened in 1999 with five themed areas.

A system of roads and two multistory parking facilities are connected by moving sidewalks to **CityWalk,** a shopping, dining, and nighttime-entertainment complex that also serves as a gateway to the **Universal Studios Florida** and **Islands of Adventure** theme parks.

LODGING AT UNIVERSAL ORLANDO

UNIVERSAL CURRENTLY HAS THREE OPERATING resort hotels. The 750-room **Portofino Bay Hotel** is a gorgeous property set on an artificial bay with an Italian coastal town theme. The 650-room **Hard Rock Hotel** is an ultracool "Hotel California" replica, with slick contemporary design and a hip, friendly attitude. The 1,000-room, Polynesian-themed **Royal Pacific Resort** is sumptuously decorated and richly appointed. All three are excellent hotels; the Portofino and the Hard Rock are on the pricey side, and the Royal Pacific ain't exactly cheap.

ARRIVING AT UNIVERSAL ORLANDO

THE UNIVERSAL ORLANDO COMPLEX can be accessed directly from I-4. Once on site, you will be directed to park in one of two multitiered parking garages. Parking runs $10 for cars and $11 for RVs. Be sure to write down the location of your car before heading for the parks. From the garages, moving sidewalks deliver you to the Universal CityWalk dining, shopping, and entertainment venue described above. From CityWalk, you can access the main entrances of both Universal Studios Florida and Islands of Adventure theme parks.

Bob

Multiday passes allow you to visit both Universal theme parks on the same day, and unused days are good indefinitely. Multiday passes also allow for early entry on select days.

Universal offers One-day, Two-day, and Annual Passes.

Passes can be obtained in advance on the phone with your credit card at ☎ 800-711-0080. All prices are the same whether you buy your admission at the gate or in advance. Prices shown below include tax.

	Adults	Children (3–9)
One-day, One-park Pass	$64	$51
Two-day, Two-park Pass	$118	All guests
Two-park Annual Preferred Pass	$193	All guests
Two-park Annual Power Pass	$129	All guests

Be sure to check Universal's Web site (**www.universalorlando.com**) for seasonal deals and specials.

The main Universal Orlando information number is ☎ 407-363-8000. Reach Guest Services at ☎ 407-224-4233, schedule a character lunch at **www.universalorlando.com,** and order tickets by mail at ☎ 877-247-5561. The numbers for Lost and Found are ☎ 407-224-4244 (Universal Studios) and 407-224-4245 (Islands of Adventure).

⌷ UNIVERSAL STUDIOS FLORIDA

UNIVERSAL STUDIOS FLORIDA OPENED IN JUNE 1990. At that time, it was almost four times the size of Disney-MGM Studios (Disney-MGM has since expanded somewhat), with much more of the facility accessible to visitors. Like its sister facility in Hollywood, Universal Studios Florida is spacious, beautifully landscaped, meticulously clean, and delightfully varied in its entertainment. Rides are exciting and innovative and, as with many Disney rides, focus on familiar and/or beloved movie characters or situations.

Universal Studios Florida is laid out in an upside-down-L configuration. Beyond the main entrance, a wide boulevard stretches past several shows and rides to Streets of America. Branching off this pedestrian thoroughfare to the right are five streets that access other areas of the studios and intersect a promenade circling a large lake.

The park is divided into six sections: Production Central, New York, Hollywood, San Francisco–Amity, Woody Woodpecker's KidZone, and World Expo. Where one section begins and another ends is blurry, but no matter. Guests orient themselves by the major rides, sets, and landmarks and refer, for instance, to "New York," "the waterfront," "over by *E.T.*," or "by Mel's Diner." The area of Universal Studios Florida open to visitors is about the size of Epcot.

The park offers all standard services and amenities, including stroller and wheelchair rental, lockers, diaper-changing and infant-nursing facilities, car assistance, and foreign-language assistance. Most of the park is accessible to disabled guests, and TDDs are available for the hearing impaired. Almost all services are in the Front Lot, just inside the main entrance.

Not to Be Missed at Universal Studios Florida	
Back to the Future–The Ride	*Earthquake*–The Big One
Jaws	*Men in Black* Alien Attack
Revenge of the Mummy	*Shrek 4-D*
Terminator 2: 3-D	

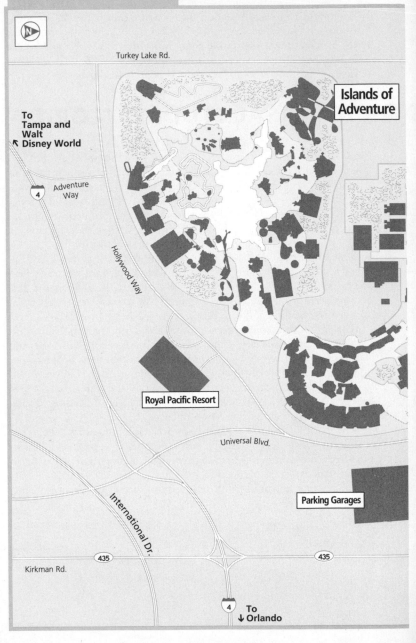

universal orlando

Turkey Lake Rd.

Islands of
Adventure

To
Tampa and
Walt
Disney World

Adventure
Way

Hollywood Way

Royal Pacific Resort

Universal Blvd.

Parking Garages

International Dr.

435

435

Kirkman Rd.

To
↓ Orlando

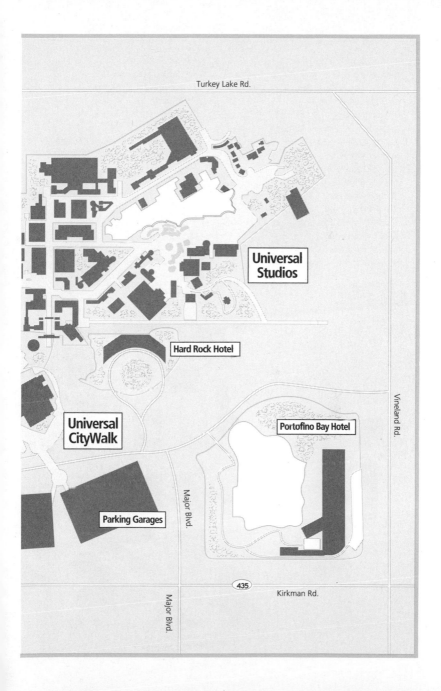

universal studios

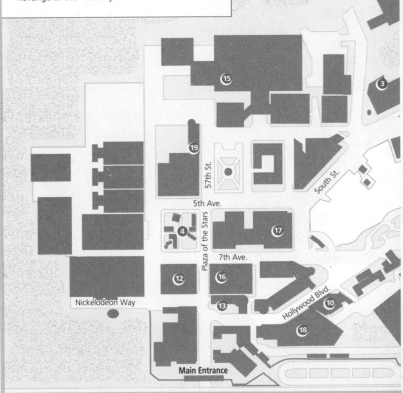

Animal Actors on Location **1**
Back to the Future—The Ride **2**
Beetlejuice's Rock 'n' Roll
   Graveyard Revue **3**
The Boneyard **4**
A Day in the Park with Barney **5**
Earthquake—The Big One **6**
E.T. Adventure **7**
Fear Factor Live **8**
Fievel's Playland **9**
The Universal Horror Make-up Show **10**
Jaws **11**
Jimmy Neutron's Nicktoon Blast **12**
Lucy, A Tribute **13**
Men in Black Alien Attack **14**
Revenge of the Mummy **15**

Shrek 4-D **16**
Sound Stage 54 **17**
Terminator 2: 3-D **18**
Twister **19**
Universal 360: A Cinesphere
   Spectacular **20**
Woody Woodpecker's KidZone **21**

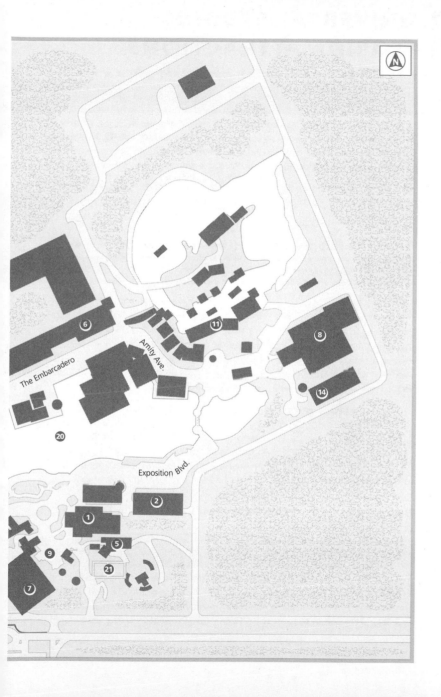

UNIVERSAL STUDIOS FLORIDA ATTRACTIONS

Animal Actors on Location (Universal Express) ★★★

APPEAL BY AGE	PRESCHOOL ★★★★	GRADE SCHOOL ★★★★	TEENS ★★★
YOUNG ADULTS ★★★		OVER 30 ★★★	SENIORS ★★★★

What it is Animal-tricks and comedy show. **Scope and scale** Major attraction. **Fright potential** Not frightening in any respect. **Bottleneck rating 4. When to go** After you have experienced all rides. **Authors' rating** Cute li'l critters; ★★★. **Duration of presentation** 20 minutes. **Probable waiting time** 25 minutes.

This show integrates video segments with live sketches, jokes, and animal tricks performed onstage. Check the daily entertainment schedule for show times.

Back to the Future—The Ride (Universal Express) ★★★★

APPEAL BY AGE	PRESCHOOL †	GRADE SCHOOL ★★★★	TEENS ★★★★
YOUNG ADULTS ★★★★		OVER 30 ★★★★	SENIORS ★★★

† Sample size too small for an accurate rating.

What it is Flight-simulator thrill ride. **Scope and scale** Headliner. **Fright potential** Frightening to all ages. **Bottleneck rating 9. When to go** First thing in the morning after Mummy and *Men in Black*. **Special comments** Rough ride; may induce motion sickness. Must be 40" tall to ride. Switching off available (page 220). **Authors' rating** Not to be missed, if you have a strong stomach; ★★★★. **Duration of ride** 4½ minutes. **Loading speed** Moderate.

An extremely intense simulator ride, guests in Doc Brown's lab get caught up in a high-speed chase through time that spans a million years. As soon as the park opens, guests stampede to Mummy, *Men in Black*, and *Back to the Future*. Our recommendation: be there at opening and join the rush.

Beetlejuice's Rock 'n' Roll Graveyard Revue ★★★ ½ (Universal Express)

APPEAL BY AGE	PRESCHOOL ★★★★	GRADE SCHOOL ★★★★	TEENS ★★★★
YOUNG ADULTS ★★★★		OVER 30 ★★★★	SENIORS ★★★★

What it is Rock-and-roll stage show. **Scope and scale** Almost major attraction. **Fright potential** Costumes and loud noises scare the under 7 crowd. **Bottleneck rating 2. When to go** At your convenience. **Authors' rating** Outrageous; ★★★½. **Duration of presentation** 18 minutes. **Probable waiting time** None.

This high-powered rock-and-roll stage show stars Beetlejuice, Frankenstein, the Bride of Frankenstein, Wolfman, and Dracula. Mercifully, this attraction is under cover.

The Blues Brothers ★★★½

APPEAL BY AGE	PRESCHOOL ★★★	GRADE SCHOOL ★★★½	TEENS ★★★½
YOUNG ADULTS ★★★½		OVER 30 ★★★★	SENIORS ★★★★

What it is Blues concert. **Scope and scale** Diversion. **Fright potential** Not frightening in any respect. **Bottleneck rating** 1. **When to go** Scheduled show times. **Authors' rating** ★★★½. **Special comments** A party in the street. **Duration of presentation** 15 minutes.

An impromptu concert featuring live singing and saxophone playing with a background track. The concert is a great pick-me-up and the short runtime keeps the energy high.

A Day in the Park with Barney (Universal Express) ★★★★

APPEAL BY AGE	PRESCHOOL ★★★★★	GRADE SCHOOL ★★★	TEENS ★★
YOUNG ADULTS ★★★		OVER 30 ★★★	SENIORS ★★★

What it is Live character stage show. **Scope and scale** Major children's attraction. **Fright potential** Toddlers may balk at Barney's size. **Bottleneck rating** 4. **When to go** Anytime. **Authors' rating** A great hit with preschoolers; ★★★★. **Duration of presentation** 12 minutes plus character greeting. **Probable waiting time** 15 minutes.

Barney, the purple dinosaur of public-television fame, leads a sing-along with the help of the audience and sidekicks Baby Bop and BJ. After the show, Barney exits momentarily to allow parents and children to gather for hugs and photos. If your child likes Barney, this show is a must. There's no line and no fighting for Barney's attention. Just relax by the rail and await your hug. There's also a great indoor play area nearby, designed especially for wee tykes.

Earthquake—The Big One (Universal Express) ★★★★

APPEAL BY AGE	PRESCHOOL ★★★	GRADE SCHOOL ★★★★	TEENS ★★★★
YOUNG ADULTS ★★★★		OVER 30 ★★★★	SENIORS ★★★★

What it is Combination theater presentation and adventure ride. **Scope and scale** Major attraction. **Fright potential** Special effects frighten 8 and unders. **Bottleneck rating** 7. **When to go** In the morning or late afternoon. **Special comments** May frighten young children. **Authors' rating** Not to be missed; ★★★★. **Duration of presentation** 20 minutes. **Loading speed** Moderate.

 Guests board a subway from Oakland to San Francisco and experience an earthquake—the big one. Experience *Earthquake* after tackling the park's other rides.

Scary Loud

E.T. Adventure (Universal Express) ★★★½

APPEAL BY AGE	PRESCHOOL ★★★★	GRADE SCHOOL ★★★★	TEENS ★★★
YOUNG ADULTS ★★★		OVER 30 ★★★★	SENIORS ★★★★

What it is Indoor adventure ride based on the *E.T.* movie. **Scope and scale** Major attraction. **Fright potential** Too intense for some preschoolers. **Bottleneck**

Thumbs Up for the Whole Family

rating 9. **When to go** Before noon; before 10 a.m. if you have small children. **Authors' rating** A happy reunion; ★★★½. **Duration of ride** 4½ minutes. **Loading speed** Moderate.

Guests aboard a bicycle-like conveyance escape with E.T. from earthly law enforcement officials and then journey to E.T.'s home planet. Lines build quickly after 10 a.m., and waits can be more than two hours on busy days. Ride in the morning or late afternoon.

Fear Factor Live ★★★

| APPEAL BY AGE | PRESCHOOL ½ | GRADE SCHOOL ★★ | TEENS ★★★★ |
| YOUNG ADULTS ★★★ | | OVER 30 ★★★ | SENIORS ★½ |

What it is Live version of the gross-out-stunt television show on NBC. **Scope and scale** Headliner. **Fright potential** Stuff of nightmares. **Bottleneck rating** 6. **When to go** 6 to 8 shows daily; crowds are smallest at the first and second-to-last shows. **Authors' rating** Great fun if you love the TV show; ★★★. **Duration of presentation** 30 minutes.

Fear Factor Live is a live stage show in which up to six volunteers compete for one prize by doing dumb and yucky things like swimming with eels and eating bugs.

Fievel's Playland ★★★★

| APPEAL BY AGE | PRESCHOOL ★★★★ | | GRADE SCHOOL ★★★★ |
| TEENS — | YOUNG ADULTS — | OVER 30 — | SENIORS — |

What it is Children's play area with waterslide. **Scope and scale** Minor attraction. **Fright potential** Not frightening in any respect. **Bottleneck rating** 1. **When to go** Anytime. **Authors' rating** A much-needed attraction for preschoolers; ★★★★. **Probable waiting time** 20–30 minutes for the waterslide; otherwise, no waiting.

Imaginative playground features ordinary household items reproduced on a giant scale, as a mouse would experience them. Walk into Fievel's Playland without waiting, and stay as long as you want. Younger children love the oversized items, and there's enough to keep teens and adults busy while little ones cut loose.

Jaws (Universal Express) ★★★★

| APPEAL BY AGE | PRESCHOOL ★★★ | GRADE SCHOOL ★★★★ | TEENS ★★★★ |
| YOUNG ADULTS ★★★★ | | OVER 30 ★★★★ | SENIORS ★★★★ |

What it is Adventure boat ride. **Scope and scale** Headliner. **Fright potential** Frightening for all ages. **Bottleneck rating** 9. **When to go** Before 11 a.m. or after 5 p.m. **Special comments** Will frighten young children. **Authors' rating** Not to be missed; ★★★★. **Duration of ride** 5 minutes. **Loading speed** Fast. **Probable waiting time per 100 people ahead of you** 3 minutes. **Assumes** All 8 boats are running.

Scary   Wet

Jaws delivers five minutes of nonstop action, with the huge shark repeatedly attacking. The attraction builds an amazing degree of suspense. It isn't just a cruise into the middle of a pond with a scary rubber fish. People on the boat's left side tend to get splashed more. If you have young children, consider switching off (see page 220).

Jimmy Neutron's Nicktoon Blast ★★★ (Universal Express)

APPEAL BY AGE	PRESCHOOL ★★★	GRADE SCHOOL ★★★★	TEENS ★★★
YOUNG ADULTS ★★★		OVER 30 ★★★	SENIORS ★★

What it is Cartoon science demonstration and simulation ride. **Scope and scale** Major attraction. **Fright potential** Ride is wild and jerky but not frightening. **Bottleneck rating** 10. **When to go** The first hour after park opening or after 5 p.m. **Authors' rating** Incomprehensible but fun; ★★★. **Duration of ride** A little more than 4 minutes. **Loading speed** Moderate to slow. **Probable waiting time per 100 people ahead of you** 5 minutes. **Assumes** All 8 simulators in use.

Motion Sickness   Rough

This ride, based on the Nickelodeon movie *Jimmy Neutron: Boy Genius,* features motion simulators that move and react in sync with a cartoon projected onto a huge screen. The attraction draws sizeable crowds primarily because it's just inside the entrance and is next door to *Shrek 4-D.* Except for avid *Jimmy Neutron* cartoon fans, in other words, it's expendable. Be aware that a very small percentage of riders suffer motion sickness. Stationary seating is available and is mandated for persons less than 40 inches tall.

Lucy, a Tribute ★★★

APPEAL BY AGE	PRESCHOOL ★	GRADE SCHOOL ★★	TEENS ★★
YOUNG ADULTS ★★★		OVER 30 ★★★	SENIORS ★★★

What it is Walk-through tribute to Lucille Ball. **Scope and scale** Diversion. **Fright potential** Not frightening in any respect. **Bottleneck rating** 0. **When to go** Anytime. **Authors' rating** A touching remembrance; ★★★. **Probable waiting time** None.

The life and career of comedienne Lucille Ball are spotlighted in this museum-like exhibit. See Lucy during the hot, crowded midafternoon or on your way out of the park.

Men in Black Alien Attack (Universal Express) ★★★★½

APPEAL BY AGE	PRESCHOOL †	GRADE SCHOOL ★★★★★	TEENS ★★★★★
YOUNG ADULTS ★★★★★		OVER 30 ★★★★★	SENIORS ★★★★

† *Sample size too small for an accurate rating.*

What it is Interactive dark thrill ride. **Scope and scale** Super headliner. **Fright potential** Dark and intense; frightens many children 10 and under. **Bottleneck rating** 9. **When to go** In the morning after Revenge of the Mummy. **Special**

comments May induce motion sickness. Must be 42" tall to ride. Switching off available (page 220). **Authors' rating** Buzz Lightyear on steroids; not to be missed; ★★★★½. **Duration of ride** 2½ minutes. **Loading speed** Moderate to fast.

  Based on the movie of the same name, the story line has you volunteering as a Men in Black (MIB) trainee. After an introduction warning that aliens "live among us" and articulating MIB's mission to round them up, Zed expands on the finer points of alien spotting and familiarizes you with your training vehicle and your weapon, an alien "zapper." Following this, you load up and are dispatched on an innocuous training mission that immediately deteriorates into a situation where only you are in a position to prevent aliens from taking over the universe. Now, if you saw the movie, you understand that the aliens are mostly giant exotic bugs and cockroaches and that zapping the aliens involves exploding them into myriad, gooey body parts. Thus, the meat of the ride (no pun intended) consists of careening around Manhattan in your MIB vehicle and shooting aliens. Each of the 120 or so alien figures has sensors that activate special effects and respond to your zapper. Aim for the eyes and keep shooting until the aliens' eyes turn red. To avoid a long wait, hotfoot it to *MIB* immediately after riding Mummy in the first 30 minutes the park is open.

Revenge of the Mummy (Universal Express) ★★★★½

APPEAL BY AGE	PRESCHOOL ★★	GRADE SCHOOL ★★★★	TEENS ★★★★★
YOUNG ADULTS ★★★★½		OVER 30 ★★★★	SENIORS ★★★½

What it is Combination dark ride and roller coaster. **Scope and scale** Super headliner. **Fright potential** Scary for all ages. **Bottleneck rating** 10. **When to go** The first hour the park is open or after 6 p.m. **Special comments** 48" minimum height requirement. **Authors' rating** Killer! ★★★★½. **Duration of ride** 3 minutes. **Probable waiting time per 100 people ahead of you** 7 minutes. **Loading speed** Moderate.

   Revenge of the Mummy is an indoor dark ride based on the *Mummy* flicks, where guests fight off "deadly curses and vengeful creatures" while flying through Egyptian tombs and other spooky places on a high-tech roller coaster. The special effects are cutting edge, integrating the best technology from such attractions as *Terminator 2: 3-D*, Spider-Man (the ride), and *Back to the Future*, with groundbreaking visuals. It's way cool. Your only prayer for a tolerable wait, however, is to be on hand when the park opens and sprint immediately to the Mummy.

Shrek 4-D (Universal Express) ★★★★½

APPEAL BY AGE	PRESCHOOL ★★★★	GRADE SCHOOL ★★★★★	TEENS ★★★★★
YOUNG ADULTS ★★★★★		OVER 30 ★★★★★	SENIORS ★★★★★

What it is 3-D movie. **Scope and scale** Headliner. **Fright potential** Loud but not frightening. Preshow area is a little macabre. **Bottleneck rating** 8. **When to go** The first hour the park is open or after 4 p.m. **Authors' rating** Warm, fuzzy mayhem; ★★★★½. **Duration of presentation** 20 minutes.

This attraction is a real winner. It's irreverent, frantic, laugh-out-loud funny, and iconoclastic. In contrast to Disney's *Honey, I Shrunk the Audience* or *It's Tough to Be a Bug!*, *Shrek 4-D* doesn't generally frighten children under age 7.

Liliane

Children under 7 might be frightened at times. Take off the 3-D glasses if it is all too scary and consider earplugs. Did you know that Shrek in German means "The Scare"?

Street Scenes ★★★★

APPEAL BY AGE	PRESCHOOL ★★★	GRADE SCHOOL ★★★★★	TEENS ★★★★★
YOUNG ADULTS ★★★★★		OVER 30 ★★★★★	SENIORS ★★★★★

What it is Elaborate outdoor sets for making films. **Scope and scale** Diversion. **Fright potential** Not frightening in any respect. **Bottleneck rating** 0. **When to go** Anytime. **Special comments** You'll see most sets without special effort as you tour the park. **Authors' rating** One of the park's great assets; ★★★★. **Probable waiting time** No waiting.

Unlike at Disney-MGM Studios, all Universal Studios Florida's back-lot sets are accessible for guest inspection. You'll see most as you walk through the park.

Terminator 2: 3-D: Battle Across Time ★★★★★

APPEAL BY AGE	PRESCHOOL ★★★	GRADE SCHOOL ★★★★	TEENS ★★★★★
YOUNG ADULTS ★★★★★		OVER 30 ★★★★★	SENIORS ★★★★

What it is 3-D thriller mixed-media presentation. **Scope and scale** Super headliner. **Fright potential** Intense; will frighten 7 and unders. **Bottleneck rating** 8. **When to go** After 3:30 p.m. **Special comments** The nation's best theme-park theater attraction; very intense for some preschoolers and grade-schoolers. **Authors' rating** Furiously paced high-tech experience; not to be missed; ★★★★★. **Duration of presentation** 20 minutes, including an 8-minute preshow. **Probable waiting time** 20–40 minutes.

Dark   Scary   Loud

The attraction, like the films, is all action, and you really don't need to understand much. What's interesting is that it uses 3-D film and a theater full of sophisticated technology to integrate the real with the imaginary. Images seem to move in and out of the film, not only in the manner of traditional 3-D but also in actuality. Remove your 3-D glasses momentarily and you'll see that the guy on the motorcycle is actually onstage. If *Terminator 2: 3-D* is the only attraction you see at Universal Studios Florida, you'll have received your money's worth. The attraction, on Hollywood Boulevard near the park's entrance, receives huge traffic during morning and early

Greatest show ever! Saw it twice on the same day and will go back for more next time I visit. From all the shows I've seen this one is the most impressive ever.

Idan

afternoon. By about 3 p.m., however, lines diminish somewhat. Though you'll still wait, we recommend holding off on *Terminator 2: 3-D* until then. Families with young children should know that the violence characteristic of the *Terminator* movies is largely absent from the attraction. There's suspense and action but not much blood and guts.

Twister (Universal Express) ★★★½

APPEAL BY AGE	PRESCHOOL ★★	GRADE SCHOOL ★★★★	TEENS ★★★★
YOUNG ADULTS ★★★★		OVER 30 ★★★★	SENIORS ★★★

What it is Theater presentation featuring special effects from the movie *Twister*. **Scope and scale** Major attraction. **Fright potential** Will frighten 7 and unders. **Bottleneck rating** 7. **When to go** Should be your first show after experiencing all rides. **Special comments** High potential for frightening young children. **Authors' rating** Gusty; ★★★½. **Duration of presentation** 15 minutes. **Probable waiting time** 26 minutes.

   Twister combines an elaborate set and special effects, climaxing with a five-story-tall simulated tornado created by circulating more than 2 million cubic feet of air per minute. The wind, pounding rain, and freight-train sound of the tornado are deafening, and the entire presentation is exceptionally intense. School children are mightily impressed, while younger children are terrified and overwhelmed. Unless you want the kids hopping in your bed whenever they hear thunder, try this attraction yourself before taking your kids.

Universal 360° (seasonal) ★★★½

APPEAL BY AGE	PRESCHOOL ★★★	GRADE SCHOOL ★★★★	TEENS ★★★½
YOUNG ADULTS ★★★★		OVER 30 ★★★★	SENIORS ★★★★

What it is Fireworks, lasers, and movies. **Scope and scale** Major attraction. **Fright potential** Fireworks and scary movie footage frighten preschoolers. **Bottleneck rating** 7. **When to go** 1 show a day, usually 10 minutes before park closes. **Authors' rating** Good effort; ★★★½. **Special comments** Movie trailers galore. **Duration of presentation** 10 minutes.

A nighttime spectacular presented daily at the Universal Studios lagoon, the presentation is a celebration of hit movies and is built around four 360-degree projection cinespheres, each 36 feet tall and 30 feet wide. The cinespheres project images relating to the chosen films, augmented by lasers and fireworks. Realize that not all of the movie clips may be suitable for young viewers. During the horror movie montage, parents may want to cover some eyes. The action movie montage is also stuffed with gunplay and gore.

The Universal Horror Make-up Show ★★★½ (Universal Express)

APPEAL BY AGE	PRESCHOOL ★★★	GRADE SCHOOL ★★★★	TEENS ★★★★
YOUNG ADULTS ★★★★		OVER 30 ★★★★	SENIORS ★★★★

What it is Theater presentation on the art of make-up. **Scope and scale** Major attraction. **Fright potential** Gory but not frightening. **Bottleneck rating** 6.

When to go After you have experienced all rides.
Special comments May upset young children.
Authors' rating A gory knee-slapper; ★★★½.
Duration of presentation 25 minutes. **Probable
waiting time** 20 minutes.

Thumbs Up for the Whole Family

Lively, well-paced look at how make-up artists
create film monsters, realistic wounds, severed limbs, and other unmentionables. Exceeding most guests' expectations, the *Horror Make-up Show* is the sleeper attraction at Universal. Its humor and tongue-in-cheek style transcend the gruesome effects, and most folks (including preschoolers) take the blood and guts in stride. It usually isn't too hard to get into.

Woody Woodpecker's Nuthouse Coaster and Curious George Goes to Town Playground ★★★

APPEAL BY AGE	PRESCHOOL ★★★★		GRADE SCHOOL —
TEENS —	YOUNG ADULTS —	OVER 30 —	SENIORS —

What it is Interactive playground and kid's roller coaster. **Scope and scale** Minor attraction. **Fright potential** Not frightening in any respect. **Bottleneck rating** 5. **When to go** Anytime. **Authors' rating** A good place to turn the kids loose; ★★★.

Rounding out the selection of other nearby kid-friendly attractions, this KidZone offering consists of Woody Woodpecker's Nuthouse Coaster and an interactive playground called Curious George Goes to Town. The child-sized roller coaster is small enough for kids to enjoy but sturdy enough for adults, though its moderate speed might unnerve some smaller children (the minimum height to ride is 36 inches). The Curious George playground exemplifies the Universal obsession with wet stuff; In addition to innumerable spigots, pipes, and spray guns, two giant roof-mounted buckets periodically dump *a thousand gallons* of water on unsuspecting visitors below. Kids who want to stay dry can mess around in the foam-ball playground, also equipped with chutes, tubes, and ball-blasters.

LIVE ENTERTAINMENT *at* UNIVERSAL STUDIOS

IN ADDITION TO THE SHOWS PROFILED ABOVE, Universal offers a wide range of street entertainment. Costumed comic-book and cartoon characters (Shrek, Donkey, SpongeBob SquarePants, Woody Woodpecker) roam the park for photo ops supplemented by movie star look-alikes, plus the Frankenstein monster, who can be said to be neither. Musical acts include Blues Brothers impersonators dancing and singing in the New York section of the park and *The Ricky and Lucy Show,* staged on Hollywood Boulevard.

UNIVERSAL STUDIOS FLORIDA TOURING PLAN

UNIVERSAL STUDIOS FLORIDA ONE-DAY TOURING PLAN FOR FAMILIES

THIS PLAN IS FOR FAMILIES. If a ride or show is listed that you don't want to experience, skip that step and proceed to the next. Move quickly from attraction to attraction and, if possible, don't stop for lunch until after Step 9. Minor street shows occur at various times and places throughout the day; check the daily schedule for details. The actual touring plan in clip-out version with map is on page 429. The touring plan is geared toward the whole family. Because there are so many attractions with the potential to frighten young children, be prepared to skip a few things and to practice switching off (works the same way as at Walt Disney World). For the most part, attractions, such as playgrounds, designed especially for young children can be enjoyed anytime. Work them into the plan at your convenience.

BUYING ADMISSION TO UNIVERSAL STUDIOS FLORIDA

THERE ARE NEVER ENOUGH TICKET WINDOWS open in the morning to accommodate the crowd. We strongly recommend you buy your admission in advance. Passes are available by mail from Universal Studios at ☎ 800-224-3838. They are also sold at the concierge desk or attractions box office of many Orlando-area hotels. If your hotel doesn't offer tickets, try Guest Services at the DoubleTree Hotel ☎ 407-351-1000, at the intersection of Major Boulevard and Kirkman Avenue.

UNIVERSAL'S ISLANDS *of* ADVENTURE

WHEN UNIVERSAL'S ISLANDS OF ADVENTURE theme park opened in 1999, it provided Universal with enough critical mass to actually compete with Disney. Universal finally has on-site hotels, a shopping and entertainment complex, and two major theme parks. Doubly interesting is that the new Universal park is pretty much just for fun—in other words, a direct competitor to Disney's Magic Kingdom, the most visited theme park in the world.

Roller coasters at Islands of Adventure are the real deal—not for the faint of heart or for little ones.

Disney and Universal officially downplay their fierce competition, pointing out that any new theme park or attraction makes central Florida a more marketable destination. Behind closed doors, however, it's a Pepsi-vs.-Coke–type rivalry

that will keep both companies working hard to gain a competitive edge.
The good news, of course, is that all
this translates into better and better
attractions for you to enjoy.

Consider yourself
warned: several at-
tractions at Islands of
Adventure will drench
you to the bone.

Liliane

BEWARE OF THE WET AND WILD

ALTHOUGH WE HAVE DESCRIBED Universal's Islands of Adventure
as a direct competitor to the Magic Kingdom, there is one major
qualification you should be aware of. Whereas most Magic Kingdom
attractions are designed to be enjoyed by guests of any age, attractions at Islands of Adventure are largely created for an under-40
population. The roller coasters at Universal are serious with a capi-
tal S, making Space Mountain and Big Thunder Mountain look
about as tough as Dumbo. In fact, seven out of the nine top attractions at Islands are thrill rides, and of these, there are three that not
only scare the bejeezus out of you but also drench you with water.

For families, there are three interactive playgrounds as well as six
rides that young children will enjoy. Of the thrill rides, only the two in
Toon Lagoon (described later) are marginally appropriate for young
children, and even on these rides your child needs to be fairly stalwart.

Not to Be Missed at Islands of Adventure

The Adventures of Spider-Man	Dueling Dragons
The Incredible Hulk Coaster	*Jurassic Park* River Adventure
Poseidon's Fury!	

GETTING ORIENTED AT ISLANDS OF ADVENTURE

BOTH UNIVERSAL THEME PARKS are accessed via the Universal
CityWalk entertainment complex. Crossing CityWalk from the park-
ing garages, you can bear right to Universal Studios Florida or left to
Universal's Islands of Adventure.

Islands of Adventure is arranged much like Epcot's World Showcase, in a large circle surrounding a lake. Unlike Epcot, however, the
Islands of Adventure themed areas evidence the sort of thematic con-
tinuity pioneered by Disneyland and the Magic Kingdom. Each land,
or island in this case, is self-contained and visually consistent in its
theme, though you can see parts of the other islands across the lake.

You first encounter the Moroccan-style Port of Entry, where you'll
find Guest Services, lockers, stroller and wheelchair rentals, ATM
banking, lost and found, and shopping. From the Port of Entry, moving clockwise around the lake, you can access Marvel Super Hero
Island, Toon Lagoon, *Jurassic Park,* the Lost Continent, and Seuss
Landing. You can crisscross the lake on small boats, but there is no
other in-park transportation.

islands of adventure

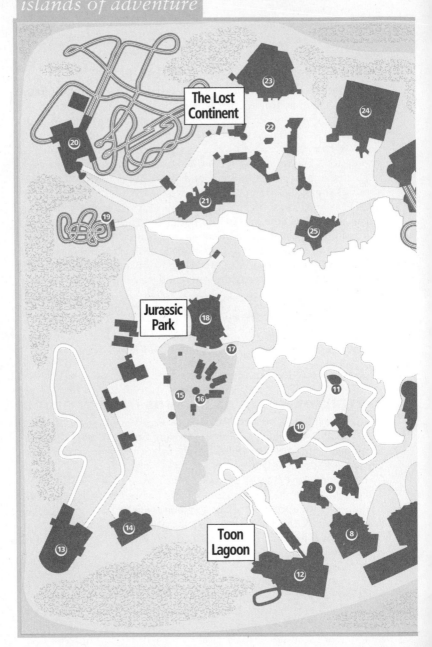

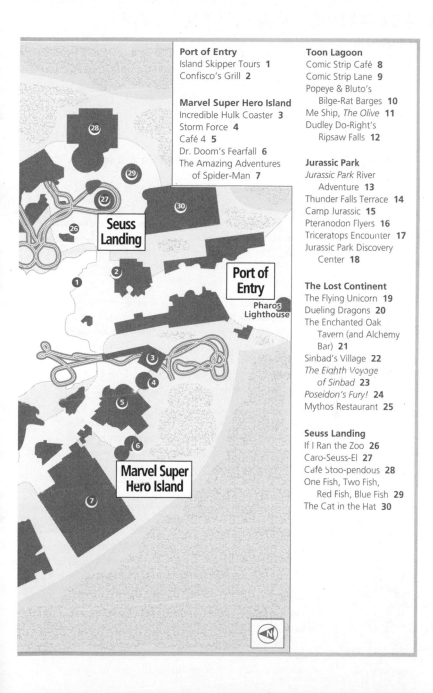

Port of Entry
Island Skipper Tours **1**
Confisco's Grill **2**

Marvel Super Hero Island
Incredible Hulk Coaster **3**
Storm Force **4**
Café 4 **5**
Dr. Doom's Fearfall **6**
The Amazing Adventures
    of Spider-Man **7**

Toon Lagoon
Comic Strip Café **8**
Comic Strip Lane **9**
Popeye & Bluto's
    Bilge-Rat Barges **10**
Me Ship, *The Olive* **11**
Dudley Do-Right's
    Ripsaw Falls **12**

Jurassic Park
Jurassic Park River
    Adventure **13**
Thunder Falls Terrace **14**
Camp Jurassic **15**
Pteranodon Flyers **16**
Triceratops Encounter **17**
Jurassic Park Discovery
    Center **18**

The Lost Continent
The Flying Unicorn **19**
Dueling Dragons **20**
The Enchanted Oak
    Tavern (and Alchemy
    Bar) **21**
Sinbad's Village **22**
*The Eighth Voyage
    of Sinbad* **23**
Poseidon's Fury! **24**
Mythos Restaurant **25**

Seuss Landing
If I Ran the Zoo **26**
Caro-Seuss-El **27**
Café Stoo-pendous **28**
One Fish, Two Fish,
    Red Fish, Blue Fish **29**
The Cat in the Hat **30**

Seuss Landing

Port of Entry

Pharos Lighthouse

Marvel Super Hero Island

N

ISLANDS *of* ADVENTURE ATTRACTIONS

MARVEL SUPER HERO ISLAND

THIS ISLAND, WITH ITS FUTURISTIC AND RETRO-FUTURE design and comic-book signage, offers shopping and attractions based on Marvel Comics characters.

The Amazing Adventures of Spider-Man ★★★★★ (Universal Express)

APPEAL BY AGE	PRESCHOOL ★★★	GRADE SCHOOL ★★★★★	TEENS ★★★★★
YOUNG ADULTS ★★★★★		OVER 30 ★★★★★	SENIORS ★★★★

What it is Indoor adventure simulator ride based on Spider-Man. **Scope and scale** Super headliner. **Fright potential** Intense; kids tall enough to ride usually take it in stride. **Bottleneck rating** 9. **When to go** Before 10 a.m. **Special comments** Must be 40" tall to ride. **Authors' rating** Our choice for the best attraction in the park; ★★★★★. **Duration of ride** 4½ minutes. **Loading speed** Fast.

Dark Scary Rough

Covering one-and-a-half acres and combining moving ride vehicles, 3-D film, and live action, Spider-Man is frenetic, fluid, and astounding. The visuals are rich, and the ride is wild but not jerky. Spider-Man is technologically on a par with Disney-MGM's Tower of Terror, which is to say that it will leave you in awe. Ride first thing in the morning after The Incredible Hulk Coaster or in the hour before closing.

Idan

An absolute must. Soar above buildings without ever leaving the ground! Kudos to Universal, this is the ultimate deception, and I loved every turn. Must ride several times to take in all the details. And do hold on to your personal belongings, as I managed to lose my room key (still wondering how I did it).

Dr. Doom's Fearfall (Universal Express) ★★★

APPEAL BY AGE	PRESCHOOL —	GRADE SCHOOL ★★★	TEENS ★★★★
YOUNG ADULTS ★★★★		OVER 30 ★★★	SENIORS —

What it is Lunch liberator. **Scope and scale** Headliner. **Fright potential** Frightening for all ages. **Bottleneck rating** 10. **When to go** Before 9:15 a.m. **Special comments** Must be 52" tall to ride. **Authors' rating** More bark than bite; ★★★. **Duration of ride** 40 seconds. **Loading speed** Slow.

Scary Lose Things

Here you are strapped into a seat with your feet dangling and blasted 200 feet up in the air and then allowed to partially free-fall back down. We've seen glaciers that move faster than the line to Dr. Doom. If you want to ride without investing half a day, be one of the first in the park to ride.

This attraction is best experienced with your mother right next to you. Hold her hand for personal comfort (it makes you look good, too) and brace for her expression of absolute terror.

Ian

The Incredible Hulk Coaster (Universal Express) ★★★★½

| APPEAL BY AGE | PRESCHOOL ★ | GRADE SCHOOL ★★★★★ | TEENS ★★★★★ |
| YOUNG ADULTS ★★★★ | | OVER 30 ★★★★ | SENIORS ★★★ |

What it is Roller coaster. **Scope and scale** Super headliner. **Fright potential** Frightening for all ages. **Bottleneck rating** 10. **When to go** Before 9:30 a.m. **Special comments** Must be 54" tall to ride. **Authors' rating** A coaster-lover's coaster; ★★★★½. **Duration of ride** 1½ minutes. **Loading speed** Moderate.

Scary   Motion Sickness   Lose Things

The Hulk is a great roller coaster, perhaps the best in Florida, providing a ride comparable to Montu (Busch Gardens) with the added thrill of an accelerated launch (instead of the more typical uphill crank). Plus, like Montu, this coaster has a smooth ride. The Hulk gives Spider-Man a run as the park's most popular attraction. Ride first thing in the morning.

You know who made me ride it, and for the duration of the ride I did lose my very polite European ways.

Liliane

Unfortunately, Liliane lost her very polite European ways at about 20 decibels. My ears hurt for days.

Bob

Storm Force Accelatron ★★★
(Universal Express)

| APPEAL BY AGE | PRESCHOOL ★★★★ | GRADE SCHOOL ★★★ | TEENS ★★★ |
| YOUNG ADULTS ★★★ | | OVER 30 ★★★ | SENIORS ★★★ |

What it is Indoor spinning ride. **Scope and scale** Minor attraction. **Fright potential** Nauseating but not frightening. **Bottleneck rating** 9. **When to go** Before 10:30 a.m. **Special comments** May induce motion sickness. **Authors' rating** Teacups in the dark; ★★★. **Duration of ride** 1½ minutes. **Loading speed** Slow.

Dark   Motion Sickness

Storm Force is a spiffed-up indoor version of Disney's nausea-inducing Mad Tea Party. Ride early or late to avoid long lines. Skip it if you're prone to motion sickness.

TOON LAGOON

TOON LAGOON IS CARTOON ART TRANSLATED into real buildings and settings. Whimsical and gaily colored, with rounded and exaggerated lines, Toon Lagoon is Universal's answer to Mickey's Toontown Fair in the Magic Kingdom. The main difference between the two toon lands is that (as you will see) you have about a 60% chance of drowning at Universal's version.

Comic Strip Lane

What it is Walk-through exhibit and shopping and dining venue. **Scope and scale** Diversion. **Fright potential** Not frightening in any respect. **Bottleneck rating** 0. **When to go** Anytime.

This is the main street of Toon Lagoon. Here you can visit the domains of Beetle Bailey, Hagar the Horrible, Krazy Kat, the Family Circus, and Blondie and Dagwood, among others. Shops and eateries tie into the cartoon strip theme. This is a great place for photo ops with cartoon characters.

Dudley Do-Right's Ripsaw Falls ★★★½ (Universal Express)

APPEAL BY AGE	PRESCHOOL ★★★	GRADE SCHOOL ★★★★	TEENS ★★★★
YOUNG ADULTS ★★★		OVER 30 ★★★★	SENIORS ★★★

What it is Flume ride. **Scope and scale** Major attraction. **Fright potential** The big drop frightens guests of all ages. **Bottleneck rating** 8. **When to go** Before 11 a.m. **Special comments** Must be 44" tall to ride. **Authors' rating** A minimalist Splash Mountain; ★★★½. **Duration of ride** 5 minutes. **Loading speed** Moderate.

Scary   Wet

Inspired by the *Rocky and Bullwinkle* cartoons, this ride features Canadian Mountie Dudley Do-Right as he attempts to save Nell from evil Snidely Whiplash. Story line aside, it's a flume ride, with the inevitable big drop at the end. Universal claims this is the first flume ride to "send riders plummeting 15 feet below the surface of the water." In reality, though, you're just plummeting into a tunnel. This ride will get you wet, but on average not as wet as you might expect (it looks worse than it is). If you want to stay dry, however, arrive prepared with a poncho or at least a big garbage bag with holes cut out for your head and arms. While younger children are often intimidated by the big drop, those who ride generally enjoy themselves. Ride first thing in the morning after experiencing the Marvel Super Hero rides.

Me Ship, *The Olive* ★★★

APPEAL BY AGE	PRESCHOOL ★★★★	GRADE SCHOOL ★★★★
TEENS —	YOUNG ADULTS —	OVER 30 —	SENIORS —

What it is Interactive playground. **Scope and scale** Minor attraction. **Fright potential** Not frightening in any respect. **Bottleneck rating** 4. **When to go** Anytime. **Authors' rating** Colorful and appealing for kids; ★★★.

The Olive is Popeye's three-story boat come to life as an interactive playground. Younger children can scramble around in Swee'Pea's Playpen, while older sibs shoot water cannons at riders trying to survive the adjacent Bilge-Rat raft ride. If you're into the big rides, save this for later in the day.

Popeye & Bluto's Bilge-Rat Barges ★★★ (Universal Express)

APPEAL BY AGE	PRESCHOOL ★★★	GRADE SCHOOL ★★★★★	TEENS ★★★★
YOUNG ADULTS ★★★★		OVER 30 ★★★★	SENIORS ★★★

What it is White-water raft ride. **Scope and scale** Major attraction. **Fright potential** Ride is wild and wet but not frightening. **Bottleneck rating** 8. **When to go** Before 10:30 a.m. **Special comments** Must be 42" tall to ride. **Authors' rating** Bring your own soap; ★★★. **Duration of ride** 4½ minutes. **Loading speed** Moderate.

  Engineered to ensure that everyone gets drenched, the rapids are rougher and more interesting, and the ride longer, than the Animal Kingdom's Kali River Rapids. But nobody surpasses Disney for visuals and theming. Use your poncho or garbage bag and ride barefoot with your britches rolled up. In terms of beating the crowds, ride the barges in the morning after experiencing the Marvel Super Hero attractions and Dudley Do-Right.

JURASSIC PARK

JURASSIC PARK (FOR ANYONE WHO'S BEEN ASLEEP for 20 years) is a Steven Spielberg film franchise about a fictitious theme park with real dinosaurs. Jurassic Park at Universal's Islands of Adventure is a real theme park (or at least a section of one) with fictitious dinosaurs.

Camp Jurassic ★★★

APPEAL BY AGE	PRESCHOOL ★★★		GRADE SCHOOL ★★★
TEENS —	YOUNG ADULTS —	OVER 30 —	SENIORS —

What it is Interactive play area. **Scope and scale** Minor attraction. **Fright potential** Not frightening in any respect. **Bottleneck rating** 3. **When to go** Anytime. **Authors' rating** Creative playground, confusing layout; ★★★.

Camp Jurassic is a great place for children to run and explore. Sort of a Jurassic version of Tom Sawyer Island, kids can explore lava pits, caves, mines, and a rain forest.

Discovery Center ★★★

APPEAL BY AGE	PRESCHOOL ★★★	GRADE SCHOOL ★★★★	TEENS ★★★
YOUNG ADULTS ★★★		OVER 30 ★★★	SENIORS ★★★

What it is Interactive natural history exhibit. **Scope and scale** Minor attraction. **Fright potential** Not frightening in any respect. **Bottleneck rating** 3. **When to go** Anytime. **Authors' rating** ★★★.

The Discovery Center is an interactive, educational exhibit that mixes fiction from the movie *Jurassic Park,* such as using fossil DNA to bring dinosaurs to life, with various skeletal remains and other paleontological displays. Cycle back after experiencing all the rides or on a second day. Most folks can digest this exhibit in 10 to 15 minutes.

 Don't skip the Discovery Center. On a hot summer day it is a great place to cool off. The best exhibit of all is the one where an animatronic raptor hatches from an egg. Young children will delight in the hatching and are afforded an opportunity to name the baby dino.

Jurassic Park River Adventure (Universal Express) ★★★★

APPEAL BY AGE	PRESCHOOL ★★★	GRADE SCHOOL ★★★★★	TEENS ★★★★★
YOUNG ADULTS ★★★★		OVER 30 ★★★★	SENIORS ★★★★

What it is Indoor-outdoor adventure river-raft ride based on the *Jurassic Park* movies. **Scope and scale** Super headliner. **Fright potential** Visuals and big drop frighten guests of all ages. **Bottleneck rating 9. When to go** Before 11 a.m. **Special comments** Must be 42" tall to ride. **Authors' rating** Better than its Hollywood cousin; ★★★★. **Duration of ride** 6½ minutes. **Loading speed** Fast.

  Guests board boats for a water tour of Jurassic Park. Everything is tranquil as the tour begins, then, as word is received that some of the carnivores have escaped their enclosure, the tour boat is accidentally diverted into Jurassic Park's maintenance facilities. Here, the boat and its riders are menaced by an assortment of hungry meat-eaters. At the climactic moment, the boat and its passengers escape by plummeting over an 85-foot drop. Young children must endure a double whammy on this ride. First, they are stalked by giant, salivating (sometimes spitting) reptiles, and then they're sent catapulting over the falls. Unless your children are fairly stalwart, wait a year or two before you spring the River Adventure on them.

Pteranodon Flyers ½

APPEAL BY AGE	PRESCHOOL ★★★	GRADE SCHOOL ★★★	TEENS ★
YOUNG ADULTS ★★		OVER 30 ★	SENIORS ★★

What it is Slow as Christmas. **Scope and scale** Minor attraction. **Fright potential** Not frightening in any respect. **Bottleneck rating 10. When to go** When there's no line. **Authors' rating** All sizzle, no steak; ½. **Duration of ride** 1 minute and 25 seconds. **Loading speed** Slower than a hog in quicksand.

This ride swings you along a track that passes over a small part of Jurassic Park. We recommend that you skip this one. Why? Because the Jurassic period will probably end before you reach the front of the line! And your reward for all that waiting? A one-minute-and-fifteen-second ride. Plus, the attraction has a name that nobody over 12 years old can pronounce.

THE LOST CONTINENT

THIS AREA IS AN EXOTIC MIX of Silk Road bazaar and ancient ruins, with Greco-Moroccan accents. (And you thought your decorator was nuts.) This is the land of mythical gods, fabled beasts, and expensive souvenirs.

Dueling Dragons (Universal Express) ★★★★

APPEAL BY AGE	PRESCHOOL —	GRADE SCHOOL ★★★★	TEENS ★★★★
YOUNG ADULTS ★★★★		OVER 30 ★★★★	SENIORS ★★

What it is Roller coaster. **Scope and scale** Headliner. **Fright potential** Frightening to guests of all ages. **Bottleneck rating 9. When to go** Before 10:30 a.m. **Special comments** Must be 54" tall to ride. **Authors' rating** Almost as good as the Hulk coaster; ★★★★. **Duration of ride** 1 minute and 45 seconds. **Loading speed** Moderate.

Scary　Lose Things　Motion Sickness

This high-tech coaster launches two trains (Fire and Ice) at the same time on tracks that are closely intertwined. Each track is differently configured so that you get a different experience on each. Dueling Dragons is the highest coaster in the park and also claims the longest drop at 115 feet, not to mention five inversions. And like the Hulk, it's a smooth ride all the way. Try to ride during the first 90 minutes the park is open or in the late afternoon.

Liliane

Richard Thompson's song puts it just right: "Let me ride on the Wall of Death one more time, you can waste your time on the other rides, but this is the nearest to being alive."

The Eighth Voyage of Sinbad (Universal Express) ★★

| APPEAL BY AGE | PRESCHOOL ★★★ | GRADE SCHOOL ★★★★ | TEENS ★★★ |
| YOUNG ADULTS ★★★ | | OVER 30 ★★★ | SENIORS ★★★ |

What It is Theater stunt show. **Scope and scale** Major attraction. **Fright potential** Special effects startle preschoolers. **Bottleneck rating** 4. **When to go** Anytime as per the daily entertainment schedule. **Authors' rating** Not inspiring; ★★. **Duration of presentation** 17 minutes. **Probable waiting time** 15 minutes.

A story about Sinbad the Sailor is the glue that (loosely) binds this stunt show featuring water explosions, ten-foot-tall circles of flame, and various other daunting eruptions and perturbations. It's billed as a stunt show, but the production is so vacuous and redundant that it's hard to get into the action. See *Sinbad* after you've experienced the rides and the better-rated shows. The theater seats 1,700.

The Flying Unicorn (Universal Express) ★★★

| APPEAL BY AGE | PRESCHOOL ★★★★★ | GRADE SCHOOL ★★★★ |
| TEENS ★★ | YOUNG ADULTS ★★ | OVER 30 ★ | SENIORS ★ |

What it is Children's roller coaster. **Scope and scale** Minor attraction. **Fright potential** Frightens a small percentage of preschool riders. **Bottleneck rating** 9. **When to go** Before 11 a.m. **Authors' rating** A good beginner's coaster; ★★★. **Duration of ride** 1 minute. **Loading speed** Slow.

A child-sized roller coaster through a forest setting, the Unicorn provides a nonthreatening way to introduce young children to the genre. This one loads very slowly. Ride before 11 a.m.

Liliane

This is a wild little thing, and just like Goofy's Barnstormer, is rough on kids and their coaster-fearing parents.

You can experience a wilder ride than this adjusting the seat of your Chevy.

Bob

Poseidon's Fury! (Universal Express) ★★★★

APPEAL BY AGE	PRESCHOOL ★★	GRADE SCHOOL ★★★★	TEENS ★★★★
YOUNG ADULTS ★★★★		OVER 30 ★★★★	SENIORS ★★★★

What it is High-tech theater attraction. **Scope and scale** Headliner. **Fright potential** Intense visuals and special effects frighten some preschoolers. **Bottleneck rating** 7. **When to go** After experiencing all the rides. **Special comments** Audience stands throughout. **Authors' rating** Much improved; ★★★★. **Duration of presentation** 17 minutes including preshow. **Probable waiting time** 25 minutes.

The Greek god Poseidon tussles with an evil wizardish guy using fire, water, lasers, smoke machines, and angry lemurs (*Note:* Lemurs are not actually used—just seeing if you're paying attention). The plot unravels in installments as you pass from room to room and finally into the main theater preshow. There's some great technology at work here. *Poseidon* is by far and away the best of the Islands of Adventure theater attractions. Frequent explosions and noise may frighten younger children, so exercise caution with preschoolers. We recommend catching *Poseidon* after experiencing your fill of the rides.

SEUSS LANDING

A TEN-ACRE THEMED AREA BASED ON Dr. Seuss's famous children's books. Like at Mickey's Toontown in the Magic Kingdom, all of the buildings and attractions replicate a whimsical, brightly colored cartoon style with exaggerated features and rounded lines. There are four rides at Seuss Landing (described below) and an interactive play area, **If I Ran the Zoo,** populated by Seuss creatures.

If you have only young children in your party, Seuss Landing is the place to spend lots of happy time. A great stop in Seuss Landing is Dr. Seuss's All the Books You Can Read bookstore. Last but not least, if your kids cannot get enough of Dr. Seuss check out **www.seussville.com.**

Liliane

Caro-Seuss-El (Universal Express) ★★★½

APPEAL BY AGE	PRESCHOOL ★★★★		GRADE SCHOOL ★★★★
TEENS —	YOUNG ADULTS —	OVER 30 —	SENIORS —

What it is Merry-go-round. **Scope and scale** Minor attraction. **Fright potential** Not frightening in any respect. **Bottleneck rating** 8. **When to go** Before 10:30 a.m. **Authors' rating** Wonderfully unique; ★★★½. **Duration of ride** 2 minutes. **Loading speed** Slow.

Totally outrageous, the Caro-Seuss-El is a full-scale, 56-mount merry-go-round made up exclusively of Dr. Seuss characters. If you are touring with young children, try to get them on early in the morning.

The Cat in the Hat (Universal Express) ★★★½

APPEAL BY AGE	PRESCHOOL ★★★★	GRADE SCHOOL ★★★★	TEENS ★★★
YOUNG ADULTS ★★★★		OVER 30 ★★★★	SENIORS ★★★★

What it is Indoor adventure ride. **Scope and scale** Major attraction. **Fright potential** Not frightening in any respect. **Bottleneck rating** 8. **When to go**

Before 11:30 a.m. **Authors' rating** Seuss would be proud; ★★★½. **Duration of ride** 3½ minutes. **Loading speed** Moderate.

Guests ride on "couches" through 18 different sets inhabited by anima-tronic Seuss characters, including The Cat in the Hat, Thing 1, Thing 2, and the beleaguered goldfish who tries to maintain order in the midst of bed-lam. Well done overall, with nothing that should frighten younger children. This is fun for all ages. Try to ride early.

One Fish, Two Fish, Red Fish, Blue Fish ★★★½ (Universal Express)

APPEAL BY AGE	PRESCHOOL ★★★★	GRADE SCHOOL ★★★★	TEENS ★★★
YOUNG ADULTS ★★★		OVER 30 ★★★	SENIORS ★★★

What it is Wet version of Dumbo the Flying Elephant. **Scope and scale** Minor attraction. **Fright potential** Not frightening in any respect. **Bottleneck rating** 10. **When to go** Before 10 a.m. **Authors' rating** Who says you can't teach an old ride new tricks? ★★★½. **Duration of ride** 2 minutes. **Loading speed** Slow.

Imagine Dumbo with Seuss-style fish instead of elephants and you've got half the story. Guests steer their fish up or down 15 feet in the air while traveling in circles trying to avoid streams of water projected from "squirt posts."

The High in the Sky Seuss Trolley Train Ride! ★★★½ (Universal Express)

APPEAL BY AGE	PRESCHOOL ★★★★	GRADE SCHOOL ★★★½	TEENS ★
YOUNG ADULTS ★★½		OVER 30 ★★½	SENIORS ★★★

What it is Elevated train. **Scope and scale** Major attraction. **Fright potential** Not frightening in any respect. **Bottleneck rating** 10. **When to go** Before 11:30 a.m. **Authors' rating** ★★★½. **Special comments** Relaxed tour of Seuss Landing. **Duration of ride** 3½ minutes. **Average wait in line per 100 people ahead of you** 11 minutes. **Loading speed** Molasses.

Trains putter along elevated tracks, while a voice reads one of four Dr. Seuss stories over the train's speakers. As each train makes its way through Seuss Landing, it passes a series of animatronic characters in scenes that are part of the story being told. The trains are small, fitting about 20 people, and the loading speed is glacial. Save the train ride for the end of the day or ride first thing in the morning.

ISLANDS *of* ADVENTURE TOURING PLAN

ISLANDS OF ADVENTURE ONE-DAY TOURING PLAN FOR FAMILIES

WE PRESENT ONE ISLANDS OF ADVENTURE TOURING PLAN geared toward the whole family. Because there are so many attrac-tions with the potential to frighten young children, be prepared to skip a few things and to practice switching off (works the same way as at Walt Disney World). For the most part, attractions, such as playgrounds, designed especially for young children can be enjoyed anytime. Work them into the plan at your convenience.

Be aware that in this park there are an inordinate number of attractions that will get you wet. If you want to experience them, come armed with ponchos, large plastic garbage bags, or some other protective covering. Failure to follow this prescription will make for a squishy, sodden day.

This plan is for families of all sizes and ages and includes thrill rides. If the plan calls for you to experience an attraction that does not interest you, simply bypass that attraction and proceed to the next step. Be aware that the plan calls for some backtracking. The plan can be found in clip-out form with a map on page 430.

SEAWORLD

MANY DOZENS OF READERS HAVE WRITTEN to extol the virtues of SeaWorld. The following are representative. An English family writes:

> *The best-organized park [is] SeaWorld. The computer printout we got on arrival had a very useful show schedule, told us which areas were temporarily closed due to construction, and had a readily understandable map. Best of all, there was almost no queuing. Overall, we rated this day so highly that it is the park we would most like to visit again.*

A woman in Alberta, Canada, gives her opinion:

> *We chose SeaWorld as our fifth day at "The World." What a pleasant surprise! It was every bit as good (and in some ways better) than WDW itself. Well worth the admission, an excellent entertainment value, educational, well run, and better value for the dollar in food services. Perhaps expand your coverage to give them their due!*

OK, here's what you need to know (for additional information, call ☎ 407-363-2613 or visit **www.seaworld.com**). SeaWorld is a world-class marine-life theme park near the intersection of I-4 and the Bee Line Expressway. It's about 10 miles east of Walt Disney World. Open daily from 9 a.m. to 10 p.m., SeaWorld charges about $67 admission for adults and $54 for children ages 3 to 9. Five-park

Discount coupons for SeaWorld admission are available in the free visitor magazines found in most (but not Disney) hotel lobbies.

Bob

Combination Passes, which include admission to SeaWorld, Universal Studios, Islands of Adventure, Wet 'n Wild, and Busch Gardens, are also available. Sea World offers some super advance purchase discounts on its Web site.

STAR RATINGS FOR SEAWORLD ATTRACTIONS

★★★★½   *Believe!* (all-new high-tech Shamu and killer whale show)

★★★★   *Seamore and Clyde* (sea lion, walrus, and otter show)

★★★★   Shark Encounter

★★★★   Kraken (roller coaster)

★★★★   Wild Arctic (simulation ride and Arctic wildlife viewing)

★★★★   *Odyssea* (Cirque du Soleil–type presentation)

★★★★   Shamu's Happy Harbor (children's play area)

★★★½   *Blue Horizons* (whale-and-dolphin show)

★★★½   *Fusion* (watersport show)

★★★½   *Pets Ahoy!* (show with performing birds, cats, dogs, and a pig)

★★★½   Pacific Point Preserve (sea lions and seals)

★★★½   Key West at SeaWorld (dolphin viewing)

★★★½   Penguin Encounter

★★★   Manatee Rescue (manatee viewing)

★★★   Journey to Atlantis (combination roller coaster–flume ride)

★★½   Clydesdale Hamlet (Budweiser Clydesdale horses)

Figure eight to nine hours to see everything, six or so if you stick to the big deals. Discovery Cove is directly across the Central Florida Parkway from SeaWorld. Parking at Discovery Cove is free.

SeaWorld is about the size of the Magic Kingdom and requires about the same amount of walking. In terms of size, quality, and creativity, it's unequivocally on par with Disney's major theme parks. Unlike Walt Disney World, SeaWorld primarily features stadium shows or walk-through exhibits. This means that you will spend about 80% less time waiting in line during eight hours at SeaWorld than you would for the same-length visit at a Disney park.

Bob

If you don't purchase your admission in advance, take advantage of the automatic admission machines located to the right of the main entrance. The machines are a pain in the rear, asking for your name, age, home zip code, and billing zip code, but if you have a credit card, the machines are a lot faster than standing in line at the ticket windows.

A daily entertainment schedule is printed conveniently on a place mat–sized map of the park. The three featured shows are:

- *Believe!* (Shamu and killer-whale show)
- *Seamore and Clyde* (sea lion, walrus, and otter show)
- *Blue Horizons* (whale-and-dolphin show)

You'll notice immediately as you check the performance times that the shows are scheduled so that it's almost impossible to see them back to back. A Cherry Hill, New Jersey, visitor confirms this rather major problem, complaining:

> The shows were timed so we could not catch all the major ones in a seven-hour visit.

Much of the year, you can get a seat for the stadium shows by showing up ten or so minutes in advance. When the park is crowded, however, you need to be at the stadiums at least 20 minutes in advance (30 minutes in advance for a good seat). All of the stadiums have "splash zones," specified areas where you're likely to be drenched with ice-cold salt water by whales, dolphins, and sea lions.

DISCOVERY COVE

SEAWORLD'S INTIMATE NEW PARK, Discovery Cove, is a welcome departure from the hustle and bustle of other Orlando parks; its slower pace could be the overstimulated family's ticket back to mental health.

Liliane

With a focus on personal guest service and one-on-one animal encounters, Discovery Cove admits only 1,000 guests per day.

The main draw at Discovery Cove is the chance to swim with their troupe of 25 Atlantic bottlenose dolphins. The 90-minute experience is open to visitors ages 6 and up who are comfortable in the water.

Other exhibits at Discovery Cove include the Coral Reef and the Aviary. Snorkel or swim in the Coral Reef, which houses thousands of exotic fish as well as an underwater shipwreck and hidden grottoes. In the Aviary, you can touch and feed gorgeous tropical birds. The park is threaded by a "tropical river" in which you can float or swim, and dotted with beaches that serve as pathways to the attractions.

Discovery Cove is open 9 a.m. until 5:30 p.m. daily. Admission is limited, so purchase tickets well in advance; call ☎ 877-4-DISCOVERY or visit **www.discoverycove.com.** Prices vary seasonally from $249 per person to $279, tax included (no children's discount). Admission includes the dolphin swim, self-parking, one meal, and use of beach umbrellas, lounge chairs, towels, lockers, and swim and snorkel gear. Discovery Cove admission also includes a seven-day pass to SeaWorld. If you're not interested in the dolphin swim, you can visit Discovery Cove for the day for $149 to $179 per person, depending on the season.

PART TWELVE

THE REST *of the* WORLD

The WATER THEME PARKS

WALT DISNEY WORLD HAS TWO SWIMMING THEME PARKS. Typhoon Lagoon is the most diverse Disney splash pad, while Blizzard Beach takes the prize for the most slides and most bizarre theme (a ski resort in meltdown). Blizzard Beach has the best slides, but Typhoon Lagoon has a surf pool where you can bodysurf. Both parks have excellent and elaborate themed areas for toddlers and preschoolers.

Disney water parks allow one cooler per family or group, but no glass and no alcoholic beverages. Both parks charge the following rental prices: towels $1, lockers are $10 small, $12 large (includes $5 refundable deposit); life jacket free with a $25 refundable deposit. Admission costs for both parks are $36 per day for adults and $30 per day for children (ages 3 to 9).

During summer and holiday periods, Typhoon Lagoon and Blizzard Beach fill to capacity on weekdays and close their gates before 11 a.m. Bob

The best way to avoid standing in lines is to visit the water parks when they're less crowded. We recommend going on a Saturday or Sunday, when most visitors are traveling, or on a Monday—very few guests go to a water park on their first day at Walt Disney World.

If you are going to Blizzard Beach or Typhoon Lagoon, get up early, have breakfast, and arrive at the park 30 minutes before opening. Wear your bathing suit under shorts and a T-shirt so you don't need to use lockers or dressing rooms. Wear shoes. The paths are relatively easy on bare feet, but there's a lot of ground to cover. If you or your children have tender feet, wear your shoes as you move around the park, removing them when you raft, slide, or go into the water. Shops in the parks sell sandals, "Reef Runners," and other protective footwear that can be worn in and out of the water.

Bob

If you have a car, drive instead of taking a Disney bus.

You will need a towel, sunblock, and money. Carry enough money for the day and your Disney resort ID (if you have one) in a plastic bag or Tupperware container. Though nowhere is completely safe, we felt comfortable hiding our plastic money bags in our cooler. Nobody disturbed our stuff, and our cash was easy to reach. However, if you're carrying a wad or worry about money anyway, rent a locker. Another great device is a waterproof card case with a lanyard to hold park tickets, a credit card, some cash, and your hotel key. You can buy them at the water parks for about $8; more sophisticated versions are available at any good outdoors/sport shop.

Personal swim gear (fins, masks, rafts, and so on) is not allowed. Everything you need is either provided or available to rent. If you forget your towel, you can rent one (cheap!). If you forgot your swimsuit or lotion, they're available for sale. So are disposable, waterproof cameras, which are especially fun to have at Typhoon Lagoon Shark Reef.

Liliane

Wallets and purses get in the way, so lock them in your car's trunk or leave them at your hotel.

Establish your base for the day. There are many beautiful sunning and lounging spots scattered throughout both swimming parks. Arrive early, and you can have your pick. The breeze is best along the beaches of the lagoon at Blizzard Beach and the surf pool at Typhoon Lagoon. At Typhoon Lagoon, if there are children younger than age 6 in your party, choose an area to the left of Mount Mayday (the one with a ship on top) near the children's swimming area.

Liliane

Lost children stations at the water parks are so out of the way that neither you nor your child will find them without help from a Disney employee. Explain to your children how to recognize a Disney employee (by their distinctive name tags) and how to ask for help.

Though Typhoon Lagoon and Blizzard Beach are huge parks with many slides, armies of guests overwhelm them almost daily. If your main reason for going is the slides and you hate long lines, try to be among the first guests to enter the park. Go directly to the slides and ride as many times as you can before the park fills. When lines for the slides become intolerable, head for the surf or wave pool or the tube-floating streams.

Both water parks are large and require almost as much walking as the major theme parks. Add to this wave surfing, swimming, and climbing to reach the slides, and you'll definitely be pooped by day's end. Consider something low-key for the evening.

It's as easy to lose a child or become separated from your party at one of the water parks as it is at a major theme park. On arrival, pick a very specific place to meet in the event you are separated. If you split up on purpose, establish times for checking in.

While I do not feel any better on a water roller coaster than I do on the dry thing, I love the water parks. My all-time favorite water ride is Teamboat Springs, the 1,200-foot white-water raft flume at Blizzard Beach.

Liliane

Children under age 10 must be accompanied by an adult. The water parks are great fun for the whole family, but if you have very young children, or if you are not a thrill-seeking water puppy, the pool of your hotel might serve just as well. The water parks, however, were made to order for teens. Note that during the winter months Disney closes Blizzard Beach and Typhoon Lagoon for refurbishing, alternating maintenance in such a way that one water park will be open at all times. If it is very wintry, Disney will close both parks. Call ☎ 407-824-4321 for current information.

FAVORITE EATS AT THE WATER PARKS

PARK	FOOD ITEM	WHERE THEY CAN BE FOUND
BLIZZARD BEACH	Snow cones	Arctic Expedition
	Hot dogs, Mickey Mouse ice-cream sandwich	Avalunch
	Popcorn and Itzakadoozie	Cooling Hut
	Danish and coffee (hot and cold)	Frosty the Joe Man Coffee Shack
	Pizza, burgers, salads, and kids' meals	Lottawatta Lodge
	Nachos and tacos	The Warming Hut
TYPHOON LAGOON	Kid's meal inside sand pail with shovel	Leaning Palms
	Caesar salad and kid's meal inside sand pail with shovel	Typhoon Tilly's
	Chicken wrap and tuna sandwich	Lowtide Lou's
	Garbage pail: Ice cream, cookies, and waffle cone. Ice-cream pieces, fudge, nuts, sprinkles, and more inside a sand pail to be scooped out with a shovel.	Happy Landings

Refillable mugs: If you or the kids enjoy soda, your best bet is to get a refillable mug, available at both water parks. For the price of the mug ($10), you are entitled to free refills throughout the day. Select locations.

HOW TO MAKE IT WORK

JUST LIKE AT THE MAJOR THEME PARKS, the key to a successful visit to the water parks is to arrive early. Plan to arrive a half hour before the scheduled opening time. If you are a Disney-resort guest,

Blizzard Beach

ATTRACTION | HEIGHT REQUIREMENT | WHAT TO EXPECT

SUMMIT PLUMMET | 48 inches | A 120-foot free fall, at 60 mph. This ride is very intense. Make sure your child knows what to expect. Being over 48 inches tall does not guarantee an enjoyable experience. If you think you'd enjoy washing out of a 12th-floor window during a heavy rain, then this slide is for you.

SLUSH GUSHER | 48 inches | A 90-foot double-humped slide. Ladies, cling to those tops—all others hang on to live.

DOWNHILL DOUBLE DIPPER | 48 inches | Side-by-side tube-racing slides. At 25 mph, the tube races through water curtains and free falls. It's a lot of fun, but rough.

CHAIR LIFT UP MT. GUSHMORE | 32 inches | Great ride even if you only go up for the view. When the park is packed, use the singles line.

TEAMBOAT SPRINGS | None | 1,200-foot white-water group raft flume. Wonderful ride for the whole family.

RUN-OFF RAPIDS | None | Three corkscrew tube slides to choose from. The center slide is for solo raft rides while the two other slides offer one-, two-, or three-person rafts. The dark enclosed tube makes the ride feel like being flushed down a toilet.

SNOW STORMERS | None | Three mat-slide flumes; down you go on your belly.

TOBOGGAN RACERS | None | Eight-lane race course. You go down the flume on a mat. The ride is less intense than Snow Stormers.

MELT-AWAY BAY | None | Wave pool with gentle, bobbing waves. The pool is great for younger swimmers.

CROSS COUNTRY CREEK | None | Lazy river circling the park; grab a tube.

TIKE'S PEAK | 4 feet and under only | Kid-sized version of Blizzard Beach. This is THE place for little ones.

SKI PATROL TRAINING CAMP | Ages 5–11 | A place for preteens to train for the big rides.

visit on a day the water park of your choice offers Extra Magic Hours. Remember, in high season the parks fill up quickly and often reach capacity by 11 a.m.

Decide if you need the locker or not. If you do, send one member in your party to stake out a base for the day while you take care of the locker business. It is easier to lose a child or become separated from your

Grab an inner tube and go on Cross Country Creek or Castaway Creek. It's best when you go with a group like your family. Sometimes I hop off the tube and find an underwater jet on the side of the bank. If you go underwater the jet will shoot you out real fast. It's a blast! Don't worry; the water isn't deep. A good trick to play on someone in your family is to push their inner tube under a cave waterfall. The water is ice cold. It's fun to watch them freak out.

Typhoon Lagoon

ATTRACTION | HEIGHT REQUIREMENT | WHAT TO EXPECT

CRUSH 'N' GUSHER | 48 inches | Water roller coaster where you can choose from among three slides: Banana Blaster, Coconut Crusher, and Pineapple Plunger, ranging from 410 to 420 feet long. This thriller leaves you wondering what exactly happened—if you make it down in one piece, that is: not for the faint of heart. If your child is new to water-park rides, this is not the place to break him in, even if he is tall enough to ride.

HUMUNGA KOWABUNGA | 48 inches | Speed slides that hit 30 mph. A five-story drop in the dark rattles the most courageous rider. Ladies should ride this one in a one-piece swimsuit.

KEELHAUL FALLS | None | Fast white-water ride in a single-person tube.

GANG PLANK FALLS | None | White-water raft flume in a multiperson tube.

MAYDAY FALLS | None | The name says it all. Wild single-person tube ride. Hang on!

STORM SLIDES | None | Three body-slides down and thru Mt. Mayday.

SHARK REEF | None | After you are equipped with fins, mask, snorkel, and a life vest, you get a brief lesson in snorkeling. Then off you go for about 60 feet to the other side of the saltwater pool where you swim with small colorful fish, rays, and very small leopard and hammerhead sharks. If you don't want to swim with the fish, visit the underwater viewing chamber anytime during the day. Surface Air Snorkeling, involving use of a "pony" tank and a small regulator as in SCUBA diving, as well as a buoyancy vest, is also offered. The fee is $20 per half hour for the first person; $15 for the second person. Participants must be at least 5 years old. To sign up and for more information, visit the kiosk near the entrance to Shark Reef.

SURF POOL | None | World's largest inland surf facility with waves up to 6 feet high. Adult supervision is required. Three mornings a week at 6:45 a.m. (before the park opens); half-hour surfing lessons are offered (surfboard provided). Cost is $140; minimum age is 8; class size is 12. Call ☎ 407-WDW-PLAY. The price does *not* include park admission.

CASTAWAY CREEK | None | Half-mile lazy river in a tropical setting. Wonderful!

KETCHAKIDDIEE CREEK | 48 inches and under only | Toddlers and preschoolers love this area reserved only for them. Say splish splash and have lots of fun.

party at one of the water parks than it is at the major theme parks. Upon arrival, pick a specific place to meet in the event you get separated.

The Slush Gusher at Blizzard Beach is really cool. It's really steep and wavy on the way down. You have to cross your arms and legs because water will rush up your swimsuit. Stay as still as possible and you will go really fast. There's a speed sign at the bottom that shows how fast you came down. Be careful, because if you try to open your eyes, water goes in, and sometimes water goes up your nose.

Ian

Remember to have fun. Experience the must-do thrill slides right away but don't overdo it; the lazy rivers at both parks are perfect for relaxation. Float through caves, beneath waterfalls, past gardens, and under bridges. Life is beautiful and the water is soothing. Did you know that in the winter months Disney actually heats all the water park pools?

BE PREPARED

CALL ☎ 407-828-3058 THE DAY BEFORE you go to find out the official park opening time. Purchase admission tickets before you arrive. Decide if you want to picnic or not, and then plan or pack accordingly.

Pets are not allowed at the water parks, and kennels are available only at the Magic Kingdom, Epcot, Disney-MGM Studios, Disney's Animal Kingdom, and Disney's Fort Wilderness Resort & Campground.

A WORD FROM THE WEATHERMAN

THUNDERSTORMS ARE COMMON IN FLORIDA. On summer afternoons, such storms often occur daily, forcing the water parks to close temporarily while the threatening weather passes. If the storm is severe and prolonged it can cause a great deal of inconvenience. The park may actually close for the day, launching a legion through the turnstiles to compete for space on the Disney resort buses. If you depend on Disney buses, leave the park earlier, rather than later, when you see a storm moving in. Most importantly though, instruct your children to immediately return to "home base" at the sight of lightning or when they hear the first rumble of thunder.

We recommend you monitor the local weather forecast the day before you go, checking again in the morning before leaving for the water park. Scattered thunderstorms are to be expected and usually cause no more than temporary inconvenience, but moving storm fronts are to be avoided.

SAFETY FIRST

TOO MUCH FUN IN THE SUN isn't a good thing if you get sunburned or become dehydrated. Drink lots of fluids, use sunscreen, and bring a T-shirt and a hat for extra protection. Read all signs and follow the rules. Lifeguards are on duty throughout the parks.

DOWNTOWN DISNEY

DOWNTOWN DISNEY COMPRISES THE Disney Village Marketplace, Pleasure Island, and Disney's West Side. All three are shopping, dining, and entertainment complexes. Admission is charged at Pleasure Island in the evening and at the entertainment venues on Disney's West Side. Otherwise, you can roam, shop, and dine without paying any sort of entrance fee.

If you have a car, use it. There is bus transportation from all the Disney resorts to Downtown Disney, and some resorts (Old Key West and Port Orleans) offer boat transportation. The problem is that buses make stops at a number of locations at Downtown Disney, so you might sit on the bus for 20 minutes or more before you finally depart for your destination. The boats are better than the buses but take about four times as long as driving your car. The boat route, however, is very pretty and a good choice if you're not in a hurry. Shops open as early as 9.30 a.m., but there is really no reason to arrive at the crack of dawn—for once.

MARKETPLACE HIGHLIGHTS

KIDS WILL PARTICULARLY ENJOY the **LEGO Imagination Center**. You'll know you're there when you see the 30-foot sea serpent made out of more than a million LEGO blocks that lives in the lake right in front of the store. Outside the store is a play area filled with LEGO blocks for children to enjoy.

Downtown Disney/LEGO Imagination Center: I love this place. You can make your own LEGO cars and drop them down a slope. Better watch out because it gets crowded with kids. One kid ran off with my car. There are cool LEGO statues outside and a LEGO dragon on the lake. It's a good place to take pictures.

Ian

World of Disney Kids stocks a wide variety of clothing, plush toys, and collectibles. The fun though is found in the two interactive rooms filled with treasures for princesses and pirates alike.

Once Upon a Toy is a joy. The biggest draw at this 16,000-square-foot store is classic toys with a Disney twist. Here you can find Mr. Potato Head with Mickey Ears or a sorcerer's hat and the classic game Clue set in the Haunted Mansion.

My all-time favorite toy here is a miniature version of Disney's Wilderness Lodge made of a Lincoln Logs building set.

Liliane

Bibbidi Bobbidi Boutique transforms your little girl into a princess, albeit for a price. A Fairy Godmother-in-training (the shop owner) and her helpers offer salon services for princesses age 3 and up. Hairstyle and makeup cost $35, adding a manicure will cost you $45, and the royal makeover (including your choice of a princess costume with accessories and a photo shoot with imaging package) will set you back $175.

I say go for the hairstyle and makeup only and take your own pictures. Disney princess costumes are available at a reasonable rate at your hometown Halloween shop (best buys just after the holiday) or on eBay. While the salon also offers a "cool dude" makeover for boys, Bibbidi Bobbidi Boutique is a serious girl's thing.

Liliane

downtown disney

N

Disney's
West Side

Village Lake

Cirque du
Soleil

House of
Blues

Pleasure Island is a
paid-access park
in the evening.

Disney
Quest

Virgin
Megastore

Specialty
Shopping

Wolfgang
Puck Cafe

Bongos
Cuban Cafe

Parking

AMC Movie
Theaters

Planet
Hollywood

Parking

Buena Vista Drive

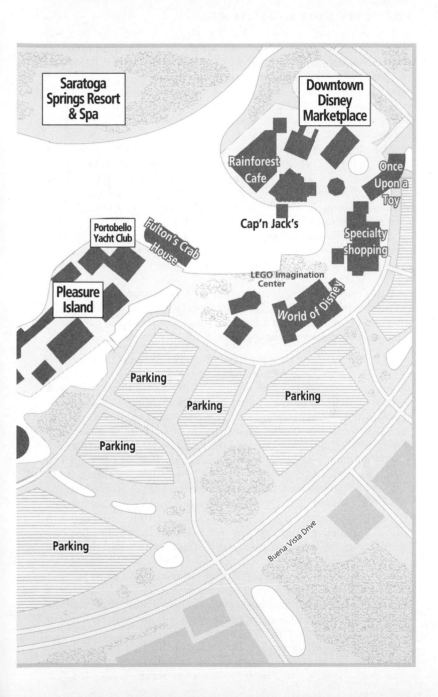

THE WEST SIDE HIGHLIGHTS

THE BEST THING AT DOWNTOWN DISNEY and probably in all of Walt Disney World is **Cirque du Soleil's _La Nouba_.** Mesmerizing, thrilling, superb, and beautiful hardly do the show justice, but it's all of those and more. Tickets range from $61 to $95 for adults and from $49 to $76 for kids ages 3 to 9 (tax not included). Florida residents are eligible for a 20% discount. If you are not familiar with Cirque du Soleil, visit their Web site at **www.cirquedusoleil.com.** You can book online or call ☎ 407-939-7600.

The **Virgin Megastore** will make the heart of any teenager beat faster. The 49,000-square-foot store offers more than 300 listening stations and over 20 DVD-viewing stations, including some that are kid-sized. The store regularly hosts live performances and autograph-signing sessions. Parents beware though, gaming tournaments are offered and your teen may never want to leave.

The place for wannabe magicians is **Magic Masters,** where the store interior is a re-creation of Houdini's personal library. If you buy a magic trick you are taken behind a hidden panel in the bookcase to learn its secret.

Catch all the latest box office hits at the **AMC Pleasure Island** state-of-the-art, 24-movie theater complex, all under one roof and offering flicks in an Art Deco setting. For information on show times and tickets, log on to **www.amctheatres.com** and select Orlando Pleasure Island 24.

DISNEYQUEST If your children are 11 or older, DisneyQuest on Disney's West Side is a special treat you might want to consider. DisneyQuest is Disney's pioneering prototype of a theme park in a box, or more literally, in a modest five-story building.

Opened in the summer of 1998, DisneyQuest contains all the elements of the larger Disney theme parks. There is an entrance area that facilitates your transition into the park environment and leads to

Bob

Weekdays before 4 p.m. are least crowded.

the gateways of four distinct themed lands, referred to here as zones. As at other Disney parks, everything is included in the price of your admission.

It takes about two to three hours to experience DisneyQuest once you get in. Disney limits the number of guests admitted to ensure that queues are manageable and that guests have a positive experience.

DisneyQuest is aimed at a youthful audience, say 8 to 35 years of age, though younger and older patrons will enjoy much of what it offers. The feel is dynamic, bustling, and noisy. Those who haunt the electronic games arcades at shopping malls will feel most at home at DisneyQuest.

From the turnstile, you enter the Departure Lobby and a "Cyberlator," a sort of "transitional attraction" (read: elevator) hosted by the genie from _Aladdin,_ that delivers you to an entrance plaza called Ventureport. From here you can enter the four zones. Like in the larger parks, each zone is distinctively themed. Some zones cover more than one floor, so, looking around, you can see things going on both above and below you. The four zones, in no particular order, are Explore Zone, Score Zone, Create Zone, and Replay Zone. In addition to the zones, DisneyQuest offers two restaurants and the inevitable gift shop.

DisneyQuest/Cyberspace Mountain. You gotta do this! Ride the rollercoaster you design on a computer. You can choose to ride in space, the jungle, or inside a volcano. Space is the coolest. I picked barrel rolls, backflips, a dive into a black hole, twists and turns, and a dip down under the track. You sit in a simulator and feel like an astronaut flying through space. And don't miss the Virtual Jungle Cruise. It's totally wild! I worked up a sweat on this one. Feels like you're in a real video game. It's a simulator raft ride and you paddle through river rapids with a group of people. Everybody is yelling and screaming as you try to paddle in the right direction. Watch out for dinosaurs and waterfalls. You will get wet, really, but not too much.

Ian

Each zone offers several attractions, most based on technologies like simulators that work well in confined spaces. The Explore Zone is representative. You enter through a re-creation of the tiger's-head cave from *Aladdin*. The headline attraction in Explore Zone is the Virtual Jungle Cruise, where you paddle a six-person raft. The raft is a motion simulator perched on top of blue air bags that replicate the motion of water. Responding to the film of the river projected before you, you can choose several routes through the rapids. The motion simulator responds to sensors on your paddle. As if navigating the river isn't enough, man-eating dinosaurs and a cataclysmic comet are tossed in for good measure.

Some DisneyQuest attractions tap your imagination. In the Create Zone, for example, you can use a computer to design your own roller coaster, including 360° loops, then take a virtual reality ride on your creation in a motion simulator. Sid's Make-a-Toy, also in the Create Zone, lets you design a toy and receive the parts to actually construct it at home. Other creative attractions include virtual beauty salon makeovers and painting on an electronic canvas.

Pinball wizard here I come! Seriously, DisneyQuest is great for a rainy day or arrival and departure days.

Liliane

Like all things Disney, admission to DisneyQuest is not cheap. But especially for teens and technology junkies, it's an eye-opening experience and a fun time.

Prices range from $29 to $35 (plus tax), and children under 10 must be accompanied by a responsible person 16 years and older. Kids under the age of 3 are admitted free of charge, but strollers are not permitted inside DisneyQuest. You can leave and re-enter anytime you want on

FAVORITE EATS AT DOWNTOWN DISNEY

SECTION	FOOD ITEM	WHERE THEY CAN BE FOUND
MARKETPLACE	Sandwich paradise	Earl of Sandwich
	Mini-donuts and coffee	Forty-Thirst Street
	Ice cream and chocolate treats	Ghirardelli Soda Fountain & Chocolate Shop
	Soups, salads, and pizza	Wolfgang Puck Express
	Burgers & kids' menu in tropical rain forest setting.* Get an idea here: **www.rainforestcafe.com**	Rainforest Cafe
WESTSIDE	Candies inside a dungeon of sweet delights	Candy Cauldron
	Pretzels with a twist	Wetzel's Pretzels
	Pizza, pasta, and salads	FoodQuest
	Cajun food and kids' menu* For shows in the music hall next door, check out **www.hob.com**.	House of Blues
	Burgers* Great for teens who will love checking out the Hollywood memorabilia.	Planet Hollywood
PLEASURE ISLAND	Irish food and live music	Raglan Road

* table service only

the day of your visit: just make sure your wrist gets stamped upon arrival. Annual passes are available.

Believe it or not, there are height restrictions at DisneyQuest, and here is the countdown: **CyberSpace Mountain:** 51 inches, **Pirates of the Caribbean—Battle for Buccaneer Gold:** 35 inches, and **Buzz Lightyear's Astro Blasters:** 51 inches.

PLEASURE ISLAND HIGHLIGHTS

PLEASURE ISLAND OFFERS SEVERAL NIGHTCLUBS with entertainment ranging from comedy to hip-hop music and various genres of rock. Admission for all clubs is $20.95 (plus tax). Single club admission is offered. If your teenager is hot to visit Pleasure Island, try **Raglan Road,** an Irish pub and restaurant featuring live Celtic music. Best of all, it is accessible without paying Pleasure Island admission or a cover charge. The rollicking pub music featured at Raglan Road can be enjoyed by all ages, making it a great choice for your teen's first-time club experience. Best of all, at Raglan Road, neither you nor the kids will feel uncomfortable or self-conscious.

Ian

Downtown Disney/Rainforest Cafe: This is like having dinner in a tree house. Tree branches are everywhere. Birds are chirping, and there are humongous mushrooms. Monkeys, orangutans, and gorillas are all around too. Don't worry. They're not real.

While you're eating, every once in a while thunder and lightning appear and a rainstorm happens. I had ribs the night we went. They were very good. You have to get the chocolate volcano for dessert. It's incredible!

Bob

Ian's tip gives you a good example of how most kids feel about the Downtown Disney Rainforest Cafe. Getting a table during normal dinner hours, however, is only slightly less difficult than eloping with Daisy Duck. If the kids are all over you to go, try the saner, more manageable Rainforest Cafe at the Animal Kingdom. You'll be done and out the door in less time than it takes to get seated at the Downtown Disney location.

HOW TO MAKE IT WORK

IT REALLY DOES NOT MATTER IF YOU MAKE Downtown Disney your destination for the day or if you decide to go on the spur of the moment. Fun can be had by all anytime. Family restrooms (with a changing and nursing area) are located in the Marketplace near Once Upon a Toy and the Art of Disney. Call ☎ 407-WDW-2NITE for Downtown Disney information.

SHOPPING There are five ATMs at Downtown Disney. All major credit cards are accepted, and if you are a Disney resort guest you can have your shopping purchases delivered to your hotel (this only works if you are not checking out the next day). Pickup is usually at the primary gift shop of your resort (no room delivery), but even so, it sure beats lugging stuff around.

BE PREPARED

DETERMINE IN ADVANCE what all members in your party want to do. Pick up a map at Guest Relations and enjoy the area. Downtown Disney is a great place to give your teenagers some space. Agree on a time and place to reunite and turn them loose. While teens enjoy DisneyQuest or the latest flick at the AMC movie theater, mom and dad can have a peaceful dinner at the Portobello Yacht Club or Wolfgang Puck Cafe.

Pets are not allowed at Downtown Disney. Kennels are available only at the Magic Kingdom, Epcot, Disney-MGM Studios, Disney's Animal Kingdom, and Disney's Fort Wilderness Resort and Campground.

THE BEST *of the* REST

UNLESS YOU'RE A GAMBLER OR A NUDIST, you'll probably find your favorite activity offered at Walt Disney World. You can fish, canoe, hike, bike, boat, play tennis and golf, ride horses, work out, take cooking lessons, even drive a real race car or watch the Atlanta Braves' spring training.

Your kids will go nuts for the **Wilderness Lodge Resort,** and so will you. While you're there, have a family-style meal at the children-friendly Whispering Canyon restaurant and rent bikes for a ride on the paved paths of adjacent Fort Wilderness campground. The outing will be a great change of pace. The only downside is that your kids might not want to go back to their own hotel.

More fun with the mouse is available at **Disney's Wide World of Sports,** a 220-acre competition and training complex. During late winter and early spring, the venue is the spring training home of the Atlanta Braves. Disney guests are welcome at the sports complex as paid spectators, but none of the facilities are available for guests to use.

To learn what events, including Major League Baseball exhibition games, are scheduled during your visit, call ☎ 407-939-1289 or visit **www.disneyworldofsports.com.**

A program called **NFL Experience** operates daily from 11 a.m. until about 5 p.m. Appealing primarily to school-age boys (girls are welcome), the NFL Experience is a supervised activity that allows kids to kick field goals, catch and throw passes, catch punts, and run through a small obstacle course, among other things. Admission is $11 for adults and $8 for children ages 3 to 9.

Located 40 to 60 minutes south of Walt Disney World is the **Disney Wilderness Preserve,** a real wetlands-restoration area operated by the Nature Conservancy in partnership with Disney. There are hiking trails, an interpretive center, and guided outings on weekends. Trails wind through grassy savannas, beneath ancient cypress tress, and along the banks of pristine Lake Russell. The preserve is open daily from 9 a.m. to 5 p.m., closed on weekends from June to September. General admission is $3 for adults and $2 for children ages 6 to 17. Guided trail walks are offered on Saturday at no extra cost, and "buggy" rides are available on Sunday afternoon. The buggy in question is a mammoth amphibious contraption, and the rides last a few hours. The buggy ride is $10 for adults and $5 for children ages 6 to 17. Reservations are highly recommended. Disney cast members and information operators don't know squat about the Wilderness Preserve, so if you're interested, call the preserve directly at ☎ 407-935-0002.

GOLF

IF GOLF IS YOUR THING call ☎ 407-WDW-GOLF for tee times and greens fees at Palm Golf Course (★★★★), Magnolia Golf Course (★★★½), Osprey Ridge Golf Course (★★★½), Eagle Pines Golf Course (★★★½), Lake Buena Vista Golf Course (★★★), or Oak Trail Golf Course (★★½). For more information call ☎ 407-WDW-GOLF.

There is, of course, golf beyond Mickey's Kingdom. The greater Orlando area has enough high-quality courses to rival better-known golfing meccas, such as Scottsdale and Palm Springs. But unlike these destinations with their endless private country clubs, Orlando is unique because almost all its courses are open for some sort of public play. We compiled a list of off-Disney golf courses for **dad's or mom's special day off:**

ARNOLD PALMER'S BAY HILL CLUB & LODGE ★★★★ **www.bayhill.com** or ☎ 407-876-2429

CHAMPIONSGATE INTERNATIONAL COURSE ★★★★ ☎ 407-787-4653

CHAMPIONSGATE NATIONAL COURSE ★★★½ ☎ 407-787-4653

CROOKED CAT ★★★★ ☎ 407-656-2626

GRAND CYPRESS GOLF CLUB ★★★★½ **www.grandcypress.com** or ☎ 407-239-4700

INDEPENDENCE ★★★★ ☎ 407-662-1100

LEGACY ★★★★½ ☎ 407-662-1100

METROWEST GOLF CLUB ★★★½ **www.metrowestgolf.com** or ☎ 407-299-1099

PANTHER LAKE ★★★★½ ☎ 407-656-2626

The 900-page *Unofficial Guide to Walt Disney World*, by Bob Sehlinger and Len Testa, contains an entire chapter on Walt Disney World and Orlando-area golf with in-depth profiles of all the best courses.

MINIATURE GOLF

CONSIDER MINIATURE GOLF FOR THE WHOLE FAMILY at **Fantasia Gardens Miniature Golf,** located across the street from the Walt Disney World Swan or at **Winter Summerland** right next to Blizzard Beach. Fantasia Gardens Miniature Golf is a beautifully landscaped garden with fountains, animated statues, topiaries, and flower beds. At Winter Summerland the Christmas holiday theme is prevalent, with ornaments hanging from palm trees. At Castle Hole watch out for a snowman that sprays water on unsuspecting guests when their golf balls pass beneath him.

Fantasia Gardens is quite demanding and not nearly as whimsical as Winter Summerland. Adults and older teens will enjoy the challenge of Fantasia Gardens, but if your group includes children younger than 12, head to Winter Summerland. Another Winter Summerland plus is that it can be reached easily via Disney transportation. To access Fantasia

Gardens you must take a bus to the Walt Disney World Swan Resort and walk to the course from there. Admission to both courses is $10.75 for adults and $8.50 for children ages 3 to 9. Opening hours are from 10 a.m. to 11 p.m. For more information call ☎ 407- WDW-GOLF.

THEME PARK TRIVIA QUIZ ANSWERS

MAGIC KINGDOM

1. (C) 2. (C) 3. (B) 4. (B) 5. (A) 6. (A) 7. (C) 8. (C) 9. (C)
10. (D) 11. (B) 12. (B) 13. (D) 14. (D) 15. (C) 16. (C)

EPCOT

1. (B) 2. (B) 3. (C) 4. (D) 5. (B) 6. (B) 7. (A) 8. (C) 9. (D)
10. (C) 11. (C) 12. (A) 13. (D)

ANIMAL KINGDOM

1. (A) 2. (B) 3. (C) 4. (A) 5. (B) 6. (C) 7. (A) 8. (C) 9. (B)
10. (D) 11. (B)

DISNEY-MGM STUDIOS

1. (A) 2. (D) 3. (B) 4. (A) 5. (C) 6. (B) 7. (C)

ACCOMMODATIONS INDEX

Note: Page numbers of hotel profiles are in **boldface** type.

RESTAURANT INDEX

Note: Page numbers in **boldface** type indicate restaurant profiles.

SUBJECT INDEX

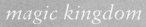

Magic Kingdom Happy Family One-Day Touring Plan

1. If you are a Disney Resort guest, arrive at the entrance to the Magic Kingdom 30 minutes prior to opening. Guests staying off-site should arrive at the TTC 40 minutes prior to opening. Obtain park maps and a copy of the daily entertainment schedule when you pass through the turnstiles.
2. **PARENTS:** As soon as the park opens, ride Dumbo the Flying Elephant in Fantasyland.
3. **TEENS:** As soon as the park opens, ride Space Mountain in Tomorrowland.
4. **FAMILY:** Ride The Many Adventures of Winnie the Pooh in Fantasyland.
5. **FAMILY:** Ride The Mad Tea Party in Fantasyland.
6. **FAMILY:** Ride Peter Pan's Flight in Fantasyland.
7. **FAMILY:** See Mickey's PhilharMagic in Fantasyland.
8. **PARENTS:** Visit Ariel's Grotto in Fantasyland.
9. **TEENS:** Ride Splash Mountain in Frontierland. If the wait exceeds 30 minutes, use FASTPASS.
10. **PARENTS:** Ride the Magic Carpets of Aladdin in Adventureland.
11. **TEENS:** Ride Big Thunder Mountain Railroad in Frontierland. Tip: Get FASTPASSes for Splash and Big Thunder now if you want to ride again later.
12. **FAMILY:** Ride Pirates of the Caribbean in Adventureland.
13. **FAMILY:** See the Enchanted Tiki Room.
14. **FAMILY:** Eat lunch. Good nearby dining choices include Pecos Bill's Tall Tale Inn and the top floor of the Columbia Harbor House.
15. **PARENTS:** After lunch, return to your hotel for a break. Be sure to get your hand stamped. We recommend allowing at least three hours.
16. **TEENS:** Ride Splash Mountain again in Frontierland. If the wait exceeds 30 minutes, use FASTPASS.
17. **TEENS:** Ride Big Thunder Mountain Railroad again in Frontierland. Tip: Get FASTPASSes for Splash and Big Thunder now if you want to ride again later.
18. **TEENS:** See the Haunted Mansion in Liberty Square.
19. **TEENS:** Explore the rest of the park, or re-visit favorite attractions until rest of the family returns.
20. **PARENTS:** Return to the Magic Kingdom and take the WDW Railroad from Main Street to Frontierland.
21. **FAMILY:** Tour Tom Sawyer Island. Allow at least 30 to 45 minutes to run around the Island. Be sure to try the barrel bridges and tour Fort Langhorn.
22. **FAMILY:** Eat dinner.
23. **FAMILY:** See the Monsters Inc. Laugh Floor Comedy Club in Tomorrowland.
24. **FAMILY:** Ride Buzz Lightyear.
25. **PARENTS:** Make your way to Toontown. As you walk through Tomorrowland, keep the Tomorrowland Speedway on your right, and you'll be at the entrance to Toontown in a couple of minutes.
26. **FAMILY:** See the evening parade and/or fireworks on Main Street. A good viewing location for Wishes is on the right-hand side of the central hub, near the walkway to Tomorrowland.
27. **FAMILY:** Depart the Magic Kingdom.

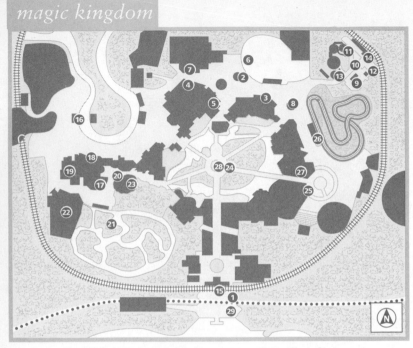

magic kingdom

Magic Kingdom One-Day Touring Plan for Grandparents with Small Children

1. Arrive at the entrance to the Magic Kingdom 30 minutes prior to opening. If you're staying outside Walt Disney World, arrive at the TTC 50 minutes prior to opening.
2. As soon as the park opens, ride Dumbo the Flying Elephant. To get to Fantasyland, go down Main Street and either through or around the castle.
3. Ride The Many Adventures of Winnie the Pooh.
4. Ride Peter Pan's Flight.
5. See *Mickey's PhilharMagic*. Take a spin on Cinderella's Golden Carrousel after *PhilharMagic*.
6. Visit Ariel's Grotto now for autographs.
7. Take the It's a Small World boat ride.
8. Give the Mad Tea Party a spin. It's located near the Winnie the Pooh ride. A less stressful choice is Pooh's Playful Spot.
9. If the kids are big enough, ride the Barnstormer in Toontown.
10. Get autographs at Toontown Hall of Fame.
11. Get Mickey's autograph in Mickey's House.
12. Experience Donald's Boat.
13. Tour Minnie's Country House.
14. Take the train from Toontown to Main Street. Eat lunch outside the park, and return to your hotel for a break of 3–4 hours.
15. Return to the Magic Kingdom and take the train from Main Street to Frontierland.
16. Take the boat to Tom Sawyer Island. Be sure to explore the bridges and Fort Langhorn.
17. Return to Frontierland for Frontierland Shootin' Arcade. Cost is $0.50 (two quarters) per play, and dollar bill changing machines are available nearby.
18. See the *Country Bear Jamboree*. If possible, send one member of your party into Adventureland to check on FASTPASSes for Jungle Cruise. If they're available for return in around an hour, get FASTPASSes for everyone.
19. Eat dinner if you've not already done so.
20. Ride the Magic Carpets of Aladdin.
21. Take the Jungle Cruise if lines are short or you have FASTPASSes, otherwise see the *Enchanted Tiki Room*.
22. Ride Pirates of the Caribbean.
23. See the Swiss Family Treehouse.
24. Find a spot for the evening parade and fireworks on Main Street. Grab the kids an ice cream and take a break. Otherwise, try the next few steps in Tomorrowland.
25. Try Buzz Lightyear in Tomorrowland. Also try the Tomorrowland Transit Authority, across from Buzz in the center of Tomorrowland.
26. Take a spin on the Tomorrowland Indy Speedway in Tomorrowland.
27. See the *Monsters Inc. Laugh Floor Comedy Club*.
28. See the evening parade and fireworks from Main Street. The right side of the central hub on Main Street is a good viewing location.
29. Depart the Magic Kingdom.

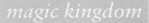

Magic Kingdom One-Day Touring Plan
for Tweens and their Parents

1. Arrive at the entrance to the Magic Kingdom 25 minutes (Disney resort guests) to 50 minutes (non-Disney resort guests) prior to opening. During days of peak attendance, the Magic Kingdom may open at 8 a.m. or earlier.

2. As soon as the park opens, ride Space Mountain in Tomorrowland.

3. Ride Buzz Lightyear.

4. Ride The Many Adventures of Winnie the Pooh in Fantasyland.

5. Ride the Mad Tea Party. Parents can abstain. Really.

6. Ride Peter Pan's Flight.

7. See The Haunted Mansion in Liberty Square.

8. Ride Splash Mountain. If the wait exceeds 30 minutes, consider using FASTPASS.

9. Ride Big Thunder Mountain Railroad.

10. Ride Pirates of the Caribbean.

11. Eat lunch. Good nearby counter-service restaurants include Pecos Bill's Tall Tale Inn and Cafe in Frontierland, and the Columbia Harbor House in Liberty Square.

12. Ride the Jungle Cruise in Adventureland. If the wait exceeds 30 minutes, use FASTPASS.

13. Tour the Swiss Family Treehouse.

14. See *Enchanted Tiki Room.*

15. See the *Country Bear Jamboree* in Frontierland.

16. Try the Frontierland Shootin' Arcade.

17. Experience *The Hall of Presidents.*

18. See *Mickey's PhilharMagic.* Use FASTPASS if the wait exceeds 30 minutes.

19. Eat dinner. The closest sit-down restaurant is Cinderella's Royal Table. For counter-service, try the Pinocchio Village Haus in Fantasyland.

20. Take a ride on the Walt Disney World Railroad. The closest station is probably in Toontown. Other stops include Main Street and Frontierland.

21. If time permits, see the *Monsters Inc. Laugh Floor Comedy Club* in Tomorrowland.

22. See the evening parade on Main Street.

23. See the evening fireworks on Main Street. A good viewing spot for *Wishes* is to the right of the central hub, on the walkway toward Tomorrowland.

24. Depart the Magic Kingdom.

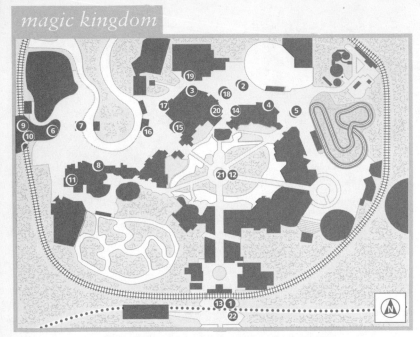

magic kingdom

Magic Kingdom Two-Day Touring Plan for Parents with Small Children - Day 1

1. If you are staying at a Disney Resort, use Disney transportation to arrive at the entrance to the Magic Kingdom 30 minutes prior to opening. Guests staying off-site should arrive at the Ticket and Transportation Center 40 minutes prior to opening. Obtain park maps and a copy of the daily entertainment schedule when you pass through the turnstiles. Stroller rentals are on the right-hand side of the entrance, near Guest Services.

2. As soon as the park opens, ride Dumbo the Flying Elephant in Fantasyland.

3. Ride Peter Pan's Flight.

4. Ride The Many Adventures of Winnie the Pooh.

5. Ride The Mad Tea Party.

6. Obtain a FASTPASS for Splash Mountain in Frontierland. Taking the train from Toontown to Frontierland will save a bit of walking, but will take longer than walking.

7. Tour Tom Sawyer Island. Allow 30 to 45 minutes to run around the Island. Be sure to try the barrel bridges and tour Fort Langhorn.

8. See the *Country Bear Jamboree.*

9. Take a round-trip on the Walt Disney World Railroad from Frontierland Station. The Frontierland station is accessed by stairs, and is located just above the entrance to Splash Mountain.

10. Ride Splash Mountain.

11. Eat lunch. Good nearby dining choices include Pecos Bill's Tall Tale Inn, with ample seating and air-conditioning. In Liberty Square, the top floor of the Columbia Harbor House is usually less crowded.

12. After lunch, return to your hotel for a mid-afternoon break. Be sure to get your hand stamped when leaving the park. We recommend allowing at least three hours, including transportation. Four hours would be even better.

13. Return to the Magic Kingdom.

14. Send one member of your party to obtain FASTPASSes for *Mickey's PhilharMagic* in Fantasyland. Have this person meet the rest of your group at the entrance to *The Hall of Presidents* in Liberty Square.

15. Experience *The Hall of Presidents* in Liberty Square.

16. Experience the *Liberty Belle* Riverboat.

17. Eat dinner. The closest counter-service restaurant is the Pinocchio Village Haus in Fantasyland. The nearest sit-down restaurant is the Liberty Tree Tavern in Liberty Square.

18. Enjoy Cinderella's Carousel in Fantasyland.

19. Ride It's a Small World.

20. See *Mickey's PhilharMagic*. This is the last attraction in today's touring. Use extra time to re-visit favorite attractions or explore the rest of the park.

21. See the evening parade and/or fireworks on Main Street.A good viewing location for *Wishes* is on the right-hand side of the central hub, near the walkway to Tomorrowland.

22. Depart the Magic Kingdom.

magic kingdom

Magic Kingdom Two-Day Touring Plan for Parents with Small Children - Day 2

1. If you are staying at a Disney Resort, use Disney transportation to arrive at the entrance to the Magic Kingdom 30 minutes prior to opening. Guests staying off-site should arrive at the Ticket and Transportation Center 40 minutes prior to opening. Obtain park maps and a copy of the daily entertainment schedule when you pass through the turnstiles. Stroller rentals are on the right-hand side of the entrance, near Guest Services.

2. As soon as the park opens, ride the Tomorrowland Speedway in Tomorrowland.

3. Ride the Astro Orbiters.

4. Ride Buzz Lightyear. In the unlikely event the wait exceeds 30 minutes, obtain FASTPASSes for each member of your party.

5. Ride the Tomorrowland Transit Authority.

6. See the *Monsters Inc. Laugh Floor Comedy Club*.

7. Make your way to Toontown. As you walk through Tomorrowland, keep the Tomorrowland Speedway on your right, and you'll be at the entrance to Toontown in a couple of minutes. In Toontown, Ride the Barnstormer at Goofy's Wiseacres Farm.

8. Tour Mickey's Country House. Have your camera and autograph book ready!

9. Experience Donald's Boat. Located outside and across the street from Mickey's Country House.

10. Tour the Toontown Hall of Fame. Parents take note: the character greeting area is housed inside a large retail space.

11. Tour Minnie's Country House.

12. Take the Walt Disney World Railroad from Toontown to Frontierland. Strollers are not permitted on the Railroad. If you've rented a Disney stroller, remove your personal possessions, name card and rental receipt from the stroller. You'll be issued a new stroller in Frontierland.

13. Ride Pirates of the Caribbean in Adventureland. While most children will take this attraction in stride, a few children may be frightened by the skeletons in some of the scenes.

14. Ride the Jungle Cruise. If the wait time exceeds 30 minutes, use FASTPASS.

15. Ride the Magic Carpets of Aladdin.

16. Eat lunch. Good sit-down restaurants include the Liberty Tree Tavern in Liberty Square, and the Crystal Palace on Main Street.

17. After lunch, return to your hotel for a mid-day break. Allow at least three hours for your break. Four hours would be better.

18. Return to the Magic Kingdom and explore the Swiss Family Treehouse in Adventureland.

19. See the *Enchanted Tiki Room*. This is the last attraction in today's touring. Use extra time to re-visit favorite attractions or explore the rest of the park.

20. If you have not already done so, see the evening parade and/or fireworks.

21. Depart the Magic Kingdom.

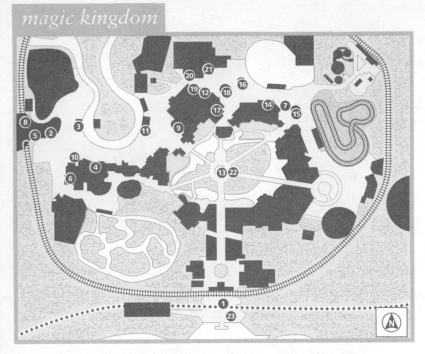

magic kingdom

Magic Kingdom Two-Day Sleepy Head Touring Plan for Parents with Small Children - Day 1

1. Arrive at the entrance to the Magic Kingdom around 11 a.m. Obtain park maps and a copy of the daily entertainment schedule when you pass through the turnstiles. Stroller rentals are on the right-hand side of the entrance, near Guest Services.
2. Obtain FASTPASSes for Splash Mountain in Frontierland.
3. Tour Tom Sawyer Island.
4. See the *Country Bear Jamboree*.
5. Ride Splash Mountain. Use the FASTPASSes obtained in Step 2.
6. Eat lunch. Good nearby dining choices include Pecos Bill's Tall Tale Inn, with ample seating and air-conditioning. In Liberty Square, the top floor of the Columbia Harbor House is usually less crowded.
7. Send one member of your party to obtain FASTPASSes for The Many Adventures of Winnie the Pooh in Fantasyland.
8. Ride the Walt Disney World Railroad from Frontierland Station. Frontierland Station is located above the entrance to Splash Mountain.
9. Experience *The Hall of Presidents* in Liberty Square.
10. See the afternoon parade from Frontierland.
11. Experience the *Liberty Belle* Riverboat.
12. Send one member of your party to obtain FASTPASSes for Peter Pan's Flight in Fantasyland. Check your FASTPASSes for Pooh for the exact time you can obtain FASTPASSes for Peter Pan.
13. Take a one hour break inside the park. Good rest areas include the second floor of the Columbia Harbor House, and the movie theater in Exposition Hall on Main Street.
14. Ride The Many Adventures of Winnie the Pooh.
15. Ride The Mad Tea Party.
16. Ride Dumbo the Flying Elephant.
17. See *Mickey's PhilharMagic*.
18. Enjoy Cinderella's Carousel.
19. Ride Peter Pan's Flight. Use the FASTPASSes obtained in Step 12.
20. Ride It's a Small World.
21. Eat dinner. Nearby choices include the Pinocchio
22. Village Haus and Cinderella's Royal Table. See the evening parade and fireworks on Main Street. A good viewing location for Wishes is on the right-hand side of the central hub, near the walkway to Tomorrowland.
23. Depart the Magic Kingdom.

Magic Kingdom Two-Day Sleepy Head Touring Plan for Parents with Small Children - Day 2

1. Arrive at the entrance to the Magic Kingdom around 11 a.m. Obtain park maps and a copy of the daily entertainment schedule when you pass through the turnstiles. Stroller rentals are on the right-hand side of the entrance, near Guest Services.
2. Explore the Swiss Family Treehouse in Adventureland.
3. Ride the Magic Carpets of Aladdin.
4. Ride the Jungle Cruise.
5. See the *Enchanted Tiki Room*.
6. Ride Pirates of the Caribbean.
7. Eat lunch. Good nearby dining choices include Pecos Bill's Tall Tale Inn, with ample seating and air-conditioning. In Liberty Square, the top floor of the Columbia Harbor House is usually less crowded.
8. Take the Walt Disney World Railroad from Frontierland to Toontown. The Frontierland station is located above the entrance to Splash Mountain. Strollers are not permitted on the Railroad. If you've rented a Disney stroller, remove your personal possessions, name card, and rental receipt from the stroller. You'll be issued a new stroller in Toontown.
9. Tour Mickey's Country House.

10. Experience Donald's Boat in Toontown.
11. Tour the Toontown Hall of Fame. Parents take note: the character greeting area is housed inside a large retail space.
12. Tour Minnie's Country House.
13. Ride the Barnstormer.
14. Take a one-hour break inside the park. A good resting spot is inside Cosmic Ray's Starlight Cafe in Tomorrowland. If possible, send one member of your party to obtain FASTPASSes for Buzz Lightyear in Tomorrowland.
15. Ride the Tomorrowland Speedway in Tomorrowland.
16. Ride the Tomorrowland Transit Authority.
17. Ride the Astro Orbiters.
18. Ride Buzz Lightyear in Tomorrowland.
19. See the *Monsters Inc. Laugh Floor Comedy Club*.
20. Eat dinner. The closest counter-service restaurant is Cosmic Ray's Starlight Cafe in Tomorrowland. Also try the Plaza Restaurant.
21. See the evening parade on Main Street.
22. Depart the Magic Kingdom.

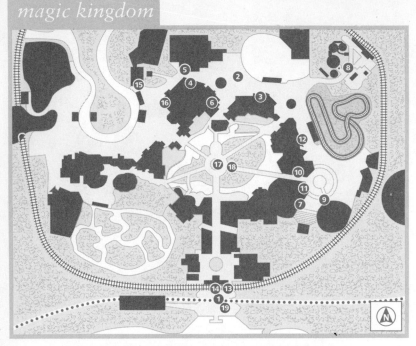

magic kingdom

Parent's Magic Kingdom Plan—One Afternoon and One Full Day (Full Day)

1. Arrive at the entrance to the Magic Kingdom 50 minutes (Disney resort guests) to 70 minutes (non-Disney resort guests) prior to opening. Rent strollers (if necessary) under the train station on Main Street.
2. As soon as the park opens, ride Dumbo in Fantasyland.
3. Ride The Many Adventures of Winnie the Pooh. Unless the wait exceeds 30 minutes, do not use FASTPASS.
4. Ride Peter Pan's Flight. Unless the wait exceeds 30 minutes, do not use FASTPASS.
5. Ride It's a Small World.
6. See *Mickey's PhilharMagic*.
7. If possible, send one member of your party to obtain FASTPASSes for Buzz Lightyear in Tomorrowland.
8. Tour Mickey's Toontown Fair in Toontown.
9. Ride the Tomorrowland Transit Authority in Tomorrowland.
10. See the *Monsters Inc. Laugh Floor Comedy Club*.
11. Ride Buzz Lightyear, using the FASTPASSes obtained earlier.
12. Eat lunch. The nearest counter-service restaurant is Cosmic Ray's Starlight Cafe, across from the Tomorrowland Indy Speedway. The seasonally

operating Tomorrowland Noodle Station has good noodle bowls and other Asian dishes. Good sandwiches can be found at the Plaza Restaurant on Main Street.

13. Leave the park for a nap back at your hotel. Allow at least 3 hours for this break—4 would be better.
14. Return to the park. If there's any ride you want to experience again, see if FASTPASSes are still available for it. Good evening rides include Splash Mountain in Frontierland and Cinderella's Golden Carrousel in Fantasyland.
15. See The Haunted Mansion in Liberty Square.
16. Eat dinner if you have not already done so. Most kids will find something they like at the Liberty Tree Tavern's character dinner. Reservations are strongly recommended.
17. See the evening parade on Main Street. Liberty Square is a good alternate viewing location if you're already there.
18. See the evening fireworks on Main Street. A good viewing spot for Wishes is to the right of the central hub, on the walkway towards Tomorrowland.
19. Depart the Magic Kingdom.

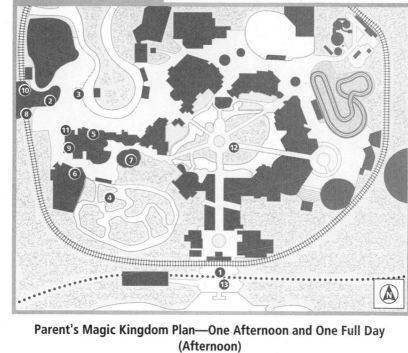

Parent's Magic Kingdom Plan—One Afternoon and One Full Day (Afternoon)

1. Arrive at the entrance to the Magic Kingdom around 2 p.m. Rent strollers (if necessary) under the train station on Main Street.

2. Obtain FASTPASSes for Splash Mountain in Frontierland. If the wait is 20 minutes or less, ride now instead of using FASTPASS.

3. In Frontierland, take the raft over to Tom Sawyer Island. Be sure to explore Barrel Bridge and Fort Langhorn. If your kids are especially adventurous, explore the caves, too!

4. Ride the Jungle Cruise in Adventureland. If the wait exceeds 30 minutes, use FASTPASS.

5. See the *Country Bear Jamboree*. It's a short walk from the Jungle Cruise if you cut through Adventureland to Frontierland. Keep the Enchanted Tiki Room on your left, Magic Carpets of Aladdin on your right, and walk straight toward Frontierland. CBJ will be on your left.

6. Ride Pirates of the Caribbean in Adventureland.

7. Explore the Swiss Family Treehouse.

8. Ride Splash Mountain, using the FASTPASSes obtained earlier.

9. Eat dinner. The closest counter-service restaurant is Pecos Bill's in Frontierland. The closest sit-down restaurant is the Liberty Tree Tavern in Liberty Square. It's a character dinner, and reservations are recommended.

10. If you want to leave the park now, take the Walt Disney World Railroad from Frontierland to Main Street. The Frontierland station is located just above the entrance to Splash Mountain.

11. See the evening parade from Frontierland. Good viewing spots are along the storefronts of Frontierland.

12. See the evening fireworks on Main Street. A good viewing spot for *Wishes* is to the right of the central hub, on the walkway towards Tomorrowland.

13. Depart the Magic Kingdom.

epcot

Epcot One-Day Touring Plan for Parents with Small Children

1. Arrive at the entrance to Epcot 30 minutes prior to opening. Pick up a park map and daily entertainment schedule when entering the park. Stroller rentals are just inside the main entrance, and to the left.

2. If your children are tall enough, ride Soarin' at the Land pavilion in Future World West. If your children aren't yet tall enough, skip this step and continue to Living with the Land.

3. Ride Living with the Land, also at the Land pavilion. Use FASTPASS if the wait exceeds 30 minutes. Exit the pavilion and turn left to get to the Living Seas.

4. See The Seas with Nemo and Friends. Be sure to catch *Turtle Talk with Crush*.

5. Ride Journey Into Your Imagination.

6. See *Honey, I Shrunk the Audience*.

7. See *The Circle of Life* in the Land pavilion.

8. Eat lunch. The closest (and best) restaurant will be Sunshine Seasons in the Land pavilion. Also consider the Electric Umbrella in Future World East.

9. Ride Universe of Energy in Future World East. This ride can also be seen after Spaceship Earth later today.

10. Ride El Rio del Tiempo at Mexico in World Showcase. Be sure to try the Kidcot Fun Stops in Mexico and Norway.

11. Ride Maelstrom at Norway. If the wait exceeds 30 minutes, consider using FASTPASS. Note that Disney rarely enforces FASTPASS return times, as long as the start of the FASTPASS return time window has past.

12. Return to your hotel for a mid-day break. Be sure to get your hand stamped for re-entry when leaving Epcot.

13. Return to Epcot and ride Spaceship Earth.

14. See the *O Canada!* film at Canada in World Showcase. Eat dinner. Le Cellier, Canada's sit-down restaurant, is a popular choice.

15. See *The American Adventure* at the United States pavilion. This is the last attraction in today's touring. Between now and *Illuminations*, consider exploring the United Kingdom and France pavilions.

16. See *Illuminations*. Excellent viewing locations can be found along the walkway between Canada and France in World Showcase.

17. Depart Epcot.

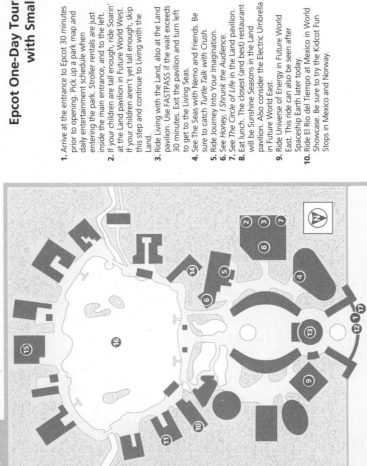

Epcot One-Day Sleepy Head Touring Plan for Parents with Small Children

1. Arrive at the entrance to Epcot around 11 a.m. Stroller rentals are just inside the main entrance, and to the left.

2. If your children are tall enough to ride, obtain FASTPASSes for *Soarin'* at the Land pavilion in Future World West. If the wait is 25 minutes or less, ride now instead of using FASTPASS.

3. Ride Living with the Land at the Land pavilion.

4. See The Seas with Nemo and Friends. Be sure to try *Turtle Talk with Crush.*

5. Ride Journey Into Your Imagination.

6. See *Honey, I Shrunk the Audience.*

7. If you have not already done so, eat lunch. Sunshine Seasons at the Land pavilion offers a decent selection of menu items.

8. Ride *Soarin',* using the FASTPASSes obtained in Step 2.

9. See *The Circle of Life,* also at the Land pavilion.

10. Ride Spaceship Earth.

11. Ride Universe of Energy in Future World East.

12. Ride El Rio del Tiempo at Mexico.

13. Ride Maelstrom at Norway. Because of the walk back, we do not recommend using FASTPASS unless the wait exceeds 45 minutes.

14. See *The American Adventure* at the United States pavilion. The Liberty Inn is a convenient counter-service restaurant.

15. Eat dinner. Good sit-down restaurants include Restaurant Marrakesh in Morocco and Le Cellier in Canada.

16. See the *O Canada!* film at Canada in World Showcase. Don't forget to stop at the Kidcot Fun Stops throughout World Showcase.

17. See *Illuminations.* The best viewing spots are along the border between Future World and World Showcase, and between Canada and France in World Showcase.

18. Depart Epcot.

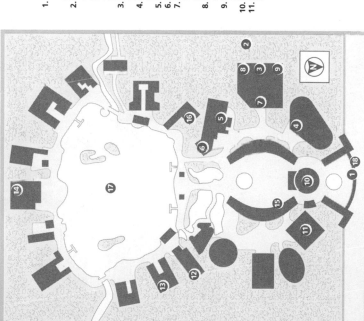

epcot

Epcot One-Day Touring Plan for Tweens and their Parents

1. Arrive at the entrance to Epcot 30 minutes prior to opening. Pick up a park map and daily entertainment schedule when entering the park.

2. As soon as the park opens, obtain FASTPASSes for Soarin' at the Land pavilion in Future World West.

3. Ride Test Track in Future World East.

4. Ride Mission: Space. Do not use FASTPASS.

5. Ride Living with the Land at the Land pavilion in Future World West.

6. Ride Soarin' using the FASTPASSes obtained in Step 2. If you want to ride Soarin' again, obtain more FASTPASSes now.

7. See The Seas with Nemo and Friends. Also check out Turtle Talk with Crush after the film.

8. See Honey, I Shrunk the Audience.

9. Tour Innoventions West.

10. Eat lunch. The Sunshine Season Food Fair in the Land pavilion has the best food in Future World. The Garden Grill is the closest sit-down restaurant.

11. Ride Universe of Energy in Future World East.

12. Ride Spaceship Earth.

13. Tour the Mexico pavilion in World Showcase. This begins a clockwise tour of World Showcase.

14. Ride Maelstrom at Norway. Also be sure to tour the stave church in Norway.

15. Tour the China pavilion.

16. See the Germany pavilion.

17. Visit the Italy pavilion.

18. See The American Adventure at the United States pavilion. Check the daily entertainment schedule for show times.

19. Explore the Japan pavilion.

20. See the Morocco pavilion.

21. See Impressions de France at the France pavilion. Younger kids rate this 2.5 stars (teens give it 3); we included this film because it is an air-conditioned, sit-down theater, and everyone might need a rest about now.

22. Eat dinner. Good sit-down restaurants include the Le Cellier at Canada and the Rose and Crown at the United Kingdom.

23. Visit the United Kingdom.

24. Tour the Canada pavilion.

25. See Illuminations. Prime viewing spots can be found all along the lagoon between Canada and France.

26. Depart Epcot.

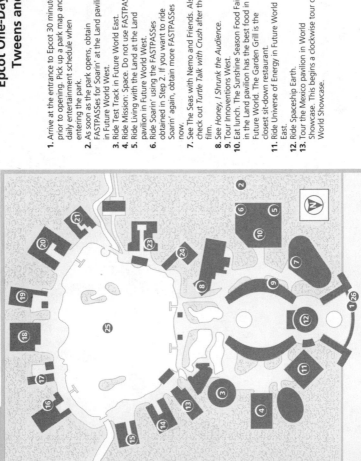

epcot

Parent's Epcot Touring Plan for an Afternoon and a Full Day (Full Day)

1. Arrive 40 minutes before official opening time. During days of peak attendance, Epcot may open at 8 a.m. or earlier. If touring during a holiday, try our holiday plans.

2. As soon as the park opens, obtain FASTPASSes for Soarin' at the Land pavilion in Future World West.

3. Ride Test Track in Future World East.

4. Ride Mission: Space. Next, make dinner reservations at Guest relations, or by calling (407) WDW-DINE.

5. In the Land pavilion, ride Living with the Land. If you wanted to ride Soarin' again, get more FASTPASSes now.

6. Ride Journey into Imagination at the Imagination pavilion.

7. See *Honey, I Shrunk the Audience.*

8. Ride Soarin' at the Land pavilion using the FASTPASSes obtained earlier.

9. Eat lunch. The best counter-service restaurant in Future World is Sunshine Seasons, at the Land pavilion. Also consider the Cantina de San Angel at the Mexico pavilion in World Showcase.

10. Experience El Rio del Tiempo at the Mexico pavilion in World Showcase. This begins a clockwise tour of World Showcase.

11. Ride Maelstrom at Norway. Use FASTPASS if the wait exceeds 20 minutes.

12. In China, see *Reflections of China.*

13. Visit the Germany pavilion.

14. Visit the Italy pavilion.

15. See *The American Adventure* at the United States pavilion.

16. Visit the Japan pavilion.

17. Visit the Morocco pavilion.

18. Depart Epcot.

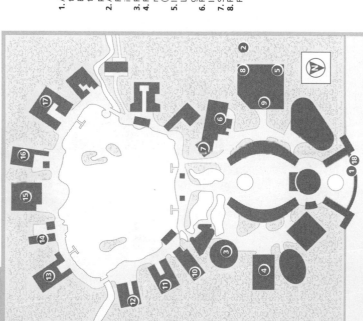

Parent's Epcot Touring Plan for an Afternoon and a Full Day (Afternoon)

1. Arrive at Epcot at 1 p.m. Get a guidemap and daily entertainment schedule. Also make dinner reservations at Guest Relations, or by calling (407) WDW-DINE.
2. Ride Spaceship Earth.
3. Tour Innoventions East.
4. See the Universe of Energy.
5. See The Seas with Nemo and Friends in Future World West. If you have young children, also see *Turtle Talk with Crush* at The Seas pavilion.
6. See *The Circle of Life* at the Land pavilion in Future World West.
7. See *O Canada!* at the Canada pavilion in World Showcase.
8. Visit the United Kingdom pavilion.
9. In France, see *Impressions de France.*
10. Eat dinner. Good nearby restaurants include Le Cellier at Canada, Restaurant Marrakesh at Morocco, and Mitsukoshi Teppanyaki at Japan.
11. See *Illuminations.* Good viewing spots can be found along the waterway between France and Canada.
12. Depart Epcot.

epcot

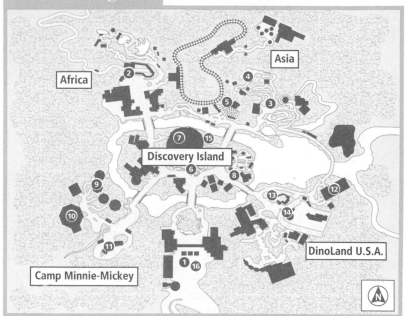

animal kingdom

Asia

Africa

Discovery Island

Camp Minnie-Mickey

DinoLand U.S.A.

Animal Kingdom One-Day Touring Plan
for Parents with Small Children

1. Arrive at the entrance to Disney's Animal Kingdom 25 minutes prior to opening. Pick up a park map and entertainment schedule. Stroller rentals are just past the entrance, to the right.
2. As soon as the park opens, experience the Kilimanjaro Safaris in Africa.
3. Ride Kali River Rapids in Asia. You will get wet. Use ponchos or plastic bags to keep dry.
4. Walk the Maharaja Jungle Trek.
5. See *Flights of Wonder.* Check the daily entertainment schedule for performance times.
6. See *It's Tough To Be a Bug* in Discovery Island. If the wait exceeds 30 minutes, use FASTPASS.
7. See the exhibits at the Tree of Life.
8. Eat lunch. Good nearby locations include Flame Tree Barbecue and Pizzafari.
9. Explore the Camp Minnie-Mickey Character Trails in Camp Minnie-Mickey.

10. See the *Festival of the Lion King.*
11. See *Pocahontas and Her Forest Friends.*
12. Check the next performance time of *Finding Nemo: The Musical* at the Theater in the Wild in Dinoland. If the next show is within 25 minutes, see Nemo now. Otherwise, see The Boneyard in Dinoland.
13. Check out The Boneyard in Dinoland.
14. Ride TriceraTop Spin in Dinoland.
15. If it's near parade time, find a good viewing spot on Discovery Island for the Afternoon Parade from Discovery Island. The parade is usually performed around 4 p.m.
16. Depart Disney's Animal Kingdom. The Animal Kingdom is a theme park to be savored. Take time to explore the exhibits and speak with the Castmembers.

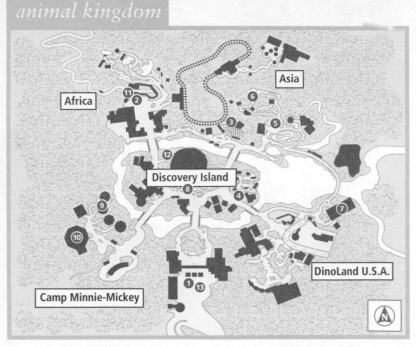

Animal Kingdom One-Day Sleepy Head Touring Plan for Parents with Small Children

1. Arrive at the entrance to Disney's Animal Kingdom around 11:00 a.m. Pick up a park map and entertainment schedule. Stroller rentals are just past the entrance, to the right.
2. Send one member of your party to obtain FASTPASSes for the Kilimanjaro Safari in Africa.
3. See *Flights of Wonder*. Check the daily entertainment schedule for show times.
4. Eat lunch. The nearest counter-service restaurants are the Flame Tree Barbecue on Discovery Island, and Restaurantosaurus in Dinoland.
5. Ride Kali River Rapids in Asia. You can leave this step for last if you'd rather not walk around the park wet.
6. Walk the Maharaja Jungle Trek in Asia.
7. Check the next performance time of *Finding Nemo: The Musical* at the Theater in the Wild in Dinoland. If the next show is within 25 minutes, see Nemo now. Otherwise, see *It's Tough to Be a Bug* first, then see Nemo.
8. See *It's Tough To Be a Bug*. Also see the exhibits at the Tree of Life in Discovery Island.
9. Explore the Camp Minnie-Mickey Character Trails in Camp Minnie-Mickey.
10. See the *Festival of the Lion King*.
11. Experience the Kilimanjaro Safaris in Africa.
12. If desired, see the Afternoon Parade.
13. Depart Disney's Animal Kingdom.

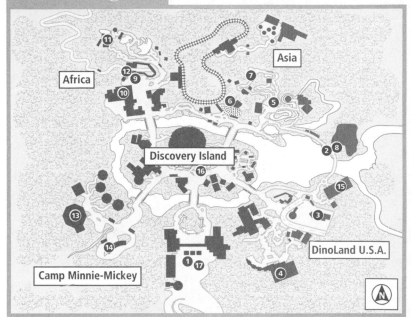

animal kingdom

Animal Kingdom One-Day Touring Plan
for Tweens and Their Parents

1. Arrive 40 minutes before official opening June 15–August 15 and during all holiday periods. At other times arrive 30 minutes early.
2. As soon as the park opens, send one member of your party to get FASTPASSes for Expedition Everest in Asia. The shortest route to Everest is from Discovery Island through Asia, not Dinoland U.S.A.
3. Ride Primeval Whirl in Dinoland U.S.A.
4. Ride Dinosaur.
5. Ride Kali River Rapids in Asia. You will get wet. Ponchos or plastic bags are advised. If you don't feel like getting soaked right now, skip this attraction or obtain FASTPASSes for later in the day.
6. See *Flights of Wonder* in Asia if the next show is within 20 minutes from now. Otherwise, walk the Maharaja Jungle Trek, then see the show.
7. Walk the Maharaja Jungle Trek in Asia if you have not already done so.
8. Ride Expedition Everest in Asia. Don't worry if your FASTPASS times have past; Disney rarely enforces the times, as long as you're not trying to get in early.
9. If possible, send one member of your party to obtain FASTPASSes for the Kilimanjaro Safaris in Africa.
10. Eat lunch. The closest counter-service restaurant is Tusker House in Africa.
11. Walk the Pangani Forest Exploration Trail.
12. Experience Kilimanjaro Safaris using the FASTPASSes obtained earlier. Don't worry if the FASTPASS return times have past; Disney rarely enforces them.
13. See the *Festival of the Lion King* in Camp Minnie-Mickey.
14. See *Pocahontas and Her Forest Friends* at Camp Minnie-Mickey. Also meet the characters at Camp Minnie-Mickey.
15. Check the next performance time of *Finding Nemo: The Musical* at the Theater in the Wild in Dinoland. If the next show is within 25 minutes, see Nemo now. Otherwise, see *It's Tough to Be a Bug* first, then see Nemo.
16. See *It's Tough to Be a Bug* on Discovery Island. Use FASTPASS if the wait exceeds 30 minutes. Also check out the exhibits at the Tree of Life.
17. Shop, snack, or repeat any attractions you especially enjoyed. Visit the zoological exhibits in The Oasis, and depart the Animal Kingdom. This plan should work well with Extra Magic Hour mornings. The only exception might be Kali River Rapids, which may open later than the rest of the attractions in Asia. If that happens, skip the attraction and return to it after all the other Asia attractions are done.

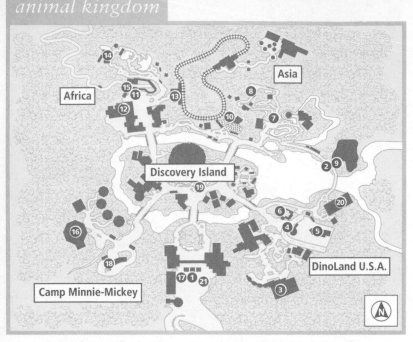

animal kingdom

Animal Kingdom Happy Family One-Day Touring Plan

1. **FAMILY:** Arrive 40 minutes before official opening mid-June through mid-August and during all holiday periods. At other times arrive 30 minutes early.
2. **TEENS:** As soon as the park opens, obtain FASTPASSes for Expedition Everest in Asia. The fastest way to Everest is through Asia, not Dinoland.
   PARENTS: Don't feel the need to rush to an attraction. Explore the Oasis on Discovery Island, pointing out any unusual animals. Hungry? Look for the Anandpur Royal Tea Company in Asia between Kali River Rapids and Expedition Everest.
3. **TEENS:** Ride Dinosaur in Dinoland U.S.A.
4. **PARENTS:** Ride TriceraTop Spin in Dinoland U.S.A.
5. **TEENS:** Ride Primeval Whirl in Dinoland U.S.A.
6. **PARENTS:** Check out the Boneyard in Dinoland.
7. **FAMILY:** If everyone's up for it, ride Kali River Rapids in Asia. You will get wet. Ponchos or plastic bags are advised. If you don't feel like getting soaked right now, save this attraction for later in the day.
8. **FAMILY:** Walk the Maharaja Jungle Trek.
9. **TEENS:** Ride Expedition Everest, using the FASTPASSes obtained earlier. Don't worry if your FASTPASS times have past; Disney rarely enforces the times, as long as you're not trying to get in early.
10. **PARENTS:** See *Flights of Wonder*. If the next show time is too far away, check out other nearby exhibits.
11. **FAMILY:** Send one member of your party to obtain FASTPASSes for the Kilimanjaro Safaris in Africa.

12. **FAMILY:** Eat lunch. The closest counter-service restaurant is Tusker House in Africa.
13. **FAMILY:** Take the Wildlife Express train to *Rafiki's Planet Watch*/Conservation Station. See the exhibits. Note the writing on the bathroom walls. Take the train back to Africa when you're done.
14. **FAMILY:** Walk the Pangani Forest Exploration Trail. If teens wanted to, they could obtain more FASTPASSes for Expedition Everest now. Meet back at the entrance to Kilimanjaro Safaris.
15. **FAMILY:** Experience Kilimanjaro Safaris using the FASTPASSes obtained earlier. Don't worry if the FASTPASS return times have past; Disney rarely enforces them.
16. **PARENTS:** See the *Festival of the Lion King* in Camp Minnie-Mickey.
17. **TEENS:** Free time. Revisit favorite attractions or explore the rest of the park.
18. **PARENTS:** See *Pocahontas and Her Forest Friends* at Camp Minnie-Mickey. Also meet the characters.
19. **FAMILY:** See *It's Tough to Be a Bug* on Discovery Island. Use FASTPASS if the wait exceeds 30 minutes. Also check out the exhibits at the Tree of Life.
20. **FAMILY:** See *Finding Nemo: The Musical*.
21. **FAMILY:** Shop, snack, or repeat any attractions you especially enjoyed. Visit the zoological exhibits in The Oasis, and depart the Animal Kingdom.

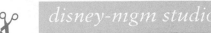

disney-mgm studios

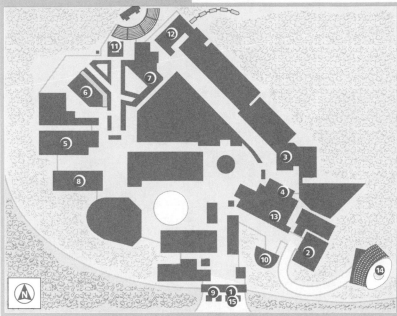

Disney-MGM Studios One-Day Touring Plan
for Parents with Small Children

1. Arrive at the entrance to Disney-MGM Studios 30 minutes prior to opening. On Extra Magic Hour mornings, arrive around 8:30 a.m.
2. If your kids are up for it, ride the Tower of Terror.
3. See *Voyage of the Little Mermaid*. If the next performance of *Playhouse Disney* is within 30 minutes, get FASTPASSes for *Mermaid* instead.
4. See *Playhouse Disney Live!* Check the daily entertainment schedule for show times. There's usually a show around 10 a.m.
5. Ride Star Tours.
6. See *Muppet-Vision 3-D*.
7. Explore the *Honey, I Shrunk the Kids Movie Set*.
8. Eat lunch. The Backlot Express and Mama Melrose's Ristorante Italiano are good nearby choices.
9. Take a mid-day break.
10. Return to the park and see *Beauty and the Beast*. There's usually a show between 4:15–5:30 p.m; check the daily schedule.
11. See the *Lights! Motors! Action! Extreme Stunt Show*. Check the daily entertainment schedule for show times. *Indiana Jones* is a good second choice.
12. If time permits, take the Backlot Tour.
13. Eat dinner. Good nearby selections include the Toluca Legs Turkey Company, Starring Rolls Cafe, and the Hollywood Brown Derby.
14. See *Fantasmic!* Plan on arriving around 25 minutes early to get good seats.
15. Depart Disney-MGM Studios.

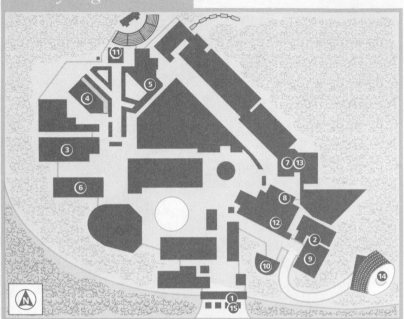

Disney-MGM Studios Sleepy Head Touring Plan for Parents with Small Children

1. Arrive at the entrance to Disney-MGM Studios around 11 a.m. Grab a park map and entertainment schedule when you enter the park. Rent strollers as needed.
2. If your kids are up for it, obtain FASTPASSes for the Tower of Terror.
3. Ride Star Tours.
4. See *Muppet-Vision 3-D.*
5. Explore the *Honey, I Shrunk the Kids* Movie Set.
6. Eat lunch. The Backlot Express and Mama Melrose's Ristorante Italiano are good nearby choices.
7. Obtain FASTPASSes for *Voyage of the Little Mermaid.*
8. See *Playhouse Disney Live!* Check the daily entertainment schedule for show times. There's usually a show around 1:30 or 2:15 p.m.

9. Ride the Tower of Terror. Use the FASTPASSes obtained in Step 2.
10. See *Beauty and the Beast.* There's usually a show between 4:15–5:30 p.m.; check the daily schedule.
11. See the *Lights! Motors! Action! Stunt Show.* Check the daily entertainment schedule for show times. The *Indiana Jones* stunt show is a good second choice.
12. Eat dinner. Good nearby selections include the Toluca Legs Turkey Company, Starring Rolls Cafe, and the Hollywood Brown Derby.
13. See *Voyage of the Little Mermaid,* using FASTPASSes obtained in Step 7.
14. See *Fantasmic!* Plan on arriving around 25 minutes early to get good seats.
15. Depart Disney-MGM Studios.

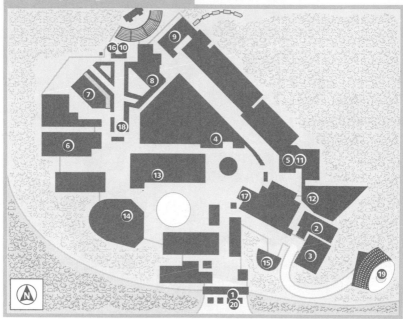

disney-mgm studios

Disney-MGM Studios One-Day Touring Plan
for Tweens and Their Parents

1. Arrive at the entrance to Disney-MGM Studios 30 minutes prior to opening. Obtain a park map and daily entertainment schedule when you enter the park.
2. As soon as the park opens, ride the Rock 'n' Roller Coaster.
3. Ride the Tower of Terror. Unless the wait time exceeds 30 minutes, do not use FASTPASS.
4. Ride The Great Movie Ride.
5. Obtain FASTPASSes for *Voyage of the Little Mermaid.*
6. Ride Star Tours.
7. See *Muppet-Vision 3-D.*
8. Eat lunch. Good nearby choices include the Studios Catering Co. and Mama Melrose's Ristorante Italiano.
9. Take the Backlot Tour.
10. If the next performance of *Lights! Motors! Action!* is within 30 minutes, get in line to see the show. Otherwise, continue to the next step.
11. See *Voyage of the Little Mermaid,* using the FASTPASSes obtained in Step 5. Obtain FASTPASSes if the wait exceeds 30 minutes.

12. Take the Magic of Disney Animation Tour.
13. See *Sounds Dangerous.* Reverse this step and step 14 if the next performance of Indy is within 30 minutes.
14. See the *Indiana Jones Epic Stunt Spectacular.* Check the daily performance schedule for show times.
15. See *Beauty and the Beast.* Check the daily entertainment schedule for show times.
16. If you've not already done so, see *Lights! Motors! Action!* Otherwise, continue to the next step.
17. Eat dinner. Good nearby choices include the Hollywood Brown Derby and the ABC Commissary.
18. Tour the Streets of America Backlot.
19. Enjoy *Fantasmic!* If getting a good seat is important to you, plan on arriving at least 60 minutes prior to show time. If two shows are performed, the second is usually less crowded.
20. Depart Disney-MGM Studios. Check the daily entertainment schedule for show times; you may be better off altering the order in which you see the shows listed in steps 13 through 16.

disney-mgm studios

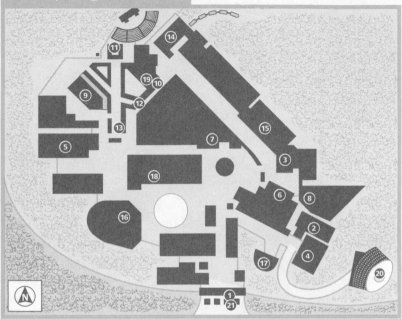

Disney-MGM Studios One-Day Happy Family Touring Plan

1. **Arrive at the park**, admission in hand, 30 to 40 minutes before official opening. Obtain a park map and daily entertainment schedule, and rent strollers and wheelchairs as needed.
2. **TEENS:** As soon as the park opens, ride the Rock 'n' Roller Coaster.
3. **PARENTS:** As soon as the park opens, see *Voyage of the Little Mermaid* in the Animation Courtyard.
4. **TEENS:** Ride the Tower of Terror. Use FASTPASS if the wait exceeds 30 minutes.
5. **TEENS:** Head in the direction of Echo Lake and ride Star Tours.
6. **PARENTS:** See *Playhouse Disney Live!* Check the daily entertainment schedule for show times, but there should be a show starting right after *Mermaid* finishes.
7. **FAMILY:** Ride the Great Movie Ride.
8. **FAMILY:** Take the Animation Tour.
9. **FAMILY:** See *Muppet-Vision 3-D.*
10. **FAMILY:** Eat lunch. The best nearby counter-service restaurant is the Studios Catering Company Flatbread Grill. Now would be a good time to check the daily entertainment schedule for show times for *Lights! Motors! Action!, Beauty and the Beast,* and *Indiana Jones.*
11. **TEENS:** See the *Lights! Motors! Action!* stunt show.
12. **PARENTS:** Explore the *Honey, I Shrunk the Kids* Movie Set.
13. **FAMILY:** Explore the Streets of America if you didn't get enough on the way to the Muppets.
14. **FAMILY:** Take the Backlot Tour.
15. **FAMILY:** See *One Man's Dream* on Mickey Avenue.
16. **FAMILY:** See the *Indiana Jones Epic Stunt Spectacular.* Check the daily entertainment schedule for show times.
17. **FAMILY:** See *Beauty and the Beast.* If you wanted to see only one show, *Indiana Jones* is rated slightly higher overall.
18. **TEENS:** See *Sounds Dangerous,* which faces Echo Lake near Indiana Jones.
19. **FAMILY:** Eat dinner. Good sit-down choices include Mama Melrose's and the Hollywood Brown Derby.
20. **FAMILY:** Tour Hollywood and Sunset Boulevards. Enjoy *Fantasmic!*
21. Depart Disney-MGM Studios.

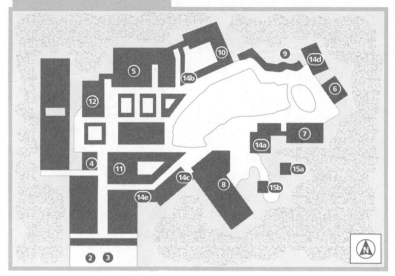

Universal Studios One-day Touring Plan

1. Call ☎ 407-363-8000 the day before your visit for the official opening time.
2. Arrive 50 minutes before opening and pick up a map and entertainment schedule.
3. Line up at the turnstile. Ask if any rides or shows are closed and adjust touring plan.
4. Ride Jimmy Neutron's Nicktoon Blast.
5. Ride *Revenge of the Mummy* if it's open.
6. Ride *Men in Black* Alien Attack.
7. Ride *Back to the Future.*
8. Ride *E.T. Adventure.*
9. Ride *Jaws.*
10. Ride Earthquake—The Big One.
11. See *Shrek 4-D.*

12. See *Twister.*
13. Take a break for lunch.
14. See *Animal Actors* on Location **(14a)**, *Beetlejuice's Rock 'n' Roll Graveyard Revue* **(14b)**, *The Universal Horror Make-Up Show* **(14c)**, and *Fear Factor Live* **(14d)** as convenient according to the daily entertainment schedule. See *Terminator 2: 3-D* **(14e)** after 3:30 p.m.
15. Take preschoolers to see Barney **(15a)** after riding *E.T.,* and then head for Woody Woodpecker's KidZone **(15b)**.
16. Revisit favorite rides and shows. See any live performances you may have missed.

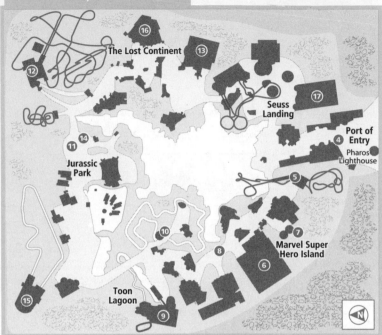

islands of adventure

Universal's Islands of Adventure
One-day Touring Plan

1. Call ☎ 407-363-8000 the day before your visit for the official opening time.
2. Arrive 50 minutes before opening time, and pick up a map and daily entertainment schedule.
3. Line up at the turnstile. Ask if any rides or shows are closed, and adjust touring plan accordingly.
4. Go straight through the Port of Entry and cross into Marvel Super Hero Island. Head for The Incredible Hulk Coaster.
5. Ride The Incredible Hulk Coaster.
6. Experience The Adventures of Spider-Man.
7. Ride Dr. Doom's Fearfall if you must.
8. Depart Super Hero Island and cross into Toon Lagoon.
9. Ride Dudley Do-Right's Ripsaw Falls.

10. Ride Popeye & Bluto's Bilge-Rat Barges.
11. Continue around the lake and pass through Jurassic Park. Head to the Lost Continent.
12. Ride both tracks of Dueling Dragons.
13. Experience *Poseidon's Fury! Escape from the Lost City.*
14. Depart the Lost Continent and go to Jurassic
15. Park.
16. Ride the *Jurassic Park* River Adventure. See The *Eighth Voyage of Sinbad* stunt show in the Lost Continent.
17. Go to Seuss Landing and ride The Cat in the Hat.
18. Revisit favorite rides and check out attractions you may have missed.